COMMENTS ON THIS EDITION

This second edition of Lisa Strelein's *Compromised Jurisprudence* brings this essential book on Australia native title up to date, but it does much more than that. In its incisive commentaries and critical analyses of the major caselaw and jurisprudence that has developed since the High Court's decision in Mabo [2], Strelein has produced a comprehensive legal treatise on native title in Australia that is of immense importance to the emerging field of comparative indigenous rights. Her book skilfully reveals both the promises, perils and pitfalls of litigating indigenous peoples' property and other fundamental human rights under the domestic law of a Western settler-state like Australia. The work of a gifted legal scholar and writer, the book contains many valuable lessons and insights that indigenous rights advocates around the world will be able to utilise in their own legal efforts aimed at decolonisation of Indigenous peoples under both domestic and international law.

Robert A. Williams, Jr., E. Thomas Sullivan Professor of Law and American Indian Studies, University of Arizona Rogers College of Law

This book is an exceptional synthesis of the major native title decisions in Australia. Strelein's deep understanding of this issue is evident on very page. It is a work of profound importance.

John Borrows, Professor and Law Foundation Chair in Aboriginal Justice, University of Victoria Law School, British Columbia, Canada

COMMENTS ON THE FIRST EDITION

A significant deficiency in native title practice in Australia has been a failure by some of the participants to come to grips with the conceptual underpinnings of native title jurisprudence. *Compromised Jurisprudence*, by confronting, analysing and challenging those underpinnings, is an important work that can assist in overcoming that deficiency.

Ron Merkel, Federal Court of Australia

Over the past decade, Strelein has been a leader in the field as one of the most concise, sober and reliable commentators on the jurisprudence of the law of native title. Practitioners, scholars, teachers and students would be well advised to add this volume to their collection.

David Ritter, Faculty of Law, University of Western Australia

In a remarkably accessible format, Strelein provides succinct and considered analyses of ten major native title decisions with considered reflections on the evolving jurisprudence. *Compromised Jurisprudence* will be invaluable to those working in the area of native title.

Garth Nettheim, Emeritus Professor, Faculty of Law, University of New South Wales

This is a much anticipated book from one of Australia's leading experts on native title. With clarity and insight, Strelein provides an overview of developments in this otherwise complex area of law.

Larissa Behrendt, Professor of Law, Jumbunna Indigenous House of Learning, University of Technology, Sydney

Compromised Jurisprudence

Native title cases since Mabo

SECOND EDITION

Lisa Strelein

Aboriginal Studies Press

First published in 2006 by Aboriginal Studies Press
Second edition published in 2009 by Aboriginal Studies Press

© Lisa Strelein 2009

All rights reserved. No part of this book may be reproduced or transmitted in any form or by any means, electronic or mechanical, including photocopying, recording or by any information storage and retrieval system, without prior permission in writing from the publisher. The *Australian Copyright Act 1968* (the Act) allows a maximum of one chapter or 10 per cent of this book, whichever is the greater, to be photocopied by any educational institution for its education purposes provided that the educational institution (or body that administers it) has given a remuneration notice to Copyright Agency Limited (CAL) under the Act.

Aboriginal Studies Press is the publishing arm of the Australian Institute of Aboriginal and Torres Strait Islander Studies.
GPO Box 553, Canberra, ACT 2601
Phone: (61 2) 6246 1183
Fax: (61 2) 6261 4288
Email: asp@aiatsis.gov.au
Web: www.aiatsis.gov.au/asp/about.html

National Library of Australia
Cataloguing-In-Publication data:

    Author: Strelein, Lisa.

    Title: Compromised jurisprudence : native title cases since Mabo / Lisa Strelein.

    Edition: 2nd ed.

    ISBN: 9780855756635 (pbk.)

    Notes: Includes index. Bibliography.

    Subjects: Native title (Australia) — Case studies.
    Jurisprudence — Australia.

    Dewey Number: 346.9404320899915

Cover image: *Into the Wanyarang sunset* © Shane Pickett, Indigenart, The Mossenson Galleries, www.indigenart.com.au.

Index by Sherrey Quinn
Printed in Australia by BPA Print Group Pty Ltd

CONTENTS

Preface	ix
Acknowledgments	xi

Introduction   1
    The law before *Mabo*   2
    The legislative responses   3
    The *Native Title Act 1993*   5
    Wik and the Ten-Point Plan   6
    Relationship between the common law and the legislation   7

1. Recognising native title in Australian law: 9
    Mabo v Queensland [No. 2]
    The consequences of settlement   10
    Establishing title   10
    The nature and content of native title   14
    Extinguishing title   16
    Wrongful extinguishment   18
    Conclusion   21

2. Coexistence and necessary inconsistency: 22
    Wik Peoples v Queensland
    Nature of the inquiry   23
    History of pastoral leases under statute   24
    Applying the rules of statutory construction   25
    The arguments in favour of exclusive possession   26
    Arguments against exclusive possession   29
    The conditional nature of the grant   30
    A presumption of beneficial construction   31
    Conclusions as to necessary extinguishment   31
    Extinguishment and the test of inconsistency   33

3. **The vulnerability of native title:** *Fejo v Northern Territory*   36
   The freehold question   37
   A 'bundle of rights'   38
   A unique title   39
   A new vulnerability   40
   Revival and extinguishment   41
   Conclusion   43

4. **Property and Crown ownership:** *Yanner v Eaton*   44
   The nature of property   44
   'Vesting' and Crown property   45
   Extinguishment, inconsistency and regulation   45
   Conclusion   48

5. **Native title offshore:** *Commonwealth v Yarmirr*   49
   Recognition of native title over the sea   50
   Crown sovereignty over the sea   50
   The public rights to navigate and to fish   52
   Non-exclusivity and enforcement   53
   Conclusion   54

6. **Redefining extinguishment:** *Western Australia v Ward*   55
   Extinguishment under the *Native Title Act 1993*   57
   The *Racial Discrimination Act* and compensation   59
   Proof of native title   61
   The 'bundle of rights' debate   61
   Connection to land   63
   Non-exclusive native title   65
   Principles for extinguishment under the *Native Title Act*   68
   Partial extinguishment and coexistence   71
   The *Wilson v Anderson* decision   72
   Conclusion   72

7. **Proof of a native title society:** *Yorta Yorta v Victoria*   74
   Tradition and continuity in *Yorta Yorta*   74
   The intersection of normative systems   76
   What has to be proved   77
   Continuity and change in tradition   78
   Conclusion   80

8. **Rules of interpretation:** *Griffiths v Minister for Lands, Planning and Environment*	82
The statutory framework	82
Public purpose and private benefit	83
The absence of clear and plain intent	84
Conclusion	86
9. **Implementing the High Court's jurisprudence:** *De Rose v South Australia [No. 2]*	87
Connection to land	88
Social and political life	89
Physical access	90
The evidence of Indigenous witnesses and the role of experts	91
Alternative determination and extinguishment	92
The Federal Court appeal	92
Who can claim native title?	94
Determining the impact of partial extinguishment	96
10. **Continuity and change:** *Bodney v Bennell*	97
The existence of a Noongar society	98
The continuity question	99
The appeal	100
Continuity and 'unacceptable' change	100
'For each generation'	105
Communal title and the recognition level	107
Connection	112
Conclusion	114
11. **The development of native title jurisprudence**	116
12. **The jurisprudence of native title:** **'Recognition' and 'protection'**	126
Native title and the assertion of Crown sovereignty	128
Non-recognition	130
The juxtaposition of recognition and denial	133
What is recognised: the nature and extent of the title	135
Sustaining recognition: the maintenance of connection	139
The 'recognition level': who holds native title?	141
The limits of protection: extinguishment of native title	144
Conclusion	148
Notes	151
Annotated case list	183
Bibliography	231
Index	242

PREFACE

Compromised Jurisprudence brings together case commentaries on the most significant native title cases in Australia and traces the development of native title law since the High Court decision in *Mabo v Queensland [No. 2]* (1992). Many of these commentaries first appeared in the AIATSIS native title issues papers and newsletters to provide immediate commentary to practitioners and policy makers in the native title field. Those papers are revisited here in a way that preserves some of their temporal perspective, and are then combined with new material to provide a complete picture of the development of case law on native title. Hence, the structure of the book provides a timeline of events that enables us to trace the development of the key doctrines of native title.

Since the first edition of *Compromised Jurisprudence* was published, the focus of the native title system has been on 'making it work', with a series of technical and institutional amendments. During this time, the number of successful native title claims has continued to increase but the process for achieving such recognition has continued to develop greater complexity and to require more resources. While the one native title decision of the High Court in the past three years — *Griffiths v Minister for Lands, Planning and Environment* (2008) (*Griffiths*) — went almost without comment, the outcome of the appeal decision in *Bodney v Bennell* (2008) (*Bennell*) has fuelled calls for changes to the *Native Title Act 1993* (Cth) (NTA) to make it easier to establish native title. The problems that plague the native title system, including the courts' interpretation of the key provisions of the NTA, have prompted calls for reform from as far up as the Chief Justice of the High Court and a number of judges of the Federal Court to overcome the inherent unfairness of the native title process for Indigenous people.[1] Further, Noel Pearson has called for the removal of section (s) 223 of the NTA altogether and for the return to the common law definition of native title.[2] In contrast, Justice Tony North has alluded to the policy role and subjectivity of judges in native title cases in his proposals for reform of the NTA.[3] This book provides the backdrop to these discussions by examining the choices that the courts have made in relation to native title and the potential for a more just native title doctrine if current reform proposals are pursued.

I acknowledge the publication of earlier versions of the following chapters: 'Recognising native title in Australian law: *Mabo v Queensland [No. 2]*' ((1993)

2 *Asia Pacific Law Review* 89); 'The vulnerability of native title: *Fejo v Northern Territory*' ((1999) 1(28) *Issues Paper*); 'Native title offshore: *Commonwealth v Yarmirr*' ((2001) 5 *Native Title News* 78); 'Proof of a native title society: *Yorta Yorta v Victoria*' ((2003) 2(21) *Issues Paper*); 'Implementing the High Court's jurisprudence: *De Rose v South Australia [No. 2]*' (6/2003 *Native Title Newsletter*); and 'Rules of interpretation: *Griffiths v Minister for Lands, Planning and Environment* (3/2008 *Native Title Newsletter*). Many of these chapters have been substantially revised from the originals. 'Redefining extinguishment: *Western Australia v Ward*' is based on a longer report prepared for the Native Title Representative Bodies in 2002.

New chapters have been added to this edition: the High Court decision in *Griffiths* (regarding compulsory acquisition); and the most controversial Federal Court case of the past two years, *Bennell* (which concerned the Noongar people's claim over the south-west of Western Australia, including Perth). Two chapters from the previous edition have been omitted ('The limits of coexistence: *Wilson v Anderson*' (2002) and 'The scope of the doctrines: *Neowarra v Western Australia*' (2003)) and the final two chapters have been revised to include discussion of the decisions of the High Court and the full Federal Court since the previous edition. Finally, the annotated case list in this edition has been updated to provide a comprehensive outline of both substantive and procedural cases related to native title jurisprudence.

The law is current as at 30 June 2009.

ACKNOWLEDGMENTS

I would like to acknowledge the assistance of staff within the Native Title Research Unit who have compiled the case list over a number of years now, and have supported and assisted the production of this book — as they do with all of my research activities.

I would like to thank the Council and Executive of the Australian Institute of Aboriginal and Torres Strait Islander Studies (AIATSIS) for the support and resources they have provided over the past ten years, including the intellectual, ethical and responsible environment in which to consider these issues. Working at AIATSIS, I have had the opportunity to participate in and learn from the networks of Indigenous communities and native title practitioners. In particular, I would like to thank the Native Title Representative Body network for its ongoing engagement and support for the activities of the Native Title Research Unit.

Introduction

> The God Malo says to you as he says to me, and has said to the rest of the world: *Tag Mauki mauki, Teter mauki mauki* ... your hands and your feet must not take you to steal what is other people's.
> David Passi, Murray Island Plaintiff[1]

The decision of the High Court of Australia in *Mabo v Queensland [No. 2]*[2] (*Mabo*) has had a profound impact on the legal, social and political reality of Indigenous–non-Indigenous relations in Australia. The result in the case was a recognition by the Australian legal system that the Meriam people hold rights to their land under their own system of law, and that those rights should enjoy the protection of the Australian law. The nature of that recognition and the extent of protection has been the subject of significant legal, policy and social debate. In each of these spheres there is significant reluctance to disturb the colonial inheritance of two hundred years of denial of the rights of Indigenous peoples.

The decision in *Mabo* was heralded as an abandonment of the 'terra nullius' myth, although this may be an overstatement of the reform that took place.[3] It was described as a 'judicial revolution' and, while bringing Australian law belatedly into line with other common law countries, attracted criticism of the High Court for taking an activist role in transforming Australian law.[4] The legal recognition of continued rights of Indigenous peoples to land in Australia plays to what is perhaps one of the country's greatest fears. Extreme public and policy responses to the recognition of native title have plagued the early years of the development of native title law.

Perhaps not surprisingly, the *Mabo* decision provoked diverse responses from industry and from pastoral and political groups; it engendered great public interest and undoubtedly some confusion. The most vocal opponents were those in the resource sector who anticipated greater constraints on their access to land for exploration and mining.[5] The hostility of the state governments was epitomised in Western Australia's resolve to 'use whatever means [they] have to nullify the effects of the decision'.[6]

The decision in *Mabo,* while it made particular directions as to the rights of the Meriam, was not restricted in its application. In reaching their conclusions, the judges relied on general propositions of common law applicable to any 'settled' colony.[7] Of greater significance was the 'declaratory' nature of the decision; that is, the High Court defined what the common law of Australia is, and therefore had always been, even if this had not been recognised until this case. This meant that not only would future dealings with Indigenous peoples' land have to change but a comprehensive review of past treatment and possible illegality was also required.

THE LAW BEFORE *MABO*

The colonial law by which Australia was annexed to the British Empire, and the reception of the common law into the colonies, rested on the legal presumption that the Indigenous inhabitants had no right to the land. This presumption had been justified on the basis that there was 'no settled law' that required the respect of the colonising power.[8] As Justice Brennan explained:

> The view was taken that, when sovereignty of a territory could be acquired under the enlarged notion of terra nullius, for the purposes of the municipal law that territory (though inhabited) could be treated as a 'desert uninhabited' country. The hypothesis being that there was no local law already in existence in the territory ... *Ex hypothesi,* the indigenous inhabitants of a settled colony ... were thus taken to be without laws, without a sovereign and primitive in their social organisation.[9]

As a result, there was seen to be no need to wrest sovereignty from the Indigenous peoples through conquest or cession; rather, the territory could be annexed by 'peaceful' settlement.[10] Until the *Mabo* decision this assumption had been upheld in Australian law and provided the basis upon which the laws of the Commonwealth and the states were drafted.

The first case in which Indigenous peoples presented evidence to challenge the notion that the continent was without law was *Milirrpum v Nabalco Pty Ltd*, which arose from a claim by the Yirrkala people of the Gove Peninsula who sought to halt mining in the area.[11] Justice Blackburn of the Supreme Court of the Northern Territory heard evidence from the Yirrkala people about their relationship to the land and their law. His Honour observed:

> a subtle and elaborate system highly adapted to the country in which the people led their lives, which provided a stable order of society and was remarkably free from the vagaries of personal whim or influence. If ever a system could be called 'a government of laws, and not of men', it is that shown in the evidence before me.[12]

Despite the evidence before the court, Justice Blackburn felt bound by the decision of the Privy Council in *Cooper v Stuart* in 1889 to conclude that no doctrine of communal title ever existed in the common law.[13] The judge therefore chose to treat the question of whether the colony was settled as a matter of law, not of fact.[14] There was no appeal from this judgment or any challenge to the law for some time. This may be partly explained by the subsequent development of land rights legislation in various states and territories. The most comprehensive legislative regime was introduced by the Commonwealth Government in the Northern Territory, under the *Aboriginal Land Rights (Northern Territory) Act 1976* (Cth).[15]

In the years after *Milirrpum*, the High Court of Australia appeared to be open to a challenge to the presumption that the acquisition of sovereignty automatically vested the ownership of land in the Crown, to the detriment of Indigenous people. Members of the Court in *Coe v Commonwealth* noted that the existence of communal title constituted an arguable question if properly raised.[16] Justice Deane had lamented in *Gerhardy v Brown* that 'the common law of this land has still not reached the stage of retreat from injustice which the Law of Illinois and Virginia had reached in 1823'.[17] Later, in *Northern Land Council v Commonwealth*, the High Court described the debate about fiduciary duties that might arise from Crown dealings with Indigenous land as of fundamental importance.[18] The impetus lay with the High Court to reassess the authorities with respect to the application of the common law to Australia and its implication for Indigenous peoples' law and their land.

The *Mabo* decision did not revisit the mode or validity of the acquisition of sovereignty, but did reconsider how the law was received in the new colonies and the consequences for the 'private rights' of the Indigenous inhabitants. The High Court rejected a domestic doctrine founded on principles of ethnocentricity that justified the 'more advanced people' in dispossessing the 'less advanced', although not entirely.[19] In so doing, the High Court rejected the assumptions upon which Australia's land law had been based and created the impetus for a review of existing legislation and statutory interpretation. In accepting responsibility for recognising the rights of Indigenous peoples to land as a part of Australian law, the High Court entered upon the considerable task of determining the extent to which law and property interests were to be affected by the recognition of native title and the extent to which the law would protect the title now recognised.

THE LEGISLATIVE RESPONSES

There were immediate calls for the implementation of a statutory or administrative scheme to deal with the uncertainties of land tenure that were unearthed by the *Mabo* decision but resolution of the issues was not conducive to a simple or quick solution. During the course of the *Mabo* litigation, the Queensland Government had sought to pre-empt the outcome of the case by passing the *Queensland Coast Islands Declaratory Act 1985* (Qld), which deemed complete beneficial ownership of all of Queensland to be in the Crown regardless of whether native title now or had ever existed.[20] The High Court declared that, should it be proved that native title in fact existed, the Queensland legislation would violate the *Racial Discrimination Act 1975* (Cth) (RDA).[21]

Putting to one side for the moment the discriminatory treatment of native title by the common law, once title had been recognised in *Mabo* the impact of the RDA put a cloud of invalidity over any dealings with land since 1975, including legislation passed concerning land management, grants made over land, especially to miners, and government activity such as public works and reservations, even the creation of national parks and townships. Over the next eighteen months, the Commonwealth Government sought to reach agreement on a legislative package that would support the recognition of native title by the courts and provide the common law title with greater protection in future dealings, while validating dealings with land prior to the recognition of native title.[22]

In December 1993, after one of the longest debates in parliamentary history, the *Native Title Act 1993* (Cth) (NTA) was introduced with the following objects:

(a) to provide for the recognition and protection of native title; and
(b) to establish ways in which future dealings affecting native title may proceed and to set standards for those dealings; and
(c) to establish a mechanism for determining claims to native title; and
(d) to provide for, or permit, the validation of past acts, invalidated because of the existence of native title.[23]

The Commonwealth also promised a measure of redress for the past dispossession through provision of a land fund for the acquisition of further land, as well as a social justice package. The land fund and an administering body, the Indigenous Land Corporation, were established by the NTA, but the social justice package has not been delivered.

In opposition to the Commonwealth's national regime, the Western Australian state government had maintained its commitment to 'nullify' the *Mabo* decision. It passed the *Land (Titles and Traditional Usage) Act 1993*, which provided for the compulsory acquisition of all native title in Western Australia and for native title to be replaced by a statutory grant of rights to access for traditional use. A constitutional challenge between the state and the Commonwealth was inevitable. The resulting decision of the High Court in *Western Australia v Commonwealth* (1995) (*Native Title Act case*) confirmed the validity of the Commonwealth legislation as being within the legislative powers of the Commonwealth to make laws for the 'persons of any race' under s 51(xxvi) of the Constitution.[24] The case also reconfirmed the decision in *Mabo v Queensland [No. 1]* (1988) (*Mabo [No. 1]*) concerning the effect of the RDA.[25] Under s 109 of the Constitution, Commonwealth legislation (enacted within power) prevails over any inconsistent state legislation. The High Court explained in the *Native Title Act case* that:

> The two-fold operation of s 10(1) [of the RDA] ensures that [Indigenous peoples] who are holders of native title have the same security of enjoyment of their traditional rights over or in respect of land as others who are holders of title granted by the Crown and that a State law which purports to diminish that security of enjoyment is, by virtue of s 109 of the Constitution, inoperative.[26]

In the result, the Court held that provisions of the *Land (Titles and Traditional Usage) Act* 1993 (WA) that purported to extinguish native title were invalid. The states were therefore bound by the Commonwealth regime and could not take an inconsistent approach.

THE *NATIVE TITLE ACT 1993*

The first object of the NTA, to 'recognise and protect native title', was thought to have been met by the statutory declaration under s 11 to the effect that native title 'is not able to be extinguished contrary to this Act'.[27] By virtue of this provision, the NTA establishes an exclusive code for extinguishment that constrains the executive and state legislatures. In the *Native Title Act case,* the High Court explained that:

> The Act removes the common law defeasibility of native title, and secures the Aboriginal people and Torres Strait Islanders in the enjoyment of their native title subject to the prescribed exceptions which provide for native title to be extinguished or impaired. There are only three exceptions: the occurrence of a past act that has been validated, an agreement on the part of the native title holders, or the doing of a permissible future act.[28]

Much is made of this 'beneficial' aspect of the NTA, but as *Mabo [No. 1]* and the *Native Title Act case* show, common law native title enjoyed significant protection against defeasibility, or extinguishment, under the RDA.[29] The primary objective of the 'protection' regime under the NTA could be argued to be the clarification of the 'exceptions'. The perceived 'vulnerability' of native title was illustrated by the treatment of the RDA by the Commonwealth Parliament in order to achieve the validation imperative. The operation of the RDA was suspended to allow the validation of past acts of extinguishment by the Commonwealth and to allow state governments to pass similar validation legislation.[30] The NTA provides for compensation but not for consent and negotiation. The effect of validation provisions was to build upon the discriminatory aspects of the common law by removing the protection of equality before the law under the RDA for the period up to the passing of the NTA.[31]

The urgency with which the Commonwealth wanted to 'resolve' native title was also evident in the objective 'to establish a mechanism for determining claims to native title'.[32] The NTA established a substantial process and infrastructure for the methodical identification of native title, including who holds it, where it exists and what it entails. Thus, potential common law native title holders were invited to seek a 'determination' that native title exists.[33] To manage this process, the National Native Title Tribunal was established with the aim of providing an environment for native title to be determined by agreement through mediation. But the process sets native title applicants in the position of having to 'explain' their claims, to assert legitimacy and to ask for recognition from potentially hundreds of 'interested' parties and often recalcitrant state governments.[34]

The remaining object of the Act, 'to establish ways in which future dealings affecting native title may proceed', is implemented through the 'future act' regime.[35] The NTA introduced the notion of 'permissible' and 'impermissible' future acts in order to meet the requirements of the RDA; that is, an act is only permissible if native title holders are treated with the same procedural rights as if they held any ordinary title, such as freehold. The provisions of the NTA in 1993 were directed primarily to the impact on the granting of mining leases, thus the future act regime provided for a 'right to negotiate' (although no right to say 'no') with governments over mining activity, within a specified period, in order to reach agreement to the doing of the act.[36]

WIK AND THE TEN-POINT PLAN

Within a year of the operation of the NTA, it was clear that there were still many aspects of the law that were unclear. One of the largest issues to be resolved was the relationship between native title and pastoral and mining leases. The balancing of these interests would determine the scope of native title on the mainland. Chapter 2 shows that the High Court determined that, in most cases, such interests should be able to coexist.[37] Of course, the decision of the High Court in *Wik Peoples v Queensland* (1996) (*Wik*) outraged pastoralist and farming industry groups, who were seeking greater 'certainty' in their tenures, which meant minimal interference with their enjoyment of property.[38] With the election of the Liberal–National Party coalition government in March 1996, these concerns found a receptive audience. The incoming federal government had already begun to implement its pre-election promise to reform the NTA to provide greater 'workability' before the *Wik* decision was handed down.[39] In response to the High Court decision in *Wik*, the government proposed a 'Ten-

Point Plan' that built upon the 'workability' proposals.[40] The plan promised to deliver 'bucket loads of extinguishment'.[41]

The resulting *Native Title Amendment Act 1998* (Cth) (the Amendments) reduced the protection afforded by the common law, the RDA and the 1993 NTA with a series of substantial reforms:

- validating new grants by state governments since the introduction of the NTA (without regard to the future act regime);[42]
- validating 'renewals' of leases issued before 1994;[43]
- 'confirmation' that extinguishment is permanent;[44]
- 'confirmation' of extinguishment in relation to freehold, leasehold and other tenures;[45]
- 'confirmation' of government authority over water and airspace;[46]
- expanding the rights of pastoralists to undertake agricultural activities;[47]
- raising the threshold for registration of applications (and thereby limiting access to procedural rights);[48]
- diminishing or removing the right to negotiate and introduction of more limited rights to notification and comment in relation to various classes of acts;[49] and
- the suspension of the RDA again to achieve this.[50]

The 1998 Amendments also introduced a detailed scheme of Indigenous Land Use Agreements that allowed greater certainty for non-Indigenous parties through the creation of binding agreements. These provisions were generally seen to be a positive element of the 1998 package but they were not enough to avoid international criticism for the discriminatory treatment of native title holders in favour of non-Indigenous interests.[51]

Further amendments to the legislation in 2007 and 2009 sought to avoid the political battles of earlier legislative interventions, focusing instead on technical and procedural reforms. During this period, the respective roles of the Federal Court and the National Native Title Tribunal were under critical review as the process for achieving settlement of native title claims continued to be time and resource intensive.

RELATIONSHIP BETWEEN THE COMMON LAW AND THE LEGISLATION

The legislature was seen to assert its role in the development and management of native title law and policy through the passing of the NTA in 1993, and particularly in light of the amendments passed in 1998. But the courts retain a central role in how native title has developed and what it could achieve. In recognising native title in the *Mabo* case, the courts took primary responsibility for determining the fundamental nature of the recognition and protection afforded to native title. The NTA incorporated common law concepts in a way that continued to require clarification of the relationship between the common law and the statute. This book examines the courts' response to this role as much as it investigates the legal concepts and contests in the jurisprudence of native title.

The primary focus of this book is the theoretical foundations of native title. The past seventeen years have been formative in terms of the evolution of the legal concept of native title from uncertain foundations to a more detailed, though arguably compromised, jurisprudence.

In this book I trace the development of the courts' thinking on the concept of native title, from the watershed decision in *Mabo* through to the significant High Court decisions in 2002 in *Western Australia v Ward* (*Ward*) and *Members of the Yorta Yorta Aboriginal Community v Victoria* (2002) (*Yorta Yorta*) and the subsequent implementation of those cases by the Federal Court in cases such as *De Rose v South Australia* (*De Rose*) *[No. 2]* (2005) and *Bodney v Bennell* (2008) (*Bennell*). Each chapter contains a discrete analysis of the most significant cases during this period, providing a timeline of events. The book concludes with a substantial overview of the legal concept of native title that identifies the underlying themes and contradictions in the law. As we will see, there are important elements of native title law that are yet to be fully realised, most significantly the issue of compensation. Moreover, the idea that the law is now 'settled' belies the number of compromises that still exist in the jurisprudence, which suggest that, while the doctrine may now be more comprehensive, it has not necessarily reached a just outcome.

A number of themes emerge when examining the development of native title jurisprudence through the twin lenses of 'recognition' and 'protection'. Perhaps most significant is the way in which the courts grapple with the notion of Indigenous societies as makers and keepers of law. Native title confronts assumptions of legal and political sovereignty that are enshrined in the law and in the thinking of lawyers and judges. A second significant observation from both the writing and the structure of this book is that the courts have made significant policy choices that have limited the potential for native title. Despite attempts to reject the continuing capacity of Indigenous peoples to make law and govern themselves, there are unavoidable acknowledgments of Indigenous society present in the reasoning of native title cases that undermine the carefully constructed doctrinal denial.

CHAPTER 1

Recognising native title in Australian law
Mabo v Queensland [No. 2]

HIGH COURT OF AUSTRALIA, 1992

In May 1982, five Murray Islanders initiated an action against the government of Queensland seeking declarations of rights to the use and enjoyment of traditional land that had been continuously occupied by the Meriam people before and since the annexation by the defendant government. To the surprise of many, the High Court decided in favour of the plaintiffs.[1] The order contained a declaration to the effect that, apart from any inconsistent grants, the Meriam people are entitled 'as against the whole world to possession, occupation, use and enjoyment of the lands of the Murray Islands', subject to the power of the state government to extinguish the title by valid exercise of legislative or executive powers.[2] Without denying its importance to the Meriam people, the greatest impact lay not in the order itself but, rather, in the context of the judgment. Each judgment considered the action in wider terms than would normally be sufficient to determine the case at hand. The principles enunciated in the judgments provided the basis for development of the law applicable to native title.

The High Court reviewed the cases decided in this and other jurisdictions, prior to and since the decision by Justice Blackburn in *Milirrpum v Nabalco Pty Ltd*,[3] on the effect of colonisation. In view of these decisions, and in spite of many of them, the Court was prepared to reject longstanding assumptions of colonial legal theory. The standards adopted at the time of acquiring sovereignty were seen to be no longer appropriate for a rule of common law. In the lead judgment, Justice Brennan said that there was a 'choice of legal principle to be made', noting that:

> it is imperative in today's world that the common law should neither be or be seen to be frozen in an age of racial discrimination … The fiction by which the rights and interests of indigenous inhabitants in land were treated as nonexistent was justified by a policy which has no place in the contemporary law of this country.[4]

COMPROMISED JURISPRUDENCE

Before Justice Brennan was prepared to enter into a review of previous authority, he was concerned not to 'fracture the skeleton of legal principle which gives the body of our law its shape and internal consistency'.[5] Justice Brennan concluded that no such fracturing of legal principle occurred in bringing the law of Australia into line with notions of justice and human rights. Although the theoretical basis of the law was not destroyed, the practical implications were yet to be understood. There was an inherent inconsistency between the new doctrine and the principles upon which Australia's land law had been based, which, no doubt, would give rise to complicated and intricate reconsideration of Australian property regimes.

THE CONSEQUENCES OF SETTLEMENT

The central question to be determined in *Mabo v Queensland [No. 2]* (*Mabo*) was whether, on acquiring sovereignty, the Crown became owner of all of the land or whether the Crown's title was burdened by any prior title.[6] The Court was not prepared to question the status of Australia as a 'settled' country, but it was prepared to examine the consequences of settlement and the way in which the common law was received into the territory. The Court in *Mabo* accepted that the settlers brought the common law with them in accordance with the settlement doctrine,[7] but 'only so much of it ... as was "reasonably applicable to the circumstances of the Colony"'.[8] The Court, in determining the content of the body of law received in the colony, reconsidered some of the conclusions that had earlier been drawn from the settlement thesis, in particular, the idea that the acquisition of sovereignty over territory automatically gave absolute beneficial ownership of land to the Crown.[9] On the principle that 'ownership could not be acquired by occupying land that was already occupied by another',[10] the way was clear of 'fictional impediments' to the recognition of Indigenous rights and interests in colonial land. Thus, the Court rejected the assertion that sovereignty invariably carries with it the beneficial title to all the lands of the territory, and determined that the pre-existing rights of the Indigenous peoples survived the acquisition of sovereignty.[11]

ESTABLISHING TITLE

In a joint judgment, Justices Deane and Gaudron described common law native title as a title derived from and conforming to traditional custom but recognised and protected by the common law.[12] As such, Justice Brennan explained, legislative or executive recognition by the sovereign is not required, and thereby, '[n]ative title, though recognised by the common law is not an institution of the common law'.[13] According to Justice Brennan (and much like his colleagues):

Native title has its origins in and is given its content by the traditional customs observed by the Indigenous inhabitants of a territory. The nature and incidents of native title must be ascertained as a matter of fact by reference to those laws and customs.[14]

The Court in *Mabo* was concerned that native title be a heterogeneous concept that reflects the diversity of Indigenous peoples' law and custom. Justices Deane and Gaudron, commenting on the accommodation of the idea of native title within Australian law, suggested that:

> Obviously, where the pre-existing native title interest was 'of a kind unknown to English law', its recognition and protection under the law of a newly settled British colony would require an adjustment either of the interests into a kind known to the common law or a modification of the common law to accommodate the new kind of interest.[15]

They concluded that the common law was capable of this accommodation. In order to assert title, Justice Brennan explained that a group of Indigenous inhabitants must show a connection with the relevant land that is maintained through continued acknowledgment of the laws and the customs of the group.[16] Justices Deane and Gaudron referred to:

> an established entitlement of an identified community, group or (rarely) an individual to the occupation or use of particular land and that that entitlement be of sufficient significance to establish a locally recognised special relationship between the particular community, group or individual and that land.[17]

On this construction, the majority argued that it was not necessary to superimpose a regime of property rights that were approximate to those known to English common law and that to do so defeated the purpose of protection and recognition.[18] The connection with the land in accordance with traditional law and custom is the source of the title. Any difficulty that arose from this characterisation could not justify non-recognition.[19] For this reason, native title was described as *sui generis,* or unique in law, because it reflects the rights of Indigenous people under their own legal system.[20]

The laws and customs are therefore considered to be a matter of fact, and their idiosyncratic details were considered irrelevant to the proof of native title.[21] Justice Toohey argued that it should be proof of a presence amounting to occupancy, which is not random or coincidental, that forms 'the foundation of the title and which attracts protection, and it is that which must be proved to establish title'.[22] The nature of occupancy should be determined by 'the demands of the land and society in question'.[23] Like Justices Deane and Gaudron, Justice Toohey held that there is therefore no separate requirement to prove the kind of society, only to prove that its presence is part of a functioning system.²⁴ Importantly, Justice Brennan (with whom Chief Justice Mason and Justice McHugh agreed) did not require that the connection include some kind of physical presence, recognising that the spiritual connection of Indigenous peoples to the land may also constitute proof of continued connection.²⁵

For Justices Deane and Gaudron, proof of occupancy was likely to provide adequate proof of the continued connection to land and the continued operation of law and custom. The two judges did not expressly separate physical presence (as proof of title) and law and custom (as the content of title). Nor did they overstate or over-prescribe the kind of evidence required. This formulation allows for circumstances in which proof of occupancy may not be the appropriate standard of proof, particularly where physical connection has been affected by the grant of other interests or the actions of others. In the result, a continuous chain of occupation is not required where there is acknowledgment of connection through law and custom.

The requirements of proof set forth in the substantive judgments of the majority can be summarised thus:

- existence of an identifiable community or group;
- traditional connection with or occupation of the land under the laws and customs of the group; and
- the substantial maintenance of the connection.²⁶

Justice Toohey most clearly expressed the qualification that, while the connection with the land must be shown to be significant, it would not be necessary to prove an exclusive relationship.²⁷ The judges contemplated a range, or continuum, of native title from a kind of title that approaches full ownership to a lesser interest that recognises limited rights to hunt or traverse the land.

In many parts of Australia, the failure of governments to satisfactorily recognise Indigenous rights to land has led to reliance by Indigenous peoples on the spiritual relationship with the land in order to assert any control over the use of that land, primarily through heritage legislation. There is no comparable experience elsewhere, with North American jurisprudence having emphasised traditional occupancy of the land, often recognised in treaties or through doctrines dating back to early contact.²⁸ Under the formulation put forward by the High Court in *Mabo*, physical presence is not the sole consideration or a condition precedent to establishing title. An arguable case can be put forward by Indigenous people who have been dispossessed or excluded from their land but maintain a connection in some other way.

Generally, native title will contain communal rights for the use and enjoyment of the group but Justices Deane and Gaudron did not rule out the 'rare' possibility of an identified individual entitled to occupation and use of a particular land where the other requirements are satisfied.²⁹ At base, those entitled to use and enjoyment under those rights are to be ascertained from the traditional laws and customs. Similarly, there was no allusion to biological determinants of ancestry in defining the membership of the group.³⁰ This was consistent with the idea that the native title is founded in the laws and customs of the group, including laws and customs in relation to membership.

In the United States, the courts have attempted to identify groups by common social, cultural or political elements. Canadian authority has developed a similar criteria: a 'distinctive cultural entity',³¹ or an 'organised society'.³² In the Inuit claim in *Hamlet of Baker Lake v Minister of Indian Affairs and Northern Development*, Justice Mahoney required that the claimants prove that 'they and their ancestors were members of an organised society'.³³ It was acknowledged that the relevant groups were not necessarily a particular anthropological construction such as a clan or tribe; rather, they were geographic groups that showed a commonality in culture and language. Similarly, Indigenous peoples in Australia organise on different levels for different purposes, from clan estates through to large cultural and linguistic groupings. The group that may be appropriate to hold a communal title, it was presumed, may vary across the continent.

In order for native title to be recognised under the common law as a burden on the radical title of the Crown, the connection with the land must be a pre-existing relationship, persisting at the time that Crown sovereignty was established. Justice Toohey pointed out that the connection need not be established long prior. If occupation is an established fact at the time of annexation, then nothing more is required.³⁴ Sovereignty over the New South Wales colony was said to have been successfully asserted by 1788.³⁵ In Western Australia, by contrast, the time that radical title was vested in the Crown appears to be 1829. In relation to the Murray Islands, it was held that sovereignty was acquired in 1895. Thus, the time of vesting is a matter of fact to be determined with reference to the legislative or executive act that annexed the particular territory to the colony.

The Court held that the group must be able to show that the connection to the land has been substantially maintained.³⁶ Failure to establish a continued connection loses the foundation of the title because, Justice Brennan explained, 'native title which has ceased with abandoning of laws and customs based on tradition cannot be revived for contemporary recognition'.³⁷ But a particular plaintiff group need not show that it is the same group that occupied the land at the time sovereignty was established if traditional law and custom contemplates the acquisition or transfer of rights, or succession of title, from one Indigenous group to another; this may extend to circumstances where a group dies out or is subsumed into a larger group.³⁸

Outside the system of traditional law, native title is inalienable except to the Crown. Justice Brennan suggested that this is consistent with Indigenous conceptions of inalienability of land.[39] He takes this further to suggest that rights and interests possessed as a native title can only be possessed by Indigenous people, more specifically by a member of the native title holding group who acknowledges and observes the traditional laws and customs.[40] Justices Deane and Gaudron expressed the inalienability of native title in terms of a right of pre-emption that was enjoyed by the Crown on acquiring sovereignty, such that native title could not be transferred outside the Indigenous system of law and customs except by surrender to the Crown.[41]

THE NATURE AND CONTENT OF NATIVE TITLE

The High Court retained the foundations of colonial property law by confirming that the underlying or radical title vested in the Crown was an assertion of sovereignty. But, through the recognition of native title, the common law conferred a beneficial interest on the Indigenous people that recognises and protects their pre-existing interests. The High Court recognised that the content of the native title interest could approximate to full ownership, which would reduce the Crown's radical title to one that 'extends to comparatively limited rights of administrative interference'.[42] The extent, or content, of native title is those rights that arise from the traditional laws and customs of the people. All other rights to deal with the land attach to the Crown's radical title. Where native title ceases to exist (for example, through surrender to the Crown), the radical title expands to create a 'plenum dominium', that is, the full beneficial as well as radical title.[43]

In *Mabo*, the High Court suggested that native title, while unique, is properly described as 'proprietary', if that idea is understood in a nondiscriminatory way. Justice Brennan said:

> If it be necessary to categorize an interest in land as proprietary in order to survive a change in sovereignty, the interest possessed by a community that is in exclusive possession of land falls in to that category.[44]

In contrast, Justices Deane and Gaudron conceived of native title as a personal or usufructuary right because of its inalienable nature.[45] Yet, they immediately recognised limitations of this characterisation, where, in all other respects, the title approached full exclusive possession. They returned to the idea, as described in *Amodu Tijani v Secretary, Southern Nigeria* [1921] (*Amodu Tijani*) and *Guerin v R* (1984) (*Guerin*), that the title should be accepted as unique.[46] While referring to native title as having a personal and usufructuary character (that is, not a right in the land itself), Justices Deane and Gaudron also imbued the title with significant strength:

> If common law native title conferred no more than an entitlement to occupy or use until the Crown or those acting on its behalf told the native title holders to cease their occupation or use[,] the term 'title' would be misleading, the 'rights' under it would be essentially illusory.[47]

Justice Brennan went so far as to suggest that 'it is not possible to admit a traditional usufructuary right without admitting a traditional proprietary title'.[48] Usufructuary rights of individuals within the group are therefore 'derived from the community laws and customs and are dependent on community title'.[49] Thus, Justices Deane and Gaudron concluded that 'rights of use and occupation conferred by the common law native title are not ... illusory. They are legal rights which are infringed if they are extinguished.'[50]

The content of native title, and hence the extent of the interests there-under, was a more difficult question. Justices Brennan, Deane, Gaudron and Toohey agreed that the content of the title and the identity of those upon whom it is conferred are to be ascertained in accordance with traditional laws and customs acknowledged and observed by the Indigenous inhabitants of the territory.[51] The Court did not therefore prescribe the content of the title.

It was further agreed by the majority in *Mabo* that, while the title crystallised at the time of annexation, the content of the title did not. The customs did not need to be frozen as at the time the territory was annexed to the Empire.[52] Where the general nature of the connection is maintained, the decision appeared to leave open the notion that the evolution of land use would include forms of contemporary sustenance and resource development.[53] This view is supported by Canadian case law.[54]

The position with respect to ownership of resources was immediately contentious. The High Court did not specifically deal with the question of ownership of resources but did consider the operation of legislation governing Crown land. Provisions of the *Land Act 1962* (Qld), which referred to the 'waste lands of the Crown', were held to constitute merely an assertion of sovereignty, not of beneficial ownership, and thus did not affect native title.[55] Legislation that reserves mineral rights to the Crown generally goes further than this to assert that sub-surface minerals and fossil fuels are 'the property of the Crown'.[56] But this was not a matter that was determined by the Court in *Mabo*. It would not be until nearly ten years later, in the *Ward* decision, that the High Court would conclusively decide whether, in asserting a proprietary claim to minerals, the Crown extinguished any claim to recover minerals as an incident of common law native title.[57] On the Court's reasoning in *Mabo*, however, the onus is on the Crown to establish a clear intention to extinguish Indigenous rights to resources.[58]

EXTINGUISHING TITLE

Justice Toohey argued that, whether personal or proprietary, the nature of native title should not determine the power of the Crown to extinguish the title unilaterally.[59] Despite the emotive statements regarding the need to reject doctrines that justify discriminatory treatment of Indigenous rights, the High Court decided that, up until the passing of the *Racial Discrimination Act* in 1975, the colonies and later the states and Commonwealth had the power to abrogate the rights of Indigenous peoples for the private benefit of non-Indigenous settlers. Justice Brennan explained that, while native title survived the acquisition of radical title, native title was exposed 'to extinguishment by a valid exercise of sovereign power inconsistent with the continued right to enjoy native title'.[60] The High Court held that native title could be lost where the traditional connection with the land has broken, had been surrendered or had become extinct. More importantly, a pre-existing title could be unilaterally extinguished by the new sovereign 'by valid exercise of sovereign power inconsistent with the continued right to enjoy native title'.[61] The majority of the Court found it unnecessary to reach a conclusion on the issue of extinguishment in the case of the Murray Islands but all of the judges engaged in some discussion of the modes of extinguishing title.[62] Where title has been extinguished through surrender, abandonment, extinction or divestiture, future generations cannot maintain a claim because, in the case of surrender, abandonment and extinction, the connection that sustains the title is lost; in the case of divestiture, recognition and protection have been unilaterally revoked by the Crown.

The possibility of surrender was proposed by Justice Brennan, although the difficulties associated with such extinguishment were not explored.[63] The surrender of native title is not a simple acquisition by the Crown under the general laws of property. That is why in other jurisdictions any such surrender to the Crown is done by treaty or treaty-style agreement.[64] Even then, because of the communal and intergenerational nature of native title, a difficulty arises in trying to identify who in the group has the capacity, and under what process they would have the power, to surrender the title in an agreement binding on the whole group and on future generations. Even if such an agreement was ratified by legislation, it is not clear that the arrangement would be beyond challenge. The advantage of voluntary surrender is the ability of the group to alienate the land under terms agreed upon by negotiation rather than the unilateral action of the Crown. It was not clear from the decision whether the doctrine established in *Mabo* explicitly precluded Indigenous people from dealing with their land without necessarily surrendering title. Nor was it conclusive whether native title land can be dealt with without requiring complete surrender. That is, so long as any divesting of interests occurred through the Crown and not through private alienation, the native title holders could surrender particular rights under their title to the Crown and retain the balance of their title on conditions that preserved their connection and control over the land. Agreements and consultation to secure access to native title land were obviously to become an integral part of land and resource development in the future and would require clarification of these matters.

Short of surrender, and without alienating native title, the community's laws may regulate the transmission of rights and access to land, as well as responsibilities and uses of land.[65] As discussed earlier in relation to connection, though the common law does not support alienability outside the system of law and custom, alienability and succession, within and between groups, can be part of native title. According to Justice Brennan, the 'incidents of a particular native title relating to inheritance, the transmission or acquisition of rights and interests … are matters to be determined by the laws and customs of the Indigenous inhabitants'.[66]

Without inheritance, acquisition or succession of title under traditional law or custom, title might be abandoned, according to the majority in *Mabo*, where the group has ceased to acknowledge their laws and customs because, in so doing, the connection between the Indigenous people and the land is lost. Similarly, the title to an area could be extinguished on the death of the last of the members of the group and native title cannot be revived if some other group subsequently acknowledges the traditional laws and customs of that group. That being said, Justices Deane and Gaudron were of the view that there could be no abandonment where there had been continuous occupation; that is, continuous occupation is sufficient evidence of continued acknowledgment.[67]

The most significant form of extinguishment, given the belated recognition of native title, was the Court's finding that the Crown has the power to extinguish title unilaterally (that is, without consent) by legislation or by executive act. This aspect of native title doctrine was a clear assertion of colonial sovereign power.

A general principle was established: specific action that purports to affect native title must show a clear and plain intention to extinguish the native title interest. Thus Justices Deane and Gaudron concluded that:

> If lands in relation to which [common law native] title exists are clearly included within the ambit of … legislation, the legislative provisions conferring executive powers will, in the absence of clear and unambiguous words, be construed so as not to increase the capacity of the Crown to extinguish or diminish the native title.[68]

Despite this general principle, native title was held to be extinguished, by necessary implication, by the grant of private rights in the land to the exclusion of the Indigenous people.[69] The rationale behind the prioritisation of the later grant was that a valid grant of an interest in land is binding on the Crown and it is unable to derogate from it.[70] The High Court contrasted the title of the Indigenous people to such grants, holding that the rights of Indigenous peoples pre-existed and burdened the radical title of the Crown upon acquisition of sovereignty. Because native title was said not to have its source in the Crown, it does not enjoy the same protection as a grant from the Crown and is therefore extinguished wherever there is a necessary inconsistency. In these cases, the clear and plain intention will be implied.[71] Similarly, title was said to be extinguished by the appropriation, reservation or dedication of land for purposes inconsistent with the title.[72]

The same reasoning was applied where the Crown has dealt with land in a manner inconsistent with the continued existence of native title. It was considered by the Court to be sufficiently clear intention if, for example, the Crown appropriated land for roadways and other permanent public utilities.[73] In contrast, uses by the Crown that are consistent with the continued enjoyment of rights under native title, such as the mere reservation of land for state forest or national parks, were considered by Justice Brennan to be consistent with the continued enjoyment by the Indigenous peoples.[74] North American decisions had already shown that regulation of Indigenous activities for the purpose of, and to the extent required for, conservation did not extinguish title. Those decisions were relied on by the High Court in *Mabo*.[75] Justice Brennan also saw the reservation of land for use by Indigenous people as consistent with the continuation of native title.[76] In the Murray Islands specifically, the activities of the state government after annexation had not shown derogatory intent. To the contrary, the system of reservation and trusteeship over the islands preserved the benefit of the native title for the Indigenous inhabitants. Thus, simply granting or reserving land for any purpose does not automatically extinguish native title; there must be actual inconsistency with continued enjoyment of native title.

In preserving the skeleton of principle of the land tenure system, the Court held that the Crown is able to grant any interest in land, including a fee simple. It was clear from the discussion by Justice Brennan that a grant of a fee simple in land would likely be sufficient to extinguish title.[77] A fee simple is the largest interest in land known to the common law, thus raising the question of whether there is any room for the continued enjoyment of rights under native title.[78] Other grants by the Crown — including leasehold interests and lesser interests (such as mining leases, exploration licences, extraction permits and leases, and interests under pastoral 'leases') — were thought unlikely to be sufficient to extinguish the title.[79]

WRONGFUL EXTINGUISHMENT

The majority in *Mabo* agreed that the legislature and executive have power to extinguish native title, though native title survives annexation. Chief Justice

1. Recognising native title: *Mabo*

Mason and Justice McHugh, in a joint judgment, identified a conflict over the issue of compensation for such extinguishment:

> The main difference between those members of the Court who constitute the majority is that, subject to the operation of the *Racial Discrimination Act 1975* (Cth), neither of us nor Justice Brennan agrees with the conclusion to be drawn from the judgements of Deane, Toohey and Gaudron JJ that, at least in the absence of clear and unambiguous statutory provision to the contrary, extinguishment of native title by the Crown by inconsistent grant is wrongful and gives rise to a claim for compensatory damages … We are authorised to say that the other members of the Court agree with what is said in the preceding paragraph.[80]

Justices Toohey, Deane and Gaudron agreed that non-statutory extinguishment, though effective, gave rise to a cause of action in equity for compensation.[81] Though acknowledging the power of the Crown to extinguish title, Justices Toohey, Deane and Gaudron held that wrongful extinguishment by inconsistent grant without clear and unambiguous legislative intent would be subject to compensation to the title holders.[82] Moreover, Commonwealth legislation is subject to the Australian Constitution. The Commonwealth Parliament has the power to legislate and to acquire property under any head of power for which it is able to legislate generally. The legislative heads of power under s 51 of the Australian Constitution are diverse, and the external affairs power (s 51(xxix)) allows an almost plenary power to legislate for any issue that is the subject of a treaty to which Australia is a signatory. Moreover, the Commonwealth Parliament has the power, under s 51(xxvi), to make laws for people of any race, including Indigenous peoples. But, in order to compulsorily acquire property, the Commonwealth Government must do so on just terms, under s 51(xxxi). This provision has been considered a constitutional guarantee, and, as a result, is construed liberally.[83] It is difficult to conceive that this guarantee was denied to Indigenous peoples by the Court. The High Court reasoning in relation to the power of the acquiring sovereign to unilaterally extinguish native title drew on a common law tradition. But that common law position should be subject to the superior law of the Constitution. Thus, in 1901, with the coming into force of the Constitution, the compulsory acquisition of native title, by the Commonwealth at least, should have been subject to compensation because, as Justices Deane and Gaudron concluded, 'any legislative extinguishment … would constitute an expropriation of property, to the benefit of the underlying estate for the purposes of s 51(xxxi)'.[84]

The difficulty arose from the authority given to Chief Justice Mason and Justice McHugh to summarise the findings of the Court.[85] The basis of their statement appears to be Justice Brennan's conclusion that the grant of an interest inconsistent with the continued enjoyment of the communal title, made with the clear intention of extinguishing that title, is valid. As the extinguishment of title was not considered to be wrongful, no right to compensation arises. But there was nothing in the judgment of Justice Brennan that inevitably denied compensatory relief. Justice Brennan expressed the view that, as a title recognised and protected by the common law, the extinguishment of traditional title was a serious consequence and, where it has not been extinguished, it remains legally enforceable.[86] Justice Brennan also cited, approvingly, a precedent for the granting of compensation, stating that the issue of compensation was not one that was to be decided in the case.[87] The decision by Justice Brennan seemed to allow scope for further development of the law and a closer review of the issue of wrongful extinguishment, which was not directly relevant to the case before the Court in *Mabo*.

Justice Toohey offered a more secure title, under which the exercise of legislative or executive action must be exercised with regard to the fiduciary relationship between the government and the title holders.[88] The duty was said to arise out of the state's power to affect the interests of the title holders, whose vulnerability gives rise to the need for the application of equitable principles. Justice Toohey pointed to the protectionist policies of the governments towards the Indigenous people as an indication of an undertaking not to act to their detriment.[89] With Justices Deane and Gaudron, Justice Toohey determined that unilateral extinguishment, while it might be valid, gave rise to compensation. Unfortunately, with the authority of the Court, the view of Chief Justice Mason and Justice McHugh stands: under the common law, the extinguishment of native title by the Crown is not subject to compensation.

In that same short judgment, Chief Justice Mason and Justice McHugh also drew attention to the impact of the *Racial Discrimination Act* (1975) (Cth) (RDA). In *Mabo [No. 1]*, the *Queensland Coast Islands Declaratory Act 1985* (Qld) was declared invalid because it was inconsistent with s 10 of the RDA.[90] As a result, it could not be relied upon by the state government to effectively terminate the proceedings.

Under the common law of native title emerging from the *Mabo* decision, any purported extinguishment of title by executive or legislative action made before 31 October 1975 was not affected by the RDA and would not be open to challenge for compensation or any other relief. However, any extinguishment of rights on or after the introduction of the RDA may be invalid or may be modified to give equal protection to Indigenous peoples in the enjoyment of their rights. The High Court's reasoning in relation to the protection provided by the RDA ensures that equal protection of the just terms clause is enjoyed by native title holders only from 1975 onwards.

State governments are not directly bound by the Commonwealth constitutional provisions, although most have their own just terms provisions. The principal limitation that the Constitution places on the state legislatures identified by Justices Deane and Gaudron is the paramountcy provision of s 109: 'When the law of a state is inconsistent with a law of the Commonwealth the latter shall prevail, and the former shall, to the extent of the inconsistency be invalid'.[91] Importantly, then, the state legislatures and executives are bound by the RDA. The RDA can operate in two ways: where legislation deprives persons of a right enjoyed by others and where the legislation confers a particular right on people generally but not on people of a particular ethnic origin. For example, the compensation provision of the *Mining Act 1978* (WA) applies in respect of the owners and occupiers of private land and certain occupiers of Crown land but not native title holders. This provision would be extended under s 10 of the RDA to apply equally to native title holders or to invalidate a grant of mining that did not guarantee compensation.

The application of the comments of the majority to past acts and existing legislation has proved to be a difficult exercise as the intention and impact of every legislative and executive act over more than two hundred years must be analysed to determine any extinguishing effect. The question of compensation remains outstanding. There is still no decision that seeks to place a value on the loss of native title.

CONCLUSION

The *Mabo* decision provided Indigenous peoples with a viable legal doctrine to protect their interests and to facilitate the preservation and strengthening of their culture. It recognised that the granting of future interests in land could coexist with the presence of native title. It merely ensured that dealings with respect to Indigenous land would be concluded in negotiation with Indigenous peoples and that their interests would be recognised by the parties involved and by the law. The movement away from bestowment of rights upon Indigenous inhabitants to the assertion of existing rights created a source of empowerment for Indigenous people that forced non-Indigenous Australians to confront their racism and the injustices of the colonising culture. This redefining of the relationship was to result in more than a decade of litigation over the extent of recognition and the limits of protection.

CHAPTER 2

Coexistence and necessary inconsistency
Wik Peoples v Queensland

HIGH COURT OF AUSTRALIA, 1996

The Wik peoples and the Thayorre people brought a claim for native title over areas of land and sea in the Cape York Peninsula on the Gulf of Carpentaria and for damages and relief for any extinguishment.[1] The country over which they asserted native title included a group of pastoral leases known as the Holroyd River Holding and the Mitchellton pastoral lease. The proceedings were initiated shortly after the High Court's decision was handed down in *Mabo v Queensland [No. 2]* (1992) (*Mabo*)[2] and prior to the enactment of the *Native Title Act 1993* (Cth) (NTA).[3] This case became the test for native title over pastoral leases and, more generally, the ability of native title to survive a grant to a third party, with a majority of the Court finding that native title and pastoral leases were capable of coexisting.[5]

Justice Gaudron summarised the dispute between the principal parties. The respondents, including the State of Queensland, the Commonwealth and the pastoralists, argued, simply, that:

> pastoral leases granted under the 1910 and 1962 [Land] Acts were true leases in the traditional common law sense and thus conferred rights of exclusive possession. Those rights, according to the argument, are inconsistent with the continued existence of native title rights and, thus, necessarily extinguished them.[6]

The Wik and Thayorre peoples claimed that their native title was not extinguished by the granting of pastoral leases; rather, it was a valid and enforceable interest in the land coexisting with the interests of the lessees. The native title applicants, according to Justice Gaudron, argued that 'pastoral leases granted under those Acts were not true leases and did not confer rights of exclusive possession but merely rights to use land for pastoral purposes'.[7]

The applicants proposed that, in any event, it was not the mere grant of a right but the exercise of that right in a manner inconsistent with native title that effected extinguishment. Argument was also put that the grant of inconsistent rights for a fixed period merely suspended native title rights, which then revived on the expiry, surrender or forfeiture of the interest. The Thayorre people offered the further argument that a fiduciary duty arose from the Crown's relationship with native title holders and that any reversion to the Crown on expiry of the leases was held in trust for the native title holders.[8]

At trial, Justice Drummond sought to deal with the question of whether native title was extinguished by the pastoral leases as a preliminary issue before deciding whether native title could be established. This approach was criticised by members of the High Court, first because it acted as an effective 'strike out' proceeding[9] and, second, because it forced the current proceedings to operate within 'a certain unreality'.[10]

Justice Drummond had determined that binding authority existed to support the conclusion that a pastoral lease granted exclusive possession, and thus extinguished native title.[11] In *North Ganalanja Aboriginal Corporation v Queensland* (1995) (*North Ganalanja*), the full Federal Court had considered a pastoral lease issued in Queensland in 1904 and concluded that it conferred exclusive possession on the grantee, although limited by duration and purpose.[12] After Justice Drummond's decision, the High Court, on appeal, had cast doubt on the decision in *North Ganalanja* and, by majority, had considered that it was premature to consider the 'pastoral lease question'.[13] Justice Drummond did recognise that the proper inquiry was not to be determined by reference to precedent, but to examine whether the particular lease conferred a right of exclusive possession or at least a right of possession sufficiently exclusive to extinguish native title.[14] Given the important principles at issue, the appeal was referred straight to the High Court, with no full Federal Court decision in the case.[15]

NATURE OF THE INQUIRY

A number of questions were drafted for consideration by the High Court.[16] The most significant question before the Court was whether the grant of a pastoral lease necessarily extinguished all native title rights.[17] Justice Toohey set out the inquiry:

1. Whether the relevant grants did in truth confer possession of land on the grantees to the exclusion of all others including the holders of native title rights.
2. Whether, if such a grant did confer exclusive possession, native title rights were necessarily extinguished, which depends on:
   a. Whether and to what extent native title rights are inconsistent with the exclusive possession; and
   b. Whether native title rights are truly extinguished or whether they are simply unenforceable.[18]

For all of the judges, the central inquiry turned on the proper construction of the *Land Act 1910* (Qld) (the 1910 Act) and the *Land Act 1962* (Qld) (the 1962 Act; together, the Land Acts) and upon the terms of the instruments that granted the pastoral leases.

For Justice Gummow, the inquiry began with a proposition that:

> for a statute such as the 1910 Act or the 1962 Act to impair or extinguish native title or to authorise the taking of steps which have that effect, it is necessary to show, at least, the intention 'manifested clearly and plainly', to achieve that result.[19]

Consistent with *Western Australia v Commonwealth* (1995) (*Native Title Act case*),[20] this intention does not refer to the state of mind of the legislators, but to the intention of the legislation: what the statute means.[21]

HISTORY OF PASTORAL LEASES UNDER STATUTE

In order to answer the questions before the Court, significant attention was paid by all of the judges to the historical context in which pastoral leases developed under Australian land law, as well as to the history of the particular interests in question in order to determine the intention behind the statute and, hence, the effect of the grant.

The first two pastoral leases were granted under the 1910 Act, in 1915 and 1919, constituting the Mitchellton pastoral lease. In 1945 a pastoral lease was granted over the Holroyd holding and a further lease was granted in 1973, under the 1962 Act. The first of the Mitchellton pastoral leases issued in 1915 lasted only three years, before being forfeited for non-payment of rent in 1918. The 1919 lease was surrendered in 1921 and neither was ever taken into possession by the lessees. Prior to the surrender, the Mitchellton pastoral leases were targeted for dedication as reserves to be held 'for benefit of Aboriginal people' in recognition of the significant community living in the area and the land had been held under similar tenure since that time.[22] The first Holroyd pastoral lease was surrendered in 1973, with the second lease being issued in 1974 for a term of thirty years. There were few improvements ever completed on the lease, despite the conditions imposed, and the land remained marginal for grazing purposes. From the perspective of the native title holders, little of significance had occurred on their land that would disturb their enjoyment. To this, Justice Kirby suggested that it would require 'a very strong legal doctrine to deprive them of their native title'.[23] While these leases were not necessarily typical, Justice Kirby used them to illustrate the purposes to which pastoral leases had been developed.

The judges in the majority surveyed the history of feudal tenures and the reception and modification of common law and property law in Australia, as well as the law of statutory interpretation.²⁴ The judges described the movement of 'squatters' into the hinterland and into areas that were unsurveyed, uncontrolled and over which they had no title.²⁵ At first, under royal prerogative (or executive power), the Governor issued occupation licences, and legislation was introduced to establish a border police force to protect persons 'lawfully occupying or being upon' Crown land outside the perimeters of the settlements.²⁶ The *Sale of Waste Lands Act 1842* (Imp) replaced the prerogative power, bringing the management and disposition of Crown lands within a statutory framework and eventually within the purview of the colonial legislatures.

From the vesting of self-government and control over Crown lands, the colonial legislators quickly began to exercise their powers to develop a multiplicity of 'new forms of tenure' specific to their circumstances.²⁷ These 'new tenures', as Justice Toohey highlighted, reflected the 'desire of pastoralists for some form of security of title and the clear intention of the Crown that pastoralists should not acquire the freehold of large area of land, the future use of which could not be readily foreseen'.²⁸

APPLYING THE RULES OF STATUTORY CONSTRUCTION

The Queensland legislature adopted the form of pastoral lease that had evolved in New South Wales and passed numerous Acts affecting and regulating pastoral leases. In none of these, apart from the use of the word 'lease', was there a clear indication of the nature of the interest conferred. Terms such as 'lease', 'licence' and 'rents' were applied in what has been described as a new, more 'generic' sense.²⁹ The judges in the majority undertook a detailed investigation of the statute and the instruments granted under it, emphasising the nature of the pastoral interest as a creature of statute, within a comprehensive legislative regime for the management of Crown lands, peculiar to the needs and circumstances of the country, and deliberately distinguished from the feudal doctrines that underpinned the common law of tenures and estates.³⁰ It would be a mistake, Justice Kirby suggested, to import such notions to statutory tenures unless necessary.³¹

The majority concluded that there was no evidence on the face of the legislation to suggest that it was intended that the pastoralists would receive possession of the land to the exclusion of the Indigenous peoples. Indeed, the judges highlighted the historical materials that indicated the degree to which the Indigenous peoples' continued access to pastoral lands, as well as their protection against violence from the squatters, was contemplated by the early legislators and executive. In particular, they noted correspondence from Secretary of State, Earl Grey, who repeatedly assured that pastoral leases were only an exclusive right to pasture cattle, not exclusive occupation, and, in particular, were not intended to exclude Indigenous peoples from the land.³² These historical statements were not taken to constitute a promise or recognition of an interest vested in Indigenous peoples but they seem to have provided some factual context that militated against the argument that there was a necessary or intended inconsistency between the enjoyment of rights under the pastoral lease and the continued occupation of the land by the native title holders.³³

THE ARGUMENTS IN FAVOUR OF EXCLUSIVE POSSESSION

All of the judges considered the central arguments supporting the respondents' contention that pastoral leases were effective to extinguish native title. There were three main arguments in favour of a presumption that exclusive possession was intended to be conveyed by the grant of a pastoral lease: the use of the term 'lease'; the need for the Crown to hold a 'reversion' in the case of the forfeiture of the lease; and the distinction drawn in the legislation between the statutory pastoral leases and other statutory licences.

1. The use of the term 'lease'

The respondents' strongest argument was that exclusive possession is an essential feature of a lease, thus, the instruments being called 'leases' confer exclusive possession. As Justice Toohey succinctly stated: 'the point is not so much that a "lease" confers exclusive possession; it is that the conferring of exclusive possession is an indication that the arrangement in question is a lease rather than, say, a licence'.³⁴ Justice Brennan, dissenting, admitted that it is a central tenet of construction that a lease is not a lease merely because it is called a lease by the parties.³⁵ He went on to suggest that, in the absence of any contrary indication, Parliament (when using a term in statute that has a defined legal meaning) should be taken to have intended that meaning. Justice Brennan concluded that the pastoral lease conveyed more than a bundle of statutory rights; it transferred a legal estate and consequently a right to exclusive possession.³⁶

The majority disagreed. For Justice Toohey, the premise that the intention of the legislature was to import notions of common law into the meaning of pastoral leases under the Land Acts was to take the intention of the Parliament too far in this instance. Justice Gaudron noted that pastoral leases had always been derived from outside the common law and had for many years been entirely anchored in statute. They conferred only the interest that the legislation authorised.³⁷ Similarly, Justice Kirby applied the rule of construction that the powers conferred by the statute are only those stated, or necessary, to achieve the stated objectives.³⁸

Referring to the principle relied upon by Justice Brennan, Justice Gaudron argued that the proposition that words with an established meaning in common law should have the same meaning in statute (unless the words of the statute indicate otherwise) is but an instance of a more general rule. Citing Justice Brennan in *American Dairy Queen (Qld) Pty Ltd v Blue Rio Pty Ltd* (*American Dairy Queen*), Justice Gaudron stated that the courts will construe statute in conformity with the common law and will not attribute to it an intention to alter the common law principles unless such an intention is manifested according to the construction of the statute.[39]

2. The Crown's reversion

The respondents placed considerable reliance on an extract from the judgment of Justice Brennan in *Mabo*, which had received some support from the Federal Court in *North Ganalanja Aboriginal Corporation v Queensland* (1996).[40] Justice Brennan, in explaining the possible effects on native title of the grant of an interest, said:

> If a lease be granted, the lessee acquires possession and the Crown acquires the reversion expectant on the expiry of the term. The Crown's title is thus expanded from the mere radical title and, on the expiry of the term, becomes a plenum dominium.[41]

Justices Deane and Gaudron in *Mabo* proposed a similar situation, although expressly referring to a lease granting exclusive possession.[42]

Justice Kirby rejected these statements as insufficient to determine the issue at hand.[43] On this analysis, Justice Kirby suggested, any dealing with Crown land would effect total extinguishment without consideration of the extent of inconsistency. Rather, the Land Acts regulated the granting of the pastoral lease and did not confer on the Crown an estate in order to grant a lease.[44] The true test, to which the majority judges referred, is found at the beginning of the passage by Justice Brennan: that is, the test of inconsistency, based on express or implied intent, clearly and plainly manifest.

The Wik and Thayorre peoples raised the alternative argument that the 'reversion' was an exercise of radical title, not of proprietary title.[45] Justice Gaudron concurred with this conclusion.[46] Justice Toohey, similarly, concluded that the grant of an estate in land does not require the Crown to assume beneficial ownership of the land. The doctrine of estates, Justice Toohey said, 'is a feudal concept in order to explain the interests of those who held from the Crown, not the "title" of the Crown itself '.[47] Pointing to the legislation itself, the majority judges held that s 135 of the 1910 Act and, similarly, s 299 of the 1962 Act ran counter to the common law tenure system, whereby the land 'reverted' to Crown land on surrender, forfeiture or expiry, and was again subject to the Land Acts, and did not vest in the Crown as a beneficial interest.[48]

3. The distinction between 'leases' and 'licences'

The respondents also relied on the argument that there was a distinction in the Land Acts between leases and licences.[49] But Justice Gummow's assessment of the Land Acts suggested that there was in fact no clear distinction between leases and licences, which for most of the relevant provisions of the Act were treated together.[50] Indeed, Justice Gummow proposed that, in creating its own remedy for ejectment available to both lessees and licensees, the statute gave some indication that the nature of the interests conferred were not exclusive possession, which at law had its own remedies.[51]

This latter provision was relied upon by the respondents and formed a central part of Justice Brennan's dissenting judgment. The 1910 Act, s 203, created an offence of trespass on Crown land (which included pastoral land under an occupation licence, s 4, but not land 'granted', s 6). Section 204 provided for warrants for removal for trespass and provided for a lessee or licensee of land granted from the Crown to make a complaint against persons in unlawful occupation. Similar provisions were contained in the 1962 Act, at ss 372(1) and 373(1).

Justice Brennan took the view that the pastoral lessee acquired a right to exclusive possession and had a right to seek to eject the native title holders under s 204. But Justice Brennan argued that the native title holders did not automatically become trespassers on the land on the grant of the pastoral lease. A pastoral lessee who took no action to exclude the Indigenous inhabitants had to be taken to have consented to their presence.[52] Unfortunately, he concluded, where the Indigenous peoples were excluded, this could only be characterised, as it was in *Mabo*, as part of the dispossession of Indigenous peoples of their land 'parcel by parcel'.[53]

The judges in the majority referred to Justice Brennan's judgment in *Mabo*, in which his Honour considered a similar provision (s 91, *Crown Lands Alienation Act 1876* (Qld)).[54] In that case, Justice Brennan argued that the provision was 'not directed to indigenous inhabitants who were or are in occupation of land by right of their unextinguished native title'.[55] Justice Gaudron interpreted this case as standing for a general proposition that words in a statute are not to be construed as extinguishing native title rights unless that intention is manifest through clear and unambiguous language. Thus, Justice Gaudron concluded that, as 's 203 did not render Aboriginal people trespassers on their own land, it follows that s 204 did not, of itself render them trespassers on land the subject of a pastoral lease'.[56]

In contrast, Justice Kirby noted that the legislature was aware of the large number of Indigenous inhabitants who were using the land and had not indicated any government policy to drive them out of the pastoral leaseholdings. Indeed, if the legislature had so intended, it may well have provided specifically for ejectment of such inhabitants.[57]

On the whole the majority judges were unconvinced that the legislation plainly conveyed exclusive possession or necessarily required the creation of an exclusive possession tenure in order to achieve the objective of managing the pastoral expansion. They also went further to examine whether there were any factors that would reinforce this presumption.

ARGUMENTS AGAINST EXCLUSIVE POSSESSION

Having determined that there was no clear indication in the statute that suggested an exclusive possession was intended to be conferred, the High Court judges variously discussed the many indicators they saw as providing evidence to the contrary. Justice Gaudron outlined a series of characteristics of the tenures granted under the 1910 Act that militated against a presumption that a traditional common law tenure was envisaged.[58]

1. The vastness of the areas over which it was intended to grant pastoral leases (evidenced by the unique calculation of rents, under s 43, on the basis of square miles rather than acres).
2. The provision for pastoral leases to be effective upon granting, under s 41, with no requirement to enter into possession or occupation, in contrast to the characteristics of common law leases (also in contrast to settlement applications, s 76).
3. Restrictions and rights of entry under the Land Acts for persons authorised to remove resources for persons riding or driving stock along stock routes.
4. The lack of distinction between pastoral leases and occupation licences, the difference seemingly the short-term nature of the licence (not the rights conferred).
5. The tenures were devised specifically to deal with the particular circumstances of the colonies and there was nothing to suggest that it was necessary or convenient to conform to the common law, nor that exclusive possession was a necessary or convenient feature.
6. Other unique tenures included in the 1910 Act diverge significantly from the common law, most notably the idea of 'perpetual leases', which could not possibly take its meaning from the common law.

The pastoral lease issued under the 1962 Act over the Holroyd land was less restrictive. This lease covered a much larger area but did not contain the proviso 'for pastoral purposes only', although it was issued under the pastoral leases provisions. The lease required the lessee to undertake certain improvements, some, though not many, of which had been made. The discretion of the minister was significant, including controlling any transfer of the interest. In other respects, the pastoral lease was similar to those under the 1910 Act, and the 1962 Act contained similar reservations. Justice Gummow found no material difference between the two Acts. But Justice Gaudron closely examined the terms of the later grant and noted that the distinctions were less starkly drawn than with respect to the earlier grants. Her Honour concluded that the purpose of the 1962 Act, evidenced by the operation of s 4(2), was to create tenures 'analogous' to those of previous Acts and should not be construed as intending to create an entirely new tenure under the same name. Indeed, the differences fell far short of a clear indication of exclusive possession.[59]

THE CONDITIONAL NATURE OF THE GRANT

The majority judges concluded that the 'strongest' indication that could be drawn from the legislation and the instruments to show that exclusive possession was not conferred was in the provisions conferring rights on third parties and authorising persons to enter on the lands for a variety of purposes, including taking of resources that would normally be the province of the lessee.[60] In particular, the three early leases were expressed to be 'for pastoral purposes only'. All of the leases contained reservations in relation to minerals (and, in all but the earliest lease, to petroleum[61]), as well as a reservation of the right of any person duly authorised by the Crown at all times to go upon the land for 'any purpose whatsoever'.[62] The grants were also expressed to be subject to the conditions and provisos under the Land Acts. Those conditions included the right of the Crown to issue licences for the removal of natural resources, such as trees, rocks, water, depasturing of travelling stock and the like.

Beyond the question of exclusive possession, Justice Gummow pointed out that the reason that it was presumed that native title was extinguished by a grant in fee simple (although it had not yet been determined) was that the fee simple is the largest estate known to the common law and confers the widest possible powers of enjoyment of land and anything found upon it. A common law lease could be presumed to similarly effect an extinguishment, as suggested by Justice Brennan in *Mabo*, on the same basis because a common law lease carries with it most of the powers of enjoyment under fee, particularly in relation to the fruits of the land. The *sui generis* statutory leases in question here did not confer these broad rights.[63]

Justice Brennan did not accept that the reservations contained in the leases indicated that a limited right had been granted; rather, he concluded that they in fact implied that the right existed. The reservations merely limited the enjoyment of the right but did not destroy it.[64] Justice Gummow explicitly rejected this argument.[65] Also arguing to the contrary, Justice Toohey warned against relying on precedents that emerged from a commercial common law context where they did not accord with the relevant statute and had no regard to the presence on the land of the Indigenous peoples.[66]

A PRESUMPTION OF BENEFICIAL CONSTRUCTION

Justice Gaudron returned to the principles of construction applied in *Mabo*, that 'general ... legislation with respect to Crown land is not to be construed, in the absence of clear and unambiguous words, as intended to apply in a way which will extinguish or diminish rights under common law native title'.[67] Similarly, Justice Kirby described this as a 'strong presumption' of beneficial construction, by which a statute would not be construed as extinguishing native title if it was at all susceptible to some other construction.[68] Both judges suggested that the presumption can be traced to the more general rule that clear and unambiguous words are required before an intention will be imputed to the legislature to extinguish valuable property rights. The presumption was also supported by the rule described above, from *American Dairy Queen*, in which an intention will not be imputed to the legislature contrary to the common law (from which native title is derived) unless clearly manifested in the language of the statute.

Thus, the grant of a pastoral lease under the 1910 Act conveyed a right to occupy the land for pastoral purposes and the right to bring an action for unlawful occupation. It did not operate to expropriate native title rights or to include a right to exclude native title holders as trespassers.[69]

CONCLUSIONS AS TO NECESSARY EXTINGUISHMENT

Having reviewed the historical material and the specific instruments, Justice Toohey returned to the operation of the legislation and the 'intention' to be properly drawn from the construction of the statute and the instrument. His Honour concluded that:

> A pastoral lease under the relevant legislation granted to the lessee possession of the land for pastoral purposes. And the grant necessarily gave to the lessee such possession as was required for the occupation of the land for those purposes. As has been seen, each lease contained a number of reservations of rights of entry, both specific and general. The lessee's rights to possession must yield to those reservations. There is nothing in the statute which authorised the lease, or in the lease itself, which conferred on the grantee rights to exclusive possession, in particular possession exclusive of all rights and interests of the indigenous inhabitants whose occupation derived from their traditional title.[70]

While Justice Brennan excluded Indigenous people from his inquiry into the construction of the statute, Justice Toohey found a place for native title within this exercise. Justice Toohey clarified, '[t]hat is not to say that the legislature gave conscious recognition to native title ... It is simply that there is nothing in the statute or grant that should be taken as a total exclusion of the indigenous people from the land'.[71] This interpretation imports the notion of a 'necessary' inconsistency and the strong beneficial construction employed by the majority.

In coming to his conclusions, Justice Brennan noted that the 'adversely discriminatory treatment suffered by the holders of native title' was not in issue.[72] In contrast, Justice Toohey noted that such a conclusion should not be drawn lightly.[73] Justice Gummow agreed, pointing to the need to 'adjust ingrained habits of thought and understanding to what, since 1992, must be accepted as the common law of Australia'.[74] Perhaps this is where Justice Brennan faltered, because it was not necessary to impute to the legislators some deliberate contemplation of native title but it was necessary to properly treat native title as the interest that arose first in time, an interest that enjoys the recognition and protection of the common law. Thus in seeking to determine whether there was a clear and plain intention to extinguish native title, Justice Gummow posed the question as to whether the incidents of the grant were such that the existing right (the native title right) could not be exercised without abrogating the statutory right. If it could not, then by necessary implication the statute extinguished the existing right.[75]

Justice Kirby summarised his findings:

> Pastoral leases give rise to statutory interests in land which are sui generis. Being creatures of Australian statute, their character and incidents must be derived from the statute. Neither of the Acts in question here expressly extinguishes native title. To do so very clear statutory language would, by conventional theory, be required. When the Acts are examined, clear language of extinguishment is simply missing.[76]

Instead, the examination of the legislation revealed several indications that the interest in land granted to the pastoralist was a limited one: for 'pastoral purposes only'. The majority expressed the view that such an interest could be exercised and enjoyed to the full without necessarily extinguishing native title interests. Justices Gaudron and Gummow concluded that the Holroyd pastoral lease did not confer a right of exclusive possession, although the inclusion of conditions for improvement might have impaired or extinguished native title rights; if so, and to what extent, were to be determined upon a hearing of the facts.[77]

In a 'postscript' authorised by the members of the majority, Justice Toohey confirmed the conclusion that all native title rights were not necessarily extinguished by the grant of the pastoral leases, but whether there was any relevant inconsistency would require an inquiry into the particular rights and interests that might be asserted and established. The postscript confirmed that to say that the pastoral leases did not grant exclusive possession was 'in no way destructive of the title of those grantees'; it merely recognised the rights of the grantees according to the pastoral lease and the statute that underpinned it. If there was inconsistency between those rights and the rights asserted by the native title holders, the latter had to yield to that extent to the rights of the grantees.[78]

EXTINGUISHMENT AND THE TEST OF INCONSISTENCY

The decision of the majority — that there was no necessary inconsistency between the non-exclusive rights of the pastoral leaseholder and the continued enjoyment of native title rights — left the issue of the extent, if any, of extinguishment to be explored in greater detail at trial. But there were a number of principles that were discussed in the context of the judgments that provided guidance to the courts and others.

Despite dissenting on the point of exclusive possession, Justice Brennan's judgment reconfirmed his views on extinguishment first articulated in *Mabo*. His Honour restated that:

> the strength of native title is that it is enforceable by the ordinary courts. Its weakness is that it is not an estate held from the Crown nor is it protected by the common law as Crown tenures are protected against impairment by subsequent Crown Grant.[79]

Justice Kirby, similarly, noted that the fact that native title was recognised to any extent in Australian law was only because it was recognised by the common law.

This understanding of the limits of common law recognition led the Court to reject the argument put by the Thayorre people, who suggested the test of inconsistency lay in the factual inconsistency, not the theoretical inconsistency found in legal instruments. Thus an investigation was required into the extent to which the two legal regimes and the concurrent enjoyment of rights could be reconciled as a matter of fact. Justice Kirby expressly rejected this argument, confirming that the law was concerned with 'title' in respect of land and the existence or otherwise of legal rights in respect of the land, not the manner of their exercise.[80] In this way, the actions of a pastoralist operating outside the powers conferred by the pastoral lease would be irrelevant to the inquiry. To do otherwise, Justice Kirby warned, would invite uncertainty in the ordering of entitlements.[81] To pay respect to the argument of the Thayorre people, what they sought was due recognition of the authority of their legal system and a negotiation of the respective interests in the land that went beyond a narrow comparison of activities carried out on land. This was the rationale for their arguments regarding 'revival'. This element of their argument was not fully engaged with by the judges.

Justice Kirby noted that, while the *Mabo* decision and the NTA may have begun a process of recognition and protection of Indigenous peoples' laws and customs, Australian law had not recognised a dual system of law or an inherent jurisdiction in Indigenous peoples, as had occurred elsewhere. Instead, the enforceability of native title within Australian courts is only as an applicable law or statute provides.[82] Thus, the native title doctrine establishes the vulnerability of native title to extinguishment.

Justice Brennan confirmed, however, that the inquiry still had to be made on the basis of actual inconsistency. His Honour explained the process of inquiry:

> Identify the particular law or act which is said to effect the extinguishment and . . apply the appropriate test to ascertain the effect of that law or act and whether that effect is inconsistent with the continued right to enjoy native title.[83]

Justice Brennan identified the relevant inconsistency for his purposes (having concluded that exclusive possession had been granted) as that between the right to exclusive possession granted to the pastoral lessee and the right of any other person to enter or remain on the land demised without the lessees' consent. His Honour continued:

> Assuming that access to the land is an essential aspect of the native title asserted, inconsistency arises precisely because the right of the lessee and the rights of the holders of native title cannot be fully exercised at the same time.[84]

Importantly, while Justice Brennan discussed extinguishment in the context of exclusive possession, he noted that 'if a holder of native title had only a non-accessory right, there may be no inconsistency'.[85] Again, in drawing conclusions on the extent of inconsistency, Justice Brennan noted that exclusive possession is inconsistent with native title (except for nonaccessory rights).[86]

For Justice Toohey, inconsistency could only be determined by identifying what native title rights in the system of rights and interests upon which the appellants rely' were asserted in relation to the land covered by the pastoral leases. This inquiry could not be a general inquiry, but had to focus on specifics. Those rights were then measured against the rights conferred on the grantees of the pastoral leases. Thus, Justice Kirby explained:

> Only if there is an inconsistency between the legal interest of the lessees (as defined by the instrument of the lease and the legislation under which it was granted) and the native title (as established by evidence) will such native title, to the extent of the inconsistency, be extinguished.[87]

In other words, to the extent of any inconsistency, the rights of the pastoralist prevail.[88]

On this last point, Justice Brennan suggested, the law could and did attribute priority to one right over another, because it could not recognise the coexistence of two rights that could not both be exercised at the same time. The Court chose to prioritise the rights of the later grantee, consistent with the discriminatory compromise reached in *Mabo*, but the extent of the impact was contained to what was necessary to give effect to the grant, using particular methods of statutory and contractual interpretation that gave due weight to the existing interests of the native title holders.

CHAPTER 3

The vulnerability of native title
Fejo v Northern Territory

HIGH COURT OF AUSTRALIA, 1998

Most observers expected that the High Court would find that native title was extinguished by the grant of a freehold estate. Yet, despite the outcome being as predicted, many Indigenous peoples were disappointed by the decision in *Fejo v Northern Territory* (*Fejo*).[1] Arguably, there was scope within the concept of native title for recognition of the interests of Indigenous peoples in freehold land in some form, and certainly in land that had been resumed as vacant Crown land. It was possible that a principle or presumption of non-extinguishment may have resulted in a more positive outcome in this case. More than this, there are aspects of the Court's reasoning in *Fejo*, and in particular the characterisation of the title, that were troubling for the doctrine of native title as a vehicle for recognising the rights of Indigenous peoples over lands.

The Larrakia people, whose country includes areas in and around Darwin, Palmerston and Litchfield in the Northern Territory, had lodged an application for a determination of native title. The action in *Fejo* was precipitated by the granting of leases, with an option to acquire freehold title, over lands that had been subdivided by the Northern Territory Government but which were within the area subject to the native title application. The Larrakia people took action against the Northern Territory Government and one of the lessees, Oilnet, with respect to the validity and consequences of the grant of such leases.

The land that was the subject of the Crown leases in dispute was once part of a tract of land granted as freehold in April 1882. The land was later acquired by the Commonwealth in 1927 for public purposes, specifically, as a quarantine station and later a leprosarium. Both public purpose proclamations were revoked in 1980. The land thus became vacant Crown land once again.

In the Federal Court, the Larrakia people sought a declaration of native title in relation to the subject lands. They argued that the Northern Territory Government was required by the *Native Title Act 1993* (Cth) (NTA) to either negotiate with the Larrakia or to compulsorily acquire their native title. The Larrakia people also sought injunctions to prevent any further development on the lands. The High Court was asked to consider a single ground of appeal: that the trial judge erred in holding that the grant of freehold was effective to extinguish all native title rights and interests in the land subject of the grant so that, upon the land being reacquired by the Crown, no native title rights and interests could then be recognised by the common law.[2]

The facts of the case, specifically the tenure history, raised two important issues that were yet to be authoritatively determined by the High Court. The first issue was whether a grant of freehold extinguished native title so that no form of native title could coexist with freehold title. The second question was whether extinguishment was permanent and absolute or whether there was potential for native title under the common law to 'revive' when the land returned to the Crown. The case also dealt with the issue of injunctive relief available outside the operation of the NTA. These issues were important for Indigenous peoples in all parts of Australia, but particularly for those in more settled regions. To this end, the Yorta Yorta, Nyungar, Wororra and Miriuwung Gajerrong peoples, among others, intervened to support the action of the Larrakia people.

THE FREEHOLD QUESTION

The grant made in 1882 was for the land, all timber, minerals and appurtenances to the grantee, 'His Heirs, and Assigns for ever'.[3] These terms were recognised to convey an estate in fee simple, commonly called a grant of freehold title. The High Court was unanimous in determining that native title was extinguished by a grant in fee simple, although Justice Kirby gave separate reasons. For Chief Justice Gleeson and Justices Gaudron, McHugh, Gummow, Hayne and Callinan, native title was extinguished by such a grant because 'The rights that are given by a grant in fee simple are rights that are inconsistent with the native title holders continuing to hold any of the rights or interests which together make up native title'.[4] An estate in fee simple was said to be the closest thing to absolute ownership that exists in the Australian system of land tenure, by which it allows 'every act of ownership which can enter into the imagination'.[5]

The conclusion that freehold extinguishes native title was foreshadowed in *Mabo v Queensland [No. 2]* (1992) (*Mabo*) when Justice Brennan explained the relationship between inconsistency and extinguishment by reference to freehold:

> Where the Crown has validly alienated land by granting an interest that is wholly or partially inconsistent with a continuing right to enjoy native title, native title is extinguished to the extent of the inconsistency. The native title has been extinguished by grants of freehold or of leases but not necessarily by the grant of a lesser interest (e.g. authorities to prospect for minerals).[6]

Similarly, Justices Deane and Gaudron stated that native title was 'susceptible of being extinguished by an unqualified grant by the Crown of an estate in fee'.[7]

In a separate judgment in *Fejo*, Justice Kirby admitted that these statements were not essential to the cases then at hand — indeed, the question had not been fully argued — and, as such, the Court in this instance was not strictly bound by previous statements.[8] Moreover, the authorities to date had given rise to a test that needed to be applied to determine whether, and to what extent, native title was extinguished by the grant of freehold title. This test focused on inconsistency as the essence of extinguishment. In *Western Australia v Commonwealth* (1995) (*Native Title Act case*), for example, the joint judgment of the majority referred to 'extinguishment or impairment' by 'a valid exercise of sovereign power inconsistent with the continued or unimpaired enjoyment of native title'.[9] As such, the extent of extinguishment or impairment would depend on the extent of any inconsistency. It was open to suggestion that, under the test, extinguishment could not be construed in a way that takes on an absolute character. This view was reinforced by the decision of the High Court in *Wik Peoples v Queensland* (1996) (*Wik*). There, the nature of the pastoral lease was examined to assess the extent of inconsistency and, indeed, was found not to be inconsistent with the continued enjoyment of some elements of native title, although the rights of the pastoralist, to the extent of any inconsistency, would prevail.[10] Therefore, the question of whether freehold title extinguished native title was open to be tested.

A 'BUNDLE OF RIGHTS'

In applying the test of inconsistency in *Fejo*, the High Court gave little or no consideration to the ways in which native title might coexist with freehold title. Instead, the way in which the two interests were characterised led the Court to conclude that there was no possibility for coexistence. There are two problems with the way in which native title was characterised. The first is the adoption of the 'bundle of rights' approach and the second is the class of rights attributed to it.

The judgments in *Fejo* gave judicial credence to the 'bundle of rights' conception of native title. In seeking to explain native title, the joint judgment stated that extinguishment does not depend upon the intention of the party making the grant but on 'the effect that later grant has on the rights which together constitute native title'.[11] Similarly, Justice Kirby referred to 'the bundle of interests we now call native title'.[12] The joint judgment then listed the rights of native title, which related to the use of land, and 'may encompass a right to hunt, to gather or to fish, a right to conduct ceremonies on the land, a right to maintain the land in a particular state or other like rights and interests'.[13] These, it was said, are 'rights and interests that are inconsistent with the rights of a holder of an estate in fee

3. Vulnerability of native title: *Fejo*

simple'.¹⁴ A fee simple estate gives the holder of that estate the right to use the land as they see fit and to exclude any and every person from access.

This prioritisation of physical access and control did not reflect the unique nature of the relationship to and interest in the land held by Indigenous peoples. Moreover, it went against those aspects of the decision in *Mabo* that embraced the spiritual and non-physical elements of Indigenous peoples' traditions, customs and laws relating to lands. Instead, the High Court superimposed non-Indigenous understandings of relations with land and the rights and interests that could attach to land over the concept of native title.

Indigenous peoples in Australia have made little or no claim to displace the rights of those who hold title under the Australia tenure system, yet they clearly see the potential for recognition of some form of native title over lands regardless of the tenure. These interests were not explored. The judgments in *Fejo*, in assuming the kind of rights asserted required physical access to and indeed control over lands, failed to appreciate the potential for recognition in the concept of native title.

A UNIQUE TITLE

The uniqueness, or *sui generis* character, of native title was undermined in *Fejo*. The importance of understanding native title as a site of mutual recognition between two peoples and two systems of law found no expression. This is not merely a reflection on *Fejo* but on the development of the doctrine of native title since the decision in *Mabo*. Drawing on the jurisprudence of *Mabo*, Chief Justice Lamer of the Supreme Court of Canada spoke of aboriginal title (as it is known in Canada) in the context of a reconciliation of prior occupation by Indigenous peoples with the assertion of Crown sovereignty. As such, Chief Justice Lamer suggested that courts need to take into account both perspectives and to accord due weight to Indigenous perspectives.¹⁵

It should be noted that the judges in *Fejo* rebuffed perceived over-reliance on overseas precedents. All of the judgments argued that decisions in other common law jurisdictions could offer little guidance to the High Court because the legal, political and historical considerations were markedly different.¹⁶ For Justice Kirby, the belated recognition of native title in this country was seen as a significant factor that negated the value of overseas authority.¹⁷ Apart from the clear denial of the extent to which native title in Australia drew upon and reflected comparative doctrines, this approach is disappointing in that it suggests that our political and legal history provides an excuse for a constrained response to the claims of Indigenous peoples.

The High Court in *Fejo* narrowed rather than enhanced the potential of native title. More and more, the unique character of native title as a concept that bridges two legal systems, showing equal respect to the perspectives of both, was replaced with a more restricted conception of an interest that reflects understandings of land and ownership that are more familiar to the courts of the coloniser.

A NEW VULNERABILITY

Despite observations in the judgments to the contrary, it appeared that native title had become a creature of the common law, as the common law attached to it characteristics of other tenures in the Australian tenure system. More devastating was that, in doing so, native title entered a hierarchy of interests and, as *Fejo* demonstrably made clear, its place was forged at the lowest point in the scale. The idea of an 'inherent vulnerability' in native title, which was emphasised by Justice Kirby, had been an undercurrent of previous judgments. In *Mabo*, for example, Justice Brennan observed that, by the assertion of sovereignty by the Crown, 'rights and interests in land that may have been indefeasible under the old regime become liable to extinction by exercise of the new sovereign power'.[18] Similarly, Justices Deane and Gaudron argued in *Mabo* that native title could be extinguished by an exercise of sovereign powers in a manner inconsistent with native title, and that native title was not protected against impairment by subsequent grant, unlike the general rules that would apply to an earlier title emerging from the non-Indigenous tenure system.[19]

Rather than explore the principle of inconsistency, Justice Kirby, in *Fejo*, placed the emphasis on the inherent vulnerability of native title as the basis for determining that native title had been extinguished by the grant of freehold title. Indeed, in rejecting any possibility of coexisting rights, Justice Kirby stated that:

> The inconsistency lies not in the facts or in the way in which the land is actually used. It lies in a comparison between the inherently fragile native title right, susceptible to extinguishment or defeasance, and the legal rights which fee simple confers.[20]

Extinguishment occurred because the titles were inconsistent in law, rather than in fact, according to the characterisation by the Court. Justice Kirby also advocated judicial restraint in this context, arguing, first, that the Court should not 'destroy or contradict' established legal principle, that is, the skeleton of principle referred to by Justice Brennan in *Mabo*.[21] A second reason for restraint was the fundamental importance attached to fee simple and exclusive possession under the law. Justice Kirby went so far as to suggest that such tenures were essential to the peace, order and economic prosperity of every society and, as such, it was not the role of the courts to make any change to those tenures. Moreover, Justice Kirby suggested that the courts should approach any claim that cast doubt on fee simple interests as a whole with particular caution.

The Court in *Fejo* unapologetically privileged non-Indigenous interests, especially freehold interests, reinforcing the status quo of colonial power relations and undermining the newly recognised rights of Indigenous peoples in Australia.

The judgments in *Fejo* rejected the need to examine the Indigenous law to see whether any native title rights could coexist with freehold title. Instead, the investigation was carried out wholly within the sphere of the Australian tenure system. Although the 'bundle of rights' attached to common law native title resembled the character of an Australian tenure, the High Court rejected any analogies between native title and other interests that have long been accepted as capable of coexisting with a fee simple interest. In rejecting such an analogy, Justice Kirby made clear the place of native title in the non-Indigenous law, taking pains to reiterate the 'inherent vulnerability' of native title and, like the majority, relied on the idea that native title has its source in, and derives its content from, a body of law outside the common law as the source of this vulnerability, asserting an inherent superiority in titles that exist under non-Indigenous law.

This characterisation reflects a 'contingent' approach to the rights of Indigenous peoples, by which the law of the coloniser recognises rights as it pleases. This goes against the notion that the rights of Indigenous peoples to their lands are inherent rights or fundamental human rights. The Court in *Fejo* adopted a vision of law based on power that comes from the capacity to dominate. The selective use of the unique status of native title in this way, in order to reinforce its susceptibility to extinguishment, is a disappointing aspect of the development of the doctrine of native title, and for the rights of Indigenous peoples in general.

REVIVAL AND EXTINGUISHMENT

Similar considerations were extended to arguments regarding the revival of native title. The Larrakia people argued that, to the extent that any inconsistency had extinguished native title, that title could be revived if the land was to return to the Crown and its essential character as unalienated Crown land was restored. Of course, this would depend upon the Indigenous people showing that native title had continued in fact. The joint judgment in *Fejo* stated that 'references to extinguishment rather than suspension of native title rights are not to be understood as some incautious or inaccurate use of language'.[22] The decision in *Fejo* determined that extinguishment was absolute and forever, regardless of the rights and interests that continued in Indigenous law from which native title derives its source and content.

While recognising that native title has its origins in, and is given its content by, the laws of Indigenous peoples, the joint judgment further undermined the status of those laws. While reaffirming that native title is neither an institution of the common law nor a form of common law title, the majority stated, succinctly, that while the existence of Indigenous law is necessary to establish native title, it is not sufficient. The existence of rights over land under Indigenous law will not be enough to receive recognition under the common law. The High Court dismissed the claim to revival as seeking 'to convert the fact of continued connection with the land into a right to maintain that connection'.[23] Surely most Indigenous peoples would argue that this is exactly the basis of their claim.

Justice Kirby took a slightly different view and did not consider that the ordinary meaning of extinguishment was sufficient basis for rejecting the appellants' arguments.[24] But Justice Kirby had already foreshadowed his opinion on this issue. In deciding that a grant of freehold extinguished native title, he had stated that:

> Doubtless the bundle of interests we now call 'native title' would continue, for a time at least, within the world of Aboriginal custom. It may still do so. But the conferral of a legal interest in land classified as fee simple had the effect, *in law*, of extinguishing the native title rights.[25]

Further, Justice Kirby argued that to recognise a 'revival' of native title in land when it returned to the Crown would be to recognise a 'new right'.

As such, Justice Kirby suggested that this outcome was incompatible with the notion that native title has its origins in Indigenous law. But this argument is fraught. To consider a revived native title as a new right, while consistent with the reasoning of the Court in terms of extinguishment, certainly does not reflect the continued existence of the laws and customs that underpin native title in the first instance. Just as the recognition of native title in 1992 did not create a new right but merely acknowledged the failure to recognise rights, so, too, the withdrawal of recognition under Australian law should be capable of re-recognition when the Crown is the beneficial holder of the estate. In the result, the decision of the Court with regard to revival combines with the reasoning of the judgments concerning inconsistency to ensure that, to be enforceable under the common law, native title must fit within the cracks left by the Australian land tenure system.

The High Court in *Fejo* makes a distinction between native title that exists in fact and where it may exist in law. With this reasoning, native title has truly become a creature of the common law because recognition and non-recognition occur wholly within that legal system. Once again a legal fiction, this time called extinguishment, is used to deny the existence of an alternative legal system that legitimately confers rights and interests and to make those rights and interests unenforceable under colonial law. As the Court moved to a bundle of rights approach — centred upon physical access — and asserted that the recognition of native title was dependent upon the common law, the idea that the source of the right lies in Indigenous law and society becomes difficult to reconcile with the doctrine of extinguishment.

CONCLUSION

In *Fejo,* Justice Kirby justified the High Court's characterisation of extinguishment by arguing that legal history, legal authority, legal principle and legal policy had combined to determine that native title was extinguished absolutely upon a grant of freehold and could never be revived.[29] For Indigenous peoples, the question remains — by whose legal history, and whose authority, are their rights taken away? Considerations of legal policy, primarily the quest for certainty for non-Indigenous interests, left Indigenous peoples' rights and interests more uncertain than ever. As the connection that Indigenous peoples maintain with their land is transformed, in law, to a 'bundle of rights' centred on physical control and as their rights, in law, become increasingly more vulnerable to the arbitrary exercise of power, Indigenous peoples again increasingly find themselves without recourse. In the *Fejo* judgments, the doctrine of native title created a hierarchy of rights and interests that, at every turn, places other interests above those of Indigenous peoples. The recognition of rights in *Mabo,* and the attempt by the High Court to reconcile the common law with Indigenous peoples' prior and continuing law and authority in *Wik* and *Fejo,* has been continually wound back to the notion of native title to accommodate non-Indigenous interests to the detriment of Indigenous peoples.

Certainty comes from the making of decisions. The decision in *Fejo* could have created certainty by recognising that Indigenous peoples' connection to land is an undeniable and essential part of Indigenous identities and societies. Over freehold land, it may be that the respect that one system can show to the other is the recognition of traditional custodianship; that is, the right to be acknowledged as the first peoples and first owners of that land. The rights and interests of the fee simple title holder could have been confirmed, as in *Wik.* But a relationship that acknowledges and respects Indigenous peoples as peoples could have been reached by recognising that Crown land, whatever its tenure history in Australian law, has to be dealt with in a way that recognises the native title holders. Respect for the law of Indigenous peoples and their struggle for survival could have been celebrated by recognising that native title cannot be extinguished absolutely in the Australian legal system where it continues to exist in Indigenous law.

CHAPTER 4

Property and Crown ownership
Yanner v Eaton

HIGH COURT OF AUSTRALIA, 1999

In allowing an appeal against a conviction for taking crocodiles without a licence, the High Court in *Yanner v Eaton* (1999) (*Yanner*) held that Marandoo Yanner was exercising a traditional right that constituted part of the native title of the Gunnamalla clan of the Gangalidda tribe.[1] Moreover, the right was not extinguished by the Queensland *Fauna Conservation Act 1974* (Qld), which provided that all fauna is the 'property' of the Crown. Yanner had used a traditional harpoon to catch two juvenile estuarine crocodiles in Cliffdale Creek in the Gulf of Carpentaria. Yanner did not hold a licence or permit under the *Fauna Conservation Act* and was charged with taking fauna contrary to s 54(1)(a). The magistrate who heard the case in the first instance accepted that the appellant's clan has a connection to the land and waters where the crocodiles were taken and that it was a traditional custom to take juvenile crocodiles. Moreover, it was determined that this practice was of 'tribal totemic significance and based on spiritual belief'.[2] The Queensland Court of Appeal set aside the order of the magistrate and the appellant was granted special leave to appeal to the High Court.

THE NATURE OF PROPERTY

The opportunity to discuss the nature of the Crown's proprietary interest in fauna led the High Court to develop a more sophisticated conception of property in the native title context. The Court noted the inherent danger in employing concepts of property that were often misunderstood and could lead to 'false thinking', noting that usually property 'is treated as a "bundle of rights". But even this may have its limits as an analytical tool or accurate description.'[3] Further, the joint judgment explained that, '"property" does not refer to a thing; it is a description of a legal relationship with a thing. It refers to a degree of power that is recognised in law as a power permissibly exercised over the thing.'[4] Justice Gummow also

44

construed the concept of property in this way, suggesting that property is an aggregate of legal relations, not of things.

This aspect of the decision is likely to have wider significance for property jurisprudence generally but its importance in the construction of native title jurisprudence has often been overlooked, including by later courts.

'VESTING' AND CROWN PROPERTY

In contrast to the judges of the dissenting minority (Justices McHugh and Callinan), the majority said that reference in the *Fauna Conservation Act* to property vesting in the Crown did not assume absolute ownership; rather, the terms may be indicative of 'all or any of the many different kinds of relationships between a person and a subject matter',[5] and therefore further investigation of the purpose of the Act was necessary.

The joint judgment outlined a number of reasons that property in this instance was not absolute ownership and concluded that the vesting of property here was 'nothing more than "a fiction expressive in legal shorthand of the importance to its people that a State have power to preserve and regulate the exploitation of an important resource"'.[6] The dissenting judgments differed in the construction of the concept of Crown property, preferring the submissions of the respondents that 'property' in the Act meant absolute ownership and therefore extinguished native title.[7] On the majority view, the 'property' referred to in the Act is 'no more than an aggregate of the various rights of control by the executive' to prohibit the taking of fauna without a licence. The property of the Crown in fauna could not be equated with private or individual property, for example, a domestic animal.[8]

EXTINGUISHMENT, INCONSISTENCY AND REGULATION

If vesting, though not 'possession', was still inconsistent with the native title rights being asserted, then native title might have been extinguished to the extent of any inconsistency, in accordance with the decision in *Wik Peoples v Queensland* (1996) (*Wik*).[9] Examining the extent of any inconsistency, the majority stated that:

> It is sufficient to say that *regulating* the way in which rights and interests may be exercised is not inconsistent with their continued existence. Indeed, regulating the way in which a right may be exercised presupposes that the right exists.[10]

Of course, the grey area between absolute prohibition and extinguishment was noted but was not considered to arise in this instance.

The majority identified that the right is further protected by s 211 of the *Native Title Act 1993* (Cth) (NTA), which preserves certain native title rights and interests on lands occupied by Indigenous peoples. In turn, the *Racial Discrimination Act 1975* (Cth) (RDA) and s 109 of the Australian Constitution further protect those rights against extinguishment by state legislation. Section 211, the majority held, necessarily assumes that a conditional prohibition does not affect the existence of the native title rights and interests in relation to which the activity is pursued.[11] Thus, s 211 removes the requirement to obtain any licence, permit or other instrument that would otherwise be necessary for the exercise or enjoyment of certain native title rights and interests by suspending the operation of any licensing regime.

In this case, Justice Gummow confirmed that the fact of native title was significantly impacted by the law of extinguishment and, in particular, by the treatment of the grant of freehold in *Fejo v Northern Territory* (1998) (*Fejo*): 'Factual findings are necessary to establish the ambit of a native title right ... The ambit of native title is a finding of law. This must be placed against the statutory rights which are said to abrogate it.'[12] His Honour explained that evidence of continued assertion or exercise of rights was not relevant:

> Where there has been a grant of a fee simple, the application of this criterion [of inconsistency] is not determined by the existence, as a matter of fact, of an indigenous community's attachment or connection to the land, whether spiritual, cultural, social or economic.[13]

But in this instance Justice Gummow concluded that:

> The exercise of the native title right to hunt was a matter within the control of the appellant's indigenous community. The legislative regulation of that control, by requiring an indigenous person to obtain a permit under the Fauna Act in order to exercise the privilege to hunt, did not abrogate the native title right. Rather, the regulation was consistent with the continued existence of that right.[14]

The joint judgment also noted that in considering the question of inconsistency, the nature of native title always had to be kept in mind. The majority held that native title rights and interests 'not only find their origin in Aboriginal law and custom, they reflect connection with the land'.[15] This may be understood as spiritual, cultural and social connection. The importance of this, especially in this case, was that regulating a particular incidence of native title would not sever the connection with the land that sustains native title.[16]

Justice Gummow also picked up on this point, when emphasising that native title is not a 'unitary concept'; that is, it varies from one case to another depending on the community's traditional laws and customs. Justice Gummow also noted the distinction between native title rights and interests, which reside with the community, and the privileges or rights that flow from that to individuals within the community:

> The native title of a community of indigenous Australians is comprised of the collective rights, powers and other interests of that community, which may be exercised by particular sub-groups or individuals in accordance with that community's traditional laws and customs. Each collective right, power or other interest is an 'incident' of that indigenous community's native title ... The exercise of rights or incidents ... is best described as the exercise of privileges of native title ... but the exercise by individuals of the privilege to hunt may be defined by the idiosyncratic laws and customs of that community.[17]

This is consistent with Justice Brennan's judgment in *Mabo v Queensland [No. 2]* (1992) (*Mabo*) where he suggested that '[i]ndeed it is not possible to admit traditional usufructuary rights without admitting a traditional proprietary title'.[18]

In *Yanner* Justice Gummow identified a relationship between these two aspects of native title, in that:

> The heterogeneous laws and customs of Australia's indigenous peoples, the [Aboriginal peoples] and Torres Strait Islanders, provide its content. It is the relationship between a community of indigenous people and the land, defined by reference to that community's traditional laws and customs, which is the bridgehead to the common law.[19]

But in regulating the exercise of that relationship, the joint judgment in *Yanner* explained that:

> an important aspect of the socially constituted fact of native title rights and interests that is recognised by the common law is the spiritual, cultural and social connection with the land. Regulating particular aspects of the usufructuary relationship with traditional land does not sever the connection of the Aboriginal peoples concerned with the land.[20]

In this case, the High Court returned to the spiritual aspects of Indigenous peoples' connection to the land that had been part of the judgments of the Court in *Mabo*. The judges incorporated these aspects into the understanding of law and custom. Justice Gummow argued that:

> The conduct of the appellant is inadequately identified in terms of the statutory definition of 'take' and its components such as 'hunt'. What was involved was the manifestation by the appellant of the beliefs, customs and laws of his community.[21]

The distinction drawn by the Court in *Yanner* between regulation and extinguishment provides greater scope for the notion of 'impairment' of the exercise of native title rights that could then be reinvigorated when the impairment was lifted. The potential was there for this idea to soften the hard edges of the *Fejo* decision, which had cast native title as a title highly susceptible to extinguishment.

CONCLUSION

This case is important for Indigenous peoples in their assertion of the right to use and control resources. It should be noted that similar language, vesting property in the Crown, is the basis for the assumption of Crown ownership of minerals in many state legislative regimes.

The decision also moves the direction away from previous discussions of 'a vulnerable title' and 'a bundle of rights' that seemed to suggest a constraining of the concept of native title (although Justice Callinan maintained this restrictive conception). The earlier focus on property no longer held the same connotations or implications, because the concept of property is construed in *Yanner* in a way that is more akin to Indigenous understandings of their relationship with land and the impact of colonial law on their connection to their country.

CHAPTER 5

Native title offshore
Commonwealth v Yarmirr

HIGH COURT OF AUSTRALIA, 2001

The appeals in *Commonwealth v Yarmirr* (2001) (*Yarmirr*) provided the High Court with the first opportunity to consider whether native title could be recognised over Indigenous peoples' sea country.¹ In the result, the High Court held that, while native title can exist offshore, as a matter of law it cannot be exclusive. This outcome was not unexpected but the decision was narrowly construed and did not provide a great deal of guidance as to the implications for the extent of rights and protections for native title holders offshore. Nor did the Court consider the substantive difference between the non-exclusive native title recognised and the qualified exclusive title that was claimed. The decision also had implications for exclusive native title onshore and took new directions in relation to the limits of common law recognition and principles of inconsistency.

The application in this case concerned the native title of the Mandilarri-Ildugij, Mangalara, Muran, Gadura, Minaga, Ngayndjagar and Mayorram over the seas in the Croker Island region off the north-west tip of Arnhem Land in the Northern Territory. While several islands, including Croker Island, are located within the claim area, they were granted as Aboriginal land under the *Aboriginal Land Rights (Northern Territory) Act 1976* (Cth) and were not included in the claim.

Hearing the case at first instance in the Federal Court, Justice Olney determined that native title exists in relation to the determination area but that such title did not confer possession, occupation, use and enjoyment of the sea and seabed within the claimed area to the exclusion of all others.² In accordance with s 225 of the *Native Title Act 1993* (Cth) (NTA), which sets out the requirements of a determination, Justice Olney considered that the rights and interests of importance were to have free access for certain purposes: first, to travel through or within the claimed area; second, to fish and hunt for the purpose of satisfying personal, domestic or non-commercial communal needs, including the purpose of observing traditional, cultural, ritual and spiritual laws and customs; third, to visit and protect places of cultural and spiritual significance; and, fourth, to safeguard cultural and spiritual knowledge. As is usual, the proposed determination stated that the native title rights and interests would be subordinate to any validly granted rights and interests. On appeal to the full bench of the Federal Court, the majority upheld the trial judge's findings.[3]

RECOGNITION OF NATIVE TITLE OVER THE SEA

As the principal respondent to the claim, the Commonwealth had argued that, despite the fact that the NTA refers to native title over 'land and waters' (including seas) and specifically refers to 'fishing' rights in s 223(1)(c), only native title 'recognised' by the common law was protected by the NTA. The majority joint judgment of Chief Justice Gleeson and Justices Gaudron, Gummow and Hayne took this as the appropriate question to begin the inquiry; that is, to determine when the common law will or will not recognise the native title rights and interests asserted.[4]

The majority joint judgment reiterated the principle finding of *Mabo v Queensland [No. 2]* (1992) (*Mabo*) that 'at common law the native title rights and interests survived the acquisition of sovereignty because only so much of the common law was brought as was applicable to the circumstances of the new colony'.[5] However, citing *Western Australia v Commonwealth* (1995) (*Native Title Act case*), the majority also suggested that an acquiring sovereign may extinguish rights and interests 'in the course of the act of State acquiring the territory'.[6] The majority concluded, therefore, that the principle issue in *Mabo* had been whether there was an 'inconsistency' between the common law and the continued recognition of native title rights and interests. The judges acknowledged that the presumption is that no extinguishment was intended but, had there been an inconsistency, the common law would have prevailed. There was no inconsistency, hence the common law 'recognised' native title and gave it effect.[7]

The judgment demonstrated how the law dealt with the coexistence of native title with the radical title of the Crown in relation to land, particularly in the *Mabo* decision, but disagreed with the contention of the Commonwealth that reference to 'radical title' is a necessary prerequisite for native title to exist.[8] Radical title, the majority suggested, is not the only (and in this case not the appropriate) analytical tool to explain the different rights and interests arising from the assertion of sovereignty over territorial sea.[9]

CROWN SOVEREIGNTY OVER THE SEA

The majority joint judgment suggested that the key to determining the possibility of recognition was to first examine the sovereign rights and interests that were, and are now, asserted by the Crown over the territorial sea.[10] At the same time, the judges said that it is notoriously difficult, inappropriate and unnecessary to attempt to describe or define the sovereignty asserted by the state.[11]

The majority argued that the assertion and international recognition of sovereignty over the sea did not amount to a claim of ownership or even radical title. They cited *R v Keyn* (1876) (*Keyn*) as authority for the proposition that, although internationally recognised as territorial sea, coastal waters were not part of the 'territory' of England and, therefore, were not owned.[12] In contrast, Justice McHugh took issue with the majority's interpretation of *Keyn,* arguing that *Keyn* and, indeed, *New South Wales v Commonwealth* (1975) (*Seas and Submerged Lands case*) stood for the proposition that the common law does not extend below the low watermark. This in essence was the basis for Justice McHugh's dissent in relation to the appeals.[13]

The majority in the joint judgment considered that the assertion of sovereignty was constituted by a right to legislate. As a corollary, they disagreed with the contentions of the Commonwealth in relation to extinguishment, saying that the passing of legislation concerning the territorial waters was an assertion of sovereignty, not ownership as in the Crown lands legislation considered in *Mabo* or the fauna legislation considered in *Yanner v Eaton* (1999) (*Yanner*).[14] Whatever the powers and title recognised by legislation under the seas and submerged lands settlement, and changes to the area considered as territorial waters over time, they had no impact upon the recognition of native title.[15]

The majority conceded that the assertion of a territorial reach to the common law may be flawed. The judges therefore avoided the question to a large degree by redirecting the inquiry under s 223(1)(c) of the NTA. They stated that it need not be demonstrated that the common law applies offshore, only that the common law is not 'inconsistent' with the continued existence of native title rights and interests offshore.[16]

The majority concluded that, apart from the important qualification in relation to exclusivity, the 'terms' upon which the assertion of sovereignty was and is made in relation to the territorial seas showed no 'necessary inconsistency' with the continued recognition of native title rights and interests.[17] The 'terms' to which the judges referred were said to be the right of innocent passage under international law (despite uncertainty in terms of the date of application) and, as a matter of municipal law, the public rights to navigate and to fish. The majority judgment held that:

> The rights and interests asserted at sovereignty carried with them the recognition of public rights of navigation and fishing and, perhaps, the concession of an international right of innocent passage. Those rights were *necessarily* inconsistent with the continued existence of any right under Aboriginal law or custom to preclude the exercise of those rights.[18]

Thus the majority held that the recognition of native title offshore was 'qualified' by the 'terms of the assertion of sovereignty' and could only reflect non-exclusive rights.[19]

THE PUBLIC RIGHTS TO NAVIGATE AND TO FISH

While Justice Olney at the trial level determined that the evidence did not establish an exclusive right to possession, occupation, use and enjoyment, the international obligation to allow innocent passage precluded exclusive native title rights in the seas in any event. Further, the public rights of navigation and fishing were described as 'skeletal principles' according to the test put forward by Justice Brennan in *Mabo*, which similarly precluded such recognition.[20] The majority of the full Federal Court had also applied the test from *Mabo* that 'recognition' of native title would be precluded where to do so would 'fracture a skeletal principle of our legal system' or be repugnant to natural justice, equity and good conscience.[21]

But the majority joint judgment applied a different test of common law recognition, explicitly rejecting the notion of 'skeletal principle' that had been generally accepted since *Mabo*.[22] Their Honours applied a simple test of inconsistency; that is, where there is an inconsistency between the rights asserted and a common law principle, the common law will prevail. There does not need to be an assessment of whether the principle is a 'skeletal' principle of the legal system or whether the inconsistency is such that it amounts to an affront to natural justice. This appears to be a much broader test of inconsistency, more akin to the doctrine of extinguishment that has developed in parallel since *Mabo*. The blurring of the two concepts was confirmed in the penultimate paragraph of their Honours' reasons, where they stated clearly that:

> Although the inconsistency does not arise as a result of the exercise of sovereign power (as in the case where a grant in fee simple extinguishes native title) the inconsistency which exists in this case between the asserted native title rights and the assertion of sovereignty is of no different quality.[23]

For such a significant shift in thinking, the concept received little attention in the judgment. The majority joint judgment simply stated that:

> there is a fundamental inconsistency between the asserted native title rights and interests and the common law public rights of navigation and fishing as well as the right of innocent passage.[24]

Until this decision, the question of recognition was assumed to be of a different order, which gave much greater respect to Indigenous rights than the extinguishment doctrine. Recognition, as opposed to extinguishment, was a contest between the normative values of the two legal systems at the point of first contact, hence the only elements of the system of law in relation to land and sea country that would not be recognised were those that are fractious or repugnant to the incoming sovereign. All other rights and interest remain in force until extinguishment by clear and plain intent by the new sovereign. To deny all elements of exclusivity on the basis of simple inconsistency in legal treatment would have justified complete nonrecognition of native title, as had occurred in *Milirrpum v Nabalco Pty Ltd* (1971).[25]

Despite the adoption of the language of extinguishment, unlike the principles applied in *Wik Peoples v Queensland* (1996) (*Wik*),[26] the Court went on to hold that:

> it is not sufficient to attempt to reconcile [the common law rights and the rights and interests under traditional law and custom] by providing that exercise of the native title rights and interests is to be subject to the other public and international rights.[27]

Instead, the Court extended the principles of 'fundamental inconsistency' expressed in *Fejo v Northern Territory* (1998) (*Fejo*), which had dispatched with the need to examine the actual extent of the inconsistency and the ability of the rights to coexist (the *Wik* test) in relation to freehold titles.[28] The joint judgment acknowledged that the 'qualified exclusivity' proposed by the claimants could have in fact accommodated the public and international rights, as well as validly granted licences and other interests, but held that the fundamental inconsistency could not be resisted. This should be directly contrasted with the conclusions of Justice Kirby in this regard.

Justice Kirby sought out the principle behind the public rights to assess whether they were principles to which the native title rights have to give way. His Honour found that behind the right of navigation and innocent passage is the fundamental principle of freedom of movement and the common heritage of humanity that is recognised under international law, as well as being a 'foundational principle of the common law'.[29] Even in relation to free passage, Justice Kirby argued that an examination of the actual extent of the inconsistency reveals that other elements of exclusivity of native title are not destroyed.[30] This interpretation that exclusivity is not an 'absolute' concept should be commended.

Justice Kirby argued that the public right to fish is of a different character amenable to regulation and the allocation of right by licensing regimes and is capable of being subject to and defeated by the underlying native title.[31]

NON-EXCLUSIVITY AND ENFORCEMENT

As Justice Kirby had taken a different view of the implications of the public right to fish and the rights of navigation and innocent passage, his Honour went further to discuss the trial judge's finding in relation to the proof of exclusivity, in particular the matter of enforcement. Justice Kirby's comments have some relevance to claims for exclusive native title over lands, as they contradict Justice Olney's findings in *Hayes* on this point.[32] Justice Kirby agreed with Justice Merkel, who was the dissenting judge in the full Federal Court appeal in *Commonwealth v Yarmirr* (1999),[33] that the existence or absence of enforcement of laws against others is clearly not determinative of exclusivity: 'It is the traditional connection arising from the acknowledgment of laws and customs of the Indigenous community, and not the recognition or acceptance by *others* of the connection which is the source of native title.'[34] Justice Kirby criticised the 'overly narrow approach' of Justice Olney as one that would always be unfavourable to the rights of claimants who, until the *Mabo* decision, could not assert and uphold their rights to their country.[35] His Honour suggested that such an approach was not only unreasonable, but discriminatory.[36] This was not a matter that the majority needed to consider in this context.

In relation to the reasoning of the joint majority, a question still remained as to the enforcement of the non-exclusive title that they had recognised. The joint judgment did not deal with the implications of its findings in relation to the rights that can be asserted under a non-exclusive native title and the protection such a title affords. Justice Kirby's discussion of the right to be consulted should be of interest in this regard. 'Presumably, non-exclusive native title affords native title holders some greater right over their traditional territory than a member of the general public may exercise on that land.[38]

CONCLUSION

In *Yarmirr* the discussion of the 'inconsistency test' for recognition in relation to the Commonwealth's appeal and the qualification on recognition in relation to the claimants' appeal are approached slightly differently. Because the Court did not clearly explain the common law's reach in relation to territorial waters, it is unclear from these two discussions whether the public rights to fish and navigate are an element of sovereignty ('the terms upon which sovereignty is asserted') or elements of the common law. Moreover, the joint majority judgment left unclear where the line is to be drawn between a question of recognition on the one hand and extinguishment on the other — a question of central importance, at least in relation to compensation.

The Court's decision in this case blurs the line between recognition and extinguishment. The High Court broadened the test for the denial of recognition to elements of native title that are merely inconsistent with a common law principle. This may occur even where, at least in the case of a public right to fish, it is admitted to be fundamentally amenable to regulation and abrogation and, indeed, has been so abrogated.[39]

CHAPTER 6

Redefining extinguishment
Western Australia v Ward

HIGH COURT OF AUSTRALIA, 2002

The decision of the High Court in *Western Australia v Ward* (2002) (*Ward*) was met with disappointment and criticism.[1] The joint majority judgment of Chief Justice Gleeson and Justices Gaudron, Gummow and Hayne broadened the extent of extinguishment and reinforced the vulnerability of native title to later grants, while illustrating the complexity of inquiry required to establish the effect of extinguishing tenures on pre-existing native title. On a number of issues, the High Court's reasoning and the resulting legal position remained unclear or ambiguous. This chapter points to a number of areas where the reasoning was open to interpretation and required further articulation by the courts. In particular, the interpretations that could lead to meaningful recognition and protection of native title have been highlighted over narrower interpretations that continue to risk leading the native title doctrine into an unworkable quagmire of impossible tests, inconsistent outcomes, incoherent theoretical underpinning and results that provide no substantive rights recognition for native title holders.

The claimed area is the traditional territory of the Miriuwung and Gajerrong peoples, an area of some 8000 square kilometres in the East Kimberley and the Northern Territory. The application was lodged in 1994, and in 1998 Justice Lee of the Federal Court confirmed that native title existed in the whole of the determination area. Justice Lee recognised a native title as right in the land itself, an underlying interest from which pendant rights, such as the right to use resources or to control access, or more narrowly defined rights such as the right to hunt, are carved.[2] So long as one right remains to be exercised, the underlying title (or root title) remains. Inconsistent grants, on this understanding, therefore have an impact on the exercise of rights and — if there is a limitation on the grant, for example, a licence for a limited time — the grant's impact on the exercise of inconsistent rights only extends until the expiry of the term of the licence. After the decision, this reasoning was contrasted with what was understood as the 'bundle of rights' conception of native title, under which native title is constituted by a bundle of freestanding independent rights, each of which can be extinguished, permanently, one by one. Justice Lee rejected this notion of partial extinguishment. In order to find absolute and permanent extinguishment, Justice Lee argued, inconsistent rights granted must be absolutely and permanently inconsistent, concluding that:

> Native title at common law is a communal 'right to land' arising from the significant connection of an Indigenous society with land under its customs and culture. It is not a mere bundle of rights. The right of occupation that is native title is an interest in land.[3]

His Honour recognised that the extent to which native title could protect the rights held under traditional laws, customs or practices was limited by the extent to which:

> legislation and by acts vesting concurrent rights in third parties in land or water of the determination area, has provided for the regulation, control, curtailment, restriction, suspension or postponement of the exercise of the rights vested in the community ... as incidents of native title.[4]

On appeal, the full Federal Court unanimously confirmed that the Miriuwung and Gajerrong peoples held native title to most parts of the claim area. But the two majority judges (Justices Beaumont and von Doussa) did not agree that native title could be characterised as an interest in land, and hence rejected Justice Lee's conclusions with regard to partial extinguishment.[5] Justices Beaumont and von Doussa acknowledged that common law native title recognises 'rights and interests in or in relation to [the] land',[6] and referred to the continuum of interests that may approach full ownership, but concluded that, whether proprietary or usufructuary, even exclusive possession native title remains a personal right.[7] They adopted the language of a bundle of rights, although in doing so they admitted that native title rights and interests in a particular case may be 'so extensive as to be in the nature of a proprietary interest in land'.[8] In any event, Justices Beaumont and von Doussa argued, it was not inaccurate to describe proprietary interests as a 'bundle of rights'.[9]

Justice North, in dissent, criticised this approach that understood native title as a collection of distinct and severable rights because it denies the necessary unifying factor, or underlying title, that is necessary to the exercise of the separate rights.[10] Instead, Justice North argued that the communal title was an interest in land and holders of native title have rights and interests that flow from the right to the land.[11] The language of a 'bundle of rights' was not, of itself, a concern in the majority judgment. As Justices Beaumont and von Doussa suggested, it is a term used in reference to interests in land, including freehold and leasehold as an abstract expression. They conceded that where native title rights comprise an exclusive right to possess, occupy, use and enjoy the land, it would be an impossible task to specify every kind of use or enjoyment that might thereby flow from native title. Where rights and interests are less than exclusive possession, 'it will be necessary to sufficiently identify them'.[12] This would be particularly apparent when determining the impact of grants of inconsistent rights. The majority held that, as inconsistent rights and interests are extinguished, the 'bundle of rights' that make up the native title are reduced accordingly.[13] The difference between Justices Beaumont and von Doussa (in the majority) and Justices North (in dissent) and Lee (at first instance) was in the scope for the suspension and revival of incidents, or more particular rights. Justice North argued for proportionality between the impact of the law and the effect on native title, such that native title should only be impaired to the extent necessary to ensure that inconsistent rights or interests can be exercised without interference.[14] This would appear to be consistent with the High Court reasoning in *Wik Peoples v Queensland* (1996) (*Wik*).[15]

The decision was appealed to the High Court, where issues for consideration concentrated on the nature and principles of extinguishment. The two questions posed were, first, whether there can be partial extinguishment and, second, what the principles are for determining extinguishment.

EXTINGUISHMENT UNDER THE *NATIVE TITLE ACT 1993*

The High Court confirmed earlier comments that the *Native Title Act 1993* (Cth) (NTA) is at the core of native title litigation where applications are brought for determination under the NTA.[16] With particular attention to the principles of extinguishment at the centre of the appeal in *Ward*, the Court highlighted that, in accordance with s 11, native title is not able to be extinguished contrary to the NTA.[17]

The High Court majority also stated that the complicated regime under the NTA for confirmation and validation of past grants had altered the position at common law.[18] Part 2, Division 2 of the NTA provides for the validation of 'past acts' that would have been invalid at common law according to the formulation of the High Court in *Mabo v Queensland [No. 2]* (1992) (*Mabo*) by the operation of the *Racial Discrimination Act 1975* (Cth) (RDA). That is, interests were granted or created after the commencement of the RDA on 31 October 1975 without equal treatment in relation to the rights of property holders.[19] Section 15 provides for (or 'confirms') the complete or partial extinguishment of native title by particular past acts, such as the grant of freehold or exclusive possession leasehold. Similarly, ss 23C and 23G provide for complete and partial extinguishment (respectively) in relation to previous exclusive possession acts and previous non-exclusive possession acts. Division 2A also introduced a validation regime for acts that took place between 1 January 1994 (the commencement of the NTA) and

December 1996 (the date of the *Wik* decision[20]), called intermediate period acts. In addition, extinguishment, whether effected by methods under the common law or provisions of the NTA, is deemed to be permanent under s 237A.

With reference to the different views among the Federal Court judges with regard to partial extinguishment, the High Court majority held that (within the legislative framework) partial extinguishment is mandated by the NTA.[21] Section 23A explains the operation of the partial extinguishment and complete extinguishment provisions:

> 23A Overview of Division
> (1) In summary, this Division provides that certain acts attributable to the Commonwealth that were done on or before 23 December 1996 will have completely or *partially extinguished* native title.
> (2) If the acts were previous exclusive possession acts (involving the grant or vesting of things such as freehold estates or leases that conferred exclusive possession, or the construction or establishment of public works), the acts will have completely extinguished native title.
> (3) If the acts were previous non-exclusive possession acts (involving grants of non-exclusive agricultural leases or non-exclusive pastoral leases), they will have extinguished native title to the extent of any inconsistency.
> (4) This Division also allows States and Territories to legislate, in respect of certain acts attributable to them, to extinguish native title in the same way as is done under this Division for Commonwealth acts.[22]

The provision links partial extinguishment (s 23A(1)) with the extent of inconsistency test (s 23A(3)). The importance of the relationship between this provision and the provision deeming extinguishment to be permanent was not clearly articulated in the majority's decision but was implicit, for example, in the treatment of particular acts, such as the Argyle project (a major mining development within the claim area). It is this notion of permanency that impinges on the potential of native title.

This is a significant disappointment in the decision because it confirms that the NTA allows the piecemeal erosion of native title. A large part of the effort in arguing against the 'bundle of rights' approach was to protect native title from unnecessary erosion over time. As the majority explained, native title may otherwise continue to exist except for the legal conclusion of extinguishment, which withdraws legal recognition of the rights conferred by native title. Justice McHugh was critical of the way in which the law operates in this circumstance to extinguish native title, regardless of the merits of the case.[23]

The joint majority judgment emphasised the importance of the suspension and revival provisions in overcoming this injustice. The majority drew attention to the operation of s 15 of the NTA, which provides for the suspension of native title rights and interests in some circumstances, through the non-extinguishment principle (defined in s 238). However, this is limited to acts that, but for the validation provisions of the NTA, would have been invalid by operation of the RDA.[24] Section 47B of the NTA also provides in certain circumstances where vacant Crown land exists that:

> (2) For all purposes under this Act in relation to the application, any extinguishment, of the native title rights and interests in relation to the area that are claimed in the application, by the creation of any prior interest in relation to the area must be disregarded.

This provision was drafted to exclude areas currently covered by reservation or dedication.

The majority joint judgment clearly indicated that the Court was only concerned with areas where extinguishment was in issue. Even here, the majority tried to emphasise that native title may survive the grant of interests to others or the exercise of executive power; for example:

- native title might survive to some extent; or
- there might be no inconsistency 'in the relevant sense' at all; and
- statute may regulate the exercise of native title without abrogating it.[25]

The majority judgment drew a distinction between extinguishment within the framework of the NTA, which is permanent, and partial inconsistency under the common law, introducing the concept of 'relevant inconsistency' in relation to extinguishment.[26] At times, the majority appeared to limit the concept of partial extinguishment to previous non-exclusive possession acts. Further exploration of the relationship between the statute and common law may reveal a basis for arguing that partial extinguishment is a concept introduced by the amendments to the NTA in 1998. This would have significant compensation implications under s 23J.

THE *RACIAL DISCRIMINATION ACT* AND COMPENSATION

At the outset, the majority joint judgment indicated that there was still no comprehensive consideration of what is meant by 'recognition' in relation to native title and what appropriate remedies and protections are afforded by the law.[27] The majority noted that compensation for the extinguishment of native title may arise under various provisions of the NTA; for example, under s 23J, compensation might be payable where validation and confirmation provisions result in extinguishment that would not have occurred at common law. This may be the case in relation to some non-exclusive leases that are deemed to extinguish native title, but compensation under the NTA is not the only remedy and protection afforded to native title under Australian law.

The majority examined the protection that might be afforded to native title as a property right and a right of inheritance protected under the RDA. *Western Australia v Commonwealth* (*Native Title Act case*) (1995) confirmed that the NTA effectively controls the scope of other laws by determining what state laws or acts are valid and the conditions of validity.[28] It also controls the effect of the RDA on validated acts (s 7) to effectively withdraw protection of the RDA in relation to past acts. Apart from this express suspension of the operation of the RDA for the purposes of validation, the RDA continues to operate in relation to any future acts.

The majority emphasised that native title is 'property' in the context of the RDA, citing *Mabo v Queensland [No. 1]* (1988) as first establishing that native title, though it has different characteristics from other forms of title (in particular, not being derived from Crown grant), cannot be treated differently from other titles.[29] The right to ownership and inheritance of property protected by the RDA is the same right regardless of the characteristics of that property. The RDA operates on discriminatory laws or laws that affect the enjoyment of rights by some but not others, or to a different extent, based on their race or ethnicity. The RDA can either make an Act or a law invalid, or 'top up' legislation to ensure non-discrimination.

The majority explained the operation of the RDA with reference to Justice Mason in *Gerhardy v Brown*.

- Where a state law omits to make enjoyment of a right universal, s 10 operates to extend that right to all on the same terms as the state law. This may occur where an Act provides for compensation only to non-native title holders (directly or in effect).
- Where a law deprives people of a particular race from the enjoyment of a particular right, s 10 confers the right thereby creating an inconsistency and therefore invalidating the discriminatory provision. This may occur where a law only extinguishes native title and leaves other titles intact (directly or in effect).
- It is also important to note that where a state law expressed in general terms forbids the enjoyment of rights by all racial groups there is no discrimination upon which the RDA can operate.[30]

The majority explained that the impact of the RDA on state legislation that authorises acts or affects native title must be considered before turning to the impact of the NTA on the particular act. If the RDA does not operate to invalidate the legislation in the first instance, the 'past acts' provisions are not engaged. This is important in determining whether the consequential compensation provisions are then engaged. Legislation may not be explicitly discriminatory, but might discriminate in its operation or effect. Thus, the RDA has an effect where the operation of the legislation is racially discriminatory in its treatment of native title holders as a class of interest holders. For example, the definition of 'occupier' under the *Mining Act 1978* (WA) does not include native title holders, but compensation provisions under that legislation will be extended to native title holders by operation of s 10 of the RDA. The RDA effectively operates to 'top up' the legislation and extend the definition of 'occupier' under the Act to include native title holders.

Section 45 of the NTA provides that compensation payments applicable to other interest holders under state legislation — such as the *Mining Act 1978* (WA), s 123(4) — that would be extended to native title holders by the operation of the RDA are brought within the compensation provisions of the NTA. The Court raised numerous possible compensation questions in this way throughout the judgment but did not draw conclusions as to any.

PROOF OF NATIVE TITLE

The High Court in *Ward* construed native title rights and interests as derived from traditional law and custom. The common law recognises those rights and interests through the concept of native title. The continued emphasis that the Court placed on traditional law and custom as defining the content of native title, rather than possession, was disappointing to some, not least because of the burden on the evidence that this has brought. The majority joint judgment confirmed that native title is defined by the NTA in s 223(1) and the statutory definition requires two inquiries. The first concerns the rights and interests possessed under traditional laws and customs, including identification of laws and customs, and identification of the rights and interest possessed under those laws. The second inquires into the connection to land or waters.[31]

The majority considered that failure to establish proof of laws and customs under s 223(1)(a) and (b) does not constitute extinguishment, although native title in such cases may be said to have ceased to exist. Instead, the Court said, 'The term "extinguishment" is most often used to describe the consequences in law of acts attributed to the legislative or executive branches of government'.[32] In this case, the conclusions of the lower courts that the Miriuwung and Gajerrong peoples had proved facts under s 223(1)(a) and (b) were not questioned[33] but the generality of the findings by the trial judge were said to make any final determination of questions of extinguishment in the High Court difficult.[34]

THE 'BUNDLE OF RIGHTS' DEBATE

The joint majority judgment only briefly discussed the 'bundle of rights' versus interest in land debate. The judges' stance on the arguments put by the parties has to be deduced from the approach underlying the reasoning in relation to extinguishment. The majority may have expressed a preference for the full Federal Court view of native title as a bundle of rights, but it should be highlighted that this was not the same as a 'list of activities'. As discussed, in property law the 'bundle of rights' metaphor is used to describe all property interests, including freehold. The 'bundle of rights' idea was said by the majority to be useful as a metaphor to illustrate that there might be more than one right or interest in a particular piece of land.[35] In addition, the 'bundle of rights' metaphor reflected the majority's view that there may be several kinds of rights and interests, not all of which are fully or accurately expressed as rights to control what others may do on land.[36] Therefore, the decision in *Ward* was not a rejection of native title ever being recognised as equivalent to or approaching freehold or an unequivocal acceptance of the 'bundle of rights' approach as it was debated in the public arena in the lead-up to the decision.

Native title as an exclusive possession title was accepted under the NTA. Indeed, s 225(e) expressly requires the determination of areas where native title confers 'possession, occupation, use and enjoyment to the exclusion of all others'. The determination of native title therefore requires the expression of this relationship in terms familiar to the common lawyer, a tendency that the Court in *Mabo* thought was capable of being avoided.[37] The High Court in *Ward* did not deal with the areas of exclusive possession within the claim, being concerned with the impact of extinguishment, but it indicated that, in the absence of extinguishing acts, native title would generally be an exclusive possession title. The majority explained the right to exclusive possession, use and enjoyment not as flowing from the fact of occupation or from the recognition of native title, but from the right to speak for country that is conferred by Indigenous law and custom.[38]

The majority joint judgment still appeared uneasy with exclusive possession native title, perhaps because of the emphasis on extinguishment. The majority was concerned, it seems, that equating native title with exclusive possession would not adequately reflect the range of rights that might survive an inconsistent grant.[39] In rejecting occupation as a basis for proving native title, the majority said that it was a mistake to assume that native title rights and interests under s 223 were necessarily a single set of rights relating to land that in every instance is analogous to a fee simple.[40] So, while accepting that the right to speak for country could be understood as equating to full rights of ownership under traditional law, the majority rejected the view that the recognition of native title resulted in communal title that could assume, as a consequence, certain rights and interests equivalent to full ownership, apart from that which was conferred by law and custom.

The positive language from the majority in relation to the right to speak for country was further undermined by the treatment of the right to minerals, where

6. Redefining extinguishment: *Ward*

the discussion reverted to the simplistic bundle of rights idea by tracing specific rights to specific laws or practices. The majority determined that any native title right to minerals was extinguished by vesting legislation. Despite this conclusion, the majority went back to consider whether there was a native title right to minerals. The High Court majority accepted the findings of the full Federal Court that the evidence did not reveal traditional laws and customs relevant to the ownership of minerals and therefore did not demonstrate a native title right to ownership or the right to use minerals and petroleum (except, perhaps, ochre).[41] The majority's reasoning in this instance was troubling. It was the only foray the majority joint judgment took into discussing the proof of particular rights and interests.

A common understanding of a right of exclusive possession or, even more narrowly, a right to the use and enjoyment of the resources of the land would be a right contemplated under native title. To expect the traditional laws and customs upon which applicants relied to establish native title to contain a 'law' in relation to the use of particular resources not yet needed reflected a 'frozen in time approach' that had been previously rejected.[42] This approach was in apparent contradiction to the majority's stated acceptance that the law is not concerned with the 'mode of use', except to cast light on the rights being asserted. Instead, the majority took a narrow view of the subject matter to which laws and customs might apply, thus masking a 'mode of use' test.

The assertion by the Crown of property in minerals was always likely to be a problematic fiction for the courts and it has to be seen as a political compromise. It is not consistent with the reasoning of the High Court in *Wik* or *Yanner v Eaton* (1999) (*Yanner*). It is one thing to resolve a conflict between rights asserted under native title and a specific interest asserted by the Crown by resorting to the extinguishment doctrine, but it is punitive to require this kind of detailed assessment to find a particular law in relation to particular sub-surface minerals.

CONNECTION TO LAND

The majority of the High Court confirmed that the 'connection to land and waters' under s 223(1)(b) of the NTA does not require physical occupation or continued use. This has been a consistent refrain from the High Court since Justice Brennan's judgment in *Mabo*. This is related to the contention that the inquiry is not directed to how Indigenous peoples use or occupy the land and is consistent with the Court's approach to native title based on the recognition of rights conferred by traditional law and custom rather than occupation. The right to exclusive possession does not therefore depend on proof of continuous presence and exclusion.[43]

The majority in *Ward* extended this reasoning to hold that the fact that claimants in the case had not exercised the rights asserted was not determinative of the claim. A failure to exercise a right does not result in the loss of the right, just as the failure to exercise a right is not indicative of a failure to acknowledge the laws and customs that sustain the right.[44] The majority held that s 223 requires consideration of what is meant by connection by traditional law and custom; that is, identifying what the traditional laws and customs say about the relationship to the land. This is part of the Court's more general push for greater particularity about the laws and customs and the rights conferred that are to be recognised by native title.

The majority determined that as there were not sufficient submissions on this latter matter, it was unnecessary to make any determination in relation to the notion of 'spiritual' connection, a term that the state of Western Australia thought to mean any non-continuous physical presence. Yet the Court reiterated that the use of land is only relevant to the extent that it reveals something about the kind of connection that exists under traditional laws or customs. The majority explicitly stated that the absence of evidence of recent use does not lead to the conclusion that there is no relevant connection.[45]

The majority sought to apply the requirement for connection to land under s 223 to the kind of rights and interests that could be recognised and protected by native title. Of particular interest was the treatment of cultural knowledge and the assertion of a right to protect. The majority noted the decision of the Federal Court in *Bulun Bulun v R&T Textiles Pty Ltd* (1998) (*Bulun Bulun*),[46] which rejected a native title right to protect works of art, drawing a long-held distinction in Anglo-Australian law between property in land (real property) and in works of art (incorporeal intellectual property). While this distinction is breaking down in many areas of property law, the NTA requires that there be a connection with land and waters, under s 223(1)(b).

In holding that protection of cultural knowledge is a native title right or interest only in so far as it relates to land and waters, the majority appeared to take a very narrow view of 'connection'. The majority used the example of denying or restricting access to sites or areas as a right relating to land. This seems to import concepts of real property under common law rather than the more ordinary meaning of connection with land that reflects the *sui generis* nature of native title and broader concepts of property law. The majority noted that controlling access may not be the defining character of 'connection to land', but suggested that greater attention has to be paid in connecting the rights and interests in cultural knowledge to the land and waters under claim. Where the boundary lies between land-related protection and unrelated assertions still requires further testing, particularly having regard to the notion that the connection need not be physical. The majority pointed to other areas of law that could be pursued to provide further protection of cultural knowledge: for example, moral rights and intellectual property law, as well as confidentiality and fiduciary duties.[47] The limits of these areas of the law to protect Indigenous rights is well documented.[48] The majority's acceptance of *Bulun Bulun* indicated a reluctance to reopen the law in this area.

NON-EXCLUSIVE NATIVE TITLE

The majority of the High Court in *Ward* accepted that the right to speak for country encapsulated the complex relationship between people and country and amounted to exclusive possession, occupation, use and enjoyment.[49] But the judges expressed concern in the context of extinguishment, particularly where the 'exclusive' character of the title may be compromised. In their view, simply equating the right to speak for country with the right to control access and use did not allow a court to assess the limits of extinguishment and the extent of the remaining native title rights and interests. The majority suggested that, although the right to be asked permission or to control access may be core concepts in traditional law and custom, they did not exhaustively describe the rights and interests conferred by the traditional law.[50]

While the majority joint judgment recognised that native title may amount to full beneficial ownership, the judges were critical of the determination by Justice Lee because it extended the broad statement of the exclusive right to control access and to make decisions about the use of the land to areas where other interests may impact on native title. A determination of exclusive occupation, use and enjoyment (subject to extinguishing acts and the validly granted rights and interests of others) was thought to be too high a level of abstraction.[51] More specificity was called for in articulating the relationship between native title and other interests.

The majority went further, holding that 'exclusive' rights (particularly the right to control access) were extinguished by virtually any grant of rights or interest to others. The High Court's readiness in this regard undermines the status of Indigenous peoples as owners of their traditional land, especially as their property rights should be prioritised as the greater interest and the first in time. The decision took the discriminatory aspects of the native title doctrine much further than that first proposed in *Mabo*. Moreover, it perpetrated unnecessary violence against the rights that flow from obligations under Indigenous law.

The majority did not say that the extinguishment of exclusive rights to control access destroyed all exclusive rights, nor all rights to control access. The majority said that (upon the exercise of authority by the new sovereign to create or assert rights to control access):

the right to be asked for permission to use or have access to the land was inevitably *confined*, if not excluded. But because native title is more than the right to be asked for permission to use or have access (important though that right undoubtedly is) there are other rights and interests which must be considered, including rights and interests in the use of land.⁵²

The High Court remitted the matter back to the Federal Court to make further findings as to how other rights and interests under native title may be affected. The Federal Court was asked to provide greater particulars as to the rights and interests conferred by native title in relation to different areas of land within the claim area. The matter was finally determined by consent in 2003.

The discussion of 'non-exclusive' in this case should be distinguished from the conclusions in *Commonwealth v Yarmirr* (2001) (*Yarmirr*) (and, in this case, in relation to exclusive fishing).⁵³ In *Yarmirr* the competing rights were public rights. In this case, many of the competing rights discussed were the limited rights of one private party. There was scope to argue that while neither the native title holders nor the other party had an exclusive right to control access by one another, they had certain rights to control access against the rest of the world. Moreover, where native title — but for the legal conclusion of extinguishment — would have amounted to exclusive possession, and the native title was affected only to the extent of the inconsistency, it would have been sensible to conclude that, together, they held rights and interests equivalent of exclusive title. The native title holders and the other interest holders were better described as co-owners in this regard.

The majority joint judgment did say that it had been difficult to characterise a non-exclusive right to make decisions about use and enjoyment, suggesting that where a right to possession was not held as against the whole world it might be doubted that there was a right to control access or make binding decisions about its use, but they did not preclude such a right existing.⁵⁴ The majority joint judgment suggested that simply stating that exclusive rights to make decisions about use and enjoyment of the land was a right that is not exclusive of the rights of others in that regard was not sufficient to identify the content of a non-exclusive right to make decisions. Defining such a right, the judgment said, required further consideration of the relationship between native title and the other interests.⁵⁵ It was an error to preclude native title holders from asserting a continuing capacity to make decisions within the scope provided by the operation of other interests.

The majority concluded that, where there are areas where native title will not amount to exclusive possession, occupation, use and enjoyment, it may be better to describe the rights and interests by reference to activities ('may', not 'must').⁵⁶ To this end, the majority seemed to prefer the differentiated statement of rights and interests originally put by the claimants, where the areas of exclusive possession, use, occupation and enjoyment were separated from areas where narrower rights were asserted.[57] Under this reasoning, it may be useful to distinguish exclusive possession areas from other areas. That is, where there are no competing interests or extinguishment issues, broad statements of rights to speak for country may not need to be further particularised. Of course, the occurrence of such areas may be limited. In areas of competing interests, there is work to be done in explaining how the right to speak for country can, and does, operate in the face of non-Indigenous users.

The difficulty lies in negotiating the confusion in the majority's reasoning between the nature of native title and the right and interests conferred by Indigenous law on the one hand, and the impacts of extinguishment on the other. The majority seemed to conceive of the continuum of rights and interests reflected by the concept of native title as different classes of title within the one claim area. Each title is *sui generis* through the operation of law and customs and the impact of extinguishment. But the Court did not adequately distinguish these two inquiries in its observations as to proof.

The majority arguably misconstrued the nature of Indigenous connection to country through law and custom. Indigenous peoples generally express their entitlement as an interest in land approaching or exceeding common law understandings of full ownership, except for the impact of extinguishment. Thus, where a group has exclusive right to speak for country under traditional law, exclusive possession (and, I would argue, Indigenous jurisdiction) should be the starting point. The High Court faltered in requiring that Indigenous peoples articulate how their law has responded to these incursions to articulate the accommodation of non-Indigenous interests within Indigenous assertions of their rights to the land. But this is not always, if ever, appropriate. As the courts have repeatedly stated, the rights and interests under Indigenous law may exist where the common law refuses to recognise them. The determination of native title is a site of contest between two systems of law and between Indigenous rights to land and non-Indigenous interests.[58]

While undermining the decision-making authority of native title holders by its readiness to imply impairment of the right to control access and make decisions about the use of land, the High Court, in insisting on the central role of law and custom, acknowledged that Indigenous peoples are lawmakers. At least as a matter of fact, the authority of Indigenous peoples within a particular sphere to make laws with respect to land was acknowledged. This authority has been reinforced by common law native title and in some respects has been given effective enforcement outside of the Indigenous group through the remedies provided by the common law and the NTA.

It is not clear in *Ward* that the High Court wished to usurp the role of the Indigenous peoples by making itself the arbiter of the application of traditional law and custom. This therefore remains an Indigenous jurisdiction, maintaining what Pearson has described as the internal aspect of native title.[59] The inquiry into traditional law and custom and the rights and interests conferred by native title should remain constrained to the purpose of identifying the extent of native title in its relationship with other interests. That is, it should still be used to establish the outer limits of native title, not the details of the internal organisation of the native title holding group.

The accommodation of non-Indigenous rights may or may not have occurred in Indigenous law or may be expressed or reflected in different ways. The majority of the High Court expressed dissatisfaction with the lack of clarity of the determination of native title by Justice Lee, which, while it reflected as far as possible under common law the interests asserted as of right by native title holders, was subject only in general terms to the interests of others. But it is in the determination process that this relationship between native title and other interests should be further articulated. The detail required by the High Court cannot and should not be found in the kinds of proof and the nature of entitlement under Indigenous law.

The title is still defined first by law and custom, and second by the relationship of native title to other interests, as demanded by the common law and the NTA. This reading of the framework for determining native title maintains that it is the rights and interests conferred by law and custom that define the title, but also maintains the idea that native title is still a form of title and not merely a list of permissible activities. The 'bundle of rights' remains as a metaphor that facilitates the articulation of the extent of the native title in question. In total, the courts are not competent to administer and articulate Indigenous law. It is therefore appropriate for native title to be treated as a plenary title from which the interests of others carve out the limits of recognition.

PRINCIPLES FOR EXTINGUISHMENT UNDER THE *NATIVE TITLE ACT*

The High Court confirmed that recognition by the NTA might cease where, as a matter of law, native title has been extinguished, even where (apart from that legal conclusion) the fact of Indigenous peoples' continued rights and interests in the land continue. This idea had been expressed in other Federal Court decisions and by the High Court as a 'withdrawal of recognition' but the majority joint judgment clearly stated that this terminology did not imply that there are 'degrees of inconsistency'.[60]

The majority agreed that 'inconsistency of incidents' was the appropriate test for determining extinguishment and coexistence. The majority affirmed that the inquiry into extinguishment and the extent of inconsistency requires a comparison of particular rights and interests conferred by native title on the one

6. Redefining extinguishment: Ward

hand and by the statutory grant or interest on the other.[61] That is, extinguishment can only be determined once the legal content of both sets of rights said to be in conflict has been established.[62]

As discussed, the majority affirmed the view of the full Federal Court majority that to describe native title as a bundle of rights, 'the separate components of which may be extinguished separately', is useful to understand the operation of the NTA in relation to extinguishment, in particular the distinction between complete and partial inconsistency.[63] The Court disagreed with arguments that native title rights and interests referred to in the NTA were necessarily a single set of rights analogous to a fee simple, requiring greater particularity. But the acceptance of the idea of 'incidents' as the keystone of the test supports the view that this decision does not reduce native title to a simple bundle of rights that result in a list of activities permitted on the land and waters. The High Court repeatedly drew a distinction, in relation to both native title and non-Indigenous interests, between the rights conferred by the title and the uses or activities pursued in the exercise of those rights.

In highlighting the inconsistency of incidents test, which looks at the impact of a grant or assertion of an interest by the Crown, the majority in *Ward* de-emphasised the clear and plain intention test. The majority argued that the requirement that legislation or an authorised act have demonstrated a clear and plain intention to extinguish native title should be understood as an objective inquiry within the context of the inconsistency of incidents test.[64]

One positive element that may be gleaned from the approach to the inconsistency of incidents test in *Ward* is the attempt to treat native title interests and other interests with the same level of scrutiny. That is, non-native title interests are also required to detail the rights and interests conferred by their title. The majority in *Ward* rejected the idea that a piecemeal accumulation of interests could be taken together and constitute some sort of 'operational inconsistency'.[65] Rather, the majority required each constituting interest to be analysed on its terms to determine the extent of inconsistency.[66] As in *Wik*, the presumptions of a grantee or the uses made of the land that may go beyond the bounds of the grant will not effect an extinguishment. But the burden of this test falls clearly on native title parties.

The majority reaffirmed the principle that an interest does not confer exclusive possession merely because it is called a lease.[67] Questions of extinguishment are questions initially for the common law and only then should attention be turned to how legislation operates.

The majority described pastoral leases under Western Australian legislation as a 'precarious' interest, even more so in some respects than leases considered in *Wik*.[68] They concluded that on no view could the pastoral leases be said to give the holder exclusive possession. The interests conferred limited rights subject to extensive reservations and exceptions permitting entry on land for a variety of circumstances.[69] The leases were held, therefore, to be non-exclusive pastoral leases within s 248B of the NTA; they were granted before the RDA came into operation and were therefore valid.[70]

The Court paid particular attention in *Ward* to the relationship between extinguishment at common law, the provision of the NTA and the operation of the RDA. For example, the Special Purposes Lease that gave effect to the Keep River National Park was held to be a grant of exclusive possession. Except for the operation of the RDA, the native title rights would have been extinguished. The lease had been subject of a specific declaration, under s 12(1) of the *Territory Parks and Wildlife Conservation Act* (NT), to be a park in respect of which no person other than the Corporation held a right, title or interest. No doubt, the majority stated, this phrase extends to any surviving native title rights and interests but such a declaration had no extinguishing effect.[71] Indeed, the rationale for the provision is to ensure that no private rights would be affected by the creation of a park, hence the absence of compensation provisions in the Act. In fact, the exercise of the power to make such a declaration was miscarried. The declaration was therefore void. This finding brought into question the status of all of the large number of parks declared in the Northern Territory since 1975.

In contrast to the result in relation to national parks in the Northern Territory, parks and reserves in Western Australia were treated differently. Much of the claim area in the Miriuwung Gajerrong application is designated as reserve lands. The *Land Act 1933* (WA) provided for the creation of reserves for public purposes, and the vesting of reserves or the placing of reserves under a board of management. The majority of the High Court in *Ward* distinguished between different types of reserves. The majority confirmed the opinion of the full Federal Court that a reservation for public purposes of itself does not affect native title, but held that consideration needed to be given to what other steps were done in relation to the land pursuant to the reservation and also what was done to bring previous interests in land to an end.[72]

Under s 33 of the *Land Act* reserves can be vested in and held by a municipality or other person in trust. The majority determined that the Crown can create an interest for itself that would be inconsistent with native title.[73] A strict legal test of inconsistency was applied to determine that, despite being vested in the Crown, the device used to achieve this was a grant of exclusive possession and therefore extinguished native title, but a reservation under s 34 that was 'vested' by simply placing it under the control of a board of management did not extinguish native title.[74]

6. Redefining extinguishment: *Ward*

PARTIAL EXTINGUISHMENT AND COEXISTENCE

The discussion of statutory leases and reservations in *Ward* appears to support the view that nothing short of an exclusive possession tenure can effect complete extinguishment without the operation of a legislative provision of the NTA. Moreover, the majority joint judgment confirmed that outside the operation of any deeming provision of the NTA, it is not the fact of exclusive possession that is determinative but the assessment that there is no capacity for coexisting rights. Thus the relationship between native title holders and the leaseholders can be understood on the basis of partial extinguishment and coexistence.

In relation to partial extinguishment, the granting of pastoral leases was an act that involved granting rights and interests inconsistent with as many of the native title rights and interests as stipulate control of access to the land that is the subject of the grant — the majority denied the native title holders the exclusive right to say who could or could not come on to the land. To that extent, those rights extinguish native title rights and interests. The right to control access apart, many other native title rights continued unaffected. The relevant inconsistency occurred at the higher level of rights and not at the level of activities conducted in the exercise of rights.[75]

In terms of coexistence, to the extent that the grant of a pastoral lease involved the grant of rights not inconsistent with native title rights and interests, the rights and interests granted by the pastoral lease and the doing of any activity in giving effect to them 'prevail' over native title rights and interests but do not extinguish them. Activities can be 'inconsistent', in the sense of competing, but there was no relevant inconsistency for the purposes of extinguishment.[76]

The majority explained the notion of prevailing rights as an issue separate from extinguishment. The native title rights cannot be exercised in a way that interferes with the exercise of inconsistent statutory rights. The law protects the holder of, for example, a mining lease, by preventing interference with the exercise of the right conferred by the lease. Once the interest is validly granted, the relationship becomes one guided by the normal rules of property law, including the idea of 'reasonable users', although this principle was mentioned in the majority judgments only by Justice Kirby.[77]

The analysis of pastoral and mining leases and, in particular, the understanding of reservations acknowledged that the native title interests are in fact the prior interest. Unfortunately, this acknowledgment is not always carried through. While native title may be vulnerable, it is a plenary interest from which the inconsistent rights of others carve away rights and interests by extinguishment. This is an important philosophical principle as much as a pivotal jurisprudential principle. For non-Indigenous people, including judges and political decision makers, native title holders are often seen as the late comers — an interest that came into being in 1992 rather than at the assertion of sovereignty by the British Crown.

The recognition of native title as the first title, as a plenary title, and as a valuable property right and inheritance right points to a more robust version of the idea of coexistence. Where native title survives to a significant degree, as is clearly the case in relation to pastoral leases and mining leases, the emphasis should be on co-ownership. This has significant implications for arrangements that have been negotiated for access to pastoral leases that have diminished the role of native title holders from co-owners to occasional visitors.

THE *WILSON V ANDERSON* DECISION

On the same day that the High Court handed down its decision in *Ward*, it also handed down the decision in *Wilson v Anderson* (2002) (*Wilson*).[78] The case concerned the traditional country of the Euahlayi-Dixon clan, over which the Crown had granted leases under the *Western Lands Act 1901* (NSW) (WLA). Here the High Court rejected the methodology of the *Wik* decision. Instead, it looked first to the operation of the 'confirmation' of extinguishment provisions of the NTA,[79] and determined that the statutory leases under the WLA were more akin to common law leases. Therefore, despite specific purpose restrictions (for grazing only), the leases were held to grant exclusive possession and were therefore deemed, by s 23B(2)(c), to extinguish native title. Chief Justice Gleeson, in separate reasons, confirmed that the Court had jettisoned the clear and plain intention test. His Honour confirmed that where a law or Act creates in a third party rights over land that are inconsistent with the anterior native title rights, native title is extinguished to the extent of the inconsistency.[80] No inquiry was required into any specific intention to extinguish native title, or any other anterior rights. The only intention to be discovered was an intention to grant exclusive possession.[81]

CONCLUSION

Before the High Court delivered its decision in the *Ward* case, it was heralded as the most important case since *Mabo* and *Wik*. It was expected that it would clarify the nature and scope of native title. Rather than espouse a coherent theory of native title, the High Court instead concentrated on the complex web of statutes that now frames native title and tried to articulate the process for determining the relationship between native title and other interests. The majority concentrated on the intricacies of determining the extinguishing effects of two hundred years of dealing with Indigenous peoples' land without consideration of their property rights.

The decision in *Ward*, bolstered by the decision in *Wilson*, confirmed that prior grants and interests could extinguish native title in part, thereby extracting particular rights and interests from native title permanently. The patchwork of tenures granted over land throughout Australia's history therefore leaves a permanent imprint on native title that cannot be removed unless statutory provision is made.

Indigenous peoples may be pleased that the High Court confirmed that native title could coexist with other interests, although it would remain subject to the rights conferred on others. In a number of respects, native title may be even more robust. Access agreements and consent determinations negotiated, at least in Western Australia, may have been negotiated on the basis of an underestimation of the strength of native title as a coexisting interest.

The exclusion of the majority of national parks from determination in Western Australia, illustrated in the Martu determination in *James v Western Australia* [2002],[82] is starkly contrasted to the reopening of negotiations over all national parks in the Northern Territory. The variation between the recognition of Indigenous peoples' legitimate claims to land based on the idiosyncrasies of tenures and legislation highlights the injustice of the extinguishment doctrine. Like the *Wik* and *Fejo* judgments before,[83] the anomaly of previous acts no longer in force was brought into relief throughout the judgment. There is surely a strong argument for greater scope for suspension and revival provisions, such as s 47B.

The judgment in *Ward* cried out for reform of the system to allow greater scope for a non-litigious examination of the merits of Indigenous peoples' claims without undue interference from historical tenures. Both Justice McHugh and Justice Callinan went so far as to call for a new process that could lead to more just outcomes for Indigenous people.[84] New processes for negotiated settlements are required to allow the return of lands and the recognition of the right to speak for country. Ideally, any such process would use the enormous investment that Indigenous peoples have made in articulating and compiling evidence of their connection to country and the investment of goodwill by many respondents to the native title process. It would be a gross injustice to allow the judicial abrogation of responsibility to permanently derail the recognition of the legitimate claims of Indigenous peoples for land justice and self-determination.

CHAPTER 7

Proof of a native title society
Yorta Yorta v Victoria

HIGH COURT OF AUSTRALIA, 2002

The decision of the High Court in *Members of the Yorta Yorta Aboriginal Community v Victoria* (2002) (*Yorta Yorta*) confirms that the gap between the aspirations of Indigenous peoples and the capacity of native title to fulfil those expectations is enormous.[1] The interpretation of the requirements of proof, and in particular the meaning attributed to the concept of 'traditional', forms a significant part of that gulf.

This is particularly pertinent for Indigenous peoples of the more settled regions of Australia. The Yorta Yorta people's lands are located along the Murray River, crossing the border between New South Wales and Victoria, in one of the most productive agricultural regions in Australia. The determination against the Yorta Yorta people raised significant questions about what is considered 'tradition' in the sense that it could sustain native title. It has been suggested that interpretation of the requirements of proof applied in *Yorta Yorta* may lead to discriminatory differentiation between one Indigenous people and another based on what are considered appropriately 'traditional' Aboriginal or Torres Strait Islander societies.[2]

TRADITION AND CONTINUITY IN *YORTA YORTA*

The way that Justice Olney posed the question of proof in *Yorta Yorta*, at first instance in the Federal Court, assumed that a historical account of the laws and customs of the original inhabitants was required.[3] The traditions and customs observed at the time of settlement were said to constitute the title that burdened the Crown and it seemed that the title survived only through continued observance of these particular customs. The forced settlement of Yorta Yorta people on missions within their traditional territories, the suppression of their language and forms of cultural expression and, importantly, the taking up of paid employment and admission of 'settling down to more orderly habits of industry'[4] were said by Justice Olney to show that by 1881, a mere forty years after European settlement of the area, the Yorta Yorta people had lost their culture and their status as a 'traditional society'. This was in large part measured against their adoption of commercial farming and settled lifestyle.[5]

The Yorta Yorta applicants did not shy away from asserting that they maintained a continuing system of custom and tradition that incorporated a traditional relationship to the land through which they maintained a traditional connection with the land, which was supported by continuous physical occupation.[6] But contemporary practices that the Yorta Yorta people saw as cultural traditions, such as protection of sites of cultural significance and involvement in the management of land and waters in their traditional areas, were rejected by Justice Olney because these practices were not of a kind that were exercised by, or of significance to, the pre-contact society. Justice Olney concluded that:

> Preservation of Aboriginal heritage and conservation of the natural environment are worthy objectives ... but in the context of a native title claim the absence of a continuous link back to the laws and customs of the original inhabitants deprives those activities of the character of traditional.[8]

To this end, it was deemed appropriate to prefer the writings of a nineteenth-century squatter over the evidence of the Yorta Yorta witnesses. The traditions and customs observed by the squatter, Curr, were said to constitute the title that burdened the Crown and it seems that only through continued observance of those particular customs could the title survive. Justice Olney observed:

> It is said by a number of witnesses that consistent with traditional laws and customs it is their practice to take from the land and waters only such food as is necessary for immediate consumption. This practice, commendable as it is, is not one which according to Curr's observations, was adopted by the Aboriginal people with whom he came into contact and cannot be regarded as the continuation of a traditional custom.[9]

The majority on appeal to the full Federal Court in *Yorta Yorta*, while not rejecting the ultimate finding of Justice Olney, did reject a strict approach to the tracing of tradition from pre-contact. Justices Branson and Katz stated their interpretation: 'The primary issue is whether the law or custom has in substance been handed down from generation to generation; that is, whether it can be shown to have its roots in the tradition of the relevant community.'[10] Therefore, despite ongoing physical presence, assertion of rights to the land, maintenance of identification as a community entitled to the land and maintenance of cultural identity, the trial judge determined that the Yorta Yorta people did not continuously occupy the land in the relevant sense. The majority of the full Federal Court supported the finding that there was a period of time between 1788 and the time of the claim during which the Yorta Yorta lost their character as a 'traditional Aboriginal community' and, as a result, native title had 'expired'.[11]

In the High Court, the claimants seized on comments from members of the Court in argument in *Commonwealth v Yarmirr* (2001) (*Yarmirr*)[12] regarding the centrality of the s 223 definition of native title and the obvious construction of the provisions in the present tense. The Court agreed that reference to native title rights and interests that 'are possessed under the traditional laws acknowledged, and the traditional customs observed' must be read as 'currently' possessed.[13]

The majority of the High Court, led by Chief Justice Gleeson and Justices Gummow and Hayne, suggested that the construction of s 223 required a different conception of tradition than is suggested by the ordinary meaning of the word. While they agreed that 'tradition' meant the transmission of law or custom from generation to generation, usually by word of mouth and common practice, they argued that more was required in the context of the *Native Title Act 1993* (Cth) (NTA).[14]

The dissenting joint judgment of Justices Gaudron and Kirby adopted the ordinary definition of tradition and agreed that the word 'traditional' in s 223 imported a sense of continuity from the past.[15] Continuity, they argued, bears upon the question whether present-day belief and practices could be said to constitute an acknowledgment of traditional laws and observance of traditional custom.[16]

THE INTERSECTION OF NORMATIVE SYSTEMS

The High Court majority judgment discussed the intersection between Indigenous and non-Indigenous systems of law that is recognised by the concept of native title. The judgment said: 'It is critically important to identify what exactly it is that intersects with the common law.'[17] The majority determined that what native title recognises is the intersection of two bodies of law — that of the prior sovereignty and that of the new sovereign. Consistent with the act of state doctrine, the extent of intersection is determined by the law of the new sovereign. The extent to which the rights and interests conferred by Indigenous society, though having their source and authority in a pre-existing and persisting sovereignty, are enforceable under the new regime depends on the degree of 'intersection' determined by the common law or legislation.[18] The jurisprudential analysis applied by the Court to determine what 'exactly' was being recognised is somewhat self-serving. The Court surmised that native title rights find their source in traditional law and custom but, because the introduction of a new legal order denied the efficacy of any other normative system or parallel law-making system, the rights and interests claimed have to have been brought into existence under that normative system when it was able to validly create new rights, interests and duties. Therefore, rights and interests created after the assertion of sovereignty that were not recognised by the common law and were not sourced in the new legal order could not be given legal effect.[19]

Through this reasoning, the Court disavowed any continuing authority within Indigenous societies capable of recognition by the courts. The majority judgment relied on the act of state doctrine, which suggests that the acquisition of sovereignty cannot be challenged by a municipal court.[20] But they denied the power of the courts to determine the implication of that acquisition and to determine the distribution of power within the state. This abdication of judicial responsibility is exacerbated by the adherence to the argument that it is the NTA that limits the ability of native title to recognise Indigenous peoples' rights to their lands, rejecting any continuing role for the common law in determining the underlying concept or framing the interpretation of the NTA.[21] Justice McHugh in dissent questioned this reasoning, stating that he was 'unconvinced that the construction that this Court has placed on s 223 accords with what parliament intended'.[22]

WHAT HAS TO BE PROVED

Armed with their analysis of the limits of the intersection of the two normative systems, the majority then turned to the NTA. Based on the idea that the source of native title is in the pre-existing normative system, the majority added two additional criteria to the meaning of 'tradition' beyond any ordinary understanding. First, the majority judgment suggested, the NTA conveys an understanding of the age of the traditions. That is, the source of the rights and interests are found in the normative rules that existed prior to the assertion of sovereignty by the Crown.[23]

Second, the Court suggested that the present tense of the provisions requires that the normative system has had a continuous existence and vitality since sovereignty.[24] The continued existence of this normative system, it was argued, depends upon its maintenance and observance by the group that has bound itself to it. In this sense, the Court suggested, the maintenance of the normative system defines the society.[25] The Court was again careful not to establish a continuous tracing of activities or rights and interests to pre-contact times. It is the 'body of law' that must have continued. The content of that body of laws may undergo evolution and development but it cannot suffer substantial interruption. The question of the relationship between the laws and customs now acknowledged and observed and those that were observed before the assertion of European sovereignty was therefore phrased, somewhat inelegantly, as necessary to a consideration of 'whether the laws and customs can be said to be the laws and customs of the society whose laws and customs are properly described as traditional laws and customs'.[26]

In their dissenting judgment, Justices Gaudron and Kirby specifically considered the idea of continuity of community. They agreed that a society has to be 'sufficiently organised' to create and sustain rights, beliefs and practices having normative influence and, as well, the society has to be sufficiently organised to adapt, modify or extend the laws.[27] A lack of continuity of community may open the way to conclude that current practices are not part of the traditional laws or customs but, Justices Gaudron and Kirby warned, communities might disperse and regroup. On this reasoning, the evidence that a community has the requisite continuity is primarily a question of whether there are people who have identified themselves and each other as members of the community in question.[28]

The dissenting judgment had a lot in common with the majority joint judgment of Chief Justice Gleeson and Justices Gummow and Hayne but differed in its assessment of Justice Olney's conclusions. Justices Gaudron and Kirby suggested that Justice Olney had not found that the Yorta Yorta people had ceased to exist as an identifiable community.[29] More fundamentally, they found that Justice Olney had not directed his inquiry to the acknowledgment of a system of laws and customs by which the group could establish a connection and, instead, had examined whether there existed laws and customs specifically related to use and occupation.[30] This preoccupation with exercise of rights and interests and laws relating to particular uses and activities was rejected by the Court in *Western Australia v Ward* (2002) (*Ward*).[31]

CONTINUITY AND CHANGE IN TRADITION

Prior to this decision, the common law had accepted that the manner in which native title rights and interests are exercised will develop and change over time. In *Mabo v Queensland [No. 2]* (1992) (*Mabo*) and since, the High Court has firmly stated that it does not expect that the laws and customs that sustain native title will be frozen in time or reflect some arcane notion of 'traditional' as meaning pre-contact activities. It is accepted that native title rights and interests are regulated by laws and customs that are internal to the group and change and evolve as the society changes and evolves.[32]

In *Yanner v Eaton* (1999) (*Yanner*), it was held that there is no prescription on the methods employed in the exercise of native title. It was generally accepted, for example, that modern methods could be employed in hunting and fishing. As Justice Gummow noted in *Yanner* and Justice Lee observed in *Ward* at first instance, it did not matter that fishing was undertaken from an outboard-motored dinghy.[33] Justices Branson and Katz, in the full Federal Court appeal in *Members of the Yorta Yorta Aboriginal Community v Victoria* (2001), also explained that the ability of traditions and customs to evolve was not limited to the mode of exercise but also applied to the subject matter, elaborating that:[34]

The primary issue is whether the law or custom has in substance been handed down from generation to generation; that is, whether it can be shown to have its roots in the tradition of the relevant community. However, for the reasons so persuasively articulated by Toohey J in *Mabo [No 2]* at 192 … it cannot be accepted that the fact that an indigenous society has adopted certain aspects of the now dominant culture means that the society has necessarily abandoned its traditional connection with land or waters.[35]

All that was required was that the general nature of the connection between the Indigenous people and the land remained.[36] Justice Brennan explained that:

so long as the people remain an identifiable community, the numbers of whom are identified by one another as members of that community, living under its laws and customs, the communal native title survives to be enjoyed.[37]

The High Court in *Yorta Yorta* confirmed that some change to or adaptation of the system of law and custom or interruption in the enjoyment of native title rights and interests is not 'necessarily' fatal to a claim, but in a particular case such changes or interruptions may take on considerable significance. While expressed in the present tense, the Court suggested that the requirements of s 223 require some continuity. This does not necessarily mean an unbroken chain of continuity but the system of law and custom must have continued 'substantially uninterrupted' since the assertion of British sovereignty.[38] The key question in this instance is whether the law and custom can still be seen to be traditional law and traditional custom.[39] To answer this question, the Court deferred to the judgment of the trial judge in assessing the evidence.

The conclusions of Justice Olney prompted strong critiques of the idea of abandonment of culture that has been read into Justice Brennan's judgment in *Mabo*.[40] The High Court's reasoning in *Ward* suggested that abandonment is not a form of common law extinguishment outside the NTA.[41]

The majority judgment in *Yorta Yorta* confirmed this, suggesting that the term 'abandonment' might be misleading in suggesting that some blame for the interruption lay with the Indigenous community.[42] The objectification of the inquiry in this way belies the fact that the Crown receives the benefit of overt disruptions to Indigenous peoples' enjoyment of the rights and interests. That benefit is reinforced by standards of proof that require claimants to establish the continuity of the system of law and custom back through to the assertion of sovereignty by the Crown.

The majority in *Yorta Yorta* stated quite frankly that the 'difficulty of the forensic task which may confront claimants does not alter the requirements of the statutory provision'.[43] The judges accepted that claimants may invite the

Court to infer from the evidence the content of the traditional laws and customs of earlier times in order to establish that they are rooted in a pre-sovereignty normative system.[44] But they also noted that the more restricted evidentiary rules introduced by the *Native Title Amendment Act* in 1998 may make such inferences much harder than under the previous provisions.

The High Court's decision in *Yorta Yorta* confirms that the legal recognition of native title continues to become more and more elusive. The need to establish a coherent and continuous society defined by a pre-sovereignty normative system creates enormous ambiguity in the requirements of proof. The nature of the group has emerged as a fundamental threshold question for native title claimants. The High Court's deference to the views of the trial judge in *Yorta Yorta* demonstrated the vagaries of an assessment based, to a significant degree, on a judge's perceptions of the group. The High Court did little to guide trial judges away from their pre-existing biases and prejudices in making such an assessment. Native title claimants must rely on the ability of a non-Indigenous judiciary to conceptualise the contemporary expressions of Indigenous identity, culture and law as consistent with the idea of a pre-sovereign normative system.

CONCLUSION

In determining that the Yorta Yorta people no longer observe the same normative system that 'burdened' the Crown's acquisition of sovereignty, the majority of the High Court expressed its self-declared 'radical' proposition that the people who came to the Court to assert native title were in fact a different Yorta Yorta society or group from those who had held native title.[45] It seemed that, although their genealogical and physical continuity and their existence as an Indigenous community bound by rules of normative content were proved, these were now rules with no source in the normative system of the 'original' Yorta Yorta people from whom they were directly descended. The majority acknowledged that the common law, in recognising native title, also recognised the rules of transmission for those interests and allowed for the development of the right in a manner contemplated by pre-existing traditional law and custom.[46] But the Court deferred to the judgment of the trial judge in determining on the facts that there had been a significant disruption in the normative system of law and custom that sustained native title. The significance of this deference to the finding of facts by the trial judge should not be understated. As a consequence, Justice Olney's prejudices in this case should not be read into the jurisprudential doctrine derived from the High Court decision. The High Court in *Yorta Yorta* supported the decision of the trial judge, not on any assessment of the change and evolution of particular laws

7. Proof of a native title society: *Yorta Yorta*

and customs or rights and interests, but on the fundamental findings in relation to the interruption to the body of law and customs, the normative system that defined the society.[47] These are very different inquiries. The High Court took a significant leap of faith in allowing Justice Olney's assessment of the facts elicited for the purpose of one inquiry to form the basis for confidently drawing the same conclusion based on the very different inquiry set out in the final appeal.

CHAPTER 8

Rules of interpretation
Griffiths v Minister for Lands, Planning and Environment

HIGH COURT OF AUSTRALIA, 2008

On 15 May 2008 the High Court of Australia, with little fanfare or media coverage, handed down a decision in its first native title case for some years. *Griffiths v Minister for Lands, Planning and Environment* (2008) (*Griffiths*) concerned a compulsory acquisition of native title by the Northern Territory Government in the Timber Creek township.[1] The case required the High Court to consider some fundamental questions of the reach of executive power to divest private citizens of their property. The case therefore has broader reach than the acquisition of native title. Indeed, while there are many issues that could have been considered in the jurisprudence of native title, the majority of the Court dealt with the case as one concerning any ordinary title.

The case was precipitated in 1997 by a request from the holder of a grazing licence to purchase the land under which the licence was held and other blocks in the Timber Creek area for development as commercial enterprises. In 2000 the Northern Territory Government issued three notices to acquire all native title rights and interests, in particular parcels of land. The traditional owners of the area lodged objections to the acquisition and lodged an application for a determination of native title over the area in response to the notices, and were successful.[2]

The notices clearly stated that the purpose of the acquisition was to grant a lease, which could be exchanged for freehold upon completion of the development. This raises a central question of the power of the Crown to acquire the private rights of one citizen (or group of citizens) for the immediate benefit of another private citizen.

THE STATUTORY FRAMEWORK

Section 43 of the Northern Territory *Lands Acquisition Act 1978* (NT) (LAA) had previously provided the Minister with power to compulsorily acquire land for 'public purposes' and, later, more simply, to 'acquire land'. In 1998 the Act was amended to allow the Minister to acquire land for 'any purpose whatsoever', so long as the 'pre-acquisition procedures' were complied with.

The 1998 amendments to the LAA took into account the amendments to the *Native Title Act 1993* (Cth) (NTA). Indeed, the provision was amended to refer to 'any purpose whatsoever' so as to ensure that the processes for acquisition of land in the Northern Territory complied with the NTA. The legislature may also have had in mind the decision of the High Court in *Clunies Ross v The Commonwealth* (1984).[3] In that case, the High Court determined that the power to acquire land for a public purpose, under the federal legislation, required that there be a proposed use or application for the land that advances a public purpose. The legislature had clearly intended to remove any fetters on the executive power to acquire land.

PUBLIC PURPOSE AND PRIVATE BENEFIT

The majority of the High Court in *Griffiths* agreed that, whether there were any ultimate limits on the broad phrasing of s 43, the LAA at least included acquisition 'for the purpose of enabling the exercise of powers conferred on the executive by another statute of the territory'; in this case, the *Crown Lands Act 1992* (NT), s 9, which provides that the Minister may grant estates in fee simple or lease Crown land.[4] The majority disregarded cases involving local government and statutory authorities that establish a clear line of authority against local governments interfering with the private title of one party for the private benefit of another.[5]

Justice Kiefel disagreed with the majority on this issue. For Justice Kiefel, the question turned on whether there was a relevant 'purpose'. Her Honour was of the view that there was no proposed use or purpose for the acquisition within any wider plan by the Northern Territory Government for the use of the land. Rather, the acquisition was simply to support the proposal of a developer for the developer's private benefit. Justice Kiefel invoked the line of authority in relation to local governments and the established principle of statutory interpretation stated in *Clissold v Perry* in 1904 that statutes 'are not to be construed as interfering with vested interests unless that intention is manifest'.[6] On her construction, the power to acquire land for a purpose requires a need for the land, and the need must be that of the acquiring agency or authority, not the needs of another private individual; that is, there must be a 'governmental' purpose at the heart of the need to acquire the land.[7] Justice Kiefel considered the processes that were required before an acquisition was approved, including the hearing by a tribunal and the right to object and additional considerations to be taken into account in relation to native title, in particular. However, her Honour argued that they were limited in their effectiveness as safeguards.[8]

The majority did not venture outside the boundaries of the statutes involved. Relying on the 'freehold equivalence' tests in the NTA, the Court dealt with this issue as simply a matter of two indistinguishable competing interests in land.[9] The Court failed to take into account common law traditions for the interpretation of legislation or agreements concerning Indigenous peoples. These rules have their roots in the common law protection of the rights of citizens against arbitrary exercises of power by the state, especially in relation to property.[10] The *Mabo* decision, while recognising the power of the state to take the property of Indigenous peoples, held that the exercise of such power 'must reveal a clear and plain intention':

> This requirement, which flows from the seriousness of the consequences to indigenous inhabitants of extinguishing their traditional rights and interests in land, has been repeatedly emphasized by courts dealing with the extinguishing of the native title of Indian bands in North America ... It is patently the right rule.[11]

As a compromise, and accommodating two hundred years of the exercise of legislative and executive power without regard for Indigenous interests, *Mabo* held that extinguishment can occur by necessary implication (for example, where inconsistent rights have been granted to another), despite the absence of an express intention to extinguish the rights of Indigenous peoples.[12]

The NTA future act regime was introduced to ensure that native title would not be extinguished without due process. But the principle of clear and plain intention and beneficial construction has been lost. Even if we can accept that native title has become a statutory right, the common law rules regarding the interpretation of legislation have been ignored.

THE ABSENCE OF CLEAR AND PLAIN INTENT

Justice Kirby and Justice Kiefel (dissenting) considered the common law tradition that protects the rights of individuals from arbitrary deprivation by the state. Justice Kirby engaged in a detailed analysis of the jurisprudence of 'clear and plain intention' generally, and in relation to native title in particular.[13] Like Justice Kiefel, Justice Kirby pointed to the strong tradition in common law that protects the basic rights of individuals from arbitrary deprivation by the state; compulsory acquisition of property has always been at the heart of this tradition. Justice Kirby agreed with Justice Kiefel that s 43 does not provide for a power to acquire land completely 'independently of purpose'. He argued that 'specificity and high particularity' in the legislation are required to permit the executive to acquire native title interests for the private benefit of another.

Justice Kirby emphasised the unique nature of native title, and, indeed, the special connection to the land it seeks to protect, as requiring additional rigours. His Honour expressed his view to this effect:

> against the background of the history of previous non-recognition; the subsequent respect accorded to native title by this Court and by the Federal Parliament; and the incontestable importance of native title to the cultural and economic advancement of indigenous people in Australia, it is not unreasonable or legally unusual to expect that any deprivations and extinguishment of native title, so hard won, will not occur under legislation of any Australian legislature in the absence of provisions that are unambiguously clear and such as to demonstrate plainly that the law in question has been enacted by the lawmakers who have turned their particular attention to the type of deprivation and extinguishment that is propounded.[14]

As a result, in his view, extinguishment must be contained within 'very specific and clear legislation that unmistakeably has this effect'.[15] Justice Kirby pointed to comparative treatment of Indigenous titles in Canada and New Zealand, where the significance of the land to the group has an impact on the legal principles to be applied.[16] He argued against the approach of the Court, which is encouraged by the 'freehold equivalence' tests in the NTA to deal with this issue as simply a matter of two indistinguishable competing interest in the land. Section 24MD (6A) gives native title holders 'the same' procedural rights as a holder of any ordinary title.

His Honour referred to his summary of the applicable principles in *Western Australia v Ward* (2002):

> Because the statutory concepts of 'recognition' and 'extinguishment' are themselves ambiguous or informed by the approach of the common law, this Court should adopt, and consistently apply, several interpretative principles in giving those concepts meaning. First, it should observe the principle that, in the case of any ambiguity, the interpretation of the statutory text should be preferred that upholds fundamental human rights rather than one that denies those rights recognition and enforcement. Secondly, so far as is possible, it should take into account relevant analogous developments of the common law in other societies facing similar legal problems. Thirdly, a clear and plain purpose is required for a statute to extinguish property rights, particularly where the legislation purports to do so without compensation.[17]

By treating native title in the same way as any other fungible property right, the law threatens the cultural survival of Indigenous peoples.

The Northern Territory Government must still comply with the provisions of the NTA. The applicants sought an alternative basis for rejecting the acquisition in the terms of the NTA. Section 24MD (2) provides for the extinguishment of native title on just terms, compensation under a Commonwealth, state or territory law if compulsory acquisition of 'all non-native title rights and interests ... is also acquired', and that native title holders suffer no greater disadvantage than is caused to non-native title holders. The appellants argued that the word 'all' meant that the provision could only be satisfied if there was a non-native title interest in existence; that is, that, as in this case, if there were no other extant interests in the land, the land could not be acquired consistently with the NTA. All of the judges agreed that 'all' should be understood as 'any and all'. Any other reading, they suggested, would have an arbitrary result.

CONCLUSION

Chief Justice Gleeson pointed out that the key purpose of the provision of the NTA in question is to avoid racial discrimination and, in relation to the specific provisions in question, to avoid extinguishment of native title rights in order to relieve other interest from any coexisting native title rights. Justices Gummow, Hayne and Heydon pointed out that if the NTA allowed such acquisition, it would fall foul of the *Racial Discrimination Act 1975* (Cth). However, the result in this case, in favour of the compulsory acquisition that would enable the granting of the lease, achieves that very effect. The rights of the native title holders have been removed to make way for the rights of the licence holder to be increased to a lease and then to freehold without seeking to reach agreement with the native title holders.

CHAPTER 9

Implementing the High Court's jurisprudence
De Rose v South Australia [No. 2]

FEDERAL COURT OF AUSTRALIA, 2005

The decision in *De Rose v South Australia [No. 2]* (2005) (*De Rose [No. 2]*) concerned a pastoral property, De Rose Hill, in the far north-west of South Australia.[1] A group of Indigenous people asserted native title over the lease area as Nguraritja, or traditional owners, for the land. The case at first instance was heard by a single judge of the Federal Court. Justice O'Loughlin determined that any physical or spiritual connection to the land by the applicants had been abandoned and had led to a breakdown in the observance of traditional customs that was fatal to their application.[2]

The decision was alarming both because the applicants had been present on the property until relatively recently, in the previous twenty years or so, and because they had a strong understanding and observance of law, customs and language of the wider Western Desert. The judge seemed to take a unique view of the legal concept of 'connection' and of the threshold for abandonment that could have set a dangerous precedent for native title cases throughout Australia.

The applicants sought a determination of native title based on their status as Nguraritja for the area and places within the pastoral station. Many applicants referred to themselves as Yunkunytjatjara; others referred to themselves, or their parents, as Pitjantjatjara or Antikirinya. The evidence of the Indigenous witnesses that the claimed area fell within Yunkunytjatjara country was accepted.[3] The claimant group was part of the Western Desert society and followed the laws and customs of the broader community. The evidence of movements of Pitjantjatjara people into the region was accepted as part of the traditional population movement throughout the Western Desert region.

The claim was not made as a communal claim, on behalf of a particular 'people' in the sense of a discrete system of laws. Nor did the applicants claim individual rights and interests. The judge, therefore, approached the claim as one in which the claimants were asserting some form of group rights.[4] This led the judge into a number of errors.

CONNECTION TO LAND

The applicants explained that the boundaries of the station were not the limits of their country, as the relationships and bases from which to assert connection under Western Desert law allow personal connections to extend throughout the region. The judge agreed that the arbitrary fixing of boundaries for the purpose of defining a claim area should not be an impediment. But the judge seemed to remain confused as to why the claimants had chosen De Rose Hill as the boundaries for the claim.[5] In trying to attach some particular significance to the station, his Honour experienced some difficulty determining the relationship to the land apart from the attachment to particular sites.[6]

Connection to the claimed area was demonstrated through personal association — whether through birth, long-term residence, knowledge or inheritance — and acceptance by the community as Nguraritja. Perhaps influenced by this, the judge failed to look at the broader system of law and custom and, instead, concentrated on the individual personal claims of each of the witnesses to their status as Nguraritja and their personal links with the station over their lifetimes.[7]

Two of the witnesses were born on De Rose Hill station; many worked or lived there for part of their lives, some for substantial periods. Most had left some time previously, with the last of the stockmen leaving the station in 1978. Occasional access for hunting had continued but there was substantial evidence of intimidation and discouragement of Indigenous people in having access to the property since that time. The judge drew the extraordinary conclusion that twenty years was a substantial period of absence, which had resulted in a failure to observe the law and custom that connected the applicants to the claim area. The breakdown in law and custom identified by the judge as a result of the lack of access was highly localised and referred primarily to observing laws and customs in relation to the physical landscape of the claim area.

The judge accepted that the absence of a physical connection to the land was not fatal to a claim, as native title could be sustained by a non-physical connection that is maintained through the acknowledgment and observance of traditional law and customs.[8] But the judge applied an idea of non-physical connection as being a 'spiritual' one, in the sense of requiring religious observance of ceremony and responsibility for the sites of significance within the pastoral station.

Justice O'Loughlin acknowledged that the claimants were actively engaged in cultural activities outside of the claim area. The judge accepted that witnesses had substantial knowledge of the sites on the claim area and activities associated with those sites — they knew and were able to perform the ceremonies, stories, dances and songs of the Tjukurpa (law) for the area. His Honour went so far as to acknowledge that such knowledge went a long way towards satisfying the Court that there was a relevant connection, but he also expressed the view that '[t]he physical activities that would have been tangible evidence of a spiritual connection to the claim area occurred long ago'.[9] He concluded that, '[s]ave for some occasional hunting trips, not one witness ... has attended to any religious, cultural or traditional ceremony or duty on De Rose Hill in almost twenty years'.[10]

The judge was unconvinced that the laws and customs were being handed down to younger generations. Nor did his Honour appreciate that the native title process would be used by knowledge holders to pass on information. The judge saw it as too late — the damage had been done; twenty years was too long.[11]

Apart from the absurdity of the timescale applied by the judge, his findings in relation to the absence of physical connection fly in the face of established High Court views. Failure to maintain physical connection to one part of a claim area does not defeat a claim as a whole. Failure to access an area over a relatively short period in a community's history should not have been treated differently merely because the claim was over a discrete part of the traditional country. The observance of law and custom in the broader region was relevant to the inquiry as to the maintenance of law and custom that sustained the community's entitlement under traditional law to the claim area and therefore to recognition of native title.

Justice O'Loughlin's reasoning also appears to be inconsistent with the findings of the High Court in *Western Australia v Ward* (2002) (*Ward*) that suggested that failure to exercise a right does not constitute an abandonment of the right.[12] These issues raise the question as to whether a different result would have been reached if the claim had been made by Yunkunytjatjara over the whole of their traditional territory as a communal claim. Such a claim may have been more familiar to the Court but obviously inappropriate to the claimants. There is a danger to be avoided in native title jurisprudence of judges developing a vision of what a native title claim should look like.

SOCIAL AND POLITICAL LIFE

In relation to social and political identity, Justice O'Loughlin found that there was no evidence of an organised community centred around the claim area. The judge found no evidence of a coherent social group since the departure from the station and no clear direction for plans to use the country if native title was recognised. He assessed the connection to the De Rose Hill station as focused on 'European style work practices' and that social interaction was dominated by that work.[13]

The judge stated that the evidence in relation to customary practices was 'not impressive when compared with the information that has been collected by early ethnographers'.[14] His Honour discussed practices in relation to body piercing and scarring, circumcision, particular magical, mystical and spiritual practices, infant betrothal and post-birth practices that were no longer carried out in the area. While no doubt these practices were part of a dynamic normative system, none of these was an essential right or interest asserted or law or custom in relation to land that was relied upon to establish native title.[15] This was a peculiar romantic fascination with 'tribalism' and a refusal to accept aspects of economic and political life as part of 'Aboriginal life'. His Honour stated, for example, that work and children's education were 'non-Aboriginal factors' in making decisions about residence.[16] The judge appeared highly critical of the applicants because their culture and laws had not held them to the claim area.

This essentialising of Indigenous peoples' relationship to land as 'spiritual' served to undermine their rights to the land as a proprietary interest. It also undermined the historical importance of opportunities to combine employment with the maintenance of connection to traditional country in ameliorating the impacts of dispossession.

The judge's perception that the applicants were not 'forcibly removed' (absent some extreme action on the part of the state or the leaseholders) did not give due weight to the impact of land and employment policies. The impact of the grant of pastoral leases on Indigenous peoples' sense of ownership over the land should not be understated. Until at least the decision of the High Court in *Wik Peoples v Queensland* (1996) (*Wik*),[17] this land was considered the pastoralists' land. The removal of employment options on pastoral leases was part of the process of dispossession.

PHYSICAL ACCESS

The judge found that the applicants had not demonstrated intent in maintaining their attachment to land. His Honour thought that access should have been found, 'surreptitiously if necessary', to perform their duties as Nguraritja.[18] This seems extraordinary when one considers the evidence of violence and intimidation that was reflected in the judgment.[19] The judge assumed that, because the most senior stockmen felt able to visit the station occasionally after they had left, this was evidence that access was available to the claimants if they had wanted it.[20] There was a lack of appreciation of the social alternatives available to the witnesses, through traditional law and historical social movements, when it came to residence. Claimants had access to and relationships with other areas of land through their relationships within Yunkunytjatjara country and also within the wider Western Desert region.

Again, Justice O'Loughlin underplayed the intimidation that claimants felt in trying to gain access to the land: intimidation not simply through the use of actual force, firearms and locked gates, but also through the historical relations of power that were implicit in the pastoralists as White bosses and the Indigenous owners as barely enjoying the status of employees. White law imposed this new conception of ownership over their own sense of ownership and allowed their effective exclusion from the land up until the recognition of native title in 1992. The idea that Indigenous people would know and enforce their rights under legislative reservations is to underestimate the influence of historical understandings of entitlement. In contrast, *Mabo v Queensland [No. 2]* (1992) (*Mabo*)[21] had a much greater impact on Indigenous peoples' sense of entitlement to assert their ownership of traditional lands. It is not surprising that the claimants exercised their economic and cultural choices to live elsewhere until they received a firm recognition of their right to be on the claim area.

THE EVIDENCE OF INDIGENOUS WITNESSES AND THE ROLE OF EXPERTS

Justice O'Loughlin commented on the question of evidence from Indigenous witnesses and the hearsay rule. His Honour was of the view that proof of the existence or otherwise of native title depended upon events that occurred in the past and the actions of earlier generations. The judge therefore accepted evidence that in other proceedings might have been considered hearsay. He held that Indigenous witnesses should be able to give evidence of their beliefs, based upon what they had been told. This was evidence not just of the fact that the witnesses believed those statements, or that the statements were made, but also, that in all probability, as evidence of the truth of the facts asserted.[22]

The judge rejected the need to establish the circumstances of Indigenous people as they existed at the time of sovereignty, noting the difficulties of proof facing Indigenous claimants seeking historical and anthropological material to support their claim. His Honour favoured the inferences drawn from the evidence of the Indigenous witnesses over the opinions of experts or historical material but he was critical of the applicants when they were unable to clearly articulate their connection to country or their laws and customs.[23] His Honour refused to accept the observations of experts in the absence of reasonable primary evidence from the claimants, complaining that:

> [t]he onus is upon the claimants, if they wish to establish their right to a determination of native title, to give the evidence that will establish that right. They had the opportunity to do that in closed session but they failed to do so.[24]

The trial judge's approach in *De Rose v South Australia* [2002] highlights the stressful burden of proof on applicants and witnesses to establish the evidence to support a native title claim even where presumptions of inference are made.

ALTERNATIVE DETERMINATION AND EXTINGUISHMENT

The judge was satisfied that a determination of native title was potentially available to the claimants if they had been able to establish the requisite connection. South Australia had originally argued that imperial legislation establishing the colony had wholly extinguished native title throughout the state but withdrew those submissions during the course of the trial. Similarly, the state, after the decision in *Ward*, did not press its argument that the pastoral leases extinguished native title.[25]

Justice O'Loughlin held that native title had not been extinguished by historical events and was not wholly extinguished by the grant of the particular pastoral leases that made up the De Rose Hill station.[26] Any extinguishment was therefore limited to partial extinguishment, to the extent of any inconsistency. Citing the full Federal Court in *Ward*, his Honour noted that the immediate consequence of the grant of a pastoral lease was that the exclusive right of the native title holders to possess, occupy, use and enjoy the land was 'Henceforth … to be [a] shared one'.[27] His Honour summarised the decision of the High Court in *Ward*, concluding that, having lost the right to exclusive possession, the native title holders also lost the exclusive native title right to control access to the land and to control the use to be made of the land.[28] The interpretation of this conclusion (for example, a decision of the lessee to refuse entry to an Indigenous person who was an invitee of the native title holders would prevail[29]) ignored any concept of reasonableness in the exercise of rights over the land and undermined any sense of 'shared' possession.

Justice O'Loughlin submitted that if he was in error in relation to the loss of connection, an appropriate determination would recognise restricted rights to live on the claim area and to have access to the claim area for hunting and gathering and for the use of water and natural resources for shelter and cultural or hunting artefacts, as well as the right to hold meetings and religious ceremonies, including the right to invite others to participate. Those rights are restricted to decisions about use and enjoyment entirely within the group and the exercise of any rights would be subject to the discretion of the pastoral leaseholder.[30] In effect, native title would provide little more than rights and interests protected under legislation.

THE FEDERAL COURT APPEAL

In December 2003, in *De Rose v State of South Australia [No. 1]* (2003) (*De Rose [No. 1]*), the applicants successfully appealed the decision of the trial judge.[31] The decision of Justice O'Loughlin was strongly criticised, including his Honour's conclusions about the failure of individual applicants to maintain their responsibilities under traditional law and custom and the extent to which 'non-aboriginal factors' such as employment and educational priorities had influenced decisions about residence away from the claim area. The full Court was critical of the trial judge for presuming to make his own judgment about the individual entitlements of the claimants under traditional law and custom, a matter that was properly internal to the Western Desert law system.[32] The trial judge's decision that in very recent history the physical or spiritual connection to the land had been abandoned and the observance of traditional law and custom had broken down was rejected by the full Court. Justices Wilcox, Sackville and Merkel instead noted the broader observance of the laws and customs of the Western Desert and the specific knowledge of law in relation to the claim area; the relatively recent and short absence from the area; the active protection of sites under heritage laws;[33] and the intimidatory exclusion from the area by the coexisting pastoral leaseholders.[34]

The full Court recognised that the applicants formed a small group within the much larger Western Desert cultural bloc and shared the same laws and customs. The applicants did not assert, and were not required to show, that they constituted a discrete society.[35] Indeed, the Western Desert bloc was the normative system upon which the claim could successfully be founded.[36] It existed at the time of sovereignty and the traditional laws and customs had continued substantially uninterrupted throughout the period.[37] This reliance on a broader normative system distinguished the circumstances of the applicants in this case from those in *Members of the Yorta Yorta Aboriginal Community v Victoria* (2002) (*Yorta Yorta*) who faced the obstacle of the trial judge's conclusion that they had 'substantial interruption' to the acknowledgment and observance of traditional law and custom that was held to have applied to the whole normative society.[38]

The full Federal Court noted that, in the *Yorta Yorta* appeal, the High Court rejected the language of 'abandonment' in favour of this concept of interruption.[39] The High Court stated that, if continuity of acknowledgment and observance was interrupted, the reasons were irrelevant.[40] However, the full Court in this appeal noted that the reasons for observance or acknowledgment being affected should be taken into consideration when assessing whether there was in fact an absence of continuity amounting to an interruption.[41]

Moreover, the High Court in *Ward* had held that physical contact is not required to maintain the connection to the claim area.[42] The full Federal Court in *De Rose [No. 1]* concluded that the judge, in determining the issue of 'connection', had placed undue weight on the physical absence.[43] The judges acknowledged that even long absence and movement due to access to food or other changes in conditions was not a new or unknown phenomenon under the traditional laws and customs of the Western Desert. In particular, the Court concluded that it might well be possible to maintain a connection with land despite moving away from the area for what the trial judge had dismissed as 'European social and work practices'.[44]

The full Federal Court found that the trial judge was wrong in law but was unable to make a conclusion as to whether the claim had been proved.[45] The applicants still needed to demonstrate that they continued to acknowledge and observe the traditional laws and customs of the Western Desert bloc and that they possessed rights and interests under those laws and customs.[46] This required further evidence about what the Western Desert law said about the applicants' entitlements.[47]

WHO CAN CLAIM NATIVE TITLE?

As Justice O'Loughlin had since retired, the matter could not be sent back for his further consideration. The full Federal Court therefore directed the parties to mediate, in order to identify what, if any, issues remained in dispute that needed to come back to the Court.[48] The parties did not resolve the issues and the Federal Court in *De Rose v South Australia [No. 2]* (2005) *(De Rose [No. 2])* was asked to reconsider the content of the laws and customs on the basis that:

> The primary Judge had correctly identified the traditional laws and customs relevant to the question of 'connection' as those of the Western Desert Bloc. He had not, however, explicitly asked in relation to any of the appellants, as s 223(1)(b) of the [*Native Title Act 1993* (Cth) (NTA)] requires, whether *by those traditional laws and customs* they had retained a connection with the claim area.[49]

In addition, the decision in *De Rose [No. 1]* had resolved that the claimants did not need to demonstrate that they constituted a discrete society in order to bring a claim under the NTA.[50] There was still some dispute among the parties as to whether the claimants could bring a 'group' claim.[51] The respondents contended that the claimants were merely individual claimants, whereas the claimants argued that they had made a group claim; no one asserted that this was a 'communal claim'.[52] An application for a determination under the NTA may be made on the basis of s 223(1), which states:

> native title or native title rights and interests means the *communal, group or individual* rights and interests of Aboriginal peoples or Torres Strait Islanders in relation to land or waters.[53]

The full Federal Court concluded, on the basis of the NTA and the common law established in *Mabo*, that the decision whether native title can be claimed or held by an individual or group is reached by reference to the body of laws and customs or the normative rules of the society that confers the rights and interests in the land.[54] The Court examined the variety of ways in which native title claim groups had been constituted in recent cases and concluded that, in this instance:

the appellants do not claim to be a discrete or functioning community and
… the normative system on which they rely for their rights and interests
is that of the wider Western Desert Bloc. But the appellants claim to
be *Nguraritja* for the claim area and, by virtue of that status, they have
common rights and responsibilities under the laws and customs of the
Western Desert Bloc in relation to the claim area.[55]

Thus the applicants were entitled to bring the claim on behalf of the native title group, being all those who are Nguraritja for the claim area.

The key argument from the respondents was that the claimants had not observed or acknowledged the laws and customs by which they asserted their rights and interests in the area. This is separate from the question of 'connection' under s 223(1)(b). As a prior question, the respondents argued that, in order to meet the requirements of proof under s 223(1)(a), the applicants needed to establish that they had acknowledged and observed the particular laws and customs that gave rise to the native title rights and interests claimed; in this case, the rules relating to their status as Nguraritja.[56] The full Federal Court entertained this idea, but concluded that it remains a question of fact and degree.[57] Moreover, the Court pointed to the difficulty of separating out which discrete laws and customs maintained the interest in land:

> given the centrality of the relationship between Aboriginal people and their country, any dichotomy between traditional laws and customs connected with rights and interests possessed in land and waters and those that are unconnected with such rights and interests may be difficult to establish.[58]

Thus, the Court concluded that s 223(1)(a) does not require claimants to establish that they have discharged their responsibilities under traditional laws and customs in relation to an area. They noted that the case may be that:

> the traditional laws and customs may provide that the holders of native title lose their rights and interests if they fail to discharge particular responsibilities. But s 223(1)(a) does not impose an independent requirement to that effect.[59]

In the result, the Court was satisfied that so long as at least one of the native title holders could establish that they possessed rights and interests in relation to the claim area under traditional laws and customs of the Western Desert bloc that are acknowledged and observed by them, the claim could succeed.[60] Peter De Rose, at least, had demonstrated all that was necessary to meet the requirements of s 223(1) and the claimants were recognised as holding native title in relation to the area.[61]

DETERMINING THE IMPACT OF PARTIAL EXTINGUISHMENT

Having found that the claimants had satisfied the requirements for proof of native title, the full Federal Court turned to the impact of the granting of the pastoral lease on the rights and interests established under traditional law and custom. The Court determined that the granting of the pastoral lease under the South Australian legislation did not extinguish all native title rights and interests.[62] But in applying *Ward*, the trial judge had concluded that the grant of a pastoral lease extinguished any exclusive native title rights to control access and use. The full Federal Court considered the extent of inconsistency in greater detail, in an attempt to clarify the application of the *Ward* decision.

In particular, as the leases in this case contained obligations to construct certain improvements, they therefore conferred a concomitant right to carry out those activities. The Court noted that, in relation to matters such as the construction of dwellings and sheds, the right conferred, 'when exercised, is clearly inconsistent with the native title rights and interests identified in the draft determination', but only in relation to the particular area of land on which the building was erected.[63] The Court highlighted the problem in applying the test in this circumstance, where the lease gave no indication where the improvements would be located. The comparison of rights that was required by the High Court in *Ward* could not clarify the precise sites over which an inconsistency arises.[64]

The Federal Court noted that the High Court in *Ward* rejected any test based on 'actual use' or 'operational inconsistency' except in so far as it focused attention on the rights conferred.[65] The Court focused attention on the High Court's comments regarding the implication of 'conditions precedent' within the terms of the lease; that is, the right is not conferred until some other act takes place.[66]

In the circumstances of the present case, the full Court decided that:

the 'operation of a grant of [the right to conduct and use improvements]' should be regarded, in effect, as subject to a condition precedent. The grant of the right could become operative in relation to a particular area of the leasehold land only when the right was exercised. The grant of the right could have an extinguishing effect only when the right was exercised, since it was only then that the precise area or areas of land affected by the right could be identified.[67]

The Court chose not to decide what might happen if an improvement was later removed but it was noted that s 237A of the NTA deemed extinguishment to be permanent.[68]

As a result of this reasoning, the final determination does not confine the activities of the native title holders to the extent proposed by Justice O'Loughlin at first instance.[69]

CHAPTER 10

Continuity and change
Bodney v Bennell

FEDERAL COURT OF AUSTRALIA, 2008

The full Federal Court decision in *Bodney v Bennell* (*Bennell*) in 2008 was a pivotal decision in the application of the High Court's jurisprudence on native title.[1] It was one of three appeals heard by a full Court of the Federal Court within the same year, which provided an opportunity for the Court to review the jurisprudence of the High Court and clarify its application in the Federal Court. The decision in *Bennell* covers some of the central issues that surround the Yorta Yorta jurisprudence. The decision in *Bennell* can be compared to the decision, shortly before, in the Larrakia appeal (*Risk v Northern Territory* (2007) (*Risk*)) and the decision in the Rubibi appeal (*State of Western Australia v Sebastian* (2008) (*Sebastian*)) shortly thereafter.[2] These decisions build on the decisions of the full Court in *De Rose v South Australia [No. 2]* (2005) (*De Rose [No. 2]*) and *Northern Territory v Alyawarr, Kaytetye, Warumungu, Wakay Native Title Claim Group* (2005) (*Alyawarr*),[3] confirming some views and elaborating on others, while leaving certain matters still unresolved.

The *Bennell* case concerned part of the single Noongar claim, lodged in September 2003 by eighty named applicants on behalf of the Noongar people, over 186,000 square kilometres of the south-west of Western Australia, including areas in and around Perth. Any areas where extinguishment has occurred (which is likely to constitute an overwhelmingly large proportion of the claim area) were expressly excluded from the claim. The proceedings were initiated in response to an underlying claim, since incorporated into the larger single Noongar claim, over the Perth metropolitan area.[4] The Western Australian Government and the Commonwealth pressed for a separate question to be resolved as to whether native title exists over the capital city. The proceedings therefore focused on whether native title exists and, if so, who holds native title, and the extent of any native title rights and interests.[5] It did not extend to determining extinguishment or the relationship of native title to any other rights or interests. The trial judge, Justice Wilcox, heard evidence about the whole single Noongar claim, including evidence of language, laws and customs, beliefs and social interaction.

The trial judge was primarily interested in whether the applicants could show two things: first, that there was a single 'community' for native title purposes (that is, a community that shared laws and customs through which they had a connection to land and waters) at the time that sovereignty was asserted by the British in 1829; and, second, whether that same community now existed and had continued to acknowledge those same laws and customs substantially uninterrupted since that time.[6]

THE EXISTENCE OF A NOONGAR SOCIETY

One of the key sources of contention between the parties was the existence of a single Noongar society. Indeed, the primary judge described the first major factual issue as the identification of the relevant society at sovereignty. The state had argued that there was insufficient cultural unity and no overarching authority binding the groups and that the relevant 'society' for native title purposes comprised smaller social units (although there was no unambiguous way of identifying these smaller groups). Moreover, the state argued that the language and laws and customs were not distinct enough to identify a normative society at the level proposed.[7] The judge agreed that if the respondents were correct and that at the time that sovereignty was asserted there was no single society, then the 'Single Noongar Claim', as presented, would fail.[8]

Justice Wilcox examined the written accounts of the time (including accounts by explorers, the military and settlers) and the expert evidence. His Honour determined that there was, indeed, a single Noongar language (although this in itself is not determinative of a normative society),[9] that there was cultural unity and similarity of laws and customs across the region, and that these laws and customs need not themselves be unique to that system.[10] The judge rejected the idea that there needed to be a centralised authority that governed all the groups or that all of the groups were known to each other.[11] Nor was there a need to show a system of sanction or enforcement.[12] What is required by the High Court's *Yorta Yorta* decision, according to the trial judge, is a common acknowledgment and observance of a system of laws and customs. This, his Honour suggested, is the relevant unifying factor required by the *Native Title Act 1993* (Cth) (NTA). The authority of the system derives its force from that observance.

The judge found that at 1829 the laws and customs governing land throughout the whole claim area were those of a single community, through shared language, shared laws and customs, internal social interaction, and internal consistency in practice and observance of laws and customs. And, Justice Wilcox concluded, it is appropriate to call this community the Noongar community.

THE CONTINUITY QUESTION

The second major factual issue addressed by the trial judge was whether the single Noongar community has continued to exist until today, with its members continuing to acknowledge and observe at least some of the traditional laws and customs in relation to land that were acknowledged and observed in 1829. Or whether, as the state contended, acts of settlement and colonisation had wrought such devastation on the Noongar people that they could not possibly have continued to exist as a normative society.

Justice Wilcox identified each of the key customs or norms and extracted the references from the evidence of the Noongar witnesses, which he said illustrated both the breadth of acknowledgment and the consistency of understanding. The consistency in the evidence in relation to rights and interests and laws and customs in relation to land lent weight to the conclusion that there was a single Noongar society in the view of the trial judge.[13] This conclusion was supported by his assessment of other customs and beliefs, which, while not directly relevant to determining native title rights and interests, did go to establishing the extent of the relevant 'society' by illustrating both the internal consistency of the group and external differentiation from other groups.

In relation to changes in laws and customs, Justice Wilcox noted four things:[14]

- in time, the laws and customs of any people will change and the rights and interests of the members of the people among themselves will change too;[15]
- universal observance is not necessary. The inquiry is directed to possession of the rights under law and customs, not their exercise;
- the rights and interests must be currently possessed and give rise to a current connection between the claimants and the land and waters claimed; and
- the acknowledgment of laws and customs must have continued substantially uninterrupted.[16]

Justice Wilcox seemed acutely aware of the comparisons that would be made between this case and the Yorta Yorta peoples' case, given the extent of non-Indigenous settlement in the lands claimed. His Honour specifically acknowledged that a native title claim may fail because of a discontinuity in acknowledgment and observance of traditional laws and customs, even though there has been a recent revival in them and current acknowledgment and observance, and he noted the decisions in *Yorta Yorta* and *Risk*.[17]

In answer to the state's arguments concerning the social disruption caused by colonial policies and the impact of settlement, the judge was more than convinced, and indeed impressed, that Noongar families, despite the impacts of colonisation, have kept in contact with each other and 'most if not all' have learned some Noongar language, traditional skills in hunting and fishing, and traditional Noongar beliefs.

Justice Wilcox held that while changes in laws and customs in relation to land were unavoidable, the key elements of connection to country remained. He held that:

- those land rules currently observed and acknowledged are a 'recognisable adaptation' of the laws and customs existing at settlement;
- Noongars continue to observe a system under which individuals obtain special rights over particular country — their *Boodjas* — through their father or mother or occasionally a grandparent; and
- Noongars maintain rules as to who may 'speak for' country.

In September 2006 Justice Wilcox determined that, subject to extinguishment, the Noongar community holds native title rights and interests in relation to the area of the separate proceeding other than offshore islands and the waters below the low water mark.[18]

THE APPEAL

The state and Commonwealth governments appealed the decision of Justice Wilcox, challenging the factual findings and the conclusions of the trial judge on each of the elements of proof under s 223 of the NTA.[19] The full Court of the Federal Court, consisting of Justices Finn, Mansfield and Sundberg, was prepared to accept the findings of the trial judge that, at the time sovereignty was asserted, there was a single Noongar society in the determination area. The judges outlined three key issues that required the full Court's attention:

- whether there has been continuity of the traditional laws and customs of the single Noongar society from sovereignty until recent times;
- whether a finding of one society or one community entails one communal title; and
- whether there was error in his Honour's approach to the issue of connection between the Noongar people and the area of the separate proceeding.[20]

CONTINUITY AND 'UNACCEPTABLE' CHANGE

The test of continuity at the heart of the first question for the appeal court links the key concepts of 'laws and customs' and 'tradition', which have become the cornerstones of the proof of native title since the *Yorta Yorta* High Court decision. That case introduced the concept of society into the native title vernacular, which was a central focus of the *Bennell* case at trial. The Court in *Yorta Yorta* had held that the term 'traditional' in s 223 of the NTA requires an additional inquiry into the age of the laws and customs, having their source in a 'normative system' or 'society' in existence at the time of the assertion of British sovereignty, when native title arose. The majority had said that: 'Law and custom arise out of and, in important respects, go to define a particular society.'[21] The full Court in *Bennell* emphasised the relationship between the normative system, the laws and customs, and the rights and interests claimed. It said that the judgment in *Yorta Yorta* speaks of 'the traditional laws and customs as constituting a normative system which possesses normative rules which give rise to rights and interests in relation to land and water'.[22]

Justice Wilcox, too, noted that the concepts of society and laws and customs are interdependent.[23] He observed that the High Court in *Yorta Yorta* adopted the term 'society' rather than 'community' to emphasise the relationship between the group and the laws and customs.[24] But it has been emphasised in *Yorta Yorta* and in more recent cases that it was not intended, by using such terms, to write into the NTA some additional test or term of art.[25] In *Alyawarr* the full Federal Court noted that the term 'society' is merely a conceptual tool to understand and apply the NTA.[26] Indeed, it reiterated the view of the High Court in *Yorta Yorta* that what is required is that the members of the group claiming native title are members of a society or community that has existed from sovereignty to the present time, as a group, united by its acknowledgment of the laws and customs under which the rights and interests claimed are said to be possessed. 'However', the High Court said, 'change or adaptation in traditional law and custom or some interruption of enjoyment or exercise of native title rights is not necessarily fatal to that continuity'.[27]

The trial judge in *Bennell* also noted the requirements of *Yorta Yorta* in this regard. In dealing with issues of continuity and change, Justice Wilcox had said:

> one should look for evidence of the continuity of the society, rather than require unchanged laws and customs. No doubt changes in laws and customs can be an indication of lack of continuity in the society; they may show that the current normative system 'is rooted in some other, different, society'. Whether or not that conclusion should be drawn must depend upon all the circumstances of the case, including the importance of the relevant laws and customs and whether the changes seem to be the outcome of the factors forced upon the community from outside its ranks.[28]

Justice Wilcox relied on the provisions of *Yorta Yorta* that define the test of 'substantial interruption': there, the High Court explained the test and, in particular, the meaning of 'substantially' maintained:

> It is a qualification that must be made in order to recognise that proof of continuous acknowledgment and observance, over the many years that have elapsed since sovereignty, of traditions that are oral traditions is very

difficult. It is a qualification that must be made to recognise that European settlement has had the most profound effects on Aboriginal societies and that it is, therefore, inevitable that the structures and practices of those societies, and their members, will have undergone great change since European settlement.²⁹

The full Court rejected the idea that any account should be taken of the 'cause' of the change in determining what is 'acceptable'; that is, the fact that any change in traditional laws and customs might arise because of the impact of colonisation was irrelevant to the inquiry.³⁰ The full Court pointed to the trial judge's conclusions on the laws and customs relating to the land estates, where Justice Wilcox acknowledged that:

> It seems to me that 'home areas' have effectively disappeared. Today's boodjas are similar in concept to — although probably larger in area than — the 'runs' of pre-settlement times. I agree this is a significant change. However, it is readily understandable. It was forced upon the Aboriginal people by white settlement. As white settlers took over, and fenced the land, Aborigines were forced off their home areas; the 'bands' or 'tribes', comprising several related families, were broken up. Surprisingly, the social links between those families seem to have survived, but the related families ceased to be residence groups, together occupying a relatively small area of land. The ability to maintain the 'home area' element of the pre-settlement normative system was lost.³¹

The full Court took issue with this approach. It said the focus must be on the particular laws and customs that give rise to the rights and interests that are recognised and protected by native title:

> An enquiry into continuity of society, divorced from an inquiry into continuity of the pre-sovereignty normative system, may mask *unacceptable change* with the consequence that the current rights and interests are no longer those that existed at sovereignty, and thus not traditional.³²

The language of the full Court here is problematic, but it is illustrative. Instead of focusing the inquiry around the seemingly objective test of 'traditionality', the Court introduced overtly judgmental language as to what is 'acceptable' and 'unacceptable' change and adaptation in Indigenous society and determined that it is the Court's role to judge this.

An alternative reading of Justice Wilcox would see the 'cause' of the change to be a relevant consideration in determining if the change is an adaptation of a traditional law to fit new circumstances, and it is in this context that his Honour refers to the change as 'understandable'. Indeed, the High Court in *Yorta Yorta* suggested as much, when it said that an examination of the reasons for change is 'important *only* to the extent that the presence or absence of reasons might influence the fact-finder's decision about whether there was such an interruption'.[33]

In any event, the trial judge's conclusion was not referable to any mitigation of otherwise unacceptable change or 'untraditional' laws. His Honour said:

> when I come back to the test stated in *Yorta Yorta*, and ask myself whether the normative system revealed by the evidence is 'the normative system of the society which came under a new sovereign order' in 1829, or 'a normative system rooted in some other, different society', there can be only one answer. The current normative system is that of the Noongar society that existed in 1829, and which continues to be a body united, amongst other ways, by its acknowledgment and observance of some of its traditional laws and customs. It is a normative system much affected by European settlement; but it is not a normative system of a new, different society.[34]

As the full Court noted in relation to the basis of inheritance, to acknowledge the impact of colonisation in precipitating change does not mean that the test as to substantial interruption is neglected.[35] Nevertheless, in relation to land tenure in particular, the full Court said that 'his Honour failed to consider, as required by *Yorta Yorta*, whether a post-sovereignty boodja was an *acceptable* adaptation of the old runs or home areas or an unacceptable change'.[36] However, the full Court reiterated that '[t]he question is whether the change means that boodjas are no longer traditional. His Honour did not find that boodjas are traditional.'[37] Thus the full Court suggested that the trial judge must make a specific finding as to whether a particular law or custom is traditional in the sense required by the NTA and *Yorta Yorta*. It appears that the full Court did not consider that it was open to the judge to conclude continuity without such a finding. The full Court not only criticised the trial judge for failing to make a specific finding as to the traditional nature of the current land tenure system, but went further to suggest that 'the evidence points against continuity with pre-sovereignty runs or home areas'.[38] The full Court concluded that:

> In the absence of any finding of permissible adaptation or change, the 'significant change' brought about by the disappearance of home areas, and apparently also the runs of pre-settlement times, is conclusive of discontinuity.[39]

The full Court did not reject the idea that laws and customs that make up that normative system may change and adapt. Indeed, it specifically rejected the state's contention that 'a new right' is never allowed under *Yorta Yorta*, and that any change in the distribution of rights is in effect the creation of new rights.[40] The judges referred to the High Court in *Yorta Yorta*, where the majority had held that 'the rights and interests in land which the new sovereign order recognised included the rules of traditional law and custom which dealt with the transmission of those interests'.[41] Moreover, the High Court had said explicitly that account may be taken of alteration and development of that traditional law and custom after sovereignty was asserted by the British, even significant adaptation, where such change is contemplated by traditional laws and customs.[42] The High Court in *Yorta Yorta* had suggested that this does not admit a parallel law-making system, but the rules of transmission and the rights in question must 'find their origin in pre-sovereignty law and custom'.[43]

The full Federal Court in *Bennell* proposed a test or measure of whether 'new rights' are asserted that would not be recognised and protected as native title rights: 'It may be that the true position is that what cannot be created after sovereignty are rights that impose a greater burden on the Crown's radical title':

> For example, in this proceeding, the evidence demonstrated that the claimants had never fished in the sea. The Crown's radical title over the sea was therefore not, at sovereignty, burdened by any native title rights to fish. If a practice of fishing in the sea had developed since sovereignty, no native title rights could attach to that practice since any such rights would constitute a greater burden on the radical title than existed at sovereignty. By definition such rights could not be traditional. On the other hand, where the Crown's radical title was burdened at sovereignty with a right to fish, a change in the number and identity of people whose rights so burden it does not necessarily mean that those current rights cannot be traditional.[44]

Thus, consistent with the views expressed by the trial judge, the full Court argued that:

> Change and adaptation will not necessarily be fatal. So long as the changed or adapted laws and customs continue to sustain the same rights and interests that existed at sovereignty, they will remain traditional.[45]

Nevertheless, the Court concluded that the trial judge had concentrated on the continuity of the 'society' to the exclusion of any consideration of the acknowledgment of laws and customs; the rationale being that it is the laws and customs, not the society, that produces rights and interests. The full Court appeared to be critical of the trial judge for being concerned with the continuity of society in the sense of 'social relations' rather than the 'normative system' that must continue. The full Court suspected that with this formulation, the primary judge may have overlooked 'unacceptable change'.[46] The trial judge's attention to the maintenance of social relations was not seen as a related or supporting observation, as he had intended, but as evidence of a much deeper flaw in the reasoning of the judge. The full Court was of the view that the judge's reasoning was 'infected' by the erroneous belief that the effect of colonisation was to be taken into account.[47]

'FOR EACH GENERATION'

The full Court accepted the Commonwealth's interpretation of the rule in *Yorta Yorta* that specified that the requirement that acknowledgment and observance of those laws and customs must have continued 'substantially uninterrupted since sovereignty' should have an additional inquiry as to whether this has been demonstrated *for each generation*.[48] In *Risk v Northern Territory of Australia* [2006], Justice Mansfield formulated the requirements of proof as:

> The acknowledgement and observance of the laws and customs has continued substantially uninterrupted by each generation since sovereignty, and the society has continued to exist throughout that period as a body united in and by its acknowledgement and observance of those laws and customs.[49]

On appeal, the full Court in *Risk* regarded Justice Mansfield's summary as an accurate reflection of the case law.[50] This addition emerges from the High Court's explanation that a 'tradition' is something handed down from one generation to the next (usually by word of mouth). The High Court in *Yorta Yorta* had explained that the normative system must have remained substantially uninterrupted, otherwise the laws and customs could not be said to be traditional; they could not have been handed down from generation to generation.[51] However, it is apparent from *Bennell* and *Risk* that the Federal Court has transformed a 'definition' into a strict requirement of proof.

The full Court in *Bennell* was strongly critical of the trial judge's disregard of the historical evidence of the colonial encounter and some evidence concerning writings of contemporary anthropologists about the changes in Noongar society. It pointed to comments made in cross-examination, as well as the treatment of the evidence in the decision.[52] The full Court suggested that the trial judge made the assumption that 'provided the pre-sovereignty society continued to exist, its members would have continued to acknowledge and observe those laws and customs'.[53] But this is an overly simplistic reading of the judgment and the treatment of the evidence by the trial judge.

The trial judge took the view that the most important material for his purposes was the material that described the situation at the time of first settlement and shortly thereafter, and the evidence about current observance or acknowledgment of laws and customs. The history of Indigenous–non-Indigenous relations through the nineteenth and twentieth centuries was 'of great interest' and proved 'fascinating (and depressing)' reading, but was not central to the inquiry.[54] The judge was interested in early writings based on identifiable facts and observations at the time as the best evidence. It was apparent to the judge that this was uniquely the case in this instance because there was so much material of this kind available. This evidence, he said, took him through to the early years of the twentieth century.

The judge was then interested in the evidence of the Noongar witnesses about their laws and customs and, in particular, from where they learned these laws and customs, and the experts' opinions on that evidence. His Honour explained how inferences are to be drawn from oral testimony as to the observance and acknowledgment of laws and customs. He drew the same parallel that was drawn by Justice Selway in *Gumana v Northern Territory*[55] about the long-held common law principle for determining custom by relying on the credible testimony of older witnesses as to the practice over their lifetime. To this end, Justice Wilcox also recognised that it was necessary to 'treat with caution' evidence from Aboriginal witnesses about their group identity or observance of laws, customs and beliefs, which may be 'tailored to suit the claim'. But his Honour noted that he was impressed with the evidence of the primary witnesses, most of whom were able to attribute their knowledge to what they had learned as children long before the resurgence of interest in native title and other land claims.[56]

In contrast, but consistent with its 'generation by generation' exercise, the full Court noted that the material the judge rejected would have been relevant to a finding of the position, for example, in 1970.[57] The full Court thus suggested that the trial judge 'deprived himself of evidence' that he could have relied upon to determine whether, 'for each generation' since sovereignty, acknowledgment and observance of the Noongar laws and customs have continued substantially uninterrupted.[58] There may be some suggestion implicit in the full Court's criticisms that, while it may be appropriate for the trial judge to draw inferences of continuity, as has been done elsewhere, the trial judge did not adequately deal with evidence that was available that may have rebutted (as well as supported) the inferences drawn. The question remains, then, whether the 'generation by generation test' has become a positive requirement of proof that must be met by native title applicants or whether it remains a more complex inquiry based on all the available evidence supported by appropriate inferences. The concern of the courts about the extraordinary burden of proof on native title applicants was reflected upon by the Chief Justice of the High Court, Robert French, prior to his departure from the Federal Court.[59] His Honour suggested that the entire process of establishing native title would be 'lightened' by a (rebuttable) presumption of continuity of laws and customs and connection.[60]

COMMUNAL TITLE AND THE RECOGNITION LEVEL

The second issue in the appeal was whether the NTA supported the idea of native title as a communal title. This relates both to how native title is proved and who holds the title. The trial judge had chosen to use the term 'community' for the purpose of identifying the claim group and recognition level in relation to communal rights and interests, rather than the term 'society', which is used specifically to indicate the level at which the laws and customs are shared, or the 'normative system' to which the native title group ascribes.

If the trial judge accepted that a Noongar society existed, and continues to exist, then the Commonwealth argued that 'it does not necessarily follow that the society is the native title holding group'.[61] This is illustrated, for example, in relation to the number of Western Desert determinations, where the normative system from which rights and interests are derived is a large 'cultural bloc' within which a number of claimant communities have successfully settled determinations. The trial judge acknowledged that the identification of the relevant society for the purposes of applying s 223(1) 'is no easy matter', as that term could apply at various levels of abstraction, but the relevant level of abstraction for native title purposes is to determine the community or group … under whose laws and customs those rights and interests were held and observed'.[62] It does not matter that there may be other smaller or larger groups that may also be called a 'society' or community for some purposes.[63]

In this case, the state and Commonwealth were arguing for some smaller societal unit, although they could not pinpoint what that group might be. In essence, both the state and Commonwealth, with other respondents, were arguing that not all Noongar people held rights in the Perth area and, therefore, the title should be held, and proof of connection (including descent) should be determined, at a different, more localised recognition level.[64] They claimed that the distribution of rights and interests should not be left to 'intramural' or internal mechanisms of law and custom, but should be determined by the Court and set out in the determination.

His Honour had rejected this argument at trial, noting that 'there are cases in which communal native title has been recognised over the whole of an area of land, notwithstanding that estate groups were found to have particular rights to parts of that land'.[65] The judge also pointed to the number of determinations, such as *Alyawarr*, where the list of rights and interests specifically include the right of the native title holding group to determine the enjoyment and distribution of rights and interests among themselves.[66] Justice Wilcox concluded that:

> In any communal native title case, it is necessary for the Court to determine whether the claimed native title extends to the whole, or any

part, of the claimed area. However, it is not necessary (and it would be inappropriate) for the Court to become involved in issues as to the intracommunal distribution of special rights over portions of the total area in relation to which native title has been established. The Court leaves it to the community to determine those issues.[67]

His Honour cited Justice Brennan in *Mabo v Queensland [No. 2]* (1992) (*Mabo*), which was reiterated in *Alyawarr*:

> A communal native title enures for the benefit of the community as a whole and for the sub-groups and individuals within it who have particular rights and interests in the community's lands.[68]

The state's argument in the Noongar case was the same argument that has consistently been rejected by the courts in Western Australian decisions. The estate group, where it may be a basis for the allocation and exercise of rights, is not generally the appropriate 'recognition level' for native title determinations.[69] The interest held by the estate group is generally referable to a broader system of law and custom that recognises those rights in relation to other groups.

It is difficult to conceive where the respondents draw the line in this argument as to what is brought within the scope of the non-Indigenous legal system by the recognition of native title. The distinction between recognition and incorporation of Indigenous law is an important conceptual difference. It impacts on where responsibility lies for determining the distribution, inheritance, exercise and resolution of disputes over rights. The approach of the state and Commonwealth would seek to remove any 'communal' character to the title, fundamentally changing the nature of native title in a way that would require the scheduling of individual interests and the codification of the internal workings of the Indigenous legal system for enforcement by the courts.

The Commonwealth objected to the trial judge's use of the term 'communal native title', suggesting that this meant that the judge had failed to consider the evidence of connection to the particular area that was the subject of the separate question currently before the Court; that is, demonstrating connection specifically to the Perth metropolitan area.[70] The full Court identified the point of contention between the parties in the appeal as a somewhat broader complaint against the perceived 'latitude' given by the Federal Court in past cases to the level of abstraction over particularity with respect to the internal distribution of rights and interests.[71]

The full Court noted that the term 'communal title' is not used in the NTA, although this is somewhat spurious because 'native title or native title rights and interests' are defined in s 223 as communal, group or individual rights and interests. The full Court returned to the reasons of Justice Brennan in *Mabo* from which these terms are drawn; in particular, it highlighted the proprietorial emphasis that Justice Brennan used to explain the unique nature of interest recognised by native title, where his Honour stated that:

> If it be necessary to categorize an interest in land as proprietary in order that it survive a change in sovereignty, the interest possessed by a community that is in exclusive possession of land falls into that category.[72]

A more sensible interpretation of the wording used in s 223 is that it sought to capture the *sui generis* nature of native title, and in particular the different descriptions of its nature used by Justice Brennan and Justice Toohey, on the one hand, and Justices Deane and Gaudron on the other; or perhaps it was the different extent of titles, envisaged by the Court in *Mabo*, some of which may approach exclusive possession and others that may be non-exclusive.

Like the majority in *Western Australia v Ward* (2002) (*Ward*), however, the full Court in *Bennell* sought to undermine the proprietary nature of the title, suggesting that the reference in s 223 to rights and interests 'in relation to land' rather than to an interest 'in land' highlights a lack of symmetry between native title rights and interests and common law conceptions of property.[73] The full Court noted, like many of the more recent decisions of the High Court, that the *Mabo* decision was a decision of the common law, and that the NTA protects only interests as defined by s 223(1).

The full Court referred to Justice Brennan's 'typology' of rights and interests of individuals and groups within the community, whose rights depend on the communal title.[74] There, his Honour said, 'it is not possible to admit [such] rights without admitting a traditional proprietary community title'.[75] But the full Federal Court was of the view that statutory native title, in contrast, is focused on 'traditional non-proprietary, usufructuary rights'.[76] The full Court in *Bennell* seemed to eschew any meaning attributable to the term 'native title' in the definition of 'native title or native title rights and interests'. Their Honours draw attention to s 223(2), which refers (without prejudice) to hunting, fishing and gathering as rights protected by native title, as further illustration of the rights and interests typology.[77]

Without making a determination that communal title does not form part of the law of native title, the full Court in *Bennell* suggested that s 225, which requires the court to articulate the nature and extent of native title rights and interests when making a determination, reinforces the 'contrivance' of s 223 inquiry to focus on rights and interests.[78] However, the full Court did not draw attention to the requirement under s 225(e) for the Court to determine whether the rights and interests confer exclusive possession.[79]

At the same time, the full Court said that the level at which recognition of native title will occur is contrived by the character of the rights and interests under traditional law and custom, including whether the rights and interests are communal, group or individual.[80] The Court agreed with the conclusions of the full Court in *De Rose [No. 2]* that a 'communal title will reflect a claim made on behalf of a recognisable community of people, whose traditional laws and customs constitute the normative system under which rights and interests are created and acknowledged'.[81] The full Court suggested that a claim by a community to all native title rights and interests in a particular area is properly described as a communal claim but questions whether it is properly characterised as a claim for communal rights and interests, which it equated with a communal title; or, the Court asked, is it to assert merely that:

> as between themselves, the members of the claimant community hold all of the rights in the claim area albeit they may hold them differentially, ie 'there is no other proprietor', so that (absent dispute over those rights) it is superfluous and unnecessary to differentiate them?[82]

The Court acknowledged that there is no doubt that 'common law native title' envisages the latter characterisation.[83] But it suggested that the idea of native titles under s 223 lends itself to the former. Nevertheless, the jurisprudence of the Federal Court is against the full Court, as it acknowledged.[84] The full Court wanted to resolve the relationship between communal rights and interests and individual or group rights and interests. To this end, it identified a number of principles that have emerged:[85]

- the so-called 'fundamental principle' that native title rights and interests are ordinarily communal in character;[86]
- communal native title holders do not necessarily possess, or need to possess, rights and interests uniformly over the entire native title determination area;[87]
- if communal native title is established, the intramural (or intracommunal) allocation of special rights to particular areas is a matter for the community itself to determine in accordance with its traditional laws and customs;[88]
- relatedly, in a communal native title claim the level of intersection — both at which common law recognition of native title rights and interests is to occur (if at all) and at which the s 225 determination is to be made — is at the level of communal rights and interests;[89] and
- group and individual rights and interests are dependent upon, and are 'carved out of', the communal native title.[90]

In the end, the full Court admitted that the 'existence, character and extent' of native title rights and interests depend on the traditional laws and customs of the community and their content. From *De Rose [No. 2]* and *Ward*, the Court reinforced that communal title will not be presumed but may emerge as the result of the evidence of the kind of rights and interests conferred by traditional law and custom. Concomitantly, to generalise about the ordinary nature of native title, it suggested, may lead to incorrect assumptions that are required to be proved.⁹¹ Thus, the Court concluded that before a claim of communal title can be made, the evidence must be capable of supporting an inference of communal ownership.⁹² The Court took issue with the trial judge for not advancing an inquiry as to whether the laws and customs of the Noongar community gave rise to a communal title, or 'only of group titles', based on a 'closer analysis' of the character of the laws and customs of the society and how the laws and customs allocated rights and interests. The Court appeared to base this 'closer inquiry' on the notion that communal title does not necessarily result in rights and interest being held 'in common'.⁹³ But this is not a revelation; it is essential to the concept of native title that a system of law and custom operates to allocate rights and interests and to regulate transmission of rights. The full Court acknowledged the High Court in *Ward*, where it was held that this internal allocation of rights and interest was a matter for the common law holders of native title to determine among themselves, in accordance with traditional law and custom.⁹⁴

However, the appeal Court suggested that if the respondent parties contest the internal distribution of rights and interests, then the Court should involve itself in determining, to some degree of specificity, the internal distribution of rights and interests.

> If there is no fundamental controversy in a communal title claim as to alleged group rights and interests, but there is serious controversy as to whether there is a community having communal title, it is understandable, if that controversy is decided favourably to the claimant community, that the native title determination be made at the level of communal rights and interests and that the s 225 rights and interests be specified accordingly. But … where the extinguishment of group rights is put in issue in a communal title claim, somewhat different considerations may well obtain.⁹⁵

This reasoning suggests that, within a broad communal title, the state may challenge the continuous acknowledgment and observance of a particular group or individual within that community. The 'typology' of individual, group and communal rights and interests has been recast here, not to provide flexibility for the claim group to define the appropriate level at which to assert itself as a 'title holding' group, but as a basis for the state to challenge individuals and groups within the claim group where there is no dispute among the Indigenous parties. This is a dangerous and inappropriate infraction on the jurisdiction and authority of the Indigenous communities to determine membership of the group and entitlement or distribution of rights and interests under their own law and custom.

CONNECTION

The third issue for the full Court in *Bennell* was the notion of connection and the proper inquiry under s 223(1)(c). The trial judge was in no doubt that the applicants must demonstrate a connection with the area that is the subject of the separate question, but that is was not necessary for the applicants to prove a connection that is 'specific' to the Perth area, distinct from their connection to the whole claim area. The trial judge repeated a well-established principle in the native title jurisprudence — 'the whole includes the parts'; that is, the Perth area was part of the claim area, and if the applicants succeeded in demonstrating connection to the whole area, or an area that included the Perth area, then they demonstrated the required connection to the Perth area.[96]

The state argued that the judge erred in law in finding that the applicants had a connection to the Perth metropolitan area by virtue of their connection to the entire claim area. It argued that the judge must make a determination that at least some of the individual claimants had a connection to the specific area and descent from original inhabitants of the area.[97]

This question relates to the discussion about the internal distribution of rights within the group and the extent to which the Court should interfere in the internal distribution of rights and interests among the native title group. The full Court acknowledged that the course of authority supporting the principle of communal title was clear, thus it conceded that if the 'fundamental principle' that native title is ordinarily communal is to be called into question, it will be in another place.[98] It was not therefore necessary for the judge to make a determination as to the distribution of group and individual rights within the communal title. But is there a distinct inquiry as to connection to various areas within the claim that may have the same effect?

The full Court on appeal in *Bennell* said that the trial judge had not separately considered the burden imposed by the connection requirements under s 223(1)(b). The full Court reviewed the jurisprudence in relation to the specific 'work' to be done by s 223(b); that is, how it adds to, rather than is subsumed by, the rights and interests in relation to land proved under s 223(a).[99] In *Ward* the High Court held that connection is not related to physical presence or particular methods of use but to a connection to land through law and custom; that is, the content and effect of traditional laws and customs that give rise to rights and interests in relation to land.[100] Similarly, law and custom can sustain a connection in the absence of physical occupation.[101] The full Court cited with approval the explanation by Justice French that connection 'involves the continuing internal and external assertion by [a claimant community] of its traditional relationship to the country defined by its laws and customs … which may be expressed by its physical presence there or otherwise'.[102]

The full Court went so far as to say that connection has no relationship to the rights and interests claimed, except in so far as their character, content and exercise may go some way to establishing connection. Thus, the Court said not only must the applicants prove that observance and acknowledgment of laws and customs has continued substantially uninterrupted but also that connection has been substantially maintained.[103] One will not automatically presume the other, although the Court noted that perhaps too little emphasis has been placed on the continued observance as evidence of connection. The full Court went on to note that the laws and customs that connect people to land are not necessarily always those that give rise to rights and interests in land.[104]

The Court also drew this discussion back to the difference between communal and group claims; that is, how does s 223(1)(b) operate in relation to communal and group claims? More importantly, how is a contest to a society's continued connection to a particular area within a claim to be treated?

> Where, as in the present matter, it is contended that connection has been lost with a particular part of the claim area, because the connection to that area by the laws and customs has not been shown to have been substantially maintained, the connection inquiry itself must address that contention and, if it is established, its significance for the communal claim to that part of the area must be assessed. To foreshadow what we have to say, the primary judge did not consider it necessary to embark upon such an inquiry in relation to the Perth Metropolitan Area and so clearly erred.[105]

In *Alyawarr* the full Federal Court reiterated that 'It does not depend upon the precise locus, within a community, of native title rights and interests intramurally allocated, provided that they can be regarded as held by the community as a whole'.[106] The full Court in *Bennell* warned that this should not lead to a 'shorthand' inquiry in which connection in relation to a communal claim is considered only at the communal level. The Court noted the inquiry undertaken in *Neowarra v Western Australia* (2003) (*Neowarra*) in relation not only to the societal or communal level, but to the estate (or Dambun) level.[107] However, it suggested the trial judge in this case did not undertake a similar inquiry, in particular in relation to the Perth metropolitan area.[108]

The Court summarised its view:

> It is not uncommon for the traditional laws and customs of a community to connect that community to a claim area by connecting groups within the community both to each other (often in complex ways) and, respectively and immediately, to their own particular portions of the claim area (in the latter case by granting rights to, and imposing responsibilities on, each such group in respect of its portion). In such cases, it is entirely

appropriate that the connection inquiry consider not merely evidence of the general connection of the claimant community to the claim area, but also the evidence of the particular connection of the particular groups and their members to their respective portions of the claim area. The latter evidence, we would suggest, will ordinarily be necessary in some degree if the claimants' assertion of connection is to be sufficiently manifest over the claim area as a whole — the more so, in communal claims, if rights and interests are held differentially across the community.[109]

Obviously, the Court was particularly concerned with the area of the separate question. But, the full Court's critique of the trial judge's line of inquiry assumes that the Perth metropolitan area is a relevant 'topographic focus' for an inquiry into connection merely because it is contested,[110] although the Court also contends that the judge did not embark on an inquiry into connection for any of the claim area in the sense required by s 223(1)(b). While the evidence may have been there, the inquiry was not.[111] The full Court emphasised finally that:

if those persons whom the laws and customs connect to a particular part of the claim area have not continued to observe without substantial interruption the laws and customs in relation to their country, they cannot succeed in a claim for native title rights and interests even if it be shown — which it has not been — that other Noongar peoples have continued to acknowledge and observe the traditional laws and customs of the Noongar.[112]

The reference to other Noongar peoples here is important. The full Court appeared to dissect the single society into smaller groups for the purposes of connection in a way that the trial judge was not prepared to do, based on the evidence of the Noongar people.

CONCLUSION

No case since *Yorta Yorta* and *Ward* in 2002 has prompted more calls for reform than the full Federal Court decision in *Bennell*. The overturning of a positive determination at first instance was unprecedented. The dissatisfaction of the full Court with the perceived lack of rigour in the trial judge's inquiries and the need for greater particularity in the judgment resulted in the case being sent back to be reconsidered by another court, but the perception that the courts had again imposed greater strictures on the requirements of proof has raised significant concern for future claims. Nevertheless, the decision stands in stark contrast to the decision in *Sebastian* only a matter of weeks later, where, again, the claimants successfully asserted their rights under traditional law and custom, including over the suburban centre of Broome. The appeal court's interpretation of the jurisprudence there remained consistent with the approach in *De Rose [No. 2]* and *Alyawarr*. No doubt the decisions in *Bennell* and *Risk* will be used as the legal benchmark for state governments in the negotiation of settlements of claims. The degree to which the courts synthesise the seemingly disparate streams of cases emerging for the full Federal Court will determine the utility of native title as a basis for recognising and protecting Indigenous peoples' rights to their traditional lands on a non-discriminatory basis.

The growing distinction between common law native title and statutory native title identified by the full Federal Court in *Bennell* is absurd but intriguing. It is certainly inconsistent with the legislative intent in 1993, which sought to capture the meaning of native title as expressed in the Mabo judgments but to allow the development of the concept at common law.[113] Perhaps the amendments to the NTA in 1998 are presumed to have heralded a new legislative intent that excluded the common law and the courts from defining native title. Consideration of the difference a common law-centred doctrine might have made over the past fifteen years may not be a purely academic exercise, if statutory native title extinguished some nascent common law right. However, and to reiterate a theme of this book, the veil of statutory interpretation cannot hide the fact that the courts have chosen interpretations of the words of the statute that have added layers of meaning and, with that, requirements of proof, without regard to the principles of non-discrimination and beneficial interpretation that should apply when considering the rights of Indigenous peoples.[114]

CHAPTER 11

The development of native title jurisprudence

The recognition of native title under the common law of Australia ensured that the courts would continue to play a central role in the development of native title law, despite the intervention of legislation seeking to clarify, regulate and institutionalise native title. The key cases discussed in the previous chapters provide a perspective on the development of — as well as the moments of confusion in — the law in the years since the decision in *Mabo v Queensland [No. 2]* (1992) (*Mabo*).[1] It is now possible to track how the central native title doctrines and concepts have developed to see how some ideas have settled, some have fallen aside and others remain dormant for possible future consideration. Indeed, some concepts considered to be settled have been rediscovered as contested ideas that may be revisited in due course.

The *Mabo* case first established the key concept of recognition and the reconsideration of the consequences of settlement. The High Court established the uneasy notion of native title as having its source in, and deriving its content from, the laws and customs of the Indigenous peoples. The declaratory nature of the common law provided not that native title was to be recognised from then on, but that, in law, it had always existed. The reordering of legal theories, land law, legislative power and private legal relations could only be guessed at the time.

Many elements of proof can be drawn from the *Mabo* decision, which determined the nature of native title as based on traditional law and custom. The *Mabo* decision determined that native title was a communal right that could be proved by an identifiable community, group or individual who was able to demonstrate a continued connection to the land through law and custom. From this same presumption, it was thought that native title, not being a creature of the common law, was not dependent on any law or statute to bring it into being, nor did it require express recognition by the sovereign. This idea did not rest easily with the apparent compromise to sovereign power at the heart of the extinguishment doctrine and the preferencing of non-Indigenous interests, which also found its source in *Mabo*.

11. Native title jurisprudence

Much of the statutory framework for the *Native Title Act 1993* (Cth) (NTA) is based on Justice Brennan's decision in *Mabo*, with which Chief Justice Mason and Justice McHugh agreed. But the prioritisation of that judgment masks the diversity of approaches of the majority. Justice Brennan's judgment was arguably the narrowest of the three substantive majority judgments in relation to some matters, particularly extinguishment and compensation, and, more fundamentally, in the scope of the concept of native title on the mainland, as was evidenced in his dissent in *Wik Peoples v Queensland* (1996) (*Wik*).[2]

Justice Brennan's reasoning in *Mabo* on other matters still remains to be explored, for example, in relation to fiduciary duty. While the idea of a freestanding fiduciary obligation upon the Crown arising out of the power to unilaterally extinguish native title has not received support, the idea of fiduciary duty emerging from particular dealings or undertakings in relation to land was mooted from early on, though it is yet to be fully argued before the High Court.[3]

In *Mabo* the idea of possessory title was considered primarily by Justice Toohey. It was not revisited in *Wik*, although the statement of claim asserted possessory title as an alternative. It was assumed that a possessory title, if found to exist, would be of no benefit to Indigenous peoples who could prove native title because it was thought to provide similar rights and protection. Given the limits placed on native title by more recent decisions, this may be an idea that could be revisited. In particular, the standards of proof required by *Members of the Yorta Yorta Aboriginal Community v Victoria* (2002) (*Yorta Yorta*)[4] and the vulnerability to extinguishment of a title without the protection of a Crown grant may distinguish native title. While the High Court in *Western Australia v Ward* (2002) (*Ward*) confirmed that native title itself was not a possessory title, the notion of an independent possessory title has not been fully argued.[5]

Before the new system for determining whether native title existed through the structures established under the NTA came into effect on 1 January 1994, a number of claims had already been lodged in the courts for recognition of common law native title. The High Court decision in *Western Australia v Commonwealth* (1995) (*Native Title Act case*) confirmed the power of the Commonwealth to pass legislation affecting native title and confirmed that, in recognising and protecting native title under legislation, the vulnerability to extinguishment by state governments had been removed.[6]

In *Wik* the High Court dealt with the appeal on the basis of common law native title, indicating that its findings in this respect might be of assistance for claims under the NTA. The idea of the parallel development of common law native title and native title under legislation is difficult to conceptualise given the extent to which the NTA relies on common law concepts and development through the courts. But in *Ward*, while the High Court confirmed that the NTA did not create a new right, the suggestion that there may be scope within the common law for the development of independent doctrines was made. This is of particular interest in relation to the compensation provisions of the NTA, which confirm that any extinguishment of common law native title caused by the legislation attracts compensation. The comments of the High Court with regard to the interrelationship between the NTA and 'common law native title' have remained ambiguous, as the two concepts appear inextricably bound. But the Federal Court has continued to draw this distinction in its decisions as it fiercely applies a textual interpretation approach to the requirements of proof under s 223(1).

The *Native Title Act case*, *Yanner v Eaton* (1999) (*Yanner*)[7] and *Wik* all highlighted the way in which the recognition of native title had changed how statutes were to be interpreted in order to provide appropriate recognition and protection of the newly recognised native title. The idea of clear and plain intention, whether express or implied, was supported by presumptions against extinguishment and the consideration of the presence and enjoyment, as of right, of native title holders. *Wik* was, of course, the high point of coexistence and a strict test of necessary inconsistency.

Beginning with *Fejo v Northern Territory* (1998) (*Fejo*) and highlighted in *Wilson v Anderson* (2002) (*Wilson*), beneficial construction and necessary implication have been put aside to a large degree.[8] In *Fejo* the joint majority judgment concluded that:

> It was sought to draw some analogy with rights recognised in English land law like rights of common or customary rights. But reference to those rights in the present context is misplaced ... That a right owing its existence to one system of law (a right of freehold tenure) may be subject to other rights created by that same legal system (such as customary rights or rights of common) is not surprising. But very different considerations arise when there is an intersection between rights created by statute and rights that owe their origin to a different body of law and traditions.[9]

Interestingly, Justice Gummow had drawn just these analogies in *Wik*.[10]

The majority in *Ward* extended this conservatism to the common law extinguishment doctrine that underpins the NTA, but the articulation in *Wik* of the extinguishment to the extent of inconsistency formed the basis for much of the current extinguishment discussion. Before *Ward* the reasoning in *Wik* made clear the process of comparing legal interests and the rights conferred by the colonial tenure or statute on the one hand, and, on the other, the rights conferred under law and custom asserted through native title and derived from a factual inquiry. The extent of inconsistency suggested a concept of partial extinguishment or impairment of aspects of native title while leaving undisturbed the enjoyment of other rights as far as possible.

11. Native title jurisprudence

Fejo also confirmed that revival or suspension of native title would not be considered. Fortunately, provisions of the amended NTA, such as ss 47A and 47B, have ameliorated the impact of this position to a large degree.[11] A paralysing vulnerability was attached to native title in a clear exercise of Crown enrichment in the guise of protecting the security of freehold tenures of private citizens. In *Fejo*, too, the 'bundle of rights' language began to emerge.

In a sense *Fejo* stood out in these early years as a correction and a move towards providing a certain or 'settled' legal status where it was possible. In *Wik* Justice Kirby had criticised the approach of Justice Drummond in effecting a 'strike out' by failing to determine the rights and interests asserted before determining the impact of the grant. Justice Kirby warned that:

> [t]he Wik [people] could only have stood to lose from the procedure adopted by Drummond J ... Any future elucidation or elaboration of such complex questions as the relationship in this case between pastoral leases and native title could be better attempted against a thorough understanding of the facts.[12]

But the Court did exactly that in *Fejo*. In order to make out the argument that the grant of freehold was inconsistent with the continued enjoyment of native title, the High Court 'assumed' what the rights asserted would be:

> For present purposes let it be assumed that those rights may encompass a right to hunt, to gather or to fish, a right to conduct ceremonies on the land, a right to maintain the land in a particular state or other like rights and interests. They are rights that are inconsistent with the rights of a holder of an estate in fee simple.[13]

The joint judgment and that of Justice Kirby in *Fejo* raised numerous policy considerations for why suspension and revival of native title rights were unable to form part of the common law of native title. In a brief respite, *Yanner* again saw the beneficial construction re-emerge, with a sophisticated consideration of concepts of property and the potential for continued enjoyment of native title. In particular, the interest of the Crown was held in check, as regulation was seen as merely the curtailing of the exercise of rights rather than as extinguishment. In effect, the reasoning in *Yanner* provided for the 'suspension' of rights in certain circumstances.

After nearly ten years, there were still aspects of the recognition of native title that remained unresolved, and *Commonwealth v Yarmirr* (2001) (*Yarmirr*) provided the test case for the issue of native title offshore, an element that had been removed from previous claims that came before the courts, including *Mabo*.[14] The case required the High Court to revisit the acquisition of sovereignty and the content of sovereign title. In *Mabo* it had been said that radical title was burdened by the pre-existing rights of the Indigenous peoples. In *Yarmirr* this was clarified, as radical title is a common law notion that applies to land, and the sovereign rights to the sea were acquired incrementally by operation of statute and international law. Native title, it was decided, burdens sovereignty. This was not a significant shift because radical title (as explained by Justice Toohey in *Wik*)[15] is the device that translates sovereignty in the international sense into sovereign power in domestic law.

The judgment in *Yarmirr* also softened the hard messages from *Mabo* about the terms upon which sovereignty was acquired in colonies already inhabited by sovereign peoples with their own societies and legal systems. In *Mabo* rights were held to survive and are recognised by the common law, 'provided those laws and customs are not so repugnant to natural justice, equity and good conscience that judicial sanctions under the new regime must be withheld'.[16] In *Yarmirr* the High Court revised the notion of 'recognition' by the common law in a way that seemed to be based more on inconvenience than abhorrence.

Partly as a result of the approach to non-recognition, *Yarmirr* is significant in its identification of a class of non-exclusive native title. Justice Kirby was critical of the majority decision in this regard, particularly the prioritisation of general public rights, such as the right to fish, which are acknowledged to be susceptible to regulation and in large part no longer exist in effect. The decision unnecessarily undermined the economic viability of native title for many coastal native title communities but, more importantly, undermined the principles upon which native title was recognised as an obligation on the acquiring sovereign.

While the passage of the NTA had not impacted substantially on the reasoning of the courts in early decisions such as *Yanner* and *Wik*, the passage of the *Native Title Amendment Act* in 1998 (the Amendments) was certainly given careful consideration in *Yarmirr* and in later decisions and was to later occupy the imagination of the lower courts. Perhaps this can be explained by the fact that cases coming before the courts since *Wik* had concerned applications under the NTA. The terms of the NTA were said to frame the inquiry into whether native title exists and to be the source of many of the incursions into the beneficial nature of native title.[17]

As *Yarmirr* was being argued before the High Court, there was already a series of further cases on appeal that dealt with the more technical details of proof and extinguishment. The issues raised in litigation in the lower courts in both *Ward* and *Yorta Yorta* revealed that these were to be the most significant native title cases since *Mabo* and *Wik*. *Ward* at first instance had provided an expansive and extensive native title determination for the Miriuwung and Gajerrong peoples but it was felt that there was insufficient guidance to determine the interaction between native title and other interests in the area, in particular the economically significant Ord River project. The case squarely raised the concept of partial extinguishment in a way that the decision in *Wik* had been unable to do, given the limited extent of the evidence in that case. The *Ward* litigation raised issues concerning the nature of native title, whether it was an interest in land or a 'bundle of rights', and what the implications of such a characterisation might mean. This debate was somewhat distracting from the more important issue of the fundamental nature of extinguishment. Issues of the permanency of extinguishment, suspension and revival were again raised for reconsideration by the High Court.

While many of these matters had been canvassed in *Wik*, the High Court in *Ward* was able to consider the impact of the 1998 Amendments to the NTA, which had been introduced largely in response to the decision in *Wik*. With undue deference to the legislature, the Court confirmed concepts such as partial extinguishment and permanent extinguishment with express reference to the legislation. Unlike *Wik*, the Court was able to examine in detail the operation of the extinguishment provisions of the NTA in relation to a raft of tenures and regulatory regimes.

The Court also had an opportunity to begin to examine the operation of the *Racial Discrimination Act 1975* (Cth) in relation to native title and the NTA. Not since the *Native Title Act case* had the Court sought to invalidate Acts or statutes on the basis of their discriminatory impact on native title. The resulting impact on national parks in the Northern Territory was a telling reminder to governments of the post-1975 issues still to be worked through. The Court only hinted at the compensation implications of some of the grants and the impact of legislation, in particular the deeming provisions of the NTA. In contrast, the beneficial construction of statutes was again constrained with the vesting and reservation of large tracts of Crown tenures in Western Australia being declared transfers of 'exclusive possession', despite being Crown-to-Crown transfers.

The Court in *Ward* demonstrated a lack of familiarity with Indigenous relationships with land and the history of the interaction of Indigenous and colonial legal systems that had characterised the membership of the Court in *Mabo* and *Wik* (Chief Justice Brennan and Justice Toohey having been Northern Territory Land Commissioners). Despite restating that pastoral leases and mining leases were 'fragile and precarious interests', the Court's unwillingness to find native title rights to anything more than subsistence activities was troubling. The Court's assertion that the 'spiritual' relationship of Indigenous peoples to their land was the primary relationship romanticised native title and provided an excuse for denying their economic rights as holders of a proprietary interest with the protection of the common law. One of the most telling aspects of the *Ward* decision was the call from the minority judges, Justices McHugh and Callinan, for a more just settlement of Indigenous peoples' claims that did not depend on the vagaries of the terms of legislation.

Despite the references to the 'precariousness' of pastoral tenures in Western Australia in the *Ward* decision, the High Court in *Wilson* confirmed that beneficial construction of statutes would no longer seek to reconcile statutory titles with the Indigenous peoples' prior and continued interests in the land. The majority joint judgment found that the NTA had changed the nature of the inquiry and that the test applied in *Wik*, of 'necessary inconsistency', was distinguished as a 'common law' test. Using the NTA definitions of exclusive and non-exclusive possession leases, the inquiry was not into whether the two could coexist, but whether the *Western Lands Act 1901* (NSW) conferred exclusive possession in relation to the 'perpetual leases' in question, which were granted for grazing purposes only. But the crux of the question was the same. The decision of the full Federal Court had found that the leases were not exclusive possession tenures and were not necessarily inconsistent with all native title rights. The full Federal Court had applied the test in *Wik* and reached the result that the granting of a statutory title for limited purpose subject to conditions and threat of forfeiture over large tracts of land did not clearly and plainly demonstrate an intention, whether express or by necessary implication, to exclude Indigenous inhabitants from pursuing all of their native title rights. Nevertheless, the High Court overturned the decision on appeal. Justice Kirby, dissenting, expressed concern at the Court's change of direction:

> This Court should be slow to reverse the steps, taken by *Mabo [No 2]* and *Wik*, in the recognition of the native title rights of Aboriginal peoples. Particularly so, because no party in this case sought to reargue the correctness of either of those decisions. Especially so, because the Federal Parliament accepted the holdings in those cases, adopted and amended the NTA accordingly and also facilitated the enactment of comparable companion legislation enacted by State and Territory legislatures throughout the country ... [T]here are already enough legal and practical impediments to the attainment of legal protection for native title rights without now eroding the principles accepted by the majority in those two cases.[18]

The majority judgments in *Wilson*, Chief Justice Gleeson's in particular, preferred the approach of Chief Justice Brennan in *Wik*,[19] an approach that made no adjustment to the 'habits of thought' employed in the judicial reasoning to take into account the recognition of Indigenous presence on, and now rights in, the land. Chief Justice Gleeson reduced the majority approach in *Wik* to 'some members' of the Court who considered the facts and related policy and legislative treatment of Indigenous peoples' continued presence on the land as relevant to the inquiry into intention.[20]

In *Ward* and *Wilson* the High Court converted the inquiry from one that was specific to whether native title holders and Indigenous inhabitants were necessarily excluded to one that placed Indigenous peoples in the same category as 'the rest of the world'. The application of the test of clear and plain intention and necessary inconsistency to a determination of whether native title has been impacted should be specific to the relationship between the rights granted and the legal rights of the native title holders. This danger, again identified by the Court — of pre-empting the findings of fact in relation to the native title rights asserted — ensured that the decision of the Court was 'clothed in an air of unreality'.[21] The Court considered only the rights conferred by the grant and its intention in excluding the rest of the world. The native title interests were assumed, thus denying the native title claimants the opportunity to present evidence of the native title rights and interests asserted.

In the lead-up to the *Ward* decision, the much more controversial proceedings in *Yorta Yorta* were also underway. The decision of the trial judge determined that, rather than having protection withdrawn by the effects of extinguishment, native title would not be recognised because the Yorta Yorta people were not a 'traditional Aboriginal society': they were found to have abandoned their traditional laws and customs and thus were unable to prove native title. Crossing outside the legal arena, the issues at the heart of the *Yorta Yorta* case concerned concepts such as tradition, authenticity, continuity and change within societies, cultures and legal systems. These issues engaged commentators from across a range of disciplines, most of whom were highly critical of the methodology and conclusions of Justice Olney.[22]

In both the Federal Court appeal and the High Court, Justice Olney's approach based on tracing pre-contact activities through to the present was regarded as a wrong-headed inquiry. Yet, on different reasoning, both appeals still supported the conclusion of the trial judge that at some point the Yorta Yorta had lost their character as a 'traditional Aboriginal society' in the sense required to establish native title. The violence perpetrated by this decision on the Yorta Yorta community continues to resonate in the public imagination.[23]

Escaping moral responsibility, the High Court again sought to emphasise that the legislature, through the enactment of the NTA, had taken control of the development of native title. For example, the meaning of tradition, the judges argued, acquired a meaning other than the ordinary meaning through s 223(1) of the NTA.[24] In order to give sense to the provision and to the conclusion of Justice Olney, the High Court introduced the concept of a 'normative society' into the native title discourse. The 'normative society' became the conceptual device to assess the source of 'traditional laws and traditional customs' and to revisit 'what exactly it is that intersects with the common law'.[25] The Court made a clumsy attempt to explain the nature of native title as a title that arose at the acquisition of sovereignty, and therefore the consequences for how it should be 'recognised' currently and reconciled with two hundred years of shared colonial history. All of this they attempted to do without admitting the ongoing existence of a parallel system of law and custom.

The influence of the trial judge — and the assessment of the evidence and the claim group at first instance — came into sharp relief in *Yorta Yorta*. Neither the Federal Court nor the High Court was prepared to disturb the findings of fact at first instance. This is a general rule in appeal proceedings. Justice Olney's factual conclusions could have been brought into question on the basis that he began with the wrong premise and instituted a wrong inquiry, as proposed by Chief Justice Black, dissenting, in the Federal Court appeal.[27] But at this stage in the development of native title doctrine, it seemed that the High Court was unwilling to require further consideration of the facts. Instead, the High Court proposed a methodology for inquiring into the elements of proof of native title for future cases, which may have led to a very different result if applied to the facts in *Yorta Yorta*. Since then, we have seen a greater preparedness on the part of the full Federal Court to review the findings of the trial judges and develop a corpus of appeal decisions at the Federal Court level.

In both *De Rose v South Australia [No. 2]* (2005) (*De Rose [No. 2]*) and *Bodney v Bennell* (2008) (*Bennell*), the full Federal Court criticised the trial judge on quite disparate bases. The trial judge in *De Rose v South Australia [No. 1]* (2003) (*De Rose [No. 1]*) was criticised for taking an extraordinarily narrow approach to the idea of abandonment, equating failure to exercise rights to a loss of connection.[28] The overturning of the decision, in *De Rose [No. 2]*,[29] was perceived as a correction of balance that demonstrated that — whatever might be the assessment of the jurisprudence of native title handed down by the High Court in *Yorta Yorta* — native title was still a meaningful concept that had not been robbed of all of its substance.

It was with great disappointment, then, that the decision of the appeal Court in *Bennell*[30] was received not only by the Noongar people, but by the sector generally. The finding of the trial judge (that, subject to extinguishment, native title existed in the area claimed by the Noongar people) was sent back to be retried. The full Court had held that the judge failed to give specific regard to the 'acceptability' of the changes in law and custom of the Noongar people (as revealed in the evidence) and failed to consider the impact of the changes on the maintenance of the requisite connection for native title purposes.

While only two cases have been considered in detail here to illustrate the application of the *Ward* and *Yorta Yorta* jurisprudence, many more could have been chosen. The full Federal Court has considered two series of appeals since these crucial cases were handed down by the High Court. The first series, in 2005, included the *De Rose [No. 2]* and *Northern Territory v Alyawarr, Kaytetye, Warumungu, Wakay Native Title Claim Group* (2005) (*Alyawarr*) decisions;[31] the second wave, in 2008, included *Risk v Northern Territory* (2007), *Bennell* and the Rubibi determination in *State of Western Australia v Sebastian* (2008) (*Sebastian*).[32] The issues that have occupied the minds of the litigants and the Federal Court have focused on interpreting the High Court's meaning in *Ward* and *Yorta Yorta*

11. Native title jurisprudence

in relation to the nature of the rights recognised and the elements of proof, in particular the ideas of tradition and connection, contained in s 223(1) and the 'recognition level' at which native title should be held. Too often, the Courts have laboured over layers of meaning and textual interpretation from the words of the NTA.

In numerous decisions since the High Court decision in *Yorta Yorta*, Federal Court judges have been able to apply the reasoning of the High Court to the circumstances before them in ways that have resulted in a large number of litigated determinations in favour of the claimant groups. The decisions of the Court in cases like *Lardil, Kaidilt, Yangkaal and Gangalidda People v Queensland* [2000], *Neowarra v Western Australia* (2003), the *De Rose* decisions, *Alyawarr* and *Sampi v Western Australia* [2005] among others, have highlighted the capacity of the courts to work with the jurisprudence of *Yorta Yorta* in the context of the facts before them.[33] However, the decisions of the full Federal Court in *Bennell, Risk v Northern Territory* (2008) and *Harrington-Smith v Western Australia [No. 9]* (2007) demonstrate the limits of the Court's flexibility.[34]

At the same time, what has also become evident in the Federal Court appeals is the lack of flexibility available in the application of the reasoning in *Ward* outside the exclusive possession native title context. The High Court's willingness to find extinguishment has been replicated by Federal Court judges at first instance, and the decision in *Neowarra* showed how the conflation of proof and extinguishment in *Ward* has created a test that has little meaning in the Indigenous context. The reasoning of the majority of the High Court in *Griffiths v Minister for Lands, Planning and Environment* (2008) (*Griffiths*)[26] reflects the gradual 'domestication' of native title in the years since *Mabo*. The majority jettisoned any reference to beneficial construction to provide protection to native title from arbitrary extinguishment.

The current inquiry into extinguishment fails to acknowledge that, having its source in a parallel normative system, the system of laws and customs that sustain native title has its own internal consistency and is not bound by, and may not adjust to or recognise, the 'extinguishing acts' under Australian law. In this way, the idea of native title as a recognition space or an intersection of two legal systems is a misleading metaphor. The courts have repeatedly shown that, in the absence of extinguishing acts, exclusive possession title is the most meaningful translation of the central relationship between Indigenous peoples and their country. But, as soon as extinguishment comes into play, the courts have sought to 'unbundle' or disaggregate the rights conferred by native title to rebuild a title from the fragments. This construction of the extinguishment doctrine fails to pay due respect and to provide due recognition and protection to native title as the interest first in time, under which the rights and interests enjoyed are as extensive as the law can allow, subject to the rights taken away by the Crown.

CHAPTER 12

The jurisprudence of native title 'Recognition' and 'protection'

The Australian law, in both the courts and parliament, has offered to recognise and protect native title. But what is meant by 'recognition'? What means of 'protection' is this title to enjoy? The answer to these questions sheds light on the place that has been provided for native title in Australian law and the degree to which the law has been able to provide the kind of 'retreat from injustice' that the High Court in *Mabo v Queensland [No. 2]* (1992) (*Mabo*) had set out to achieve.[1]

If we begin with the objective of the native title doctrine, at base, native title is a common law doctrine aimed at 'recognising and protecting' the interests of Indigenous peoples, arising from their own normative system, to the land over which they once enjoyed sovereignty and continue to assert rights. The legislature, through the objects of the *Native Title Act 1993* (Cth) (NTA), has in turn undertaken to augment the objective of the common law by providing for 'the recognition and protection of native title'.[2] While the High Court has clearly placed the NTA at the centre of the inquiry, the common law retains its significance in determining the threshold for recognition and protection. Justice McHugh has argued that:

> The stipulation in s 223(1)(c) that the common law must recognise those rights and interests inevitably poses questions as to where, when and in what circumstances the common law will recognise and enforce those rights and interests.[3]

The High Court has, on numerous occasions, explained that native title in Australia does not recognise a 'dual system of laws'.[4] But the courts have struggled with the juxtaposition of recognising the existence of a normative system, as a matter of fact, and denying its authority as part of the law of Australia. In *Commonwealth v Yarmirr* (2001) (*Yarmirr*), the majority, in a joint judgment, explained that recognition does not operate under the principles of 'conflict of laws', but went on to note that native title allows, even requires, two systems of law to operate together. The majority remarked that:

It is inappropriate to see the present issues as engaging the common law rules of choice of laws because the Act requires no resolution of any conflict or competition between two systems of law. The Act presupposes that, so far as concerns native title rights and interests, the two systems — the traditional law acknowledged and traditional customs observed by the relevant peoples, and the common law — can and will operate together. Indeed, not only does it presuppose that this will happen, it requires that result.[5]

Similarly, for Justices Deane and Gaudron in *Mabo*, the purpose of native title was to leave room for 'the continued operation of some local laws and customs among the native people and even the incorporation of some of those laws and customs as part of the common law'.[6]

Interestingly, the doctrine of native title that has developed in South Africa has taken this approach further. The Constitutional Court of South Africa in 2003 upheld a decision of the Supreme Court of Appeal (SCA) recognising communal title on a similar foundation to other common law native title. The SCA had relied on the decision of the High Court in *Mabo* and the suite of cases upon which *Mabo* relied.[7] The Constitutional Court went further, with the aid of constitutional recognition of 'indigenous law', to declare that the customary law of the Indigenous inhabitants of South Africa was not simply recognised by the law of South Africa, but was part of that law. The Court stated that:

> While in the past indigenous law was seen through the common law lens, it must now be seen as an integral part of our law ... the Constitution acknowledges the originality and distinctiveness of indigenous law as an independent source of norms within the legal system.[8]

In Australia the terms upon which Indigenous law will operate is asserted to be the province of the 'new sovereign'. The common law doctrine of native title and the legislative response do not give the same authority to Indigenous law as that afforded by constitutional recognition in South Africa. In *Wik Peoples v Queensland* (1996) (*Wik*), Justice Kirby, in a less conventional presentation of the relationship between the two systems of law, concluded that:

> The theory accepted by this Court in *Mabo [No. 2]* was not that the native title of indigenous Australians was enforceable of its own power or by legal techniques akin to the recognition of foreign law. It was that such title was enforceable in Australian courts because the common law in Australia said so.[9]

Thus, the place of native title in Australian law is determined, according to the joint judgment of the majority in *Yarmirr*, on two bases: first, what is meant by 'recognition of native title' and, second, what is meant by 'the assertion of sovereignty' by the Crown.[10]

NATIVE TITLE AND THE ASSERTION OF CROWN SOVEREIGNTY

The implications of the acquisition of sovereignty by the British on the rights of the Indigenous peoples of the colonised territory was the central question for the High Court in *Mabo*. The Court examined the consequences of the acts of state that established the colonies in Australia while seeking to leave undisturbed the basis for asserting sovereignty by way of settlement. The Court relied on the principle, articulated in *New South Wales v Commonwealth* (1975) (*Seas and Submerged Lands case*), that '[t]he acquisition of territory by a sovereign state for the first time is an act of state which cannot be challenged, controlled or interfered with by the courts of that state'.[11]

In *Yarmirr* the High Court adopted the understanding of sovereignty expressed by Justice Jacobs in the *Seas and Submerged Lands case*:

> [s]overeignty under the law of nations is a power and right, recognised or effectively asserted in respect of a defined part of the globe ... External sovereignty, so called, is not mere recognition by other powers but is a reflection, a response to, the sovereignty exercised within the part of the globe. Looked at from the outside, the sovereignty ... is indivisible because foreign sovereigns are not concerned with the manner in which a sovereign state may under the laws of that sovereign state be required to exercise its powers or with the fact that the right to exercise those powers which constitute sovereignty may be divided vertically or horizontally in constitutional structure within the State. Therefore, although a sovereignty among nations may thus be indivisible, the internal sovereignty may be divided under the form of government which exists.[12]

The internal ordering of authority is not an international matter; rather, it is a matter for the courts, the legislature and the executive.[13] For the courts, then, 'the critical question ... is what reach the Sovereign claims for *itself*, not what reach other Sovereigns may concede to it'.[14] But the deference of the courts to the interests of the state creates a level of judicial impotence and a self-fulfilling jurisprudence if the 'reach' of the claims of the sovereign are not subject to checks and balances under the rule of law.[15]

In the *Mabo* decision, the High Court was prepared to check the claims of the sovereign to the lands of Indigenous peoples. Justice Brennan explained that there is a clear distinction between the Crown's title to a colony and the Crown's ownership of land in the colony. The Court reconfirmed in *Western Australia v Commonwealth* (1995) (*Native Title Act case*) that:

> Although an acquiring Sovereign can extinguish such rights and interests in the course of the act of State acquiring the territory, the presumption in the case of the Crown is that no extinguishment is intended. That

presumption is applicable by the municipal courts of this country in determining whether the acquisition of the several parts of Australia by the British Crown extinguished the antecedent title of the Aboriginal inhabitants.[16]

The legal device used to explain how the pre-existing title survived the assertion of sovereignty relied on a long history of case law from other colonial territories. The idea of a 'native title' that 'qualifies' or 'burdens' the radical title of the Crown emerged from the 1921 judgment of Viscount Haldane in *Amodu Tijani v Secretary, Southern Nigeria*:

> A very usual form of native title is that of a usufructuary right, which is a mere qualification of or burden on the radical or final title of the Sovereign where that exists. In such cases the title of the Sovereign is a pure legal estate, to which beneficial rights may or may not be attached.[17]

Having separated the Crown's acquisition of sovereignty over land from 'ownership' of it, Justice Brennan explained that:

> On acquisition of sovereignty over a particular part of Australia, the Crown acquired a radical title to the land in that part ... The rights and privileges conferred by native title were unaffected by the Crown's acquisition of radical title.[18]

Importantly, the Court held that an express act of recognition by the new sovereign was not necessary for recognition.[19]

The issue was raised again in *Yarmirr*; the emphasis on radical title in the reasoning in *Mabo* and the links with property law did not make for a straightforward inquiry into whether native title would be recognised offshore. The majority of the Court in its joint judgment explained its understanding of the nature of the inquiry:

> it is of the very first importance to bear steadily in mind that native title rights and interests are not created by and do not derive from the common law. The reference to radical title is, therefore, not a necessary pre-requisite to the conclusion that native title rights and interests *exist*.[20]

Radical title was explained as the relevant tool of legal analysis to determine the Crown's interest in land over which it asserted sovereignty in order to judge whether the Crown's interest could coexist with native title rights.[21] For the Court in *Yarmirr*, the anterior question to be considered was as follows: what was meant by the claim of sovereignty and, further, what rights and interests were asserted over the territory (whether land or sea)?[22]

From *Yarmirr* we can conclude that native title is a burden or qualification on the sovereignty of the Crown. It limits the extent to which the new sovereign can exercise authority over the territory — it limits the reach of the assertion of sovereignty. This is consistent with the discussion in *Mabo* with reference to acquisition of sovereignty by settlement of inhabited territories. The consequences of settlement are no different from those of conquered territories, at least with respect to the recognition of continuing rights to enjoy communal lands under traditional law and custom.

Native title, then, is a recognition by the new sovereign that the acquired territories were the territories of another sovereign, taken by force without consent, if not always by violence. A 'mere change in sovereignty' does not extinguish the rights and interests of those prior societies to enjoy their territories as communities according to their own laws and customs, at least until those rights are abrogated by force of law. So much we know from *Mabo*. The wresting of sovereignty from a people should not come without consequence. The seizing of territories 'parcel by parcel' should not be easy.[23] There is a legal, as well as a moral, burden on the sovereign to recognise and protect the rights of those over which it has asserted authority.

As is evident in the decision of the High Court in *Griffiths v Minister for Lands, Planning and Environment* (2008) (*Griffiths*), the seriousness with which the Court in *Mabo* considered the obligations of the acquiring sovereign appears to have been lost as the practice of native title and its curtailment becomes a more mundane business.[24] But it remains the courts that stand between the citizen and the Crown. The presumptions in favour of the recognition and protection of native title need to maintain their robustness.

NON-RECOGNITION

It was envisaged in *Mabo* that there may be circumstances in which the common law would not recognise the rights of the Indigenous inhabitants under their own laws. Justice McHugh in *Yarmirr* usefully summarised the findings of Justice Brennan in *Mabo*, in relation to circumstances in which the common law will recognise native title:

> In appropriate circumstances, as *Mabo [No. 2]* expressly held, the common law of Australia recognises and enforces by appropriate remedies rights and interests, possessed under traditional laws and customs, in respect of areas of land. In general terms, it will do so if:
> - at the date when the Crown acquired sovereignty over a particular territory, the indigenous inhabitants of the territory possessed those rights or interests in land in the territory 'under the traditional laws

acknowledged by and the traditional customs observed by the indigenous inhabitants';
- since the acquisition of sovereignty, the indigenous inhabitants and their descendants have continued to enjoy those rights and interests under their traditional laws and customs even if the laws and customs have undergone some change since sovereignty was acquired;
- the rights and interests have not been surrendered to or been extinguished by acts of the Crown or abandoned at any stage since sovereignty was acquired; and
- the rights and interests are not 'so repugnant to natural justice, equity and good conscience' or so inconsistent with 'a skeletal principle of our legal system' that the courts will refuse to enforce them. If these conditions are met, the common law will recognise and enforce the particular native title rights and interests claimed in respect of land in a given case.[25]

There is a presumption that the Court would recognise native title unless it was abhorrent to the common law to do so, or if to do so would 'fracture the skeleton of legal principle which gives the body of our law its shape and internal consistency'.[26] In relation to the former, this is generally understood to refer to particular rights or laws and customs rather than the system as a whole.[27] The latter, if *Mabo* is read more closely, was a threshold question as to whether the Court would recognise any surviving rights at all, if to do so after two hundred years of settlement required a rejection of legal authority and revision of legal principles that would create an insoluble dilemma for the law. In *Mabo* the skeletal principle that Justice Brennan was most concerned to leave intact was the land tenure system that underpinned Australian land law.[28] It may be, as the High Court said in *Yarmirr*, pointless to try to determine what is and is not part of the skeleton of legal principle.[29] But, as discussed in Chapter 5, the Court tried to frame the bases for withholding recognition in terms similar to the test for withdrawing recognition of rights and interests once recognised (extinguishment), and did so on far too broad terms. The Court misread the reasoning in *Mabo* by suggesting that the basis for withholding recognition was simply one of inconsistency. The majority referred to the judgment of Justices Deane and Gaudron in *Mabo* to conclude that:

> the question about continued recognition of native title rights requires consideration of whether and how the common law and the relevant native title rights and interests could co-exist. If the two are inconsistent, it was accepted in *Mabo [No. 2]* that the common law would prevail. (The central issue for debate in *Mabo [No. 2]* was whether there was an inconsistency.) If, as was held in *Mabo [No. 2]* in relation to rights of

the kind then in issue, there is no inconsistency, the common law will 'recognise' those rights.[30]

The justification for this approach was somewhat confused by what was said in the joint judgment in the *Native Title Act case:*

> At common law, a mere change in sovereignty over a territory does not extinguish pre-existing rights and interests in land in that territory. Although an acquiring Sovereign can extinguish such rights and interests in the course of the act of State acquiring the territory, the presumption in the case of the Crown is that no extinguishment is intended.[31]

The idea that the sovereign could extinguish rights in the course of acquiring the territory was not explained, although normal rules of extinguishment presumably were in mind; that is, a manifestly clear and plain intention to extinguish rights or interests that otherwise burden the sovereignty of the Crown and are recognised and protected by the common law.

As noted in Chapter 5, the Court concluded in *Yarmirr* that the recognition of native title offshore was a qualified recognition:

> there was no *necessary* inconsistency between the rights and interests asserted by Imperial authorities and the continued recognition of native title rights and interests. The qualification is required because the rights and interests asserted at sovereignty carried with them the recognition of public rights of navigation and fishing and, perhaps, the concession of an international right of innocent passage. Those rights were necessarily inconsistent with the continued existence of any right under Aboriginal law or custom to preclude the exercise of those rights.[32]

It was held that it was insufficient to simply reconcile the two assertions by suggesting that the exercise of native title is subject to the other public and international rights, despite the common understanding that native title is subject to laws of general application and can be regulated.[33] This was borne out by the decision of the High Court in *Northern Territory of Australia v Arnhem Land Aboriginal Land Trust* (2008) (*Blue Mud Bay*).[34] There, the High Court held that the title granted under the *Aboriginal Land Rights (Northern Territory) Act 1976* (Cth) confers exclusive possession over tidal waters. This decision confirmed that waterways are susceptible to ownership and that the common law rights to fish and navigate are susceptible to regulation or derogation and are not a skeletal part of our system of law.

The High Court in *Yarmirr* seemed to provide two alternative rationales for its approach. One is perhaps defensible and consistent with the seriousness of the consequences of wresting sovereignty; the other is not. First, it could be read from the majority joint judgment that the assertion of sovereignty of the Crown over the territorial waters was inherently limited because the public and international rights referred to come from a source outside the control of the sovereign legal system, therefore constraining the ability of the Crown to recognise native title to the full extent. The judges argued, for example, that the '[a]ssertion of sovereignty, on *those* terms, is not consistent with the continuation of a right in the holders of a native title to the area for those holders to say who may enter the area'.[35] On the other hand, they posed the test of inconsistency on the same terms as the extinguishment doctrine:

> Although the inconsistency does not arise as a result of the exercise of sovereign power (as is the case where a grant in fee simple extinguishes native title) the inconsistency which exists in this case between the asserted native title rights and the assertion of sovereignty is of no different quality. At its root, the inconsistency lies not just in the competing claims to control who may enter the area but in the expression of that control by the sovereign authority in a way that is antithetical to the continued existence of the asserted exclusive rights.[36]

On this latter understanding the formulation of the grounds upon which recognition will be withheld in *Yarmirr* goes much further than the judgment in *Mabo*. The idea of a skeletal principle implies that it would be impossible for the law to change and adjust to the new circumstances. In *Yarmirr* it does not have to. The common law principle, that only so much of the law should be imported as necessary and appropriate, is undermined by this approach. It disguises the denial of protection under the veil of 'recognition'. In any event, the result is the same. The Court has claimed greater power for the Crown and greater privilege for non-Indigenous interests.

THE JUXTAPOSITION OF RECOGNITION AND DENIAL

In 1996 Noel Pearson sought to explain the concept of recognition:

> The High Court tell us in *Mabo* that native title is not a common law title but it is instead a title recognised by the common law. What they fail to tell us, and something which we have failed to appreciate, is that neither is native title an Aboriginal law title. Because patently Aboriginal law will recognise title where the common law will not. Native title is therefore the space between the two systems, where there is recognition. Native title is, for want of a better formulation the recognition space between the common law and Aboriginal law which [is] now afforded recognition in particular circumstances.[37]

In a similar vein, explaining the formulation of Justice Brennan in *Mabo*, the joint majority judgment in *Fejo v Northern Territory* (1998) (*Fejo*) said that '[t]here is, therefore, an intersection of traditional laws and customs with the common law'.[38] But the capacity of the courts to accept an intersection with a parallel normative system has proved limited. In *Members of the Yorta Yorta Aboriginal Community v Victoria* (2002) (*Yorta Yorta*), the High Court attempted to resolve the meaning of this 'intersection', as discussed in Chapter 7, by interrogating exactly what it is that intersects with the common law.[39]

The conceptual difficulty presented by the jurisprudence of the *Yorta Yorta* case is the High Court's treatment of the consequences of the acquisition of sovereignty on the Indigenous normative system. The idea of native title as an intersection of two normative systems, which 'requires the two systems to operate together',[40] is jettisoned in an effort to preserve the internal ordering of authority. The Court identified the central importance of understanding the 'consequences of sovereignty', stating that:

> Upon the Crown acquiring sovereignty, the normative or lawmaking system which then existed could not thereafter validly create new rights, duties or interests. Rights or interests in land created after sovereignty and which owed their origin and continued existence *only* to a normative system other than that of the new sovereign power, would not and will not be given effect by the legal order of the new sovereign.[41]

This is a clear statement of 'what the sovereign claims for itself'.

The Court concluded that the intersection is, indeed, an intersection between two systems of law. However, the purpose of the recognition of native title is limited to rights and interests in land. The joint majority explained that the 'relevant intersection' for the purposes of native title concerns 'rights and interests in land', thus:

> What survived were rights and interests in relation to land or waters. Those rights and interests owed their origin to a normative system other than the legal system of the new sovereign power; they owed their origin to the traditional laws acknowledged and the traditional customs observed by the indigenous peoples concerned.[42]

Through this conceptualisation, the High Court limits 'recognition' to rights and interests in land. Immediately the inquiry into the existence of native title begins, the theory becomes unsustainable. In order to give meaning to recognition, the High Court in *Yorta Yorta* explained that '[t]he rights and interests in land which the new sovereign order recognised included the rules of traditional law and custom which dealt with the transmission of those interests'.[43] In addition, account can be taken of the alteration and development, even significant adaptations, of traditional law and custom after sovereignty, so long as the burden on the Crown's title is not increased.[44] As a result the jurisprudence of native title is forced to admit that native title is not a recognition of rights and interest that existed at sovereignty as the 'consequences of sovereignty' argument suggests, but recognition of current rights and interests that have their source in a normative system that existed at the point of colonisation.⁴⁵

The fundamental disjunction identified in Chapter 7 is, of course, that — while denying the authority of any parallel law-making system — the High Court required proof of a 'system that has had a continuous existence and vitality since sovereignty'.⁴⁶ Issues of transmission, change and adaptation are central to the inquiry into the existence of native title in Australia. The belated recognition of native title in Australia and the requirement that Indigenous peoples now prove that a normative system exists, in order to prove that native title burdened the Crown's acquisition of sovereignty, reveal the flaw in the jurisprudence. The idea that 'the assertion of sovereignty by the British Crown *necessarily* entailed ... that there could thereafter be no parallel law-making system in the territory'⁴⁷ is simply false. Had the legal consequences of settlement really given equal protection to the inhabitants of a territory regardless of the mode of acquisition at international law, then the approach of the South African Constitutional Court would be apt, with or without constitutional recognition.

WHAT IS RECOGNISED: THE NATURE AND EXTENT OF THE TITLE

The High Court in *Western Australia v Ward* (2002) (*Ward*) specifically rejected the approach, perhaps best expressed by Pearson,⁴⁸ that native title is best described as a possessory title and should be based on proof of occupation.⁴⁹ The Court held to the vision of Justice Brennan in *Mabo* that native title 'has its origin in and is given its content by the traditional customs observed by the indigenous inhabitants of a territory'.⁵⁰ The preamble to the NTA reflects this view, stating that 'the common law of Australia recognises a form of native title that reflects the entitlement of the indigenous inhabitants of Australia, in accordance with their laws and customs, to their traditional lands'. The definition under s 223(1), which the courts say now guides the determination of native title, incorporates this idea.

Despite the courts' insistence, it is false to say that native title is not a creature of the common law. It is a common law doctrine that is centuries old. It emerges from the common law rules for the acquisition of territories articulated by Blackstone and dating back to *Calvin's case* in 1608.⁵¹ The rights and the interests that it seeks to protect, it may be correctly said, arise from the Indigenous peoples' parallel systems of law; it may also be correct to say that those rights and interests burden the Crown's claim to sovereignty. But the Court's comments in relation to terms on which recognition will be given, and in particular how protection will be provided, clearly illustrate that this is very much a non-Indigenous legal construct. It is the courts and the legislature that have invested the doctrine of native title with the vulnerability and contradictions that limit its capacity to protect the interests of Indigenous peoples.

A number of High Court judges have held to the idea that finding the source of native title in the laws and customs of Indigenous peoples means that there is a continuum or spectrum of native title rights that defines the extent and content of the title in the particular circumstances of each group, depending on the scope of their traditional laws and customs.[52] For example, Justice Gummow in *Wik* reiterated that:

> The content of native title, its nature and incidents, will vary from one case to another. It may comprise what are classified as personal or communal usufructuary rights involving access to the area of land in question to hunt for or gather food, or to perform traditional ceremonies ... At the opposite extreme, the degree of attachment to the land may be such as to approximate that which would flow from a legal or equitable estate therein.[53]

This is the accepted jurisprudence despite the evidence that, but for extinguishment, native title has generally been found to be equivalent to full ownership and recognised where possible as exclusive possession native title. Attention was paid in Chapter 6 to the treatment of native title as an interest in land, or a proprietary right, in contrast to the 'bundle of rights' approach to defining native title. As argued there, to describe native title as a bundle of rights, even after *Ward*, does not necessarily deny it having a proprietary character, most obviously in relation to exclusive possession native title.

There is a danger here, not in the bundle of rights construction in itself, but in the way the courts have combined it with traditional law and custom to articulate what rights and activities are expected to be carried out on native title land. The approach denies a level of abstraction that we readily accept in other common law tenures. Chief Justice Brennan (dissenting), in *Wik*, illustrated this bias most dramatically. In rejecting the suspension of native title rights, he argued that this equated native title with an estate in fee simple, which it is not.[54] At the same time, his Honour complained that the approach of the majority in that case treated pastoral leases as a mere statutory bundle of rights, denying it the character of a legal estate and therefore exclusive possession.[55] The privileging of interests that derive from common law tenures and estates is a nonsense in Australia, where property law has diverged so radically from these roots.[56]

Despite some academic angst, the courts seem satisfied with the uncertainty surrounding the character of native title. The majority joint judgment of the High Court in *Yarmirr* concluded that:

12. 'Recognition' and 'protection'

Even if difficulties about the meaning of the word 'property' were resolved, it would be wrong to start consideration of a claim under the Act for determination of native title from an a priori assumption that the only rights and interests with which the Act is concerned are rights and interests of a kind which the common law would traditionally classify as rights of property or interests in property. That is not to say, however, that native title rights and interests may not have such characteristics. The question is where to begin the inquiry. The relevant starting point is the question of fact posed by the Act: what are the rights and interests in relation to land or waters which are possessed under the traditional laws acknowledged and the traditional customs observed by the relevant peoples?[57]

To use an analogy or comparison with common law tenures (or even the sovereign rights over property analysed in *Yanner v Eaton* (1999) (*Yanner*)[58]) in order to gauge the protection of native title should still be useful, provided, as identified by Justice Merkel in the full Federal Court decision in *Yarmirr*, it does not deflect the Court from the task it has set for itself of defining native title by reference to traditional laws and customs rather than the common law.[59] But a central premise remains that native title should be treated equally to other interests, at least since the introduction of the *Racial Discrimination Act 1975* (Cth) (RDA).

The problem with the uncertainty surrounding the 'extent' of native title is that, while the courts have been at pains to stress that analogies with common law concepts should be avoided, they have demonstrated that their alternative has done greater violence.[60] As discussed in Chapter 3, the *sui generis* nature of native title — the idea that its source is not in the Crown — has given the courts an excuse on which to hang their discriminatory treatment of native title.

In Chapter 10 we saw the Federal Court in *Bodney v Bennell* (2008) (*Bennell*) attempt to place greater emphasis on the statutory 'contrivance' of the inquiry, towards a greater emphasis on rights and interests over proprietary title. I agree with Noel Pearson, and with the approach taken by the applicants in *Neowarra v Western Australia* (2003) (*Neowarra*),[61] that the correct understanding of native title is as the right of 'ownership'.[62] At the assumption of sovereignty the Crown was unable to take absolute beneficial title because the land was not 'ownerless': there was someone with a better, pre-existing title that, though subject to defeasance, survived the acquisition of sovereignty. At that moment, as Justice Brennan observed in *Mabo*, the Indigenous peoples were in exclusive possession, communally, against the world. In this instance, as discussed in Chapter 1, 'If it be necessary to categorize an interest in land as proprietary in order to survive a change in sovereignty, the interest possessed by a community that is in exclusive possession of land falls into that category'.[63] Indeed, as Kent McNeil has noted, otherwise '"title" would be a misnomer'.[64]

For Pearson, native title recognises the occupation by Indigenous peoples of land at the time that sovereignty was acquired and seeks to protect their right to continued occupation — this is implicit in the relationship between native title and Crown title.[65] Native title, Pearson claims, is therefore a communal title to exclusive possession, the content of which is a right to possession.[66] Native title, he continues, is a uniform concept from the outside, the exercise of rights and interests in accordance with the traditional laws and customs being a separate, internal dimension.[67] The variability in native title is a result of extinguishment and derogation, not because the titles were originally diverse.[68]

The judgment of Justice Sundberg in *Neowarra* reflected this approach when stating that, in the absence of extinguishing acts, the right to speak for country, the highest abstraction of the native title holder's claim over their territory, would sustain a right to exclusive possession native title.[69] The claimed right was underpinned by the evidence of the system of laws and customs under which the claimants lived and by which they determined rights and interest in land among themselves.

Of course, this argument admits a role for traditional law in determining the internal ordering of affairs within the Indigenous group. Justice Brennan in *Mabo* acknowledged that:

> The incidents of a particular native title relating to inheritance, the transmission or acquisition of rights and interests on death or marriage, the transfer of rights and interests in land and the grouping of persons to possess rights and interests in land are matters to be determined by the laws and customs of the indigenous inhabitants.[70]

This was a central element of the decision in *De Rose v South Australia [No. 1]* (2003) (*De Rose [No. 1]*).[71] It is not the role of the courts to determine the conferring and transmission of rights and interests under native title.[72] The full Federal Court in *Bennell*, however, suggested that if the internal ordering of rights and interests is contested, then the court should involve itself to some degree in specifying the allocation of rights and interests among the claim group.[73] In cases such as *Rubibi Community v Western Australia [No. 5]* [2005] (*Rubibi*) and, more recently, the Ngarluma and Yindjibarndi appeal in *Moses v State of Western Australia* (2007), the courts have been asked to determine whether a smaller group is part of a larger native title holding group or holds native title in its own right at a more local level.[74] The courts have generally preferred the 'fundamental principle' that native title will ordinarily be communal in character,[75] although this is a conclusion to be drawn from the evidence.[76] The extent to which the courts can and should intervene to determine the internal ordering of rights and interests is an issue of serious concern. The need to resolve the dispute before the court, particularly in determining the existence of native title, must be carefully weighed against the risks of non-Indigenous courts carrying out the functions of the traditional Indigenous laws and decision makers.

Importantly, there is also a role for law and custom in proving connection, and the right to possession, when actual possession has been interfered with.[77] Again, we see an example in *De Rose v South Australia [No. 2]* (2005) (*De Rose [No. 2]*) of the Federal Court's acceptance of the impacts of colonisation on Indigenous peoples' ability to exercise rights that they continue to acknowledge and assert.[78]

SUSTAINING RECOGNITION: THE MAINTENANCE OF CONNECTION

The greatest risk in a jurisprudence that relies on Indigenous law and custom as the source of title lies in the need to manage and overcome the perceptions and biases of the courts as to what a 'normative society' might or should look like and how the Indigenous people before them have inherited their communal right to ownership since the acquisition of sovereignty. The development of the jurisprudence of recognition as the intersection of two normative systems was precipitated by one judge's conclusion that a native title claim group was so far removed from its pre-sovereignty customs and culture that he refused to recognise the group as a 'traditional Aboriginal society'. Justice Olney in *Yorta Yorta* concluded, as we have seen, that the people who once held native title had lost their title by abandoning the normative rules that bound them as a society. A society might exist, but the change in their normative system had been so profound as to be fatal to their claim. The majority joint judgment of the High Court in *Yorta Yorta* concluded that:

> it must be shown that the society, under whose laws and customs the native title rights and interests are said to be possessed, has continued to exist throughout that period as a body united by its acknowledgment and observance of the laws and customs.[79]

The idea that adaptation could be so profound as to result in a society no longer existing seems to be an aspect of the *Yorta Yorta* decision that is distinguished more often than it is applied.[80]

In the Wotjobaluk determination in Victoria, although determined by consent, Justice Merkel made observations about the notion of continuity and change in settled areas, concluding that:

> The outcome of the present claim is testimony to the fact that the 'tide of history' has not 'washed away' any real acknowledgement of traditional laws and any real observance of traditional customs by the applicants and has not, as a consequence, resulted in the foundation of their native title disappearing. Indeed, the evidence in, and the outcome of, the present case is a living example of the principle that is now recognised in native

title jurisprudence that *traditional* laws and customs are not fixed and unchanging. Rather, they evolve over time in response to new or changing social and economic exigencies to which all societies adapt as their social and historical contexts change.[81]

A number of judges have highlighted the severity of the loss of connection that would have to be demonstrated to meet the High Court's test in *Yorta Yorta*. The applicants are required to establish that connection with the land has been substantially maintained through the acknowledgment and observance, only so far as is practicable, of traditional laws and customs.

The 'practicability' of exercising rights or observing customs is acknowledged as a reality of assessing the facts in each case. In the full Federal Court decision in *Western Australia v Ward* (2000), Justices Beaumont and von Doussa applied this criterion to determine whether substantial maintenance of connection had been demonstrated:

> With the arrival of European settlement, the ways in which the indigenous people were able to possess, occupy, use and enjoy their rights and interests in the land underwent major change ... The evidence paints a clear picture of it being impracticable after European settlement for members of the indigenous population to maintain a traditional presence on substantial parts of the determination area. However, it does not follow that the surviving members of the indigenous population have not substantially maintained their connection with the land.[82]

The decisions of the full Federal Court in *Risk v Northern Territory* (2007) *(Risk)* and *Bennell* stand in contrast to the approach of the Court in other cases. In *Bennell* the full Federal Court was critical of the trial judge for taking the question of 'practicability' too far, taking into account the impacts of colonisation and settlement in determining what were 'understandable' changes in traditional laws and customs relating to land.[83] The full Court said that the cause of the change was irrelevant — what was important was whether the change is 'unacceptable'.[84] The absolution of the coloniser for acts that impact on Indigenous peoples' capacity to prove native title has led one judge to propose that changes to law and custom caused by, or in response to, colonial acts (including, for example, forced removal to reserves or the removal of children) should be disregarded in order to overcome the fundamental injustice of native title that sees those most affected by colonisation least able to seek redress.[85]

In addition, the courts have moved away from the particularity that burdened Justice Olney's inquiry. In *De Rose*, among the arguments against connection having been maintained, the suggestion had been put that the laws and customs that were currently acknowledged and observed were unconnected to land. The full Federal Court rejected this argument, commenting that, given the 'centrality of the relationship' between Indigenous people and their country, 'any dichotomy between traditional laws and customs connected with rights and interests possessed in land and waters and those that are unconnected with such rights and interests may be difficult to establish'.[86] In *Neowarra* Justice Sundberg noted that, although he would examine the laws and customs individually to determine the rights and interests that may be protected by native title, the system had to be examined as a whole in order to obtain an accurate picture.[87] The full Federal Court in *Bennell* was wary of replacing the inquiry into whether the society continues to exist as a social system, as it is the laws and customs, not the society, that gives rise to rights.[88]

In *Gumana v Northern Territory* (2005) (*Gumana*) Justice Selway observed what is now well established, that the 'connection' with the land and waters referred to in s 223(1)(b) may be a spiritual, cultural or social connection.[89] *Rubibi*, too, was interesting in this regard, as the judge was not concerned with the content of native title or the extent of extinguishment, leaving those issues for further mediation between the parties. Instead, Justice Merkel was concerned only with determining whether native title had been proved under s 223.[90] He reiterated the comments from *De Rose* and *Gumana* to conclude that:

> there is no simple dichotomy between traditional laws and customs that are connected with land and waters and those that are not. Nonetheless, it is clear from the above findings that, by almost all of the laws and customs acknowledged and observed by the members of the Yawuru community, the members of that community have the requisite spiritual, cultural and social connection to land and waters in the Yawuru claim area.[91]

In *Gumana* the Court recognised the practicalities of proof in native title by adopting an inference of continuity of laws and customs back to the time that sovereignty was asserted based on the oral testimony of the witnesses.[92] But this inference was rejected by the full Federal Court in *Bennell* in favour of a strict requirement that connection be established 'generation by generation' from the acquisition of sovereignty to the present.[93] This restrictive requirement again prompted others within the judiciary to call for legislative intervention. To this end, the High Court Chief Justice Robert French has proposed a presumption of continuity that would effectively reverse the onus of proof in native title cases.[94]

THE 'RECOGNITION LEVEL': WHO HOLDS NATIVE TITLE?

An analysis of the application of the native title doctrine by the Federal Court in *De Rose [No. 2]* and *Bennell* raises the question of who is recognised as holding native title. This issue centres on the nature of the group that holds native title and the group's relationship to the normative society from which native title rights are said to derive. The notion in the *Mabo* decision that native title might be held by 'a community group or individual' was incorporated into the language of s 223 and the requirements for a determination in s 225.[95] In *De Rose [No. 2]* the full Federal Court held that:

> communal native title presupposes that the claim is made on behalf of a recognisable community of people, whose traditional laws and customs constitute the normative system under which rights and interests are created and acknowledged. That is, the traditional laws and customs are those of the very community which claims native title rights and interests. By contrast, group and individual native title rights and interests derive from a body of traditional laws and customs observed by a community, but are not necessarily claimed on behalf of the whole community. Indeed, they may not be claimed on behalf of any recognisable community at all, but on behalf of individuals who themselves have never constituted a cohesive, functioning community.[96]

As was particularly pertinent in *De Rose [No. 2]*, the groups that claim native title as a native title holding group have varied considerably. Not all have been discrete claims on behalf of the whole society. In most cases this has not unduly confused the inquiry into the recognition of native title. In *Neowarra* Justice Sundberg referred to this as determining the 'recognition level'.[97] The judge was not concerned with the idea that the 'Wanjina-Wunggurr' community might have been an anthropological construct or of recent origin as a descriptive label, and accepted that it need not even be a term used by the claimants themselves.[98] While the claimants identified as Ngarinyin, Wororra and Wunambul, and by their Dambun (clan) relationships, they also clearly articulated the extent of the society with which they shared a system of law and custom, particularly in relation to land, and that was the extent of the Wanjina-Wunggurr community.[99]

Despite repeated objections from respondent parties, various kinds of groups have been accepted in determinations under the NTA. Justice Sundberg suggested that the reasoning of the High Court and lower courts in *Ward* was directly comparable, in which the Miriuwung Gajerrong community had been accepted as the appropriate native title holding group.[100] In *Hayes v Northern Territory* (1999), in the determination over Alice Springs, three estate groups had been recognised as holding title;[101] in *Commonwealth v Yarmirr* (2001) (*Yarmirr*) five clans had claimed a communal title over Croker Islands sea country;[102] similarly, in *Lardil, Kaidilt, Yangkaal and Gangalidda People v Queensland* [2000], a composite of groups had been recognised as sharing laws and customs that defined them as a group for the purposes of native title over the Wellesley Island sea country.[103]

Justice Sundberg described this inquiry as the question of the 'native title recognition level' when determining whether rights are held as 'communal, group or individual' rights and interests under s 223(1) of the NTA. The judge determined that it was appropriate for the community to claim communal rights to the area, within which certain groups and individuals hold various rights and interests as determined by the laws and customs that define the broader Wanjina-Wunggurr community. Moreover, he suggested that a determination at any lower level would not fully reflect the basis upon which rights and interests are conferred or transmitted.[104]

In *Ward* the Miriuwung and Gajerrong societies were found to hold native title together. Prior to contact the Miriuwung and Gajerrong were found to be distinct 'organised societies', although they shared particular dreamings and cooperated in trade and religious activities.[105] But it was accepted that the two groups had developed a closer association post-contact, and in recent times, through marriage and population movement, the communities had come to be regarded as a composite community with shared interests and shared laws and customs.

In *Sampi v Western Australia* [2005] (*Sampi*),[106] Justice French warned against the application of concepts of 'societies' (from various social or scientific schools of thought) that are not required by the NTA and may restrict the beneficial application of the NTA.[107] But in *Sampi* Justice French distinguished *Ward*, arguing that, having been determined before the decision of the High Court in *Yorta Yorta*, the decision did not give due consideration to the need to establish the normative society.[108] In contrast, the judges in *Neowarra* and *De Rose [No. 2]* (cases that were also determined after *Yorta Yorta*) affirmed the reasoning in *Ward* in defining the 'recognition level' of a native title holding group.

In the final result in *Sampi*, Justice French found that the current construction of the Bardi-Jawi society was not a composite community; instead, despite the contrary understanding of the Indigenous witnesses, the Bardi society had subsumed the Jawi members (but not their territory) and the Jawi society had not survived. This decision should be contrasted with the decision in the *Rubibi* appeal in *State of Western Australia v Sebastian* (2008)[109] in relation to a neighbouring claim. There, although distinct in some ways, the smaller groups were considered part of the larger group, both in determining the relevant normative society and the appropriate native title holding group. Alternatively, succession of the larger group was accepted by the Court and native title was found to exist over the entire territory.

Respondents have repeatedly pressed the argument that native title should be determined at the narrower level of estate groups. While in some instances this has been the approach taken by the native title applicants,[110] this view has generally been rejected by the courts in favour of a larger normative system. In *Sampi* Justice French stated that the rejection of the state's contention affirms the 'unitary' character of the laws and customs that give rise to the native title rights and interests. Justice French stated that 'the communal nature of native title ... is not to be lost sight of by an undue concentration on the fractal detail of inter-societal allocations of rights and interests or the modes of their enjoyment'.[111] In *De Rose [No. 2]* the full Federal Court characterised estate group claims and the claim in *De Rose* as 'group' claims, which are recognisable under s 223(1) only if the traditional laws and customs allow rights and interests to be claimed in that way.[112] This is not to say that the traditional laws and customs label the rights and interests in this way. The Court in *De Rose [No. 2]* recognised this as a 'statutory construct' derived from the language in *Mabo*.[113] But if a clear distinction was necessary, the Court suggested that 'communal' native title presupposes that the claim is made on behalf of a recognisable community of people (or peoples) who constitute the normative society. By contrast, a group or individual native title claim asserts interests that are derived from a body of laws and customs but are not necessarily claimed on behalf of the whole community.[114] This is perhaps best illustrated by the claims in the Western Desert that draw from the broad cultural bloc. The reasoning in *De Rose [No. 2]* was reaffirmed in *Northern Territory v Alyawarr, Kaytetye, Warumungu, Wakay Native Title Claim Group* (2005) (*Alyawarr*) and, as discussed in Chapter 10, was accepted by the full Federal Court in *Bennell*, although somewhat begrudgingly.

The corollary is that claimants should not need to show that every individual or every estate group has maintained connection to the claim area or observes and acknowledges laws and customs.[115] That is a matter to be considered by the group. *Bennell* has confused the jurisprudence to some extent, with the full Court's emphasis on establishing connection to particular areas where contested.[116] But the consistent view of the courts is that 'All depends on the body of normative rules of the relevant society which gives rise to rights and interests in land and waters'.[117] As with the distribution of rights and interests among the group, the courts should not place themselves as arbiters of Indigenous law and custom in defining the group. Significant weight needs to be given to the view of elders, the claimants and Indigenous witnesses as to the construction of both the normative society and the appropriate recognition level for the native title group.[118]

THE LIMITS OF PROTECTION: EXTINGUISHMENT OF NATIVE TITLE

Recognition of the survival of the rights of Indigenous peoples to their land, however compromised, is meaningless unless that recognition is given effect. The High Court in *Yarmirr* explained the relationship between recognition and enforceability, saying that the common law:

will, by the ordinary processes of law and equity, give remedies in support of the relevant rights and interests to those who hold them. It will 'recognise' the rights by giving effect to those rights and interests owing their origin to traditional laws and customs which can continue to co-exist with the common law the settlers brought.[119]

Indeed, Chief Justice Brennan in *Wik* had said that the one strength that native title had was the protection it received from the law:

> The strength of native title is that it is enforceable by the ordinary courts. Its weakness is that it is not an estate held from the Crown nor is it protected by the common law as Crown tenures are protected against impairment by subsequent Crown grant.[120]

The weakness to which Chief Justice Brennan referred defines the place of native title in Australian law. The recognition of native title in *Mabo* was said to be grounded in non-discrimination and equality before the law. The High Court held that the laws of Australia would no longer tolerate discriminatory treatment of Indigenous rights to land and rejected any interpretation of the consequences of settlement that arbitrarily refused to recognise the pre-existing rights of Indigenous peoples over their lands upon the acquisition of sovereignty.[121] The rights and interests recognised by native title were made enforceable against the world. The majority also argued that the introduction of the RDA in 1975 provided protection against the arbitrary abrogation or appropriation of native title rights and guaranteed the same protections that are afforded to non-Indigenous interest holders against the arbitrary deprivation of rights by the state.[122] But wedged between these two statements is a plainly discriminatory treatment of Indigenous peoples' rights in relation to extinguishment.[123] The Court held, as we have seen, that — up until the passing of the RDA — the Crown, whether in right of the states or the Commonwealth, had virtually unfettered power to abrogate the rights of Indigenous peoples in favour of the non-Indigenous population or for its own purpose.[124]

To achieve this, the legal maxim that the Crown cannot derogate from a grant once made, rather than providing protection to native title holders, was used to underscore the doctrine of extinguishment. Because native title is held to have its source in another legal system, it is said not to enjoy the protection of this rule. Instead, the rule protects grants made in conflict with native title land. Kent McNeil has questioned the Court's interpretation of this rule, arguing that it is part of a broader rule and 'that the Crown in its executive capacity cannot derogate from or interfere with the vested rights of its subjects'.[125] Taken at this more general level, it is immaterial whether those rights are granted by the Crown or emerge from another source.

In *Fejo* the capacity of the common law to withdraw recognition was well illustrated. The case revealed the disjunction between the fact of Indigenous peoples holding interests in the land and the circumstances in which those interests would be protected. The majority joint judgment argued that 'The underlying existence of the traditional laws and customs is a *necessary* pre-requisite for native title but their existence is not a *sufficient* basis for recognising native title'.[126] Extinguishment, then, occurs wholly within the non-Indigenous law, whether in the common law doctrine or by the NTA. It is best understood as a withdrawal of recognition and protection, and the courts and the legislature determine the circumstances under which protection will be withdrawn. This understanding of extinguishment has been accepted by the courts; for example, by Justice Olney, in the Alice Springs determination, who explained that:

> In the event that the claimant group establishes the existence of traditional rights and interests in relation to the claimed land, it will then be necessary to consider the extent, if any, to which those rights and interests are recognised by the common law.[127]

In *Wik* the inquiry into extinguishment was based on a test of necessary inconsistency. By this test, once the rights that made up native title had been established, any existing grant extinguished native title only to the extent of any inconsistency. Where there was any inconsistency, the High Court preferred the leaseholder's rights to prevail and the native title rights to yield to that extent.[128] But, in undertaking the inquiry into inconsistency, the Court held to strict rules of statutory construction to determine the clear and plain intent of the legislation.

The decision of the High Court in *Griffiths*, discussed in Chapter 8, confirmed that the presumptions in favour of the continued recognition and protection of Indigenous rights have not survived the development of the law since *Ward*. In *Ward* we witnessed the preference for partial extinguishment over curtailment and impairment, rejection of suspension and revival in favour of permanent extinguishment, and the profound readiness to find extinguishment of exclusivity, equating that with the absence of any decision-making role in relation to land. While the Court may trace the choices back to the language of the NTA, the effect of legislation is largely determined by the interpretation of the courts as to what constitutes extinguishment; that is, while the NTA may deem extinguishment to be permanent, it is the courts that determine if a particular act is 'inconsistent'.

The focus now, as was so well illustrated in *Neowarra*, in the current approach to determining the extinguishment of rights and interests confuses the inquiry into proof (and the details of the laws and customs of the group) with the extinguishment of rights and interests that are inconsistent with competing grants and interests. There, Justice Sundberg had concluded that, in the absence of any extinguishment or other interests, native title was a comprehensive right that was sufficiently described as 'possession, occupation use and enjoyment, as against the world', but, as there were other interests, this comprehensive right had to be 'unbundled'.[129]

Part of the High Court's concern in *Ward* with the approach of Justice Lee and Justice North was the assumption that to adopt the idea of an interest in land or exclusive possession model is an all-or-nothing affair — that somehow, in doing so, the Court would reduce the instances in which native title could survive inconsistent grants. Arguably, the Court's current doctrine does much more violence in that regard than the approach proposed by the applicants. The concept of partial extinguishment under the NTA does not necessitate the kind of inquiry that the High Court articulated in *Ward*. Instead, the 'exclusive possession minus' methodology is the sensible approach (consistent with the NTA) that sits comfortably with traditional common law tenure and estate concepts while reinvigorating the presumption of non-extinguishment. On that approach, exclusive possession native title is reduced only by the extent of the interests granted or appropriated by the Crown. The Court has to assess the rights and interests conferred by the non-Indigenous interest and the native title is extinguished only to the extent necessary to give effect to the right.[130]

The unique character of native title as an intersection of two normative systems and, more importantly, as a recognition and protection of the rights of Indigenous peoples should not result in the unquestioning assertion of dominance of one legal system over the other based purely on the excuse that 'it can'. As the doctrine of extinguishment has been constructed and applied, it unnecessarily perpetuates precisely the discrimination that the recognition of native title should seek to eliminate. The common law foundations in *Mabo* provided a model and an excuse for the legislature to protect only so much of the rights and interests of Indigenous peoples as was necessary and convenient. The uniqueness of native title has been relied upon to attribute weakness to the title. The idea that native title is inherently vulnerable and fragile is inextricably linked to its susceptibility to extinguishment. The emphasis by the courts on the interpretation of the NTA shields the discriminatory foundations of the doctrine of native title. The continued uncoupling of 'statutory native title' from its common law source raises questions as to what 'common law native title' might look like.[131]

The decision of the High Court in *Mabo* that the unilateral extinguishment of native title under common law was neither wrongful nor compensable, nor subject to the Constitutional guarantee of just terms for the appropriation of property, was a profoundly discriminatory judicial act. But in recognising that protection was afforded by the RDA, the Court ensured that compensation remains a sleeping giant. The NTA ensures that any acts that may have been invalidated by the operation of the RDA are converted into compensation claims under the NTA. As the principles for calculating compensation await a determination by the courts, the large number of commercial agreements for the authorisation of future acts is beginning to create an economic environment from which the value of native title, and its loss, can begin to be quantified.

The doctrine of extinguishment should not serve to deprive Indigenous people of native title unnecessarily. Justice North in his dissent in *Ward* warned that the origin of the notions of extinguishment upon which the courts rely should be kept in mind. In particular, the policy setting in which the early common law of native title was developed was concerned with achieving a compromise that allowed the expansion of the Crown's dominion. We do, or should, operate in a different social setting, in which greater respect is afforded to the interests of native title holders.[132] Since the validation of past grants in the NTA and the *Native Title Amendment Act 1998* (Cth), the need to prioritise the interests of non-native title holders should no longer take primacy as a public policy objective of the courts in interpreting native title. There is a need to contain the discriminatory aspects of the common law and to prioritise the principles of non-discrimination in order to return some balance to the judicial compromise of extinguishment.

CONCLUSION

The declaratory power of the common law allowed the High Court to reach back in time to determine the implications of the acquisition of sovereignty, the legal outcome of which is within the purview of the common law to decide. This created unique and difficult problems with which the colonial legal system and the traditions of common law are ill equipped to deal.[133] Nevertheless, the task of revisiting the terms upon which sovereignty was acquired has begun. Justice Kirby in *Yarmirr* noted that, as a result, 'for nearly a decade, the Australian legal system has been adjusting to new legal principles'.[134]

In 2001, before the pivotal cases of *Ward* and *Yorta Yorta* were decided, I posed three central issues that should be considered when seeking to understand the concept of native title: first, we must understand 'how' the common law seeks to recognise native title within Australian law; second, 'what' it is that the common law is recognising; and, third, and more fundamentally, 'why' the common law recognises native title. This last issue seeks to understand the purpose to which recognition is directed and the policy or jurisprudential foundation for native title. This 'principled' approach should provide the tether as the courts negotiate Justice Kirby's 'native title jungle'.[135] At that time I proposed that the purpose of native title was as a settlement between competing sovereignties, or, as Chief Justice Lamer of the Canadian Supreme Court described in *Delgamuukw v*

British Columbia [1997], the reconciliation of the prior sovereignty of Indigenous peoples with the assertion of sovereignty by the Crown.[136] Native title is the burden of colonisation, not simply another property interest.

The settlement reached in *Mabo* was compromised. The discriminatory treatment of Indigenous peoples' rights undermined its foundations as a just settlement of the acquiring sovereign with those from whom sovereignty was wrested. The doctrine that the courts have developed since then, using the legislation as a cloak, builds upon those discriminatory aspects. The denial of Indigenous law as an ongoing normative system that continues to allocate rights and interests, together with judgments about authenticity and the vulnerability invested in native title by the rules of extinguishment, compromises the coherence of the native title jurisprudence. Placing this compromised jurisprudence at the centre of the inquiry into whether 'native title' exists ensures that the recognition and protection afforded by native title to the rights and interests of Indigenous peoples is also compromised. Recognition and protection of native title, as we have witnessed, will be afforded by the Australian law on its own terms on the basis of convenience if the reach of the sovereign to claim benefit for itself remains unchecked.

The courts play a significant role both in setting the context in which legislation operates and interpreting the words and legal concepts contained within the legislation. More importantly, some of the judiciary who deal directly with determinations have used the scope and flexibility provided by the High Court's jurisprudence to push the law into providing justice in the circumstances before them. But there are obvious limits. Parties have already begun to look for ways to work around the doctrinal constraints of native title, although the minimal outcomes achievable through the current native title law seem to narrow the vision of what is possible or, indeed, appropriate. In particular, the emergence of 'alternative settlement' negotiations seeks to provide an alternative to, or augmentation of, the native title determination process. This was the case in relation to the Wotjobaluk and Gunditjmara settlements in Victoria, which involved an alternative settlement package, secured through Indigenous Land Use Agreements, to support more limited consent determinations.[137] This led to the development of a new approach to land settlements in Victoria that does not depend on native title at all.[138] In this context, the law may no longer lead the way in the development of native title, as it did when *Mabo* and *Wik* were decided, but may need to keep step with the needs and expectations of the community.

Judges and commentators alike have called for reforms to the NTA, and to the requirements of proof in s 223 in particular. But these calls obfuscate the responsibility of the courts for the state of native title law in Australia and underestimate their capacity to change it. To consider the law as settled is to misunderstand the common law process. It is true that the law is more certain and comprehensive after seventeen years of considered decisions on key contested ideas; but so long as the native title jurisprudential settlement compromises the equal enjoyment of rights by Indigenous peoples, there is reason to contest the current state of the law. As other countries continue to reach more just settlements through the common law, or through a mixture of common law and statute or constitutional provision, the settlement with Indigenous peoples that has been reached in Australia should continue to be critically examined.

NOTES

Preface

1. Chief Justice Robert French, 'Lifting the Burden of Native Title: Some modest proposals for improvement', (2009) 93 *Reform* 10.
2. Noel Pearson, 'Defining the Problem', presentation to the 's223 workshop', Agreements Treaties and Negotiated Settlements Project, Melbourne University, May 2009.
3. Justice Tony North, 'Disconnection — The gulf between law and justice', paper presented at the National Native Title Conference 2009: Spirit of Country — Land, Water, Life, 3–5 June 2009.

Introduction

1. Reverend David Passi quoted in Nonie Sharp, 'Contrasting Cultural Perspectives in the Murray Island Case' (1990) 8 *Law in Context* 1, 28.
2. (1992) 175 CLR 1.
3. See David Ritter, 'The "Rejection of Terra Nullius" in *Mabo*: A critical analysis' (1996) 18 *Sydney Law Review* 1, 5, 63. The treatment of 'terra nullius' by the High Court has been the subject of much critical debate, even a decade from the judgment: see, for example, Asa Wahlquist, 'Judge under Fire over Mabo Ruling', *The Australian* (Sydney) 27 February 2006, 5.
4. The contrast in views is perhaps best summarised in the title of Garth Nettheim's article, '*Mabo*: Judicial revolution or cautious correction? *Mabo v Queensland*' (1993) 16 *University of New South Wales Law Journal* 1. See, for example, P. H. Lane, 'The Changing Role of the High Court' (1996) 70 *Australian Law Journal* 246; S. E. K. Hulme, 'Aspects of the High Court's Handling of *Mabo*' (1993) 87 *Victorian Bar News* 29; and P. Connolly, 'Should the Courts Determine Social Policy', *The High Court of Australia in Mabo*, Association of Mining and Exploration Companies Inc (1993) 5. Contrast Hal Wooten, '*Mabo* — Issues and challenges' (1994) 1 *Judicial Review* 303; and Noel Pearson, 'Wik: Whither the separation of powers', *The Australian* (Sydney), 2 January 1997, 11.
5. See, for example, Richard Gluyas, 'Big Miners Fight Mabo Claims', *The Australian* (Sydney), 8 March 1993, 25; Richard Owen, 'Mabo a Threat to Recovery: MIM chief', *The Australian* (Sydney), 30 March 1993, 41; see also Liz Tickner, 'Cattlemen in Rage as Land Claims Loom', *The West Australian* (Perth), 19 April 1993, 13.
6. The West Australian Liberal–National parties government reported in Jane Hammond, 'Diamond Drilling Sparks First Mabo Case', *The Australian* (Sydney), 30–31 January 1993, 8. See also Jane Hammond, 'West Plots to Stop Mabo Claims', *The Australian* (Sydney), 27 May 1993; and Sally Fisher and Jennifer Sexton, 'Backyards for Grabs: Kennett', *The Australian* (Sydney), 10–11 July 1993, 3.

8. *Mabo v Queensland [No. 2]* (1992) 175 CLR 1, 179 (Toohey J); 77 (Deane and Gaudron JJ); 26, 69 (Brennan J).
8. *Cooper v Stuart* (1889) 14 App Cas 286, 291.
9. *Mabo v Queensland [No. 2]* (1992) 175 CLR 1, 36 (footnotes omitted).
10. ibid.; Justice Toohey notes the irony of the concept of 'peaceful annexation' of the colonies of New South Wales and later annexations 'in light of what we now know', implying the violent nature of colonial acquisition, at 181. See also Gordon Brysland, 'Rewriting History 2: The wider significance of *Mabo v Queensland*', (1992) 17 *Alternative Law Journal* 162.
11. *Milirrpum v Nabalco Pty Ltd* (1971) 17 FLR 141.
12. ibid. 267.
13. ibid. 244–5.
14. ibid. 244. Later Canadian and other North American cases cast doubt on the correctness of Justice Blackburn's conclusion. See, for example, *Calder v Attorney General of British Columbia* (1973) 34 DLR (3rd) 145.
15. Western Australia is the notable exception. See also *Pitjantjatjara Land Rights Act 1981* (SA) and *Maralinga Land Rights Act 1984* (SA); *Aboriginal Land (Lake Condah and Framlingham Forest) Act 1987* (Cth) (re lands in Victoria); *Aboriginal Land Rights Act 1983* (NSW); *Aboriginal Land Act 1991* (Qld) and *Torres Strait Islander Land Act 1991* (Qld); and *Aboriginal Lands Act 1995* (Tas).
16. *Coe v Commonwealth* (1979) 118 ALR 193.
17. *Gerhardy v Brown* (1985) 159 CLR 70, 149, referring to the decision of Marshall CJ in *Johnson v M'Intosh* (1823) 8 Wheat 543, 574.
18. *Northern Land Council v Commonwealth* (1987) 61 ALJR 616, 620.
19. *Mabo v Queensland [No. 2]* (1992), 175 CLR 1, 39–41.
20. *Queensland Coast Islands Declaratory Act 1985* (Qld), s 3.
21. *Mabo v Queensland [No. 1]* (1988) 166 CLR 186. A majority of four judges determined that the Queensland Act denied the Meriam people rights in their lands while other Australians were unaffected by the legislation. Therefore the legislation was contrary to the principle of equality before the law enshrined in s 10 of the *Racial Discrimination Act*: 218 (Brennan, Toohey, Gaudron JJ). The primary difference in the reasoning of the majority and the minority was not whether the legislation was discriminatory, but whether the claim could be entertained prior to a determination of rights to land being made: 196 (Mason CJ); 243 (Dawson J); contra 206 (Wilson J).
22. For a detailed discussion of the political context of the development of the legislation, see Richard Bartlett, *Native Title in Australia* (2nd edn, Lexis Nexis Butterworths, Sydney, 2005), 33–42.
23. NTA s 3. These objects now contain the term 'intermediate period acts' within the validation clause (s 3(d)).
24. *Western Australia v Commonwealth* (1995) 183 CLR 373, 459 [96]. With the exception of (then) s 12, which purported to give the common law of native title the force of a law of the Commonwealth. This would have effectively given judges 'legislative' power in future decisions and was thus a breach of the separation of powers between parliament and the courts. See 485–6 [148–9].
25. *Mabo v Queensland [No. 1]* (1988) 166 CLR 186. See note 21 above.

Notes (pages 5–9)

26. *Western Australia v Commonwealth* (1995) 183 CLR 373, 438 [42].
27. ibid. 453 [79].
28. ibid. 459 [93].
29. ibid. 453 [80].
30. NTA s 7(2).
31. For more, see Bartlett above n 22, 40.
32. NTA s 3(c).
33. Potential native title holders may make an application under NTA s 61 for a determination of native title under s 225.
34. As at 31 December 2008, of the 82 determinations that native title exists, 71 determinations have been reached by consent. See <www.nnttt.gov.au>.
35. An 'act', whether a past or future (or, under the amended NTA, intermediate period) act, includes the making, amending or repealing of any legislation; the exercise of any executive power; and the grant, creation, variation or extinguishment of any interest in land or other rights: NTA s 226.
36. NTA s 31.
37. *Wik Peoples v Queensland* (1996) 187 CLR 1.
38. See Bartlett above n 22.
39. See Office of Indigenous Affairs, Department of Prime Minister and Cabinet, Commonwealth of Australia, Canberra, 'Towards a More Workable Native Title Act', discussion paper, May 1996.
40. An initial Native Title Amendment Bill was introduced in June 1996, with further amendments added in June 1997.
41. This infamous quote was from Tim Fischer, Deputy Prime Minister and Minister for Trade, quoted in J. Brough, 'Wik Draft Threat to Native Title', *The Sydney Morning Herald* (Sydney), 28 June 1997, 3. See also Aboriginal and Torres Strait Islander Social Justice Commissioner, *Native Title Report – July 1996–June 1997* (Human Rights and Equal Opportunity Commission, Sydney, 1997), 59–100.
42. NTA ss 21–22H.
43. NTA ss 24IA–24ID.
44. NTA s 237A.
45. NTA ss 23A–23JA; schedule 1.
46. NTA s 24HA.
47. NTA ss 24GA–24GE.
48. NTA s 190B.
49. NTA ss 24 HA, 24KA–26D, 36A, 42A, 43A.
50. For a detailed summary of the 1998 Amendments see Bartlett above n 22, 52–64.
51. See Lisa Strelein, Michael Dodson and Jessica Weir, 'Understanding Non-discrimination: International criticisms of Australia's compliance with human rights standards' (2001) 3 *Balayi: Culture, Law and Colonialism* 113.

1. Recognising native title in Australian law: *Mabo v Queensland [No. 2]*

1. *Mabo v Queensland [No. 2]* (1992) 175 CLR 1.
2. The decision was supported by a majority of six of the seven judges. Justice Brennan wrote what is considered the lead judgment in the case, to which Chief Justice

Mason and Justice McHugh wrote a brief concurring judgment, which itself was said to have the authority of the majority. Justices Deane and Gaudron wrote a joint judgment, Justice Toohey gave separate reasons and Justice Dawson was the sole dissenting judge.
3. (1971) 17 FLR 141.
4. *Mabo v Queensland [No. 2]* (1992) 175 CLR 1, 41–2 (Brennan J).
5. ibid. 29. Justices Deane and Gaudron were also persuaded by the fact that the circumstances of this present case made it unique; had it been merely an ordinary case, they would not have felt justified in 'reopening the validity of fundamental propositions which have been endorsed by long established authority', 109.
6. The decisions of the majority of the High Court consider the effect of colonisation for the Crown's proprietary sovereignty. The assumption that colonisation gave the imperial power sovereignty was not challenged by the plaintiffs in the case, but the effect of that acquisition was a justiciable question.
7. *Mabo v Queensland [No. 2]* (1992) 175 CLR 1, 34–8 (Brennan J, Mason CJ and McHugh J agreeing), 79–80 (Deane and Gaudron JJ), 122 (Dawson J), 206 (Toohey J).
8. ibid. 79 (Deane and Gaudron JJ).
9. ibid. 45.
10. ibid.
11. ibid. 69 (Brennan J).
12. ibid. 87–8 (Deane and Gaudron JJ).
13. ibid. 59 (Brennan J).
14. ibid. 58 (Brennan J).
15. ibid. 87 (Deane and Gaudron JJ).
16. ibid. 59–60. See Richard Bartlett, 'Aboriginal Land Claims at Common Law' (1982) 12 *University of Western Australia Law Review* 293.
17. *Mabo v Queensland [No. 2]* (1992) 175 CLR 1, 85–6.
18. Cases that imposed such world views were expressly rejected by the majority in *Mabo*. Most notable of these was *Cooper v Stuart* (1889) 14 App Cas 286 and *Milirrpum v Nabalco Pty Ltd* (1971) 17 FLR 141.
19. *Mabo v Queensland [No. 2]* (1992) 175 CLR 1, 58 (Brennan J).
20. ibid. 88–9 (Deane and Gaudron JJ).
21. ibid. 187 (Toohey J); also Justices Deane and Gaudron, at 87–8.
22. ibid. 188 (Toohey J).
23. ibid.
24. ibid. 187.
25. ibid. 59–60 (Brennan J).
26. This formulation has a commonality with Canadian and United States law, e.g. *Hamlet of Baker Lake v Minister of Indian Affairs and Northern Development* (1979) 107 DLR (3d) 513.
27. *Mabo v Queensland [No. 2]* (1992) 175 CLR 1, 189–90 (Toohey J); for discussion see Deane and Gaudron JJ, at 85–6.
28. A form of aboriginal title was recognised in the United States in 1823, in New Zealand in 1847 and in Canada in 1973; *Johnson v M'Intosh* (1823) 8 Wheat 543; *R v Symonds* [1847] NZPCC 387; *Calder v Attorney General of British Columbia*

(1973) 34 DLR (3d) 145). The first treaty in North America between the Iroquois and the British Crown was signed in 1664: the Treaty of Albany.
29. *Mabo v Queensland [No. 2]* (1992) 175 CLR 1, 85–6 (Deane and Gaudron JJ).
30. ibid. 61 (Brennan J).
31. *Calder v Attorney General of British Columbia* (1973) 34 DLR (3d) 145, 190 (Hall J).
32. ibid. 156 (Judson J).
33. *Hamlet of Baker Lake v Minister of Indian Affairs and Northern Development* (1979) 107 DLR (3d) 513, 542.
34. *Mabo v Queensland [No. 2]* (1992) 175 CLR 1, 189 (Toohey J).
35. ibid. 26, 38 (Brennan J).
36. ibid. 59–60 (Brennan J); 110 (Deane and Gaudron JJ).
37. ibid, 60 (Brennan J).
38. *Mabo v Queensland [No. 2]* (1992) 175 CLR 1, 60, 70 (Brennan J); 88, 110 (Deane and Gaudron JJ). For an account of the anthropology of succession in Australian Indigenous societies, see Peter Sutton, *Native Title and the Descent of Rights* (National Native Title Tribunal, Perth, 1998). For a recent application of the principle see *Rubibi Community v Western Australia [No. 6]* (unreported decision, FCA, Merkel J, 13 February 2006).
39. *Mabo v Queensland [No. 2]* (1992) 175 CLR 1, 51 (Brennan J).
40. ibid. 59, 60.
41. ibid. 88 (Deane and Gaudron JJ); cf 194 (Toohey J). This reasoning is consistent with *Johnson v M'Intosh* (1823) 8 Wheat 543, 574 and *R v Symonds* [1847] NZPCC 387.
42. *Mabo v Queensland [No. 2]* (1992) 175 CLR 1, 60 (Brennan J).
43. ibid. 90–1, (Deane and Gaudron JJ); 60 (Brennan J).
44. ibid. 51 (Brennan J).
45. ibid. 88–9, 101 (Deane and Gaudron JJ). This view relied in part on earlier Canadian decisions: *Attorney General (Quebec) v Attorney General (Canada)* [1921] 1 AC 408, 411, *St Catherine's Milling Case* (1888) 14 App Cas 54.
46. *Mabo v Queensland [No. 2]* (1992) 175 CLR 1, 89 (Deane and Gaudron JJ); *Amodu Tijani* [1921] 2 AC 404–5; *Guerin v R* (1984) 13 DLR (4th) 321.
47. *Mabo v Queensland [No. 2]* (1992) 175 CLR 1, 91 (Deane and Gaudron JJ).
48. ibid. 51 (Brennan J).
49. ibid.
50. ibid. 110 (Deane and Gaudron JJ).
51. ibid. 58 (Brennan J, with whom Mason CJ and McHugh J agreed); 110 (Deane and Gaudron J); 187 (Toohey J).
52. ibid. 70 (Brennan J); 110 (Deane and Gaudron JJ); 187 (Toohey J).
53. ibid. 61 (Brennan J); 110 (Deane and Gaudron JJ).
54. The Supreme Court of Canada in *Guerin v R* (1984) 13 DLR (4d) 321, 339 (Dickson J); approved the reasoning of *Amodu Tijani* [1921] 2 AC 404–5, which was similarly relied upon by the High Court of Australia.
55. *Mabo v Queensland [No. 2]* (1992) 175 CLR 1, 75 (Brennan J); 117–18 (Deane and Gaudron JJ); Justice Toohey agreed with Justice Brennan, at 197.
56. For example, *Mining Act 1978* (WA) s 9; 24 *Petroleum Act 1967* (WA).
57. *Western Australia v Ward* (2002) 213 CLR 1. See Chapter 6.

58. *Mabo v Queensland [No. 2]* (1992) 175 CLR 1, 111 (Deane and Gaudron JJ).
59. ibid. 195 (Toohey J).
60. ibid. 69 (Brennan J, Mason CJ and McHugh J agreeing). See also 80–3 (Deane and Gaudron JJ), 180–4 (Toohey J).
61. ibid. 69 (Brennan J).
62. ibid. 71–3 (Brennan J); 118 (Deane and Gaudron JJ); 196–7 (Toohey J).
63. ibid. 60 (Brennan J).
64. Surrender is arguably a domesticated version of 'cession' or ceding of territories by one sovereign to another, usually by treaty. The tradition of treaty making in North America continues in present-day 'comprehensive agreement processes' in Canada. See, generally, Sean Brennan, Larissa Behrendt, Lisa Strelein and George Williams, *Treaty* (Federation Press, Sydney, 2005).
65. *Mabo v Queensland [No. 2]* (1992) 175 CLR 1, 59 (Brennan J); 88 (Deane and Gaudron JJ).
66. ibid. 61 (Brennan J).
67. ibid. 110 (Deane and Gaudron JJ).
68. ibid. 111.
69. ibid. 68 (Brennan J).
70. ibid. 64.
71. ibid. 64 (Brennan J); 111 (Deane and Gaudron JJ); 193 (Toohey J); Justice Brennan did not decide the matter.
72. ibid. 68 (Brennan J).
73. ibid. This was seen to be the case with respect to the lease of two acres (just under one hectare) on Murray Island to the London Missionary Society in 1882.
74. ibid. 64, 68.
75. *Sparrow v R* (1990) 3 Canadian Native Law Reporter 160; *Guerin v R* (1984) 13 DLR (4th) 321.
76. *Mabo v Queensland [No. 2]* (1992) 175 CLR 1, 64–8 (Brennan J).
77. ibid. 69, also Justices Deane and Gaudron, at 110.
78. For example, *Mining Act 1978* (WA), s 9; *Petroleum Act 1967* (WA), s 9; *Land Act 1933* (WA).
79. Though called 'leases', the rights under the *Land Act 1933* (WA) are more akin to a licence. See also Henry Reynolds, '*Mabo* and Pastoral Leases' (1992) 12(59) *Aboriginal Law Bulletin* 8.
80. *Mabo v Queensland [No. 2]* (1992) 175 CLR 1, 15–16 (Mason CJ and McHugh J).
81. ibid. 193 (Toohey J); 111 (Deane and Gaudron JJ).
82. ibid. 111, 112, 119 (Deane and Gaudron JJ). They assumed, however, that limitation periods would apply to bar the claim after a certain period, which in many instances has long passed.
83. *Clunies Ross v The Commonwealth* (1984) 155 CLR 193, 202.
84. *Mabo v Queensland [No. 2]* (1992) 175 CLR 1, 111 (Deane and Gaudron JJ).
85. The statement by Chief Justice Mason and Justice McHugh must be given careful consideration in applying the decision. Although it could be considered as merely one judgment of the majority, it is carefully worded to carry the full authority of the Court. This goes one step further than the similar statement by the High Court in *Commonwealth v Tasmania (Tasmanian Dams case)* (1983) 158 CLR 1, 58–9, where

it was said that the summary was published only for convenience and was not an authoritative statement.
86. *Mabo v Queensland [No. 2]* (1992) 175 CLR 1, 61–2 (Brennan J): 'where an indigenous people (including a clan or group), as a community, are in possession of land under a proprietary native title, their possession may be enforced by a representative action brought on behalf of the people by a subgroup or individual who sues to protect or enforce rights or interests which are dependent on the communal native title'.
87. *Adeyinka Oyekan v Musendiku Adele* [1957] 1 WLR 876, 880 (Lord Denning); referred to in *Mabo v Queensland [No. 2]* (1992) 175 CLR 1, 56 (Brennan J). Neither is the issue contained in Justice Brennan's summary of his conclusions, at 68–70.
88. *Mabo v Queensland [No. 2]* (1992) 175 CLR 1, 200–3.
89. ibid. 200–1.
90. 166 CLR 186.
91. *Mabo v Queensland [No. 2]* (1992) 175 CLR 1, 111–12 (Deane and Gaudron JJ).

2. Coexistence and necessary inconsistency: Wik Peoples v Queensland

1. *Wik Peoples v Queensland* (1996) 187 CLR 1. The Wik peoples brought the initial claim. The Thayorre people were joined as a party when they claimed native title over part of the land subject to the Wik claim.
2. 175 CLR 1.
3. *Wik Peoples v Queensland* (1996) 187 CLR 1, 167–8: Justice Gummow noted that while the litigation 'stands outside the system for determination of native title claims established by the Native Title Act[,] … it raises issues which may have importance for the operation of that statute'. In particular, his Honour noted that if acts done before the commencement of the *Racial Discrimination Act 1975* (Cth) were effective to extinguish or impair native title, then the NTA did not undo that result, referring to the majority joint judgment in *Western Australia v Commonwealth (Native Title Act case)* 183 CLR 373, 454.
4. The Wik and Thayorre peoples also originally included a claim to possessory title, but this was not pressed: see procedural history outlined by Kirby J, *Wik Peoples v Queensland* (1996) 187 CLR 1, 209, 210–13. The Wik peoples also sought to challenge the effectiveness of two mining agreements that had been enshrined by statute, and given the force of law. This matter was dealt with by Kirby J, 251–61, with whom Toohey, Gaudron and Gummow JJ agreed.
5. The majority on the substantive issue of the pastoral leases was constituted by Toohey, Gaudron, Gummow and Kirby JJ, who all gave separate reasons. Brennan J dissented, with Mason CJ and McHugh J agreeing.
6. *Wik Peoples v Queensland* (1996) 187 CLR 1, 134 (Gaudron J).
7. ibid. See also 102 (Toohey J).
8. ibid. 70. On this point, Brennan J considered that no freestanding fiduciary duty arose out of the relationship between the Crown and native title holders, by virtue of the power of the Crown to adversely affect native title. That required a particular action or function to be exercised that gave rise to a fiduciary duty, or a discretionary power, whether statutory or otherwise, that required the executive or legislature to act on behalf of, or in the interests of, another, 9–10.

9. ibid. 213 (Kirby J).
10. ibid. 103 (Toohey J).
11. *Wik Peoples v Queensland* (1996) 134 ALR 637, 666 (Federal Court).
12. ibid, citing *North Ganalanja Aboriginal Corporation v Queensland* (1995) 61 FCR 1 (Full Court, Federal Court).
13. *North Ganalanja Aboriginal Corporation v Queensland* (1996) 135 ALR 225 (High Court).
14. *Wik Peoples v Queensland* (1996) 134 ALR 637, 666 (Federal Court).
15. The full Federal Court may remove a matter to the High Court under s 40(1) of the *Judiciary Act 1903* (Cth).
16. The questions were outlined, in full, in the judgment of Brennan J, *Wik Peoples v Queensland* (1996) 187 CLR 1, 65–7.
17. ibid. 108 (Toohey J); 170 (Gummow J); 209 (Kirby J). For the treatment of remaining questions see above n 4.
18. ibid. 108 (Toohey J).
19. ibid. 168 (Gummow J).
20. 183 CLR 373.
21. *Wik Peoples v Queensland* (1996) 187 CLR 1, 168 (Gummow J).
22. ibid. 137 (Gaudron J).
23. ibid. 232 (Kirby J).
24. See discussion by Toohey J, ibid. 108–15; 137–44 (Gaudron J); 136–44 (Gummow J); 226–33 (Kirby J).
25. ibid. 109 (Toohey J); 226 (Kirby J). Queensland became a separate colony in June 1859. The laws of New South Wales applied and remained in force until repealed or varied by the Queensland legislature.
26. The *Crown Lands Unauthorized Occupation Act 1839* (NSW), s 25. For details of occupation licences granted of the Mitchellton lands, see *Wik Peoples v Queensland* (1996) 187 CLR 1, 136 (Gaudron J).
27. *Wik Peoples v Queensland* (1996) 187 CLR 1, 174 referring to *Stewart v Williams* (1914) 18 CLR 381, 406 (Isaacs J).
28. *Wik Peoples v Queensland* (1996) 187 CLR 1, 111.
29. ibid. 148 (Gaudron J); 174 (Gummow J), referring to *O'Keefe v Malone* [1903] AC 365, 377. See also *Wade v New South Wales Rutile Mining Co Pty Ltd* (1969) 121 CLR 177, 192, re 'mining leases' under the *Mining Act 1906* (NSW).
30. *Wik Peoples v Queensland* (1996) 187 CLR 1, 111–12, 115 (Toohey J); 226 (Kirby J).
31. ibid. 243–4 (Kirby J).
32. ibid. 115–16 (Toohey J); 140–1 (Gaudron J); 215–16 (Kirby J).
33. Gummow J discussed the lack of a judicial 'taxonomy' or way of dealing with the unique situation presented by native title in the 'interpretation' of history: see ibid. 182.
34. ibid. 116 (Toohey J).
35. ibid. 75 (Brennan J), referring to *Radaich v Smith* (1959) 101 CLR 209, 22. Compare Gaudron J on this point, *Wik Peoples v Queensland* (1996) 187 CLR 1, 153.

36. *Wik Peoples v Queensland* (1996) 187 CLR 1, 96–8 (Brennan J). The effect of Justice Brennan's conclusion with regard to exclusive possession, he admits, would constitute a 'significant moral shortcoming' in the law that could only be rectified by legislation or the acquisition of an estate that would allow the Wik and Thayorre people to continue to exercise their traditional rights on their country.
37. ibid. 149–51 (Gaudron J).
38. ibid. 249 (Kirby J).
39. ibid. 51 (Gaudron J), citing *American Dairy Queen (Qld) Pty Ltd v Blue Rio Pty Ltd* (1981) 147 CLR 677, 682–3.
40. *North Ganalanja Aboriginal Corporation v Queensland* (1995) 61 FCR 1, 55–6.
41. *Mabo v Queensland [No. 2]* (1992) 175 CLR 1, 68 (Brennan J).
42. ibid. 110 (Deane and Gaudron JJ).
43. *Wik Peoples v Queensland* (1996) 187 CLR 1, 223 (Kirby J).
44. ibid. 244 (Kirby J).
45. This was the basis of the applicants' argument regarding the suspension and revival of native title temporarily impacted by inconsistent grant. As a result of the conclusion that no necessary extinguishment had occurred, except perhaps by the conditions under the Holroyd lease, and the construction of the reversion by Gaudron and Gummow JJ, the issue of revival was not considered, ibid. 204.
46. ibid. 155.
47. ibid. 128 (Toohey J).
48. ibid. 156 (Gaudron J); 190 (Gummow J); 240 (Kirby J).
49. ibid. 151 (Gaudron J).
50. ibid. 195 (Gummow J), for example in relation to s 204 of the 1910 Act, and s 373(1) of the 1962 Act, concerning unlawful occupation.
51. ibid.
52. ibid. 71 (Brennan J).
53. ibid. referring to *Mabo v Queensland [No. 2]* (1992) 175 CLR 1, 69 (Brennan J).
54. *Wik Peoples v Queensland* (1996) 187 CLR 1, 146–7 (Gaudron J); 191 (Gummow J).
55. *Mabo v Queensland [No. 2]* (1992) 175 CLR 1, 66 (Brennan J).
56. *Wik Peoples v Queensland* (1996) HCA 40 (23 December 1996), 147.
57. ibid. 247 (Kirby J).
58. ibid. 147–55 (Gaudron J).
59. ibid. 154.
60. ibid. see also 229 (Kirby J).
61. The *Petroleum Act* (Qld) was passed in 1915.
62. *Wik Peoples v Queensland* (1996) 187 CLR 1, 105 (Toohey J).
63. ibid. 176–7 (Gummow J).
64. ibid. 73–4 (Brennan J). His Honour relied on comments from Mason J in *Goldsworthy Mining Ltd v Federal Commissioner of Taxation* (1973) 128 CLR 199.
65. *Wik Peoples v Queensland* (1996) 187 CLR 1, 201 (Gummow J).
66. ibid. 117, 118 (Toohey J).
67. ibid. 154–5, citing *Mabo v Queensland [No. 2]* (1992) 175 CLR 1, 111 (Deane and Gaudron JJ).
68. *Wik Peoples v Queensland* (1996) 187 CLR 1, 247 (Kirby J).

69. ibid. 201 (Gummow J).
70. ibid. 122 (Toohey J).
71. ibid.
72. ibid. 71 (Brennan J).
73. ibid. 122 (Toohey J).
74. ibid. 177 (Gummow J); see also 219 (Kirby J).
75. ibid. 185, referring to *Corporation of Yarmouth v Simmons* (1878) 10 Ch D 518, 423 (Fry J).
76. *Wik Peoples v Queensland* (1996) 187 CLR 1, 242–3 (Kirby J).
77. ibid. 166–7. The final determination in relation to the pastoral leases was reached by consent: *Wik Peoples v Queensland* [2004] FCA 1306.
78. ibid. 133 (Toohey J, for the majority (Gaudron, Gummow and Kirby JJ)).
79. ibid. 84 (Brennan J).
80. ibid. 236–7 (Kirby J).
81. ibid. 237.
82. ibid. 215.
83. ibid. 87 (Brennan J).
84. ibid.
85. ibid.
86. ibid. 73.
87. ibid. 243 (Kirby J).
88. ibid. 126 (Toohey J for the majority (Gaudron, Gummow and Kirby JJ)).

3. The vulnerability of native title: *Fejo v Northern Territory*

1. *Fejo v Northern Territory* (1998) 195 CLR 96.
2. This single ground of appeal was removed directly to the High Court without a full Federal Court decision, under s 18 of the *Judiciary Act 1903* (Cth).
3. *Fejo v Northern Territrory* (1998) 195 CLR 96, 117.
4. *Fejo v Northern Territory* (1998) 195 CLR 96, 126 [43] (joint judgment).
5. *Commonwealth v New South Wales* (1923) 33 CLR 1, 42 (Isaacs J).
6. 175 CLR 1, 69 (Brennan J).
7. ibid. 89 (Deane and Gaudron JJ), see also 110 (Deane and Gaudron JJ); *Western Australia v Commonwealth* (1995) (*Native Title Act case*) 183 CLR 373, 422 [11]; *Wik Peoples v Queensland* (1996) 187 CLR 1, 176 (Gummow J), 250 (Kirby J).
8. *Fejo v Northern Territory* (1998) 195 CLR 96, 148 [100] (Kirby J).
9. 183 CLR 373, 439, per (Mason CJ, Brennan, Deane, Toohey, Gaudron and McHugh JJ).
10. *Wik Peoples v Queensland* (1996) 187 CLR 1.
11. *Fejo v Northern Territory* (1998) 195 CLR 96, 128 [47].
12. ibid. 151 [106].
13. ibid. 128 [47].
14. ibid.
15. *Delgamuukw v British Columbia* [1997] 3 SCR 1010, [81–2]; *R v Van der Peet* [1996] 2 SCR 507, [42, 49–50].
16. *Fejo v Northern Territory* (1998) 195 CLR 96, 130 [54] (joint judgment).
17. ibid. 150 [103], 154 [111].
18. *Mabo v Queensland* [No. 2] (1992) 175 CLR 1, 63 (Brennan J).

Notes (pages 40-50)

19. ibid. 89 (Deane and Gaudron JJ).
20. *Fejo v Northern Territory* (1998) 195 CLR 96,151 [105] (Kirby J).
21. *Mabo v Queensland* [No. 2] (1992) 175 CLR 1, 43 (Brennan J).
22. *Fejo v Northern Territory* (1998) 195 CLR 96, 127 [45] (joint judgment).
23. ibid. 128 [46].
24. ibid. 153 [110].
25. ibid. 151 [106] (Kirby J) (emphasis added).
26. ibid. 151-2 [107].

4. Property and Crown ownership: *Yanner v Eaton*

1. *Yanner v Eaton* (1999) 201 CLR 351. In a joint majority judgment, Gleeson CJ and Gaudron, Kirby and Hayne JJ allowed the appeal, with Gummow J also in the majority allowing the appeal though offering separate reasons.
2. ibid. 361 [4].
3. ibid. 366 [17] (Gleeson CJ, Gaudron, Kirby, and Hayne JJ).
4. ibid.
5. *Yanner v Eaton* (1999) 201 CLR 351, 367.
6. ibid. 369 [28], citing *Toomer v Witsell* (1948) 334 US 385, 402.
7. *Yanner v Eaton* (1999) 201 CLR 351, 375 [47-9] (McHugh J); 405-6 [143] (Callinan J).
8. ibid. 370 [30].
9. 187 CLR 1.
10. *Yanner v Eaton* (1999) 201 CLR 351, 372, [37] (original emphasis).
11. ibid. 373 [39].
12. ibid. 396 [109] (Gummow J).
13. ibid. 395 [107] (Gummow J).
14. ibid. 397 [115].
15. ibid. 373 [37] (Gleeson CJ, Gaudron, Kirby, and Hayne JJ).
16. ibid. 373 [38].
17. ibid. 383-4 [73-4] (Gummow J).
18. 175 CLR 1, 51 (Brennan J).
19. 201 CLR 351, 382-3 [72] (Gummow J).
20. ibid. 373 [38] (Gleeson CJ, Gaudron, Kirby and Hayne JJ).
21. ibid. 382 [69].

5. Native title offshore: *Commonwealth v Yarmirr*

1. 208 CLR 1.
2. *Mary Yarmirr and Others v Northern Territory and Others* [1998] 771 FCA (6 July 1998) (Olney J).
3. *Commonwealth v Yarmirr* (1999) 101 FCR 171 (Beaumont and von Doussa JJ, Merkel J dissenting) (Full Court Federal Court).
4. *Commonwealth v Yarmirr* (2001) 208 CLR 1, 47-8 [40] (Gleeson CJ, Gaudron, Gummow and Hayne JJ).
5. ibid. 48 [41].
6. ibid. citing *Western Australia v Commonwealth (Native Title Act case)* (1995) 183 CLR 373, 422-3, in turn citing *Mabo v Queensland [No. 2]* (1992) 175 CLR 1, 95 (Deane and Gaudron JJ); 193-4 (Toohey J).

7. *Commonwealth v Yarmirr* (2001) 208 CLR 1, 49 [42] (Gleeson CJ, Gaudron, Gummow and Hayne JJ).
8. ibid. 51 [48] (Gleeson CJ, Gaudron, Gummow and Hayne JJ). Contra 99 [207] (McHugh J).
9. ibid. 51 [50] (Gleeson CJ, Gaudron, Gummow and Hayne JJ).
10. ibid.
11. ibid. 52–3 [52].
12. (1876) 2 Ex D 63.
13. *Commonwealth v Yarmirr* (2001) 208 CLR 1, 91 [181] (McHugh J), referring to *New South Wales v Commonwealth (Seas and Submerged Lands case)* (1975) 135 CLR 337. McHugh J, at 69 [104], states the argument simply: 'The Act does not recognise native title unless the common law recognises it. The *Seas and Submerged Lands case*, applying *R v Keyn*, held that the common law of Australia has no operation below the low water mark' (footnotes omitted). See also Callinan J at 150 [340]: 'the Act ... does not create native title'. In this context, their Honours refer to the 'possibility' that native title 'might' exist offshore to explain the various references in the Act to 'waters' and 'fishing', cf. 74 [122] (McHugh J).
14. *Mabo v Queensland [No. 2]* (1992) 175 CLR 1, 66 (Brennan J); *Yanner v Eaton* (1999) 201 CLR 351, 372 [37].
15. *Commonwealth v Yarmirr* (2001) 208 CLR 1, 59 [70] (Gleeson CJ, Gaudron, Gummow and Hayne JJ).
16. ibid. at 60 [76]. Again, McHugh J, at 107 [232], explicitly rejected the majority's approach on this point. Kirby J, in contrast, while clearly considering that the common law extends to the sea, did not need to discuss the proposition because his Honour took the view that the NTA expressly contemplates and allows for the recognition of native title offshore and that effect should be given to that intention, at 113 [253]. Kirby J was, in turn, expressly critical of the approach of McHugh J to the interpretation of the various references to 'waters' and 'fishing' rights in the NTA as merely speculative, at 114–15 [256–8].
17. ibid. 56 [61] (Gleeson CJ, Gaudron, Gummow and Hayne JJ).
18. ibid. (original emphasis).
19. ibid. also at 60 [75].
20. *Mary Yarmirr and Others v Northern Territory and Others* [1998] 771 FCA (6 July 1998), [129] (Olney J).
21. *Commonwealth v Yarmirr* (2001) 208 CLR 1, 55–6 [58–62] (Gleeson CJ, Gaudron, Gummow and Hayne JJ), following *Mabo v Queensland [No. 2]* (1992) 175 CLR 1, 59, 43 respectively (Brennan J).
22. *Commonwealth v Yarmirr* (2001) 208 CLR 1, 68 [97] (Gleeson CJ, Gaudron, Gummow and Hayne JJ).
23. ibid. 68 [100].
24. ibid. 68 [98].
25. *Milirrpum v Nabalco Pty Ltd* (1971) 17 FLR 141.
26. 187 CLR 1.
27. *Commonwealth v Yarmirr* (2001) 208 CLR 1, 68 [98] (Gleeson CJ, Gaudron, Gummow and Hayne JJ).
28. 195 CLR 96.
29. *Commonwealth v Yarmirr* (2001) 208 CLR 1, 124 [278–9] (Kirby J).
30. ibid. 125 [281].

Notes (pages 53-58)

31. ibid. 125 [282].
32. *Hayes v Northern Territory* (1999) 97 FCR 32.
33. 101 FCR 171 (Full Federal Court).
34. *Commonwealth v Yarmirr* (2001) 208 CLR 1, 137 [307] (Kirby J) (original emphasis).
35. ibid. 140 [316], 137 [309].
36. ibid. 140–1 [317].
37. ibid. 139 [313].
38. This decision has been applied in *Lardil, Kaidlilt, Yangkaal and Gangalidda People v Queensland* [2000] FCA 1548; *Gumana v Northern Territory* [2005] FCA 50; *Sampi v Western Australia* [2005] FCA 777 and *Rubibi Community v Western Australia [No. 5]* [2005] FCA 1025 (the latter claims concerned land and sea).
39. *Mary Yarmirr and Others v Northern Territory and Others* [1998] 771 FCA (6 July 1998), [137] (Olney J), citing *Harper v Minister for Sea Fisheries* (1989) 168 CLR 314 at 330.

6. Redefining extinguishment: *Western Australia v Ward*

1. *Western Australia v Ward* (2002) 213 CLR 1.
2. *Ward on behalf of the Miriuwung and Gajerrong People v Western Australia* (1998) 159 ALR 483 (Lee J).
3. ibid. 508.
4. ibid. 639.
5. *Western Australia v Ward and Others* (2000) 99 FCR 316.
6. ibid. 337 [55] (Beaumont and von Doussa JJ).
7. ibid. 338 [59] (Beaumont and von Doussa JJ).
8. ibid. 346 [97] (Beaumont and von Doussa JJ).
9. ibid. (Beaumont and von Doussa JJ).
10. ibid. 515 [784] (North J).
11. ibid. 487 [683] (North J).
12. ibid. 373 [210] (Beaumont and von Doussa JJ).
13. ibid. 345 [91] (Beaumont and von Doussa JJ).
14. ibid. 489 [689] (North J).
15. *Wik Peoples v Queensland* (1996) 187 CLR 1.
16. *Western Australia v Ward* (2002) 213 CLR 1, 60 [2] (Gleeson CJ, Gaudron, Gummow and Hayne JJ).
17. ibid. 64–6 [13, 16] (Gleeson CJ, Gaudron, Gummow and Hayne JJ).
18. See *Native Title Act 1993* (Cth), Pt 2 Div 2 — Validation of Past Acts; and Div 2B — Confirmation of Past Extinguishment of Native Title by Certain Valid or Validated Acts.
19. *Mabo v Queensland [No. 2]* (1992) 175 CLR 1 has been interpreted as finding that, prior to the introduction of the *Racial Discrimination Act 1975* (Cth), discrimination against native title holders on the basis of race was lawful under the common law.
20. *Wik Peoples v Queensland* (1996) 187 CLR 1.
21. *Western Australia v Ward* (2002) 213 CLR 1, 63 [9] (Gleeson CJ, Gaudron, Gummow and Hayne JJ). See NTA s 23G — Previous Non-Exclusive Possession Acts (PNEPAs); and s 4(6).
22. NTA s 23A. Emphasis added. Original emphasis removed.

23. *Western Australia v Ward* (2002) 213 CLR 1, 240 [561] (McHugh J).
24. Past acts that were no longer in force on 1 January 1994, and are not Previous Exclusive Possession Acts (PEPA) or Previous Non-Exclusive Possession Acts (PNEPA), would fit this category.
25. *Western Australia v Ward* (2002) 213 CLR 1, 69 [26] (Gleeson CJ, Gaudron, Gummow and Hayne JJ).
26. ibid. 69 [26, 27] (Gleeson CJ, Gaudron, Gummow and Hayne JJ).
27. ibid. 66–7 [20–1] (Gleeson CJ, Gaudron, Gummow and Hayne JJ).
28. *Western Australia v Commonwealth* (1995) 183 CLR 373, 468–9.
29. *Western Australia v Ward* (2002) 213 CLR 1, [116–17] (Gleeson CJ, Gaudron, Gummow and Hayne JJ), citing *Mabo v Queensland [No. 1]* (1988) 166 CLR 186.
30. *Western Australia v Ward* (2002) 213 CLR 1, [104–8] (Gleeson CJ, Gaudron, Gummow and Hayne JJ), citing *Gerhardy v Brown* (1985) 159 CLR 70, 98–9 (Mason J).
31. *Western Australia v Ward* (2002) 213 CLR 1, 66 [18] (Gleeson CJ, Gaudron, Gummow and Hayne JJ).
32. ibid. 70 [26].
33. ibid. 70 [28].
34. ibid. 82 [49–51].
35. ibid. 95 [95].
36. ibid. 91 [82].
37. ibid. 64–5 [14]; cf. *Mabo v Queensland [No. 2]* (1992) 175 CLR 1.
38. *Western Australia v Ward* (2002) 213 CLR 1, 94–5 [93].
39. ibid. 95 [94].
40. ibid. 91 [82].
41. ibid. 185 [382] (Gleeson CJ, Gaudron, Gummow and Hayne JJ).
42. ibid. 243 [570]. Kirby J argued that the NTA provides the recognition of native 'title', not a list of activities, but expressed concern that the approach of the majority on the question of minerals verged on this latter approach.
43. Compare *Hayes v Northern Territory* (1999) 97 FCR 32.
44. *Western Australia v Ward* (2002) 213 CLR 1, 85 [64] (Gleeson CJ, Gaudron, Gummow and Hayne JJ).
45. ibid.
46. *Bulun Bulun v R & T Textiles Pty Ltd* (1998) 86 FCR 244, 256 (von Doussa J).
47. *Western Australia v Ward* (2002) 213 CLR 1, 84–5 [59–61] (Gleeson CJ, Gaudron, Gummow and Hayne JJ).
48. e.g. Terri Janke, *Our Culture: Our Future: Report on Australian Indigenous cultural and intellectual property rights* (AIATSIS/Michael Frankel, Canberra, 1998).
49. *Western Australia v Ward* (2002) 213 CLR 1, 93 [88] (Gleeson CJ, Gaudron, Gummow and Hayne JJ).
50. ibid. 93–4 [90–1] (Gleeson CJ, Gaudron, Gummow and Hayne JJ).
51. ibid. 70 [29] (Gleeson CJ, Gaudron, Gummow and Hayne JJ).
52. ibid. 93–4 [91] (Gleeson CJ, Gaudron, Gummow and Hayne JJ).
53. *Commonwealth v Yarmirr* (2001) 208 CLR 1.

54. *Western Australia v Ward* (2002) 213 CLR 1, 82 [49] (Gleeson CJ, Gaudron, Gummow and Hayne JJ).
55. ibid.
56. It is not clear, however, how this sits with the discussion of minerals highlighted above n 41 and accompanying text.
57. *Western Australia v Ward* (2002) 213 CLR 1, 82 [49] (Gleeson CJ, Gaudron, Gummow and Hayne JJ).
58. e.g. *Wik v Queensland* (1996) 187 CLR 1, 214 (Kirby J); cited in *Commonwealth v Yarmirr* (2001) 208 CLR 1, 46–7 [37].
59. Noel Pearson, 'Concept of Native Title at Common Law', in *Land Rights — Past, present and future: 20 years of land rights, our land is our life*, Conference Proceedings (Northern Land Council and Central Land Council, Canberra, 1996) 119.
60. *Western Australia v Ward* (2002) 213 CLR 1, 91 [82]. Contra *Western Australia v Ward* (2000) 99 FCR 316 at 487–8 [684] (North J).
61. *Western Australia v Ward* (2002) 213 CLR 1, 89 [78] (Gleeson CJ, Gaudron, Gummow and Hayne JJ).
62. ibid. 114 [149] (Gleeson CJ, Gaudron, Gummow and Hayne JJ).
63. ibid. 89 [76] (Gleeson CJ, Gaudron, Gummow and Hayne JJ).
64. ibid. 89 [78] (Gleeson CJ, Gaudron, Gummow and Hayne JJ). At 88–9 [74–80], the majority summarily rejected any application of the stricter test of adverse dominion adopted by Lambert JA of the Canadian Supreme Court in *Delgamuukw v British Columbia* (1993) 104 DLR (4th) 470 at 670–2 (Lambert JA), which would require an express intention by parliament that was permanently and actually adverse to the continued enjoyment of native title.
65. This was highlighted in the treatment of the Ord Project, which the majority held must be considered on the basis of the rights conferred by each of the diverse titles making up the project: *Western Australia v Ward* (2002) 213 CLR 1, 112 [143].
66. ibid. 114–15 [148–51] (Gleeson CJ, Gaudron, Gummow and Hayne JJ).
67. ibid. 158 [287] (Gleeson CJ, Gaudron, Gummow and Hayne JJ). It should be noted that the deeming provisions of the Previous Exclusive Possession Act (PEPA) Regime ignore this fundamental principle.
68. ibid. 123 [170] (Gleeson CJ, Gaudron, Gummow and Hayne JJ). Mining leases, too, were considered not to grant exclusive possession, at 165 [306]. The exclusive right to mine is a limited purpose that is not wholly inconsistent with continued access and use by native title holders.
69. ibid. 128 [184] (Gleeson CJ, Gaudron, Gummow and Hayne JJ). This finding should be compared to the Court's decision in *Wilson v Anderson* (2002) 213 CLR 401, decided on the same day. In that case, a class of New South Wales grazing leases was said to confer exclusive possession and therefore fall within the PEPA provisions (NTA s 23B).
70. They are a PNEPA within the definition of the NTA s 23F. As a state 'act', s 12M of the State Validation legislation applies. That section parallels s 23G of the NTA.
71. *Western Australia v Ward* (2002) 213 CLR 1, 206 [458] (Gleeson CJ, Gaudron, Gummow and Hayne JJ).
72. ibid. 132 [200] (Gleeson CJ, Gaudron, Gummow and Hayne JJ).
73. ibid. 115 [151] (Gleeson CJ, Gaudron, Gummow and Hayne JJ).

74. ibid. 143–5 [238–41] (Gleeson CJ, Gaudron, Gummow and Hayne JJ).
75. ibid. 131 [192] (Gleeson CJ, Gaudron, Gummow and Hayne JJ).
76. ibid. 131 [193] (Gleeson CJ, Gaudron, Gummow and Hayne JJ).
77. ibid. 250 [590] (Kirby J).
78. *Wilson v Anderson* (2002) 213 CLR 401 (8 August 2002). The case was brought by Michael Anderson on behalf of the Euahlayi-Dixon clan in relation to its traditional lands in western New South Wales.
79. NTA (Pt 2 Div 2B), especially s 23B(2)(viii) and s 248A. See also *Native Title (New South Wales) Act 1994* (NSW). The effect of these provisions and any compensation payable may operate outside the common law and RDA: NTA s 23J; *Wilson v Anderson* (2002) 213 CLR 401, 431-2; [50-51] (Gaudron, Gummow and Hayne JJ).
80. ibid., 420 [14] (Gleeson CJ).
81. ibid., 419-20 [13-14] (Gleeson CJ). A significant aspect of the leases in question, to the reasoning of the Court, was that they were granted 'in perpetuity', which arguably goes only to the length of time, not exclusive possession. Unlike *Wik*, the Court did not consider the *sui generis* status of the statutory titles emerging from the WLA. Compare *Wilson v Anderson* (2002) 213 CLR 401, 481; [204] (Callinan J) and full Federal Court: *Anderson v Wilson* (2000) 97 FCR 453, 484; also *Wik Peoples v Queensland* (1996) 187 CLR 1.
82. *James on behalf of the Martu People v Western Australia* [2002] FCA 1208.
83. *Wik Peoples v Queensland* (1996) 187 CLR 1; *Fejo v Northern Territory* (1998) 195 CLR 96.
84. *Western Australia v Ward* (2002) 213 CLR 1, 240 [561] (McHugh J); 398 [970] (Callinan J).

7. Proof of a native title society: *Yorta Yorta v Victoria*

1. 214 CLR 422.
2. Noel Pearson, discussant on questions of proof raised by the *Yorta Yorta* case, The Past and Future of Land Rights Conference, AIATSIS, Townsville 28–31 August 2001.
3. *Members of the Yorta Yorta Aboriginal Community v Victoria* (1998) 1606 FCA.
4. Referring to the 1881 Petition to the Governor General of New South Wales signed by 42 residents of Maloga Mission who requested that lands be reserved for them so as to 'support ourselves by our own industry'. Rather than being seen as evidence of the ongoing struggle for the return of lands, as it was tendered by the applicants, it was adjudged evidence of abandonment of laws and customs.
5. This approach immediately began to be replicated in other native title cases: See Chapter 9, which discusses *De Rose v South Australia* [2002] 1342 FCA (1 November 2002).
6. *Members of the Yorta Yorta Aboriginal Community v Victoria* (2002) 214 CLR 422, 435–6 [17–20], summary of claimants' arguments (Gleeson CJ, Gummow and Hayne JJ).
7. *Members of the Yorta Yorta Aboriginal Community v Victoria* (1998) 1606 FCA, [121–5] (Olney J).
8. ibid. [128].
9. ibid. [123].

10. *Members of the Yorta Yorta Aboriginal Community v Victoria* (2001) 110 FCR 244, 279 [127] (Branson and Katz JJ).
11. ibid. [191] (Branson and Katz JJ).
12. 208 CLR 1.
13. *Members of the Yorta Yorta Aboriginal Community v Victoria* (2002) 214 CLR 422, 455–7 [85]. See also *Members of the Yorta Yorta Aboriginal Community v Victoria* (2001) 110 FCR 244, 282 [140–1] (Branson and Katz JJ, Black CJ dissenting).
14. *Members of the Yorta Yorta Aboriginal Community v Victoria* (2002) 214 CLR 422, 444 [46].
15. ibid. 463 [112], 459 [101] (Gaudron and Kirby JJ).
16. ibid. 463 [111].
17. ibid. 439–40 [31] (Gleeson CJ, Gummow and Hayne JJ).
18. ibid.
19. ibid. 443–4 [43-4].
20. ibid. 441 [37].
21. ibid. 440 [32].
22. ibid. 467 [129] (McHugh).
23. ibid. 444 [46] (Gleeson CJ, Gummow and Hayne JJ).
24. ibid. 444-5 [47].
25. ibid. 445 [49].
26. ibid. 447 [56].
27. ibid. 464 [116] (Gaudron and Kirby JJ).
28. ibid. 464 [117].
29. ibid. 465 [119].
30. ibid. 465–6 [121].
31. 213 CLR 1.
32. 175 CLR 1, 110 (Deane, Gaudron JJ); 192 (Toohey J).
33. *Yanner v Eaton* (1999) 201 CLR 351, 381–2 [68] (Gummow J); *Ward on behalf of the Miriuwung and Gajerrong People v Western Australia* (1998) 159 ALR 483. See also *Campbell v Arnold* (1982) 565 FLR 382 (NTSC), concerning the *Crown Lands Act 1978* (NT) regarding the use of firearms in hunting.
34. *Members of the Yorta Yorta Aboriginal Community v Victoria* (2001) 110 FCR 244, 279, [127] (Branson and Katz JJ).
35. ibid.
36. *Mabo v Queensland [No. 2]* (1992) 175 CLR 1 61, 70 (Brennan J), 110 (Deane and Gaudron JJ). See also Gummow J in *Yanner v Eaton* (1999) 201 CLR 351, 381–2 [68], who referred to 'evolved or altered form of traditional behaviour'.
37. *Mabo v Queensland [No. 2]* (1992) 175 CLR 1, 61 (Brennan J).
38. *Members of the Yorta Yorta Aboriginal Community v Victoria* (2002) 214 CLR 422, 456 [87], 456–7 [89]. Compare the dissenting judgment of Gaudron and Kirby JJ. They rejected the requirement that connection be 'substantially maintained', suggesting that this term finds no expression in the NTA.
39. ibid. 455 [83].
40. Pearson suggested what may seem a radical approach: that the requirements for proof should begin with the perceptions of the contemporary society — do the Indigenous people identify as a social and cultural group, defined by their status as Indigenous and their history as the original owners of the area claimed? On this test, Justice Olney's decision can only be interpreted as suggesting that the Yorta Yorta

have fabricated their identity. Noel Pearson, discussant on questions of proof raised by the *Yorta Yorta* case, The Past and Future of Land Rights Conference, AIATSIS, Townsville, 28–31 August 2001. A similar view was expressed by Justice Kirby in arguments before the Bench, *Members of the Yorta Yorta Aboriginal Community v Victoria*, M128/2001 (24 May 2002) transcript: 'when Australia began to accept their [Indigenous peoples'] entitlement to a separate identity, it [traditional society] flourished again, it came again. Now, the question is: was there abandonment in that history or was it simply the reality of those times that they had to face up to?'

41. That is, native title cannot be extinguished contrary to the Act. Abandonment is not a basis for extinguishment contemplated by the NTA and cannot be introduced through reference to the definition of native title in s 223, which requires that native title be 'recognised by the common law': s 223(1)(c).
42. *Members of the Yorta Yorta Aboriginal Community v Victoria* (2002) 214 CLR 422, 457 [90].
43. ibid. 454 [80] (Gleeson CJ, Gummow and Hayne JJ).
44. ibid. 453–4 [80, 77].
45. ibid. 458 [96].
46. ibid. 443–4 [44].
47. ibid. 458 [95–6].

8. Rules of interpretation: *Griffiths v Minister for Lands, Planning and Environment*

1. *Griffiths v Minister for Lands, Planning and Environment* (2008) 235 CLR 232.
2. *Griffiths v Northern Territory* (2007) 243 ALR 72.
3. (1984) 155 CLR 193.
4. *Griffiths v Northern Territory* (2007) 243 ALR 72, [30] (Gummow, Hayne and Heydon JJ, with Gleeson CJ and Crennan J agreeing).
5. *Werribee Council v Kerr* [1928] HCA 41; (1928) 42 CLR 1 at 33.
6. *Clissold v Perry* [1904] HCA 12; (1904) 1 CLR 363 at 373.
7. *Griffiths v Minister for Lands, Planning and Environment* (2008) 235 CLR 232, [173].
8. ibid. [178–9].
9. NTA s 24MD(6A) gives native title holders 'the same' procedural rights as a holder of any ordinary title.
10. See, for example, *Clissold v Perry* [1904] HCA 12; (1904) 1 CLR 363, 373; *Balog v Independent Commission against Corruption* (1990) 169 CLR 625, 635-36; *Davis v The Commonwealth* (1988) 166 CLR 79; *Coco v the Queen* (1994) 179 CLR 427, 436-37; *Bropho v Western Australia* (1990) 171 CLR 1, 18.
11. *Mabo v Queensland [No. 2]* (1992) 175 CLR 1 [75]. Brennan J cites cases from those jurisdictions, including *Calder v Attorney General of British Columbia* (1973) SCR, 404; (1973) 34 DLR (3d), 210; *R v Sparrow* (1990) 1 SCR.1075, 1094; (1990) 70 DLR (4th) 385, 401; *United States v Santa Fe Pacific Railroad Co.* (1941) 314 US 353, 354; *Lipan Apache Tribe v United States* (1967) 180 Ct Cl 487, 492; *Te Weehi v Regional Fisheries Officer* (1986) 1 NZLR 680, 691–2.
12. *Mabo v Queensland [No. 2]* (1992) 175 CLR 1 [81].

13. *Griffiths v Minister for Lands, Planning and Environment* (2008) 235 CLR 232, [107].
14. ibid. [109].
15. ibid. [109].
16. ibid. [107–8].
17. *Western Australia v Ward* (2002) 213 CLR 1 [557]. See also *Griffith* [107].

9. Implementing the High Court's jurisprudence: *De Rose v South Australia [No. 2]*

1. *De Rose v South Australia [No. 2]* (2005) 145 FCR 290.
2. *De Rose v South Australia* [2002] 1342 FCA [911] (O'Loughlin J).
3. Although early ethnographic maps show the land as Antikirinya country: ibid [297–9].
4. ibid. [320].
5. ibid. [203].
6. ibid. [331].
7. ibid. [206].
8. ibid. [377].
9. ibid. [905].
10. ibid. [106].
11. Compare commentary from Justice Kirby from the bench, in *Members of the Yorta Yorta Aboriginal Community v Victoria*, M128/2001 (24 May 2002) transcript.
12. 213 CLR 1, 85–6 [64].
13. *De Rose v South Australia* [2002] FCA 1342 [901].
14. ibid. [302].
15. Indeed, had such laws and practices continued, they may have fallen short of recognition by the common law under the 'repugnancy' rule: see ibid. [508, 512].
16. ibid. [681].
17. *Wik Peoples v Queensland* (1996) 187 CLR 1.
18. *De Rose v South Australia* [2002] FCA 1342 [106].
19. ibid. [436].
20. ibid. [439].
21. 175 CLR 1.
22. *De Rose v South Australia* [2002] FCA 1342 [270–1].
23. e.g. ibid. [372, 570].
24. ibid. [342].
25. ibid. [237, 245].
26. ibid. [541].
27. ibid. [531], citing *Western Australia v Ward* (2002) 213 CLR 1, 168 [316].
28. *De Rose v South Australia* [2002] FCA 1342 [541], citing *Western Australia v Ward* (2002) 213 CLR 1, 196 [417].
29. *De Rose v South Australia* [2002] FCA 1342 [558].
30. ibid. [922].
31. *De Rose v South Australia [No. 1]* (2003) 133 FCR 325 (Wilcox, Sackville and Merkel JJ).
32. ibid. [312–13].
33. ibid. [145].

34. ibid. [322].
35. ibid. [282].
36. ibid. [275].
37. ibid. [279].
38. ibid. [281]; distinguishing *Members of the Yorta Yorta Aboriginal Community v Victoria* (2002) 214 CLR 422.
39. *De Rose v South Australia [No. 1]* (2003) 133 FCR 325 [312]; citing *Members of the Yorta Yorta Aboriginal Community v Victoria* (2002) 214 CLR 422, 457 [90].
40. *Members of the Yorta Yorta Aboriginal Community v Victoria* (2002) 214 CLR 422, 457 [90].
41. *De Rose v South Australia [No. 1]* (2003) 133 FCR 325 [326].
42. *Western Australia v Ward* (2002) 213 CLR 1, 85 [64]; also *Western Australia v Ward* (2000) 99 FCR 316, 382 [243].
43. *De Rose v South Australia [No. 1]* (2003) 133 FCR 325 [316–17].
44. ibid. [328].
45. ibid. [330].
46. ibid. [281].
47. ibid. [331].
48. ibid. [312–13].
49. *De Rose v South Australia [No. 2]* (2005) 145 FCR 290, [8(2)] (Wilcox, Sackville and Merkel JJ) (original emphasis).
50. ibid. [8(1)].
51. ibid. [24].
52. The classification may be relevant in determining the content of the determination order under s 225. Also, the amended NTA requires application to be made on behalf of the native title group and to be authorised: ss 61(1), 253. See *De Rose v South Australia [No. 2]* (2005) 145 FCR 290, 302–4 [46–50].
53. NTA s 223(1). Original emphasis removed; emphasis added.
54. *De Rose v South Australia [No. 2]* (2005) 145 FCR 290, 300 [31].
55. ibid. [44]; see discussion, at [35–43].
56. ibid. [52].
57. ibid. [59–60]; at [57–8] the Court compared the two extremes: it was true that an individual or group who had never acknowledged or observed laws and customs in relation to the area could succeed merely because 'other Aboriginal peoples' had observed laws and customs and maintained a connection with the area, but it was also true that a claim could succeed only if every member of the claimant community or group had acknowledged and observed the relevant traditional laws and customs.
58. ibid. [60].
59. ibid. [63].
60. ibid. [65].
61. ibid. [108].
62. The rights of the pastoral leaseholders were contained in the terms and conditions of three Crown leases and in the *Pastoral Land Management and Conservation Act 1989* (SA).
63. *De Rose v South Australia [No. 2]* (2005) 145 FCR 290 [149]. The Court concluded that the non-extinguishment principle that applied to activities done pursuant to a

grant (s 44H NTA) did not apply to rights conferred by a grant that extinguished native title rights and interests. That is, s 44H confirmed the exercise of 'coexisting rights': [159–60].
64. ibid. [150].
65. ibid.
66. ibid. [156] citing *Western Australia v Ward* (2002) 213 CLR 1, 114–15 [150].
67. ibid.
68. *De Rose v South Australia [No. 2]* (2005) 145 FCR 290 [31], though noting the ambiguity in the High Court's treatment in *Ward* of the Western Australian mining lease's impermanent structures, see *Western Australia v Ward* (2002) 213 CLR 1, 165–6 [308].
69. Leave to appeal by the pastoralists was rejected by the High Court: *Fuller and Another v De Rose and Others* (unreported decision, HCA A37/2005, Hayne, Gummow and Crennan JJ, 10 February 2006).

10. Continuity and change: *Bodney v Bennell*

1. *Bodney v Bennell* (2008) 167 FCR 84.
2. *Risk v Northern Territory* (2007) 240 ALR 75; *State of Western Australia v Sebastian* (2008) 173 FCR 1.
3. *De Rose v State of South Australia [No. 2]* (2005) 145 FCR 290; *Northern Territory v Alyawarr, Kaytetye, Warumungu, Wakay Native Title Claim Group* (2005) 220 ALR 431, [78].
4. For discussion see Stuart Bradfield, 'Settling Native Title: Pursuing a comprehensive regional agreement in south west Australia' in M. Langton et al. (eds), *Settling With Indigenous Peoples* (Federation Press, Sydney, 2006). For a short summary of the history of this process, see Lisa Strelein and Stuart Bradfield, 'The Single Noongar Claim: Negotiating native title in the south west' (2004) *Indigenous Law Bulletin* 36.
5. See Bradfield op. cit. Compare Manuhuia Barcham, 'Regional Governance Structures in Indigenous Australia: Western Australian examples', *CIGAD Working Paper Series No. 1/2006* (CIGAD, Massey University, Palmerston North, 2006).
6. *Bennell v State of Western Australia* (2006) 153 FCR 120 (per Wilcox J), statement at the handing down of the decision.
7. ibid. [266]. However, under cross-examination the state's anthropologist, Ron Brunton, conceded that there was a considerable degree of similarity in culture, beliefs, customs and laws; indeed, this had been his working assumption when preparing an earlier report for the state in response to the combined metropolitan claim before the Single Noongar Claim had been lodged, [322], [349].
8. ibid. [83(e)]. This would not mean that native title did not exist in the whole area or the Perth area but that it is held by a different group.
9. ibid. [273]–[275]. See also see *Neowarra v Western Australia* (2003) 134 FCR 208, [393].
10. *Bennell v State of Western Australia* (2006) 153 FCR 120, [409–10].
11. ibid. [330], [395], [430], [437] relying on *De Rose v State of South Australia [No. 2]* **(2005) 145 FCR 290.**

12. *Commonwealth v Yarmirr* (2001) 208 CLR 1 [16]; *Neowarra v Western Australia* 134 FCR 208 [310], *Northern Territory v Alyawarr, Kaytetye, Warumungu, Wakay Native Title Claim Group* (2005) 220 ALR 431, [156], *Rubibi Community v State of Western Australia [No. 6]* (2006) 226 ALR 676 [115].
13. *Bennell v State of Western Australia* (2006) 153 FCR 120 [284].
14. ibid. [68–9].
15. Referring to *Mabo v Queensland [No. 2]* (1992) 175 CLR 1, 61 (Brennan J).
16. See *Members of the Yorta Yorta Aboriginal Community v Victoria* (2002) 214 CLR 422 [85]–[89].
17. *Risk v Northern Territory* [2006] FCA 404.
18. *Bennell v State of Western Australia* (2006) 153 FCR 120. His Honour dismissed competing applications of C. R. Bodney.
19. *Bodney v Bennell* (2008) 167 FCR 84 [42].
20. ibid. [43].
21. *Members of the Yorta Yorta Aboriginal Community v Victoria* (2002) 214 CLR 422 [49], (Gleeson CJ, Gummow and Hayne JJ). Cited by Wilcox J, *Bennell v State of Western Australia* (2006) 153 FCR 120 [64], and by the full Court, *Bodney v Bennell* (2008) 167 FCR 84 [46].
22. ibid. [46].
23. *Bennell v State of Western Australia* (2006) 153 FCR 120 [64].
24. ibid. [65].
25. *Sampi v Western Australia* [2005] FCA 777 [1042].
26. *Northern Territory v Alyawarr, Kaytetye, Warumungu, Wakay Native Title Claim Group* (2005) 220 ALR 431 [78].
27. ibid. [77].
28. *Bennell v State of Western Australia* (2006) 153 FCR 120 [776] citing *Members of the Yorta Yorta Aboriginal Community v Victoria* (2002) 214 CLR 422.
29. ibid. [89].
30. *Bodney v Bennell* (2008) 167 FCR 84 [81]. Reiterated at [97].
31. *Bennell v State of Western Australia* (2006) 153 FCR 120 [785].
32. *Bodney v Bennell* (2008) 167 FCR 84 [74] (emphasis added).
33. *Members of the Yorta Yorta Aboriginal Community v Victoria* (2002) 214 CLR 422 [90] (per Gleeson CJ, Gummow and Hayne JJ).
34. *Bennell v State of Western Australia* (2006) 153 FCR 120 [791].
35. *Bodney v Bennell* (2008) 167 FCR 84 [116].
36. ibid. [79] (emphasis added).
37. ibid. [82].
38. ibid.
39. ibid. [80].
40. ibid. [117]–[119].
41. *Members of the Yorta Yorta Aboriginal Community v Victoria* (2002) 214 CLR 422 [44].
42. ibid. See also *State of Western Australia v Sebastian* (2008) 173 FCR 1.
43. *Bodney v Bennell* (2008) 167 FCR 84 63.
44. ibid. [121].
45. ibid.
46. ibid. [74], also [79].

47. ibid. [97].
48. ibid. [70].
49. *Risk v Northern Territory* [2006] FCA 404, [97(c)]. Compare *Members of the Yorta Yorta Aboriginal Community v Victoria* (2002) 214 CLR 422 [87].
50. *Risk v Northern Territory* (2007) 240 ALR 75 [78]–[79].
51. *Members of the Yorta Yorta Aboriginal Community v Victoria* (2002) 214 CLR 422 [87].
52. *Bodney v Bennell* (2008) 167 FCR 84 63.
53. ibid. [77].
54. *Bennell v State of Western Australia* (2006) 153 FCR 120 [88].
55. [2005] FCA 50, [195], referring to Jessell MR in *Hammerton v Honey* (1876) 24 WR 603 at 604.
56. *Bennell v State of Western Australia* (2006) 153 FCR 120 [449–50].
57. *Bodney v Bennell* (2008) 167 FCR 84 [89]. The full Court observed that there is no doubt that the evidence is *prima facie* admissible under s 79 of the *Evidence Act* and an expert may rely on 'facts' that would otherwise be hearsay, for example, contained in the writing of others and thus not in evidence as such. Those facts become admissible as relevant to the basis of the experts' opinion, but they are not evidence of the truth of the facts themselves: *Evidence Act* s 60. This includes reputable publications and materials in their area of expertise. However, the weight to be attributed to the evidence is a matter for the Court.
58. *Bodney v Bennell* (2008) 167 FCR 84 [95].
59. Robert French, 'Lifting the Burden of Native Title: Some modest proposals for improvement', presentation to the Federal Court Native Title User Group, Adelaide, 9 July 2008.
60. French, ibid. [27]–[30].
61. *Bennell v State of Western Australia* (2006) 153 FCR 120, [77].
62. ibid. [425].
63. ibid. [424], making reference to similar comments by French J in *Sampi v Western Australia [No. 2]* [2005] FCA 1567.
64. This argument was carried through to the appeal: *Bodney v Bennell* (2008) 167 FCR 84 [75]–[77]. It should be noted, of course, that the ultimate argument of the state and Commonwealth was that native title did not exist in the area of the separate question.
65. See *Western Australia v Ward* (2000) 99 FCR 316 (first Full Court decision), [203]–[204], *Neowarra v Western Australia* (2003) 134 FCR 208 [393] and *Northern Territory v Alyawarr, Kaytetye, Warumungu, Wakay Native Title Claim Group* (2005) 220 ALR 431 [69]–[71]. See also *Lardil, Kaidilt, Yangkaal and Gangalidda People v Queensland* [2000] FCA 1548. Interestingly, his Honour referred to the idea of individual and groups rights being 'carved out of' (to use Brennan's words) or as 'incidents of' (to cite Gummow J in *Yanner v Eaton* (1999) 201 CLR 351 [73]) the communal title.
66. *Bennell v State of Western Australia* (2006) 153 FCR 120, *Northern Territory v Alyawarr, Kaytetye, Warumungu, Wakay Native Title Claim Group* (2005) 220 ALR 431 [78]: see [81], [110-12] and paras 2 and 6 of the formal determination, which is set out at [504]–[505]. See also *Western Australia v Ward* (2000) 99 FCR 316 [202].

67. *Bennell v State of Western Australia* (2006) 153 FCR 120 [82].
68. *Mabo v Queensland* [No. 2] (1992) 175 CLR 1, 62; cited in *Northern Territory v Alyawarr, Kaytetye, Warumungu, Wakay Native Title Claim Group* (2005) 220 ALR 431 [69] and Wilcox J in *Bennell v State of Western Australia* (2006) 153 FCR 120 [61].
69. Recognition level was the term used in *Neowarra v Western Australia* (2003) 134 FCR 208. For examples of the courts' rejection of the estate group argument see also *Sampi v Western Australia [No. 2]* [2005] FCA 1567; and *State of Western Australia v Sebastian* (2008) 173 FCR 1.
70. *Bodney v Bennell* (2008) 167 FCR 84 [131].
71. ibid. [142].
72. *Mabo v Queensland [No. 2]* (1992) 175 CLR 1, 51 [53].
73. *Bodney v Bennell* (2008) 167 FCR 84 [139].
74. ibid. [152].
75. *Mabo v Queensland [No. 2]* (1992) 175 CLR 1, 51 (Brennan J).
76. *Bodney v Bennell* (2008) 167 FCR 84 [139].
77. ibid. [139].
78. ibid. [142]. Though they 'note in passing' that the High Court has not used the term 'communal title': [141].
79. The provision refers to 'rights to possession, occupation, use and enjoyment to the exclusion of all others'.
80. ibid. [143].
81. *De Rose v State of South Australia [No. 2]* (2005) 145 FCR 290 [38].
82. *Bodney v Bennell* (2008) 167 FCR 84 [149].
83. ibid. [150].
84. The full Court cites *Sampi v Western Australia [No. 2]* [2005] FCA 1567 [955]; *Northern Territory v Alyawarr, Kaytetye, Warumungu, Wakay Native Title Claim Group* (2005) 220 ALR 431 [69]–[71]; *Western Australia v Ward* (2002) 213 CLR 1 [7]; and *De Rose v State of South Australia [No. 2]* (2005) 145 FCR 290 [29]–[30], and notes that communal native title claims have been made regularly: see, for example, *Yarmirr v Northern Territory [No. 2]* (1998) 82 FCR 533, 601–602; and *Gumana v Northern Territory* (2007) 158 FCR 349 [144]–[161].
85. *Bodney v Bennell* (2008) 167 FCR 84 [147].
86. Citing, for example, *Sampi v Western Australia* [2005] FCA 1567, [955]; *Northern Territory v Alyawarr, Kaytetye, Warumungu, Wakay Native Title Claim Group* (2005) 220 ALR 431, [71].
87. Citing *Western Australia v Ward* (2000) 99 FCR 316 [239].
88. ibid. [202]; *Northern Territory v Alyawarr, Kaytetye, Warumungu, Wakay Native Title Claim Group* (2005) 220 ALR 431 [79].
89. Citing *Western Australia v Ward* (2000) 99 FCR 316 [205]–[206]; cf. *De Rose v State of South Australia [No. 2]* (2005) 145 FCR 290 [45]–[47]; see, for example, *Neowarra v Western Australia* (2003) 134 FCR 208 [384] ff.
90. Citing *Mabo v Queensland [No. 2]* (1992) 175 CLR 1, 62.
91. *Bodney v Bennell* (2008) 167 FCR 84 [148].
92. ibid. [152].
93. ibid. [154].
94. See *Western Australia v Ward* (2002) 213 CLR 1 [202].

95. *Bodney v Bennell* (2008) 167 FCR 84 [156].
96. *Bennell v State of Western Australia* (2006) 153 FCR 120 [82].
97. *Bodney v Bennell* (2008) 167 FCR 84 [161].
98. ibid. [158].
99. ibid. [162] ff. See *Northern Territory v Alyawarr, Kaytetye, Warumungu, Wakay Native Title Claim Group* (2005) 220 ALR 431 [87]; *Sampi v Western Australia [No. 2]* [2005] FCA 1567 [1079]; and *Harrington-Smith on behalf of the Wongatha People v Western Australia (No. 9)* [2007] FCA 31; (2007) 238 ALR 1, [1880]. For the source of s 233(1)(b) see *Mabo v Queensland [No. 2]* (1992) 175 CLR 1, 59–60.
100. *Western Australia v Ward* (2002) 213 CLR 1 [64].
101. *Bodney v Bennell* (2008) 167 FCR 84 [172]–[173].
102. *Sampi v Western Australia [No. 2]* [2005] FCA 1567 [1079] cited in *Bodney v Bennell* (2008) 167 FCR 84 [174].
103. *Bodney v Bennell* (2008) 167 FCR 84, 63 [168].
104. ibid. [169] citing *Neowarra v Western Australia* (2003) 134 FCR 208 [352].
105. *Bodney v Bennell* (2008) 167 FCR 84 [168], references omitted.
106. *Northern Territory v Alyawarr, Kaytetye, Warumungu, Wakay Native Title Claim Group* (2005) 220 ALR 431 [111].
107. *Bodney v Bennell* (2008) 167 FCR 84 [170].
108. This also extends to the question of direct descent, which the judges note is relevant only in relation to its relationship to laws and customs that connect people to land: ibid. [189].
109. ibid. [178] (references omitted).
110. ibid. [179].
111. ibid. [181]–[184].
112. *Bodney v Bennell* (2008) 167 FCR 84 [186].
113. Noel Pearson, 'Defining the Problem', presentation to the 's223 workshop', Agreements Treaties and Negotiated Settlements Project, Melbourne University, May 2009.
114. See Lisa Strelein, 'A Captive of Statute' (2009) 93 *Reform* 48–51.

11. The development of native title jurisprudence

1. 175 CLR 1.
2. 187 CLR 1.
3. Early attempts to bring an argument concerning fiduciary duty include *Bodney v Westralia Airports Corporation* (2000) 109 FCR 178. In a different context *Kruger v Commonwealth* (1997) 190 CLR 1 sought to establish a fiduciary duty arising from the policies that forcibly removed Indigenous children from their families.
4. 214 CLR 244.
5. 213 CLR 1. Any such argument must overcome the position taken by Brennan CJ in *Wik* that Indigenous peoples' possession of land under native title was not wrongful and therefore not adverse to the Crown: *Wik Peoples v Queensland* (1996) 187 CLR 1, 11 (Brennan CJ).
6. 183 CLR 373, 453 (Mason CJ, Brennan, Deane, Toohey, Gaudron and McHugh JJ).
7. 201 CLR 351.

8. *Fejo v Northern Territory* (1998) 195 CLR 96; *Wilson v Anderson* (2002) 213 CLR 401.
9. *Fejo v Northern Territory* (1998) 195 CLR 96, 130 [53]. References omitted.
10. *Wik Peoples v Queensland* (1996) 187 CLR 1, 177–9 (Gummow J).
11. *Hayes v Northern Territory* (1999) 97 FCR 32; most recently, see *Dale v Moses* [2007] FCAFC 82 [206], [308–9]; *State of Western Australia v Sebastian* (2008) 173 FCR 1, [282], [288–93].
12. *Wik Peoples v Queensland* (1996) 187 CLR 1, 213.
13. *Fejo v Northern Territory* (1998) 195 CLR 96, 128 [47].
14. 208 CLR 1.
15. *Wik Peoples v Queensland* (1996) 187 CLR 1, 127–8 (Toohey J).
16. *Mabo v Queensland [No. 2]* (1992) 175 CLR 1, 61; see also 43 (Brennan J, Mason CJ and McHugh J agreeing).
17. *Commonwealth v Yarmirr* (2001) 208 CLR 1, [7]; *Western Australia v Ward* (2002) 213 CLR 1, [16]; *Members of the Yorta Yorta Aboriginal Community v Victoria* (2002) 214 CLR 422, [32].
18. *Wilson v Anderson* (2002) 213 CLR 401, 467 [169–70].
19. ibid. 416–17 [4–6] (Gleeson CJ).
20. ibid. 419–20 [13] (Gleeson CJ) referring to *Wik Peoples v Queensland* (1996) 187 CLR 1, 120 (Toohey J), but see also 177 (Gummow J); 219 (Kirby J).
21. *Wilson v Anderson* (2002) 213 CLR 401, 426–7 [34–6]. I have borrowed this phrase from *Wik Peoples v Queensland* (1996) 187 CLR 1, 103: 'clothe the principal questions with a certain unreality'.
22. T. Murray, 'Conjectural Histories: Some archaeological and historical consequences of Indigenous dispossession in Australia' in Ian Lilley (ed.), *Native Title and the Transformation of Archaeology in the Postcolonial World, Oceania Monograph* (2000) 50; Rod Hagen, 'Ethnographic Information and Anthropological Interpretation in a Native Title Claim: The Yorta Yorta experience' (2001) 25 *Aboriginal History* 216; James Weiner, 'Diaspora, Materialism, Tradition: Anthropological issues in the recent High Court Appeal of the Yorta Yorta' (2002) 2(18) *Land, Rights, Laws: Issues of Native Title* 1; Heather Bowe, 'Linguistics and the Yorta Yorta Native Title Claim' in John Henderson and David Nash (eds), *Language in Native Title* (Aboriginal Studies Press, Canberra, 2002) 101; Clare Land, 'Representations of Gender in E. M. Curr's "Recollections of Squatting in Victoria": Implications for land justice through the native title process' (2002) 5(19) *Indigenous Law Bulletin* 6; Greg McIntyre, 'Native Title Rights after Yorta Yorta' (2003) 9 *James Cook University Law Review* 268; Daniel Lavery, 'A Greater Sense of Tradition: The implications of the normative system principles in Yorta Yorta for native title determination applications' (2003) 10(4) *Murdoch University Electronic Journal of Law*.
23. See, for example, Ann Arnold, 'Turning Back the Tide of History', *The Sunday Age: Extra* (Melbourne), 8 January 2006, 18.
24. *Members of the Yorta Yorta Aboriginal Community v Victoria* (2002) 214 CLR 422, 444 [46].
25. ibid. 439 [31].
26. *Griffiths v Minister for Lands, Planning and Environment* (2008) 235 CLR 232.
27. *Members of the Yorta Yorta Aboriginal Community v Victoria* (2001) 110 FCR 244 [91–2] (Black CJ).

28. *De Rose v State of South Australia [No. 1]* (2003) FCAFC 286 (16 December 2003).
29. *De Rose v State of South Australia [No. 2]* (2005) 145 FCR 290 (8 June 2005).
30. *Bodney v Bennell* (2008) 167 FCR 84 (23 April 2008).
31. *Northern Territory v Alyawarr, Kaytetye, Warumungu, Wakay Native Title Claim Group (Alyawarr)* (2005) 220 ALR 431 [78].
32. *State of Western Australia v Sebastian* (2008) 173 FCR 1.
33. *Lardil, Kaidilt, Yangkaal and Gangalidda People v Queensland* [2000] FCA 1548; *Neowarra v Western Australia* (2003) 134 FCR 208 (*Neowarra*); *Alyawarr; Sampi v Western Australia* [2005] FCA 777; see also, *Gumana v Northern Territory* (2007) 158 FCR 349; *Griffiths v Northern Territory* (2007) 243 ALR 72; *State of Western Australia v Sebastian* (2008) 173 FCR 1; among others. From 2002 to 2008 there were more than fifteen litigated determinations that native title exists.
34. *Risk v Northern Territory* (2007) 240 ALR 75; *Harrington-Smith v Western Australia [No. 9]* (2007) 238 ALR 1.

12. The jurisprudence of native title: 'Recognition' and 'protection'

1. *Mabo v Queensland [No. 2]* 175 CLR 1.
2. NTA s 3(a).
3. *Commonwealth v Yarmirr* (2001) 208 CLR 1, 90 [176] (McHugh J). See also *Members of the Yorta Yorta Aboriginal Community v Victoria* (2002) 214 CLR 422, 444 [45], where the Court held that the NTA does not create a new right called 'native title', but seeks to recognise the same rights and interests recognised by the common law.
4. *Wik Peoples v Queensland* (1996) 187 CLR 1, 214 (Kirby J).
5. *Commonwealth v Yarmirr* (2001) 208 CLR 1, 46–7 [37] (Gleeson CJ, Gaudron, Gummow and Hayne JJ).
6. *Mabo v Queensland [No. 2]* (1992) 175 CLR 1, 79 (Deane and Gaudron JJ).
7. *Richtersveld Community and Others v Alexkor Ltd and Another* [2003] (6) BCLR 583 (SCA).
8. *Alexkor Ltd and Another v Richtersveld Community and Others* [2003] Case CCT 19/03 (14 October 2003).
9. *Wik Peoples v Queensland* (1996) 187 CLR 1, 237–8.
10. *Commonwealth v Yarmirr* (2001) 208 CLR 1, 47 [39].
11. 135 CLR, 388 (Gibbs J), cited with approval in *Mabo v Queensland [No. 2]* (1992) 175 CLR 1, 31 (Brennan J, Mason CJ and McHugh J agreeing).
12. *Commonwealth v Yarmirr* (2001) 208 CLR 1, 53 [52], citing *New South Wales v Commonwealth* (1975) 135 CLR 337, 479 (Jacobs J).
13. *Mabo v Queensland [No. 2]* (1992) 175 CLR 1, 32.
14. *Commonwealth v Yarmirr* (2001) 208 CLR 1, 52 [51] (original emphasis).
15. For a discussion of the relevance of the relationship between the courts and the parliament, the separation of powers and the rule of law, see Lisa Strelein, 'The "Courts of the Conqueror": The utility of the courts for the assertion of Indigenous selfdetermination claims' (2000) 5(3) *Australian Indigenous Law Reporter* 1.
16. 183 CLR 373, 422–3 [12] (footnotes omitted). The presumption referred to here has its source in *Adeyinka Oyekan v Musendiku Adele* [1957] 2 All ER 785, 788.

17. [1921] 2 AC 399, 403. See also *St Catherine's Milling and Lumber Company v R* (1888) 14 App Cas 46.
18. *Mabo v Queensland [No. 2]* (1992) 175 CLR 1, 69 (Brennan J, with Mason CJ and McHugh J agreeing). See also 80–3 (Deane and Gaudron JJ), 180–4 (Toohey J).
19. Subject of course to the compromise in favour of Crown power to extinguish: ibid. 55–7 (Brennan J, with Mason CJ and McHugh J agreeing); 97–9 (Deane and Gaudron JJ); 182–3 (Toohey J); confirmed in *Western Australia v Commonwealth* (1995) 183 CLR 373, 422 (Mason CJ, Brennan, Deane, Toohey, Gaudron and McHugh JJ).
20. *Commonwealth v Yarmirr* (2001) 208 CLR 1, 51 [48] (original emphasis).
21. ibid. 51 [49].
22. ibid. 51 [50].
23. *Mabo v Queensland [No. 2]* (1992) 175 CLR 1, 82 (Brennan J).
24. *Griffiths v Minister for Lands, Planning and the Environment* (2008) 235 CLR 232.
25. *Commonwealth v Yarmirr* (2001) 208 CLR 1, 90 [178] (McHugh J) (references omitted). See also 115–16 [258] (Kirby J). The use of the term 'abandonment' was later rejected as a basis for extinguishment in *Members of the Yorta Yorta Aboriginal Community v Victoria* (2002) 214 CLR 422.
26. *Mabo v Queensland [No. 2]* (1992) 175 CLR 1, 30. Deane and Gaudron JJ were also persuaded by the fact that the circumstances of the case at hand made it unique; had it been merely an ordinary case, they would not have felt justified in 'reopening the validity of fundamental propositions which have been endorsed by long established authority', 109.
27. Thus, in *The Case of Tanistry* (1608) Davis (80 ER); 4th ed. Dublin (1762) English translation, 94–9, the Irish custom of tanistry under Brehon law (as the basis for inheritance) was held to be void because it was founded in violence and thus precluded from recognition by the common law. Referred to by Brennan J in *Mabo v Queensland [No. 2]* (1992) 175 CLR 1, 65.
28. See ibid. 47 (Brennan J).
29. *Commonwealth v Yarmirr* (2001) 208 CLR 1, 68 [97].
30. ibid. 49 [42], citing *Mabo v Queensland [No. 2]* (1992) 175 CLR 1, 95; they also cite Toohey J, at 193–4.
31. *Western Australia v Commonwealth* (1995) 183 CLR 373, 422–3 [12] (footnotes omitted).
32. *Commonwealth v Yarmirr* (2001) 208 CLR 1, 56 [61] (original emphasis).
33. ibid. 68 [98].
34. *Northern Territory of Australia v Arnhem Land Aboriginal Land Trust* (2008) 236 CLR 24.
35. ibid. 68 [99] (original emphasis).
36. ibid. 68 [100].
37. 'Concept of Native Title at Common Law' in *Land Rights — Past, present and future: 20 years of land rights, our land is our life*, Conference Proceedings (Northern Land Council and Central Land Council, Canberra, 1996) 119, 120.
38. 195 CLR 96, 128 [46] (Gleeson CJ, Gaudron, McHugh, Gummow, Hayne and Callinan JJ).
39. *Members of the Yorta Yorta Aboriginal Community v Victoria* (2002) 214 CLR 422, 439–40 [31].

40. *Commonwealth v Yarmirr* (2001) 208 CLR 1, 46–7 [37].
41. *Members of the Yorta Yorta Aboriginal Community v Victoria* (2002) 214 CLR 422, 443 [43] (original emphasis).
42. ibid. 441 [37]. Whether this is due to the intervention of the NTA remains unclear until we better understand whether there is in fact a parallel common law doctrine of recognition. The language and the majority joint judgment is ambiguous: 'An application for determination of native title requires the location of that intersection, and it requires that it be located by reference to the *Native Title Act*. In particular, it must be located by reference to the definition of native title in s 223(1).'
43. ibid. 443–4 [44].
44. *Bodney v Bennell* (2008) 167 FCR 84 [121].
45. ibid. The joint majority explained that 'the only rights or interests in relation to land or waters, originating otherwise than in the new sovereign order, which will be recognised after the assertion of that new sovereignty are those that find their origin in pre-sovereignty law and custom'.
46. ibid. 444–5 [47].
47. ibid. 443–4 [44] (original emphasis).
48. See Noel Pearson, 'Land is Susceptible of Ownership' in M. Langton et al. (eds), *Honour Among Nations?* (Melbourne University Press, 2004) 83.
49. *Western Australia v Ward* (2002) 213 CLR 1.
50. *Mabo v Queensland [No. 2]* (1992) 175 CLR 1, 58 (Brennan J); Deane and Gaudron JJ, similarly observed that 'the content ... will of course, vary according to the extent of the pre-existing interest of the relevant individual, group or community', at 88.
51. William Blackstone, 1 *Commentaries on the Laws of England* 104 (Legal Classics Library 1983) (1823); *Calvin's case* (1608) 77 Eng. Rep. 377, 398.
52. Originally expressed by Toohey J in *Mabo v Queensland [No. 2]* (1992) 175 CLR 1, 189–90.
53. *Wik Peoples v Queensland* (1996) 187 CLR 1, 169 (Gummow J). See also 126–7 (Toohey J).
54. ibid. 90 (Brennan J).
55. ibid. 25 (Brennan J).
56. See the Torrens system for the registration of titles introduced in Australia in the 1850s and 1860s and the Property Law Acts in each state and territory: for example, *Real Property Act 1862* (NSW); *Real Property Act 1861* (Qld); *Real Property Act 1858* (SA); *Real Property Act 1862* (Tas); *Real Property Act 1862* (Vic); and the *Transfer of Land Act 1874* (WA). See generally M. A. Neave, C. J. Rossiter and M. A. Stone, *Sackville and Neave, Property Law: Cases and materials* (6th edn, Butterworths, Sydney, 1999) 408–562.
57. *Commonwealth v Yarmirr* (2001) 208 CLR 1, 48 [14–15].
58. 201 CLR 351.
59. See *Commonwealth v Yarmirr* (1999) 101 FCR 171, 249–50 [325].
60. See *Mabo v Queensland [No. 2]* (1992) 175 CLR 1, 89 (Deane and Gaudron JJ); affirming *Amodu Tijani* [1921] 2 AC, 404–5; and *Guerin v R* (1984) 13 DLR (4th), 339. See also *Commonwealth v Yarmirr* (2001) 208 CLR 1, 48 [12].
61. *Neowarra v Western Australia* (2003) 134 FCR 208.

62. Without denying the anterior jurisprudential question of whether the common law should also recognise jurisdiction.
63. *Mabo v Queensland [No. 2]* (1992) 175 CLR 1, 51 (Brennan J). Toohey J, at 207, argued that the term 'title' described 'the group of rights which result from possession but which survive its loss; this includes the right to possession'.
64. 'The Post-*Delgamuukw* Nature and Content of Aboriginal Title' (Draft #3), *Delgamuukw* National Process Papers (May 2000), 12.
65. Pearson, 'Land is Susceptible of Ownership', see n 48, 9–11.
66. ibid. 11.
67. Pearson also finds support for his argument in the work of Kent McNeil, see Kent McNeil, 'Aboriginal Title and Aboriginal Rights: What's the connection?' (1997) 36 *Alberta Law Review*,117. See also Brian Slattery, 'The Metamorphosis of Aboriginal Title' (2006) 85 *The Canadian Bar Review* 255.
68. Pearson, 'Land is Susceptible of Ownership', see n 48, 12.
69. *Neowarra v Western Australia* (2003) 134 FCR 208, [380–1].
70. *Mabo v Queensland [No. 2]* (1992) 175 CLR 1, 61 (Brennan J).
71. *De Rose v South Australia* [No. 1] (2003) 133 FCR 325.
72. See *Western Australia v Ward* (2002) 213 CLR 1 [202]; *Alyawarr, Kaytetye, Warumungu, Wakay Native Title Claim Group v Northern Territory* (2004) 207 ALR 539, [79].
73. *Bodney v Bennell* (2008) 167 FCR 84, [156].
74. *Moses v State of Western Australia* (2007) 160 FCR 148.
75. *Sampi v Western Australia [No. 2]* [2005] FCA 1567 [955].
76. *Bodney v Bennell* (2008) 167 FCR 84 [152].
77. *De Rose v South Australia [No. 2]* (2005) 145 FCR 290.
78. ibid.
79. *Members of the Yorta Yorta Aboriginal Community v Victoria* (2002) 214 CLR 422, 456–7 [89].
80. For example, see *Clarke on behalf of the Wotjobaluk, Jaadwa, Jadawadjali, Wergaia and Jupagulk Peoples v Victoria* [2005] FCA 1795 (13 December 2005); *Rubibi Community v Western Australia [No. 5]* [2005] FCA 1025 (29 July 2005), 376; and *De Rose v South Australia [No. 1]* (2003) 133 FCR 325.
81. *Clarke on behalf of the Wotjobaluk, Jaadwa, Jadawadjali, Wergaia and Jupagulk Peoples v Victoria* [2005] FCA 1795 (13 December 2005) [11] (original emphasis).
82. *Western Australia v Ward* (2000) 99 FCR 316, 381–2 [241], also 383 [244–5]. See also *De Rose v South Australia [No. 1]* (2003) 133 FCR 325, [169].
83. *Bodney v Bennell* (2008) 167 FCR 84, [81], [97].
84. ibid. [74].
85. Justice Tony North, 'Disconnection — The gulf between law and justice', paper presented at the National Native Title Conference 2009: Spirit of Country — Land, water, life, 3–5 June 2009.
86. *De Rose v South Australia [No. 2]* (2005) 145 FCR 290, [60].
87. *Neowarra v Western Australia* (2003) 134 FCR 208, [162].
88. *Bodney v Bennell* (2008) 167 FCR 84, [74].
89. *Gumana v Northern Territory* (2005) 141 FCR 457, [226–8]; see also *De Rose v South Australia [No. 1]* (2003) 133 FCR 325, [168]; and *Western Australia v Ward* (2000) 99 FCR 316, 382 [243].

90. *Rubibi Community v Western Australia [No. 5]* [2005] FCA 1025 (29 July 2005).
91. *Rubibi Community v Western Australia [No. 5]* [2005] FCA 1025 (29 July 2005) 376, reiterated in the determination of connection: *Rubibi Community v Western Australia [No. 6]* (2006) 226 ALR 676), [7].
92. *Gumana v Northern Territory* (2005) FCA 50, [195].
93. *Bodney v Bennell* (2008) 167 FCR 84 [70]; relying on Mansfield J in *Risk v Northern Territory* [2006] FCA 404, [97(c)].
94. Robert French, 'Lifting the Burden of Native Title: Some modest proposals for improvement' (2009) 93 *Reform* 10. See also Tony North 'Disconnection — The gulf between law and justice', paper presented at the National Native Title Conference 2009: Spirit of Country — Land, water, life, 3–5 June 2009.
95. NTA s 225 provides: 'A determination of native title is a determination whether or not native title exists in relation to a particular area (the determination area) of land or waters and, if it does exist, a determination of: (a) who the persons, or each group of persons, holding the common or group rights comprising the native title are …'
96. *De Rose v South Australia [No. 2]* (2005) 145 FCR 290, [38].
97. *Neowarra v Western Australia* (2003) 134 FCR 208, [387].
98. *Neowarra v Western Australia* (2003) 134 FCR 208 [393–8]; see also *Western Australia v Ward* (2000) 99 FCR 316, [239].
99. *Neowarra v Western Australia* (2003) 134 FCR 208 [393].
100. ibid. [392–3].
101. *Hayes v Northern Territory* (1999) 97 FCR 32.
102. *Commonwealth v Yarmirr* (2001) 208 CLR 1.
103. *Lardil, Kaidilt, Yangkaal and Gangalidda People v Queensland* [2000] FCA 1548.
104. *Neowarra v Western Australia* (2003) 134 FCR 208 [387].
105. *Western Australia v Ward* (1997) 76 FCR 492.
106. (2005) FCA 777.
107. ibid. [969].
108. ibid. *Western Australia v Ward* (1997) 76 FCR 492 [971]. In particular, he suggested that Lee J at first instance relied on the 'ancestral connection', which in light of *Yorta Yorta* would not be sufficient to establish 'the necessary societal continuity', [972].
109. *State of Western Australia v Sebastian* (2008) 173 FCR 1.
110. Particularly in the Northern Territory: see *Hayes v Northern Territory* (1999) 97 FCR 32, *Alyawarr, Kaytetye, Warumungu, Wakay Native Title Claim Group v Northern Territory* (2004) 207 ALR 539.
111. *Sampi v Western Australia* [2005] FCA 777 [954]. To do so, he remarked, would be the antithesis of the policy of the legislation and the process of recognition that it seeks to advance.
112. *De Rose v South Australia [No. 2]* (2005) 145 FCR 290, 291 [31].
113. ibid. 301 [38].
114. ibid.
115. ibid. 302 [45].
116. *Bodney v Bennell* (2008) 167 FCR 84, [179].
117. *De Rose v South Australia [No. 2]* (2005) 145 FCR 290, 291 [31].
118. See *Rubibi Community v Western Australia [No. 6]* (2006) 226 ALR 676, [24].
119. *Commonwealth v Yarmirr* (2001) 208 CLR 1, 49 [42].

120. *Wik Peoples v Queensland* (1996) 187 CLR 1, 84 (Brennan CJ).
121. See *Mabo v Queensland [No. 2]* (1992) 175 CLR 1, 41–2 (Brennan J).
122. ibid. 53 (Brennan J); with Mason CJ and McHugh J concurring, at 15.
123. Lisa Strelein, 'Conceptualising Native Title' (2001) 23 *Sydney Law Review* 95, 122.
124. *Mabo v Queensland [No. 2]* (1992) 175 CLR 1, 71 (Brennan J), 41–2.
125. See McNeil, 'Native Title and Extinguishment', paper presented to the FAIRA Native Title conference, 11 May 1995, 30, 37.
126. *Fejo v Northern Territory* (1998) 195 CLR 96, 128 [46] (Gleeson CJ, Gaudron, McHugh, Gummow, Hayne and Callinan JJ) (original emphasis).
127. *Hayes v Northern Territory* (1999) 97 FCR 32, 12.
128. *Wik Peoples v Queensland* (1996) 187 CLR 1, 133 (Toohey J with the authority of Gaudron, Gummow and Kirby JJ).
129. *Neowarra v Western Australia* (2003) 134 FCR 208, [382]; Justice Sundberg concluded that where the evidence sustains a comprehensive right to the land, in the absence of any other non-Indigenous interests, s 225(b) would not require any greater particularity.
130. *Wik Peoples v Queensland* (1996) 187 CLR 1,179–84.
131. Lisa Strelein, 'A Captive of Statute', (2009) 93 *Reform* 48–51.
132. *Griffiths v Minister for Lands, Planning and Environment* (2008) 235 CLR 232, [107–9] (Kirby J).
133. *Commonwealth v Yarmirr* (2001) 208 CLR 1, [240].
134. See ibid., n 306 and accompanying text (Kirby J).
135. Lisa Strelein, 'Conceptualising Native Title (2001) 23 *Sydney Law Review* 95.
136. *Delgamuukw v British Columbia* [1997] 3 SCR 1010.
137. *Clarke on behalf of the Wotjobaluk, Jaadwa, Jadawadjali, Wergaia and Jupagulk Peoples v Victoria* [2005] FCA 1795 (13 December 2005); *Lovett on behalf of the Gunditjmara People v State of Victoria* [2007] FCA 474.
138. This is manifest to some extent in a proposed alternative settlement framework developed in Victoria: see *Report of the Steering Committee for the Development of a Victorian Native Title Settlement Framework*, December 2008, available online at <www.justice.vic.gov.au>. See Office of Native Title Western Australia, 'Towards an Alternative Settlement Framework', Consultation paper, October 2005.

ANNOTATED CASE LIST

The following list of cases provides a brief summary of the key findings and precedential value of the most significant native title cases. The list aims to be comprehensive but is not exhaustive. The cases are arranged according to the year in which the case was decided, and then by alphabetical order. Where cases have been appealed, reference is made to the final appeal and readers should refer to the appeal entry for the final result. Where cases are the subject of a substantive chapter of this book, reference is made to that chapter. Citations include authoritative reference or citations for the online Australia Legal Information Institute (Austlii) archive, which can be accessed at <www.austlii.edu.au>.

The case list contains cases up until 30 June 2009. For cases after this date, readers may refer to the AIATSIS Native Title Research Unit monthly web resource 'What's New', which is available at <ntru.aiatsis.gov.au/publications. html#whatsnew>, the Butterworths periodic publication *Native Title News* (edited by G. Hiley and M. McKenna), or the National Native Title Tribunal website at <www.nntt.gov.au>, which lists determinations.

PRE-1993

Cooper v Stuart **(1889) 14 App Cas 286 (Privy Council)** The Privy Council held that there was no land law or tenure existing at the time of annexation to the Crown. Their Lordships declared that the colony of New South Wales was peacefully annexed to the Crown, describing it as territory 'practically unoccupied, without settled inhabitants or settled law'.

Mabo v Queensland [No. 1] **(1988) 166 CLR 186 (HCA Mason CJ, Wilson, Brennan, Deane, Toohey and Gaudron JJ)** The Queensland Government sought to defeat a common law claim by the Meriam people by enacting legislation to extinguish any native title rights that might exist. The High Court held that the Queensland Act was invalid due to the paramountcy of Commonwealth laws under s 109 of the Constitution and the operation of the *Racial Discrimination Act 1975* (Cth) (RDA).

Milirrpum v Nabalco Pty Ltd **(1971) 17 FLR 141 (NTSC Blackburn J)** Applied *Cooper v Stuart* (1889). The appellants claimed that at common law, rights held by Indigenous communities to land under their laws and customs persisted after the acquisition of sovereignty unless and until validly terminated by the Crown. While Justice Blackburn recognised the social rules and customs of the appellants as a system of law, he reasoned that Indigenous land laws were incapable of recognition because they lacked essential elements that define a proprietorial interest in the Australian legal system: rights to alienate, and to exclude others.

Coe v Commonwealth **(1979) 24 ALR 118 (HCA Gibbs, Jacobs, Murphy, Aickin JJ)** The majority refused leave to amend a statement of claim that asserted, among other points, that there is an 'Aboriginal nation' that has sovereignty over Australia. The Court did, however, suggest that the existence of native title would be 'arguable ... if properly raised'.

Mabo v Queensland [No. 2] **(1992) 175 CLR 1 (HCA Mason CJ, Brennan, Deane, Dawson, Toohey, Gaudron and McHugh JJ))** By a majority of six to one, the Court upheld the native title claim of the Meriam people, declaring that they were entitled against the whole world to the possession, occupation, use and enjoyment of the Murray Islands. Justice Brennan's judgment included the following key points: acquisition of sovereignty cannot be challenged in an Australian municipal court; Indigenous peoples' rights and interests in land, under their own law and custom, survived acquisition of sovereignty by the Crown; the Crown's radical title is burdened by those interests; those rights and interests are recognised and protected by common law through the doctrine of native title; and native title is susceptible to extinguishment by the Crown. (See Chapter 1.)

1993

Coe v Commonwealth **(1993) 118 ALR 193 (HCA Mason CJ)** Chief Justice Mason followed Justice Gibbs in *Coe v Commonwealth* (1979) in rejecting the contention that an Indigenous nation held sovereignty or a residual sovereignty in the form of a 'domestic dependent nation', or was entitled rights and interests other than those created or recognised by the laws of the Commonwealth.

Pareroultja v Tickner **(1993) 42 FCR 32 (FCA Lockhart, O'Loughlin and Whitlam JJ)** The Federal Court held that there was no fundamental inconsistency between the rights and interests of native title holders and statutory owners of a grant under the *Aboriginal Land Rights (Northern Territory) Act 1976* (Cth); statutory title and native title are capable of coexisting over the same area of land.

1994

Djaigween v Douglas **(1994) 48 FCR 535 (FCA Carr J)** Held that s 213(2) of the NTA confers jurisdiction on the Federal Court to provide injunctive relief to protect the subject matter of claims while the Registrar is considering whether or not to register a claim under s 190A.

Ejai v Commonwealth **(1994) (Unreported, SCWA, 18 March 1994, 1774/93)** Proceedings may be conducted in a culturally sensitive manner, for example to minimise disclosure of details of sensitive matters in an open forum where disclosure would otherwise be prohibited. Evidence can be taken before trial on certain issues.

Mason v Tritton **(1994) 34 NSWLR 572 (NSWCA Gleeson CJ, Kirby P and Priestley JA)** The applicants asserted that they were exercising native title rights to hunt or fish in defence to charges under the relevant fisheries or flora legislation. It was recognised that as a matter of common law there was 'no bar to the recognition' of a native title right to fish.

1995

Brandy v Human Rights and Equal Opportunity Commission **(1995) 183 CLR 245 (HCA Mason CJ, Brennan, Deane, Dawson, Toohey, Gaudron and McHugh JJ)** The statutory scheme established under the RDA, by which determinations made by the Human Rights and Equal Opportunity Commission were to be registered in the Federal Court, was held to be invalid as the determination of complaints was a judicial function that had to be exercised by a court. The case raised constitutional questions over the power provided to the National Native Title Tribunal (NNTT) to make determinations of native title even where all parties agreed. After the decision in *Brandy*, significant amendments were made to the native title determination process so that the NNTT would continue to mediate applications but under the direction of the Federal Court.

Western Australia v Commonwealth **(1995) 183 CLR 373 (*Native Title Act case*) (HCA Mason CJ, Brennan, Deane, Dawson, Toohey, Gaudron and McHugh JJ)** Western Australia challenged the Commonwealth *Native Title Act 1993* (NTA) and the Wororra peoples relied on the RDA and s 109 of the Constitution to challenge the extinguishment of native title in Western Australia under the *Land (Titles and Traditional Usage) Act 1993* (WA). The High Court held that the RDA and the NTA were valid (except s 12 NTA). The Western Australian legislation was held to be invalid as a result of being inconsistent with the RDA and NTA.

1996

Members of the Yorta Yorta Aboriginal Community v Victoria **(1996) 1 AILR 402 (FCA Olney J)** (See annotation HCA appeal *Members of the Yorta Yorta Aboriginal Community v Victoria* (2002) and Chapter 7.)

North Ganalanja Aboriginal Corporation v Queensland **(1996) 185 CLR 595 (*Waanyi case*) (HCA Brennan CJ, Dawson, Toohey, Gaudron, McHugh, Gummow and Kirby JJ)** The majority overturned the decision of the President of the NNTT (*Waanyi People's Native Title Application* (1994) 129 ALR 100 (NNTT French J)) to reject an application over an area formerly subject to a pastoral lease for failing to make out a *prima facie* case. The majority determined that the functions performed by the NNTT Registrar were administrative (not judicial) in character. The NNTT Registrar could not refuse to accept a claim

Annotated case list

while there was legal doubt about whether native title may or may not exist over pastoral leases.

Walley v Western Australia (1996) 67 FCR 366 (FCA Carr J) In the context of provisions of the NTA regarding expedited procedures, Justice Carr confirmed that the discharge of the state's obligation to negotiate in good faith was a condition precedent for arbitral decision by the NNTT regarding the doing of the future act.

Ward v Western Australia (1996) 69 FCR 208 (FCA Carr J) Parties to proceedings before the NNTT relating to whether an act attracts the expedited procedure have 'no burden of proof' or 'evidential burden of a legal nature'. A 'commonsense approach to evidence' should be followed. (See annotation *Daniel v Western Australia* (2000).)

Wik Peoples v Queensland (1996) 187 CLR 1 (HCA Brennan CJ, Dawson, Toohey, Gaudron, McHugh, Gummow and Kirby JJ) The majority (four to three) held that pastoral leases issued under the Queensland *Land Acts* of 1910 and 1962 did not 'necessarily extinguish all incidents of aboriginal title'. Where an inconsistency arises between the rights enjoyed by native title holders and the rights conferred upon the lessee, native title rights must yield to the extent of the inconsistency to the rights of the lessee. The Court recognised that native title could coexist with the interests of other parties in particular land. (See annotation *Wik Peoples v Queensland* [2004] and Chapter 2.)

1997

Buck v New South Wales (Unreported FCA, 7 July 1997, Lockhart J) (Consent determination [1997] FCA 1624, 7 April 1997) The first consent determination of native title, recognising that native title existed in the entire determination area. As a result of this consent determination, the Dunghutti people became the first determined holders of native title on the Australian mainland. Native title was immediately surrendered to facilitate development, in return for compensation.

Deeral v Charlie [1997] FCA 1408 (FCA Beaumont J) First consent determination in Queensland (Hopevale), recognised that native title exists in the entire determination area. The claimants were the Gamaay, Dingaal, Nugal, Thuubi, Nguurruumungu, Dharrpa, Binhthi, Thiithaarr and Tha peoples.

Derschaw v Sutton (1997) AILR 11; (1997) 2 AILR 53 (FCWASC Franklin, Wallwork and Murray JJ) A right to fish based on traditional laws and customs is a recognisable form of native title defended by common law but a stringent standard of proof of traditional laws and customs is required.

Members of the Yorta Yorta Aboriginal Community v Victoria [1997] FCA 1181 (FCA Olney J) Evidence of a non-Indigenous person's attachment to an area is not relevant to the proceedings.

Western Australia v Ward (1997) 76 FCR 492 (FCA Hill, Branson and Sundberg JJ) Upheld the power of the court to make orders excluding parties, legal representatives and experts of a particular gender from attending the taking of evidence and from being informed of the content of the evidence where such information was traditionally subject to gender restrictions (s 82(2) NTA as originally enacted). Section 82 of the NTA was subsequently amended; the Court is no longer required to take cultural and customary concerns into account, though it has discretion to do so (cf. *Daniel v Western Australia* (2000)).

Yarmirr and Others v Northern Territory (Unreported FCA 4 April 1997) (FCA Olney J) Refused to join a person claiming native title rights because he had not lodged a claimant application under the NTA (contra *Munn v Queensland* [2002]). Held no power to exclude a party from a hearing merely by reason of the party's gender. (Contra *Western Australia v Ward* (1997) above.)

1998

Dillon v Davies (1998) 145 FLR 111 (SCT Underwood J) Concerned the taking of undersize abalone and affirmed that, in order to rely on the exercise of native title rights as a defence, the evidence must be sufficient to demonstrate a number of matters, including that the appellant 'had ... continued, uninterrupted, to observe the relevant traditional laws and customs and ... the conduct' in fishing for abalone was an exercise of those traditional laws and customs. Despite genealogical evidence of biological descent and the ancestral connection, the Court did not accept that the fishing in question was an exercise of particular rights according to traditional laws and customs.

Fejo v Northern Territory (1998) 195 CLR 96 (HCA Gleeson CJ, Gaudron, McHugh, Gummow, Kirby, Hayne and Callinan JJ) Held unanimously that native title was extinguished by a freehold grant of fee simple. Also confirmed that the extinguishment is permanent, rather than being a matter of mere suspension of native title. (See Chapter 3.)

Jones v Queensland [1998] QSC 11 (SCQ Ambrose J) Concluded that the Court had jurisdiction to entertain a claim to the extent that it related to coastal waters and submerged lands within three miles (4.8 kilometres) of the low-water mark on the coast of Queensland, but had no jurisdiction to entertain the claim to waters and submerged lands beyond the three-mile limit (contra *Commonwealth v Yarmirr* (2001)).

Members of the Yorta Yorta Aboriginal Community v Victoria [1998] FCA 1606 (FCA Olney J) Justice Olney held that the 'tide of history' had washed away any acknowledgment or observance of traditional laws and customs of the Yorta Yorta people. Yorta Yorta people were no longer a traditional Indigenous society and had abandoned native title. On procedural matters, it was held that an applicant for an exploration licence did not have a sufficient interest to be a party to an application for a determination of native title. (See annotation HCA appeal *Members of the Yorta Yorta Aboriginal Community v Victoria* (2002) and Chapter 7.)

Mualgal v Queensland (1998) 90 FCR 303 (FCA Drummond J) When the Court makes a determination of native title under s 55 of the NTA, it must 'at the same time' commence to implement the procedures of s 56 or s 57, to establish a prescribed body corporate that may not be completed until after the pronouncement of the determination under s 55.

Ward on behalf of the Miriuwung and Gajerrong People v Western Australia (1998) 159 ALR 483 (FCA Lee J) Justice Lee found that the Miriuwung and Gajerrong peoples, as a community, held native title over most of the claimed area as exclusive possession, subject to extinguishing acts. (See annotation FCA appeal *Western Australia v Ward* (2000); HCA appeal *Western Australia v Ward* (2002) and Chapter 6.)

Western Yalanji Peoples v Pedersen [1998] 1269 FCA (FCA Drummond J) Consent determination that native title exists in parts of the determination area (second consent determination in Queensland).

Yarmirr v Northern Territory (1998) 82 FCR 533 (FCA Olney J) Native title found to exist in relation to the sea and seabed in the vicinity of the Croker Island in the Northern Territory. The rights granted were 'non-exclusive' and 'non-commercial'. Where land in the intertidal zone (i.e. between the high-water and the low-water marks) has been the subject of a freehold grant, it remained possible to make a claim under the NTA for native title rights and interests in the waters that flow periodically over that land. Justice Olney held that the native title holders had no right to trade in the resources of the area, despite evidence that they had traded in the past. A right to trade in goods did not meet the definition of 'native title' because it was not a right in relation to land or waters. Procedurally, Justice Olney noted that determinations of native title can be made only after the procedures prescribed by s 13 and Part 3 of the NTA have been met and a native title applicant is not able to amend an application to increase the area of land or waters claimed because any such claim is a fresh claim and all of the procedures of the NTA must be complied with. (See annotation HCA appeal *Commonwealth v Yarmirr* (2001) and Chapter 5.)

1999

Adnyamathanha People v South Australia **[1999] FCA 402 (FCA O'Loughlin J)** When an application to combine two or more claimant applications is made, notice of the application to amend needs to be given to any registered native title claimants who have overlapping claims (regardless of whether or not they are parties in the proceedings). It is not appropriate to use the Court's general power to refer a matter to mediation under s 53A of the *Federal Court Act 1976* (Cth) when these specific powers are provided under the NTA.

Commonwealth v Yarmirr **(1999) 101 FCR 171 (FCA Beaumont, von Doussa and Merkel JJ)** Upheld Justice Olney's finding that only 'non-exclusive cultural and subsistence rights' could be recognised because exclusive possession of, or rights to control access to, the claimed area would 'fracture the skeletal principle of the freedom of the seas' by conflicting with Australia's international obligation to permit innocent passage of ships. Their Honours held the tentative view that a right to trade could be an integral aspect of a broader right to exclusive possession, but as this broader right was not applicable, it was not necessary to decide. Fishing, hunting or gathering, though specifically mentioned in s 223(2), are not necessarily native title rights and interests in every case. (See annotation HCA appeal *Commonwealth v Yarmirr* (2001) and Chapter 5.)

Daniel v Western Australia **[1999] FCA 686 (FCA, Nicholson J)** Amendments to a native title determination application have to comply with ss 61 and 62 (authorisation) of the NTA as amended in 1998 regardless of the date the application was lodged. The applicant's state of knowledge is relevant to determining s 62(2) compliance. (See annotation *Daniel v Western Australia* (2002).)

Hayes v Northern Territory (1999) 97 FCR 32 (FCA Olney J) Pastoral leases granted in the area (in and around Alice Springs, Northern Territory) did not extinguish native title, but were capable of coexisting with native title.

Lardil Peoples v Queensland (1999) 95 FCR 14 (FCA Cooper J) The possibility that an act may affect native title does not impose obligations to observe procedural steps relating to ss 24HA or 24NA (that is, if it is subsequently established that native title exists and that the act is therefore a future act, compensation may apply). (See annotation FCA appeal *Lardil Peoples v Queensland* (2001).)

Mualgal People v Queensland [1999] FCA 157 (FCA Drummond J) Consent determination in the Torres Strait recognised that native title exists in the entire determination area.

Saibai People v Queensland [1999] FCA 158 (FCA Drummond J) Consent determination in the Torres Strait recognised that native title exists in the entire determination area.

Thorpe v Kennett [1999] VSC 442 (VSC Warren J) Held that genocide is not a criminal offence in Victoria.

Wilkes v Johnsen (1999) 21 WAR 269 (WASC Kennedy, White and Wheeler JJ) The full Court allowed an appeal against a conviction of being in possession of 'totally protected fish' (under s 36(b) *Fish Resources Management Act 1994* (WA)) on the grounds that s 211 of the NTA offers some protection for native title rights to hunt, fish, gather or engage in cultural or spiritual activities. The Court held that exemption regime under s 7 of the *Fish Resources Management Act 1994* (WA) fell within s 211(2) of the NTA.

Wotjobaluk People v Victoria [1999] FCA 961 (FCA North J) What forms part of the application and what does not are matters for the applicant.

Yanner v Eaton (1999) 201 CLR 351 (HCA Gleeson CJ, Gaudron, Gummow, Kirby, Hayne, McHugh and Callinan JJ) Majority held that the *Fauna Conservation Act 1974* (Qld), declaring fauna to be the property of the Crown, did not extinguish native title. Hunting and fishing with modern technology were endorsed by the majority. Regulation of the exercise of a native title right does not extinguish the right. (See Chapter 4.)

2000

Anderson v Western Australia (2000) FCA 1717 (FCA Black CJ) A determination of native title has to comply with s 225 of the NTA. Consent determination that native title exists in parts of the determination area of the Pula Nguru/Spinifex people.

Anderson v Wilson (2000) 97 FCR 453 (FCA Black CJ, Beaumont and Sackville JJ) Held that exclusive possession is not the sole factor in determining whether a grant or interest is inconsistent with the continued existence of native title. There was nothing in the lease or the *Western Lands Act 1901* (NSW) that was necessarily inconsistent with the exercise of every incident of native title that may exist in relation to the leased land. (See annotation HCA appeal *Wilson v Anderson* (2002).)

Bodney v Westralia Airports Corporation Pty Ltd (2000) 109 FCR 178 (FCA Lehane J) Following *Fejo v Northern Territory* (1998), grant of a freehold estate to the Crown extinguishes native title. Wherever an estate in fee simple is vested in the Crown, native title is wholly extinguished. The claimants argued for a general fiduciary or trust relationship owed by the Crown but Justice Lehane concluded that there is no firm basis for the assertion of fiduciary duty of the kind contended for. The determination found that native title does not exist.

Bropho v Western Australia (2000) 96 FCR 453 (FCA French J) The Court held that s 66 of the NTA requires that all those whose interests may be affected by a determination should have reasonable opportunity to become aware of and to become parties to the application if they so wish.

Daniel v Western Australia (2000) 178 ALR 542 (FCA Nicholson J) Section 82(1) of the NTA amends s 82(3) of the NTA as originally enacted by providing that the rules of evidence apply to native title applications except where the Court orders otherwise. Justice Nicholson determined first whether (hearsay) evidence proposed to be led was admissible under the *Evidence Act 1995* (Cth) and next considered whether the Court could properly exercise its discretion under s 82 of the NTA to dispense with the rules.

Dauan People v Queensland [2000] FCA 1064 (FCA Drummond J) Consent determination in the Torres Strait recognised that native title exists in the entire determination area.

Harris v Great Barrier Reef Marine Park Authority (2000) 98 FCR 60 (FCA Heerey, Drummond and Emmett JJ) The notification requirement in s 24HA(7) of the NTA imposes no obligation to comply with the common law rules of procedural fairness. The NTA defines the extent of procedural rights, leaving no room for further rights to be implied. For example, there is no obligation to provide additional information beyond that of the notice, and in particular no obligation to provide information that applicants for permits had submitted. Also held that the 'opportunity to comment' conferred on notice recipients under s 24HA(7)(b) is not a right to veto or be involved in the decision-making process, but rather an opportunity to 'proffer information and argument to the decision maker that it can make such use of as it considers appropriate'.

Hayes v Northern Territory [2000] FCA 671 (FCA Olney J) Found that native title existed in all of the determination area, which included parcels of land in and around Alice Springs. The first determination of native title relating to areas within a town. The Court made interim orders at the same time as making an approved determination of native title, thus allowing the common law holders a period of time in which to nominate a prescribed body corporate in accordance with ss 56(2)(b) and 57(2)(b).

Lardil, Kaidilt, Yangkaal and Gangalidda People v Queensland [2000] FCA 1548 (FCA Cooper J) Incorporates discussion of procedural rights and future acts. The rules of evidence apply unless there are circumstances that persuade the Court that the rules should not, or to a limited extent, apply to all of the evidence sought to be tendered or particular categories of that evidence.

Mabuiag People v Queensland [2000] FCA 1065 (FCA Drummond J) Consent determination in the Torres Strait recognised that native title exists in the entire determination area.

Masig and Damuth People v Queensland [2000] FCA 1067 (FCA Drummond J) Consent determination in the Torres Strait recognised that native title exists in the entire determination area.

Smith v Western Australia (2000) 104 FCR 494 (FCA Madgwick J) Consent determination recognised that native title exists in parts of the determination area, the Upper Murchison and Gascoigne in Western Australia. The claimants were the Nharnuwangga, Wajarri and Ngarla peoples. Large areas of the 50,000 square kilometres of the claim area were excluded from the determination.

Contains discussion of the Court's discretion, once jurisdictional preconditions are established, to make or not make the orders sought.

Wandarang v Northern Territory **(2000) 104 FCR 380 (FCA Olney J)** Litigated determination recognised that native title exists in parts of the determination area and is held by the Wandarang, Alawa, Marra and Ngalakan peoples (St Vidgeon's claim). (See annotation *Wandarang, Alawa, Marra and Ngalakan Peoples v Northern Territory* [2004].)

Warrabur and Poruma People v Queensland **[2000] FCA 1066 (FCA Drummond J)** Consent determination in the Torres Strait recognised that native title exists in the entire determination area.

Western Australia v Ward **(2000) 99 FCR 316 (FCA Beaumont, von Doussa and North JJ)** Partially overturned Justice Lee's decision, challenging his findings on the nature of native title and the way it may be extinguished. This resulted in a major reduction in the area over which native title was recognised. The majority of the full Federal Court held that native title should be viewed not as an interest in land but as a 'bundle of rights' in relation to land and waters. 'Partial extinguishment' of native title will occur where only some of the rights are extinguished, thereby reducing the 'bundle of rights' that make up native title. Justice North, dissenting, agreed with Justice Lee that native title is a fundamental right to land that would only be extinguished where there is a 'fundamental, total or absolute' inconsistency between the rights or interests created by a legislative or executive act and the underlying right of Indigenous people to the land. The majority declared the inconsistency of incidents test requires a comparison between the legal nature and incidents of the statutory right that has been granted and the native title rights being exerted. The majority also considered that any rights to resources excluded petroleum and minerals on the basis that 'the evidence did not establish any traditional Aboriginal law, custom or use relating to minerals', apart from ochre. The majority concluded that exclusive possession is the key to determining inconsistency and grants conferring exclusive possession automatically extinguish native title. The majority held that there were two inquiries required by the statutory definition in s 223(1) of the NTA: (i) case for the rights and interests possessed under traditional laws and customs; and (ii) for connection with land or waters by those laws and customs. Rejected submission that physical occupation of the land is a necessary requirement for continuing connection with the land. Held that no other applications for a determination of native title can be made to an area that already has an approved determination of native title. An approved native title determination is a judgment *in rem*, binding against the whole world. An approved determination may be varied or revoked under s 13 where the determination fails to recognise an existing interest or where legislation comes into force after the determination and affects native title in a way that contradicts the determination. The majority held that the Court making a native title determination has to apply s 47 with the consequence that native title in areas to which the section applies is not extinguished. Requirement to 'occupy' in s 47A(1)(c) is met where a member of the claimant group is one of many people who share occupancy, and that the land might be relevantly occupied even though the person is rarely present on the land, so long as the person makes use of the land for the reserved purpose as and when the person wishes to do so. A person (or group) who becomes a party to a claim under s 84(5) of the NTA may seek a determination that they are a native title holder even though they are not a member of the claim group. The Court retains discretion to be exercised in the interests of justice to decline to exercise jurisdiction to make a determination that native title does not exist where the parties before the Court claiming that native title exists have failed to make a positive case, but the evidence fails to disclose that native title does not exist. Identification of native title holders does not require the name of each member of the native title holding group. There is no need to separately specify the rights and interests; it is a matter internal to the group according to traditional laws and customs. Where the native title right is not a right to possession (right to control access and decide how land will be used), it will be preferable to express the rights by reference to the activities that may be conducted, as of right, on or in relation to the land and waters. (See annotation HCA appeal *Western Australia v Ward* (2002) and Chapter 6.)

***Wik Peoples (McNaught Ngallametta) v Queensland* [2000] FCA 1443 (FCA Drummond J)** Consent determination recognised that native title exists in the entire determination area. Under s 86EN of the NTA, the Federal Court may request the NNTT to provide reports on the progress of any mediation and may specify when the report is to be provided. Justice Drummond considered that while 'an agreed resolution' is 'preferable to a Court imposed result', the Court cannot allow the claim to be subject to protracted negotiations. The cost benefits would be illusory, the uncertainty would be unacceptable to the public interest and interest of all the parties, and the continued uncertainty might destroy the willingness of the parties to compromise.

***Yarmirr v Northern Territory* [2000] FCA 48 (FCA Beaumont, von Doussa and Merkel JJ)** Upheld the trial judge's conclusion that non-exclusive native title exists in respect of intertidal waters. Also found that failure of a party to participate in proceedings may be used by the Court as an indication that the party did not oppose the rights being asserted by claimants. (See annotation HCA appeal *Commonwealth v Yarmirr* (2001) and Chapter 5.)

2001

***Arnhemland Aboriginal Land Trust v Director of Fisheries (NT)* (2001) 109 FCA 488 (FCA Mansfield J)** Held that the intertidal zone is not 'adjoining Aboriginal land' under s 73(1)(d) of the *Aboriginal Land Rights (Northern Territory) Act 1976* (Cth) and is not claimable.

***Brown v Western Australia* [2001] FCA 1462 (FCA French J)** Consent determination recognised that native title exists in the entire determination area in the Gibson Desert, Western Australia. The native title holders are the Kiwirrkurra people.

***Commonwealth v Yarmirr* (2001) 208 CLR 1 (HCA Gleeson CJ, Gaudron, McHugh, Gummow, Kirby, Hayne and Callinan JJ)** Confirmed that native title rights are recognised in Australia's territorial sea out to 12 nautical miles (22.2 kilometres), subject to important limitations upon their content. Native title rights and interests cannot be recognised to the extent that they are inconsistent with the terms upon which sovereignty is asserted. The majority upheld the decision that there could be no native title right to exclusive possession, occupation, use and enjoyment of areas of the territorial sea, even if described as being 'subject to' the public rights of navigation and fishing and the right of innocent passage. The majority argued that attention must be directed to the nature and extent of the inconsistency between the asserted native title rights and interests and the relevant common law principles. No conclusion was expressed as to the recognition of native title beyond 12 nautical miles. The majority held that although native title existed in relation to the sea and seabed, this did not include a right to trade in the resources of the area. Traditional laws and customs must have a normative content, but it is not necessary to show enforcement of exclusion. The objectives of the NTA as stated in the preamble reveal that the NTA is to be given a beneficial construction. (See Chapter 5.)

***Congoo v Queensland* [2001] FCA 868 (FCA Hely J)** Consent determination recognised that native title exists in parts of the determination area in the Atherton Tablelands of Queensland. The native title holders are the Bar-Barrum people.

Kaurareg People v Queensland (2001) 6 (2) AILR 41 (FCA Drummond J) Consent determination in the Torres Strait recognised that native title exists in parts of the determination area.

Kelly on behalf of the Byron Bay Bundjalung People v New South Wales Aboriginal Land Council [2001] FCA 1479 (FCA Branson J) Consent determination recognised that native title does not exist in the determination area. Native title rights and interests in relation to land or waters may be surrendered to the Commonwealth, a state or a territory (and hence extinguished) under two forms of Indigenous Land Use Agreement (ILUA): body corporate agreements and area agreements. An ILUA takes effect according to its terms and will generally take effect as a contract at common law binding the parties to the agreement.

Lardil, Kaidilt, Yangkaal and Gangalidda People v Queensland [2001] FCA 464; *Lardil Peoples v Queensland* (2001) 108 FCR 453 (FCA French, Merkel and Dowsett JJ) Considered that it may not be possible to determine if an act is a future act before it is carried out. If native title has already been extinguished, an act affecting that area cannot be a future act because it cannot affect native title. The applicants for an injunction had agreed not to seek an order that native title existed, and made no attempts to establish any effect on native title but relied solely on the registration of the claim. A permanent, as opposed to an interlocutory, injunction will not be granted unless native title has been established or determined to exist. Interlocutory relief preserving the status quo may be available because registration indicates the case is arguable. Also considered whether failure to comply with procedural requirements affects the validity of the future act.

Members of the Yorta Yorta Aboriginal Community v Victoria (2001) 110 FCR 244 (FCA Black CJ, Branson and Katz JJ) The majority upheld the decision that the claimants had ceased to observe their traditional laws and customs, with the consequence that the foundation of native title no longer existed. All of the members of the Federal Court considered the definition of 'native title rights and interests' in s 223 of the NTA, and agreed that this section allowed for the evolution and change of traditional laws and customs. They differed as to what should be seen as 'traditional'. The majority (Justices Branson and Katz) endorsed an 'objective test' to determine whether a law acknowledged or a custom observed is a traditional law or custom. Their Honours held there was sufficient evidence to support the trial judge's finding that there was a period of time during which the relevant community lost its character as a traditional Indigenous community. (See HCA appeal *Members of the Yorta Yorta Aboriginal Community v Victoria* (2002) and Chapter 7.)

Munn v Queensland **(2001) 115 FCR 109 (FCA Emmett J)** After the jurisdictional preconditions are established, the Court retains a discretion as to whether or not to make the orders sought.

Ngalakan People v Northern Territory **(2001) 112 FCR 148 (FCA O'Loughlin)** Considered whether a person can be part of the claimant group through adoption and incorporation into the community. The Ngalakan people identified a tradition of adoption through 'growing up' a child and of incorporation 'as a result of ceremonial involvements or residence or skin affiliation'. Held that absence of biological or adoptive descent does not create a problem in an application for a determination of native title if a particular person can show that they are a member of the claimant group by virtue of the traditional laws acknowledged and the traditional customs observed by that group. Declared that 'the onus of proof proving extinguishment, was clearly on the Crown'.

Ngalpil v Western Australia **[2001] FCA 1140 (FCA Carr J)** Consent determination recognised that native title exists in parts of the determination area. Determination made provision for a variation application to the High Court in the event that the High Court overturned the ruling of the full Federal Court in *Western Australia v Ward* (2000) 99 FCR 316 with respect to ownership of minerals and petroleum. Held that it was appropriate to order that reports prepared and used in the course of proceedings could not be copied or their contents disclosed without either the permission of the applicants or an order of the Court.

Passi on behalf of Meriam People v Queensland **[2001] FCA 697 (FCA Black J)** Consent determination recognised native title exists in the entire determination area of the Murray Islands in the Torres Strait. Section 47A(1)(b)(i) of the NTA was applied to a reserve set apart for the use of the Indigenous inhabitants and prior extinguishment disregarded.

Rubibi Community v Western Australia **(2001) 112 FCR 409 (FCA Merkel J)** Concerned the Yawuru people's claim to 300 acres (121 hectares) of traditional men's law ground, currently a reserve, near Broome. Held native title exists in relation to the area and confers, among other rights, the exclusive right of occupation, use, possession and enjoyment of the area for 'ceremonial purposes'. The native title includes the right to control the access of others to

the area and the right to control the use and enjoyment of others to the area (excluding minerals, petroleum and gas). Held for the purposes of s 47A(1)(c) of the NTA, the following constituted occupation of the claim area:
- continuing supervisory and protective activities of the senior Yawuru men in relation to the claim area;
- holding of traditional ceremonies on the claim area as and when the senior law men authorised those activities;
- continued storage of sacred objects on the claim area;
- occupancy of the Leregon structures constructed on the claim area by members of the Lee family, who were acknowledged to be members of the Rubibi claimant group.

Considered the meaning of 'prior interest' in s 47A NTA. Justice Merkel appeared to accept the concession by Western Australia that the making of by-laws with respect to depasturing of stock and other activities on the land fell within the definition of 'interest' in s 253 NTA and thus under s 47A(2)(b) the making of the by-laws was to be disregarded. The Rubibi applicants were ordered to mediate with the other parties to determine their rights and interests and relationship to the remainder of the claim area.

***Smith on behalf of the Gnaala Karla Booja People v Western Australia* (2001) 108 FCR 442 (FCA French J)** Considered the legislative intention of the amendments to s 237 NTA. Agreed the intention was to require a predictive assessment of the effect of the proposed future act. Rejected argument that the requirement of a predictive assessment mandates 'that interference or major disturbance of the kind contemplated by the section must be established or negated on the balance of probabilities'. The word 'likely' requires a risk assessment by the tribunal that will exclude from the expedited procedure any proposed act that would involve a real chance or risk of interference or major disturbance of the kind contemplated by s 237. In assessing the risk of direct interference generated by a future act, the Tribunal is entitled to have regard to other factors that so affect community or social activities that the impact of the proposed future act is 'insubstantial'.

2002

***Anderson v Western Australia* [2002] FCA 1558 (FCA French J)** Considered evidence of authorisation in regard to notification of meetings to authorise replacement of applicants. Attempt to replace the applicants in the Ballardong claimant application failed to show that the applicants were no longer authorised as required by s 66B. Adding applicants is not 'replacement' of applicants.

Daniel v Western Australia **(2002) 194 ALR 278 (FCA French J)** Justice French summarised five conditions that a person applying to replace an applicant under s 66B has to establish: there is a claimant application; each applicant for an order under s 66B is a member of the native title group; the person to be replaced is no longer authorised by the claimant group; alternatively, the person to be replaced has exceeded the authority given to him or her by the claimant group; and persons making the application under s 66B are authorised by the claim group to make the application and to deal with matters arising under it.

De Rose v South Australia **[2002] FCA 1342 (FCA O'Loughlin J)** Held that while the applicants might satisfy s 223(1)(a) NTA being Nguraritja (traditional owners) under traditional laws acknowledged and traditional customs observed and while some claimants once had a relevant connection with the claim area, they had since abandoned that connection by failing to carry out obligations in relation to sites and ceremonies and did not constitute a distinct society. Determined that native title did not exist in the area. (See annotation FCA appeal *De Rose v South Australia* (2003) and Chapter 9.)

James on behalf of the Martu People v Western Australia **[2002] FCA 1208 (FCA French J)** Consent determination recognised that native title exists in the entire determination area in the Pilbara, Western Australia. The claimants are the Martu and Ngurrara peoples.

Kennedy v Queensland **(2002) 190 ALR 707 (FCA Sackville J)** The first successful non-Indigenous non-claimant determination. The plaintiff sought an order that native title does not exist. Justice Sackville ruled that the Court must have regard to the objects and purposes of the NTA in applying s 86G(1) NTA dealing with unopposed applications. The Court must be satisfied that the application is unopposed and that an order that native title does not exist is within the power of the Court. Considered the general principles that the Court must exercise where any declaratory order involving public rights is sought.

Members of the Yorta Yorta Aboriginal Community v Victoria **(2002) 214 CLR 422 (HCA Gleeson CJ, Gaudron, McHugh, Gummow, Kirby, Hayne and Callinan JJ)** Appeal by the Yorta Yorta people was dismissed by a majority (Justices Gaudron and Kirby dissenting). Native title does not exist in the determination area. The majority held that traditional laws and customs must have normative content so as to be capable of giving rise to rights and interests. The word 'traditional' under s 223 of the NTA referred not only to a means for the transmission of laws and customs, but also conveyed the age of the traditions, being derived from laws and customs that originated in normative rules existing before the assertion of sovereignty by the British Crown. The statutory requirement that the rights or interests be 'possessed' under traditional laws and customs requires that the normative system under which the rights and interests are possessed is a system that has had a continuous existence and vitality since sovereignty. The only rights or interests in relation to land or water, originating other than in the new sovereign order, that will be recognised after the assertion of that new sovereignty are those that find their origin in pre-sovereignty law and custom. Held substantial interruption is a matter of fact and degree. If the traditional laws and customs of a society ceased at some point in time after the acquisition of sovereignty, a later adoption of them by a new society will not re-enliven the old laws and customs. But the fact that there has been some alteration of traditional law or custom or some interruption of enjoyment or exercise of native title rights and interests in the period between the Crown asserting sovereignty and the present is not necessarily fatal to a native title claim. The rights recognised and protected are not new rights or interests created by the NTA. (See Chapter 7.)

Munn v Queensland [2002] FCA 486 (FCA Emmett J) Held that a person who claims to hold native title in respect of an area covered by a native title claim may have sufficient interest to warrant being joined in proceedings under s 84(5) of the NTA.

Nangkiriny v Western Australia (2002) 117 FCR 6 (FCA North J) A determination of native title must comply with s 225. Following *Munn v Queensland* (2001) 115 FCR 109, Justice North noted that the Court would not make an order unless the agreement was entered into freely without duress, fraud or misrepresentation.

Ngalakan People v Northern Territory (Unreported, FCA, 7 February 2002, O'Loughlin J) Litigated determination that native title exists in parts of the determination area.

Rubibi v Western Australia (2002) 120 FCR 512 (FCA Merkel J) Allowed a subgroup of the applicants, who wished to contend that native title rights were held by their subgroup alone, to join in the application to oppose some of the rights claimed by the larger claimant group.

Ward v Northern Territory [2002] FCA 171 (FCA O'Loughlin J) Outlined what an affidavit supporting a s 66B application should deal with in providing evidence of an authorisation meeting. The power to order the replacement of an applicant in s 66B(2) is discretionary; even if the conditions have been met, the Court is not required to make the order.

Ward v Northern Territory **(2002) 196 ALR 32 (FCA Mansfield J)** Determined that the applicants were no longer authorised, in contentious circumstances where the applicants did not appear and were unrepresented.

Western Australia v Ward **(2002) 213 CLR 1 (HCA Gleeson CJ, Gaudron, McHugh, Gummow, Kirby, Hayne and Callinan JJ)** The first opportunity for the High Court to determine questions of extinguishment after the 1998 NTA amendments. Clarified that certain interests in land completely extinguish native title and that the NTA allows for partial extinguishment of native title. The test for extinguishment begins with the NTA, although the NTA provides for the common law to retain a role. A claimed right may fall outside the statutory definition because it is not in relation to land and waters under s 223(1) (e.g. the right to maintain, protect and prevent the misuse of cultural knowledge). Rights and interests to which s 223(1) refers are not necessarily 'a single set of rights relating to land that is analogous to a fee simple'; nor are those rights and interests confined to control over access. The rights are usefully described as a 'bundle of rights'. Justice Kirby, reluctantly in the majority, warned against the creation of a list of rights and interests in relation to land. Resolved that the test for extinguishment is a test of 'inconsistency of incidents' that is an objective inquiry and requires identification of and comparison between the two sets of rights. Partial extinguishment occurs when the incidents are inconsistent. Whether there is a relevant connection depends, in the first instance, upon the content of traditional law and customs. Section 223(1)(b) is not directed to 'how Aboriginal peoples use or occupy land and waters'. Previous acts that took effect in earlier times are not 'past acts' if they are not to any extent invalid by operation of the RDA. Held native title rights are property for the purposes of protection under s 10 of the RDA. Interference with enjoyment of native title rights amounts to discrimination and has implications for extending rights of compensation to native title holders. (See Chapter 6.)

Wilson v Anderson **(2002) 213 CLR 401 (HCA Gleeson CJ, Gaudron, McHugh, Gummow, Kirby, Hayne and Callinan JJ)** Leases executed under the *Western Lands Act 1901* (NSW) in the Western Division of New South Wales conferred exclusive possession and so extinguished native title.

2003

Attorney-General of the Northern Territory v Ward **(2003) 134 FCR 16 (FCA Wilcox, North and Weinberg JJ)** Consent determination in relation to the Miriuwung Gajerrong native title application recognised that native title exists in parts of the determination area. Following the decision of the High

Court in *Western Australia v Ward* (2002) 213 CLR 1, the Court confirmed that the definition of native title holders and the definition of non-exclusive native title rights and interests had to be defined exhaustively, rather than inclusively. Also made orders that non-exclusive rights and interests could not include a right to occupy.

Daniel v Western Australia **[2003] FCA 666 (FCA RD Nicholson J)** Finalised the claim over almost 25,000 square kilometres of the Pilbara region, 100 kilometres south-west of Port Hedland. Held that the Ngaluma/Injibandi held non-exclusive native title rights over parts of their claim area. In relation to the rights given to pastoral leaseholders, native title rights are not to be considered as inconsistent or extinguished only because the leaseholder may want to exercise rights at the same location as the native title holder. The 'true test' is whether at that location at that time, the exercise of native title rights and interests would prevent the leaseholder's rights from prevailing.

De Rose v South Australia [No. 1] **(2003) 133 FCR 325 (FCA Wilcox, Sackville and Merkel JJ)** The Court upheld appeal by the native title applicants and strongly criticised the decisions of trial judge. Concluded that, although the trial judge had correctly identified the traditional laws and customs relevant to the question of 'connection' as those of the Western Desert bloc, he took the wrong approach to the question of whether the claimants were connected to the claim area by reference to those laws and customs. Unable to remit the case to the trial judge, since he had retired, the appropriate course was for the parties to identify the remaining issues in dispute and for the Court to hold a further hearing to allow these issues to be fully argued. (See annotation *De Rose v South Australia [No. 2]* (2005) and Chapter 9.)

James on behalf of the Martu People v Western Australia [No. 2] **[2003] FCA 731 (FCA French J)** Determination of prescribed body corporate for the Martu people. It is desirable that the membership class of a prescribed body corporate be textually aligned precisely with the definition of the native title holders in the relevant native title determination.

Neowarra v Western Australia **(2003) 134 FCR 208 (FCA Sundberg J)** Native title was held to exist in parts of the determination area. Following *Members of the Yorta Yorta Aboriginal Community v Victoria* (2002) 214 CLR 422, the judge considered the nature of the 'normative society'. Consideration of the 'recognition level' of the native title holding group. A number of groups under a single system of law can be a native title holding group. A law or custom does not have to be distinctive of the claimant group. The normative content of traditional laws and customs does not need to be mandatory or obligatory. There does not have to be complete uniformity of practice by the claimants; breach of a rule, where such a breach is met with disapprobation, is evidence that the rule exists; s 223(1) of the NTA requires that rights and interests held under laws and customs must be in relation to land and waters (not the laws and customs themselves).

Rubibi v Western Australia [2003] FCA 62 (FCA Merkel J) Granted leave for a non-legally qualified person to represent an Indigenous respondent, upon certain conditions (in this case, funding difficulties).

Wilkes v Western Australia [2003] FCA 156 (FCA Beaumont J) The Federal Court is bound by the rules of evidence except to the extent it otherwise orders (s 82(1) NTA). Orders may be sought to restrict evidence for reasons unrelated or not solely related to gender, for example, because people are from other areas and not entitled to visit the sites in question. Made orders excluding two unrepresented Indigenous respondents from the hearing of evidence about sites claimed to be sacred, as these respondents had 'as yet undefined interests'.

2004

Alyawarr, Kaytetye, Warumungu, Wakay Native Title Claim Group v Northern Territory (2004) 207 ALR 539 (FCA Mansfield J) Determination recognised that native title exists in the entire determination area. Area of claim reserved for the Town of Hatches Creek, which was never effected; the claimants were found to have exclusive rights for this area. Non-exclusive right to control the access of others to the claim area, including land subject to pastoral lease. (See annotation *Northern Territory v Alyawarr, Kaytetye, Warumungu, Wakay Native Title Claim Group* (2005).)

David on behalf of the Iama People and Tudulaig v Queensland [2004] FCA 1576 (FCA Cooper J) Consent determination recognised that native title exists in the entire determination area, incorporating land and waters landward of the high-water mark of Yam Island, Zagai or Jeaka Island, Tudu Island and Cap or Mukar or Mugquar Islet.

Djabugay People v Queensland [2004] FCA 1652 (FCA Spender J) Consent determination recognised that native title exists in the entire determination area, incorporating land and waters in the Barron Gorge National Park.

Gale on behalf of the Darug People v Minister for Land and Water Conservation for New South Wales [2004] FCA 374 (FCA Madgwick J) Found that there was insufficient evidence that the claim group was a society or that it or any member of it exercised rights and interests in accordance with traditional laws and customs. There was no cause to doubt the claimants' Indigenous identity, their descent from relevant ancestors, their self-identification as Indigenous people, nor their aspirations for factual and moral recognition, but these were found to fall short of the requirements to establish native title.

Gibuma on behalf of the Boigu People v Queensland [2004] FCA 1575 (FCA Cooper J) Consent determination recognised that native title exists in the entire determination area, described as those lands and waters landward of the high-water mark comprising (subject to specified exceptions) Boigu Island in the Torres Strait.

Lardil Peoples v Queensland [2004] FCA 298 (FCA Cooper J) Despite the fact that the majority of people did not live on country and did not live a 'traditional' lifestyle, his Honour was satisfied that none of the groups had lost its identity or existence as a society. Determination recognised non-exclusive rights to access the land and waters in accordance with traditional laws and customs. Considered the claimants' relationship to the land and waters as one of 'sustenance and religious and spiritual belonging' and as such the native title rights and interests had to reflect this. Did not accept that the claimants had exclusive control of access to this area. Further held that claimants did not control access to the fish, dugong and turtles within the claim area.

Lawson v Minister for Land and Water Conservation [2004] FCA 165 (FCA Whitlam J) Concerning an application for a determination of native title and compensation (covering the same area) in the region of Lake Victoria in New South Wales. Determined that native title does not exist. The 1922 appropriation was a previous exclusive possession act under the *Public Works Act 1912* (NSW), which resulted in extinguishment of native title. Compensation was not payable under the NTA.

Mye on behalf of the Erubam Le v Queensland [2004] FCA 1573 (FCA Cooper J) Consent determination concerning Erub Island in the Torres Strait; recognised that native title exists in the entire determination area.

Nangkiriny v Western Australia [2004] FCA 1156 (FCA North J) Consent determination recognised that native title exists in parts of the determination area. Commented on the Court's role in implementing a consent determination: the Court needs to be satisfied that it is appropriate to make a consent determination; the Court will be guided by the fact that the parties had freely entered into the proposed determination; the Court is not required to resolve issues that remain open, but rather can implement the parties' compromises. Expressed concern at the lack of funding provided for the proposed prescribed body corporate (PBC), noting that this could affect the operation of the PBC, particularly in regard to future act matters.

Neowarra v Western Australia [2004] FCA 1092 (FCA Sundberg J) Final determination based on findings of fact (2003) FCA 1402.

Newie on behalf of the Gebaralgal v Queensland [2004] FCA 1577 (FCA Cooper J) Consent determination recognised that native title exists in the entire determination area, the land and waters landward of the high-water mark of the island known as Gebara, Gabba or Two Brothers Island.

Nona on behalf of the Badulgal v Queensland [2004] FCA 1578 (FCA Cooper J) Consent determination recognised that native title exists in the entire determination area, incorporating the land and waters landward of the high-water mark in relation to most of Badu Island in the Torres Strait.

Stephen on behalf of the Ugar People v Queensland [2004] FCA 1574 (FCA Cooper J) Consent determination recognised that native title exists in the entire determination area, incorporating all land and waters landward of the high-water mark in relation to Stephens or Ugar Island, Campbell Island and Pearce Cay.

Wandarang, Alawa, Marra and Ngalakan Peoples v Northern Territory [2004] FCAFC 187 (FCA Black CJ, Moore and Hely JJ) Consent determination resolved an appeal in relation to pastoral leases, making amendments to the proposed native title determination removing the right to possess and occupy the determination area and the right to make decisions about the use and enjoyment of the determination area. The consent determination also made explicit the recognition of public rights in tidal rivers within the determination area.

Warria on behalf of the Kulkalgal v Queensland [2004] FCA 1572 (FCA Cooper J) Consent determination recognised that native title exists in the entire determination area, incorporating land and waters on the landward side of the high-water mark of Aureed Island in the Torres Strait.

Wik Peoples v Queensland [2004] FCA 1306 (FCA Cooper J) First consent determinations made in Queensland over land subject to pastoral leases. Consent determinations recognised exclusive and non-exclusive native title exists in the entire determination area. The nature and extent of the native title rights and interests in relation to the flowing, tidal and underground waters of the determination area are, subject to certain rights and interests, non-exclusive rights. (See Chapter 2.)

2005

Clarke on behalf of the Wotjobaluk, Jaadwa, Jadawadjali, Wergaia and Jupagulk Peoples v Victoria [2005] FCA 1795 (FCA Merkel J) First consent determination and first determination recognising native title in Victoria. The three consent determinations made by the Court determined that the Wotjobaluk, Jaadwa, Jadawadali, Wergaia and Jupagulk peoples have non-exclusive native title rights over Area A (limited to some Crown reserves along the banks of the Wimmera River with Yarriambiak Creek); and no native title rights in Area B (the remainder of the claim area).

Daniel v Western Australia (2005) 141 FCR 426 (FCA Nicholson J) First determination of native title in the Pilbara region of Western Australia. Court held that the Ngarluma and Indjibarndi peoples hold non-exclusive native title rights over parts of the claim area.

De Rose v South Australia [No. 2] (2005) 145 FCR 290 (FCA Wilcox, Sackville and Merkel JJ) Held that native title exists in relation to De Rose Hill station and is held by the Indigenous people who are Nguraritja (traditional owners) according to the relevant traditional laws and customs of the Western Desert bloc people. Considered issues in relation to 'connection' under s 223(1) of the NTA. The trial judge's statements of the principles underlying s 223(1)(b) were correct but incorrectly applied. Noted the claimants' broader observance of the laws and customs of the Western Desert bloc and the specific knowledge of law in relation to the claim area; the relatively and recent short absence of the claimants from the area; the claimants' active protection of sites under heritage laws; and the existence of intimidatory exclusion from the area by coexisting pastoral leaseholders. Also considered whether the claim is group, communal or individual. The native title rights and interests recognised in the determination area are non-exclusive rights to use and enjoy the land and waters in accordance with traditional law and custom. The Court upheld the trial judge's determination that native title has been wholly extinguished in land subject to certain pastoral improvements but improvements considered condition precedent to conferring of rights inconsistent with native title. Native title not extinguished prior to construction. (See Chapter 9.)

Gumana v Northern Territory [No. 2] [2005] FCA 1425 (FCA Mansfield J); *Gumana v Northern Territory* [2005] FCA 50 (Selway J) The principal claim was for a determination of native title in respect of an area in and around Blue Mud Bay in coastal remote East Arnhem Land, north-west of Groote Island. The second claim involved a challenge to the power of the Northern Territory to issue commercial fishing licences in relation to the intertidal zone of Indigenous land. The reasons for judgment were given by Justice Selway and the matter concluded by Justice Mansfield. Held that there cannot be a native title right to exclusive possession of small areas of sea and seabed. In relation to whether the public rights to fish and navigate and statutory rights of fishing apply to the intertidal zone around the relevant areas of Blue Mud Bay, Justice Selway set out reasons to find in favour of the claimants but felt bound by the decision of the Full Court in *Commonwealth v Yarmirr* (1999) 101 FCR 171. Lastly Justice Selway found that s 47A of the NTA does not revive a native title right of exclusive possession in the intertidal zone within the outer boundaries of the fee simple, where no statutory fishing licences under Northern Territory legislation have any validity. The determination recognised that native title exists in the entire determination area.

Jack Billy on behalf of the Poruma People v Queensland and Others (2005) 223 ALR 447 (FCA Black CJ) Consent determination recognised that native title exists in the entire determination area.

Mervyn and Others on behalf of the Peoples of the Ngaanyatjarra Lands v Western Australia [2005] FCA 831 (FCA Black CJ) Largest determination of native title to be made in Australia, covering approximately 187,000 square kilometres of land and waters in Western Australia. Consent determination found that native title exists in parts of the determination area. Exclusive possession native title was recognised over most of the claim area, including special leases; reserves held in trust for the use and benefit of Indigenous people; and unallocated Crown land. Non-exclusive possession native title was recognised over the Warburton Range stock route.

Nona on behalf of the Saibai, Dauan, Mabuiag, Badu and Boigu Peoples v Queensland [2005] FCA 1118 (FCA Black CJ) Consent determination recognised that native title exists in the entire determination area.

Annotated case list

***Northern Territory v Alyawarr, Kaytetye, Warumungu, Wakay Native Title Claim Group* (2005) 220 ALR 431 (FCA Wilcox, French and Weinberg JJ)** Unanimous decision allowed in part the Northern Territory's appeal and the claimants' cross-appeal. The Court upheld the definition of native title holders as one community comprising seven estate groups and the trial judge's holding that the relevant title is communal rather than severally held by the estate groups. Affirmed their exclusive native title rights over the Hatches Creek 'town' area. Rejected a right to control access where possession and occupation is not exclusive. Removed the rights to trade (insufficient evidence) and to control the disclosure of spiritual beliefs and practices (not a right in relation to land and waters) from the determination. The decision considered issues relating to the composition of native title rights and interests that can survive the grant of pastoral leases in the Northern Territory. Also significant for its application of s 47B of the NTA within town boundaries.

***Sampi v Western Australia [No. 3]* [2005] FCA 1716 (FCA French J)** The Bardi, and those Jawi with traditional rights in Bardi territory, succeeded in establishing native title over part of the area claimed: Lombadina and One Arm Point, Northern Dampier and King Sound regions, West Kimberley. Since then the parties have been finalising the terms of the determination. Orders include recognition of exclusive native title rights over parts of the land claimed and non-exclusive native title rights over areas below the mean high-water mark. A determination that native title does not exist was made over Brue Reef. Recognised exclusive possession over those areas identified as Bardi, the bulk of the claim area, but rejected the self-definition of the claimant group and consequently did not make a determination over those areas identified as Jawi. Justice French made no positive determination as to the existence of a Jawi society at the time of sovereignty and concluded that he was unable to identify a distinct Jawi society in the present. Distinguished *Ward* in which the claimants, the Miriuwung and Gajerrong peoples, were accepted as a single native title group while being distinct 'organised societies', arguing that as a pre-*Yorta Yorta* decision, the determination in *Ward* did not pay due consideration to the need to establish the normative society.

***Thaiday on behalf of the Warraber, Poruma and Iama Peoples v Queensland* [2005] FCA 1116 (FCA Black CJ)** Consent determination recognised that native title exists in the entire determination area, incorporating Sassi Island (Long Island) and surrounding islets in Torres Strait.

***Warria on behalf of the Poruma and Masig Peoples v Queensland* (2005) 223 ALR 62 (FCA Black CJ)** Consent determination recognised that native title exists in the entire determination area.

2006

Bennell v State of Western Australia (2006) 153 FCR 120 (FCA Wilcox J) A preliminary determination of fact regarding whether, putting aside the question of extinguishment, native title existed in an area approximately 9000 square kilometres in and around metropolitan Perth. The area formed part of the Single Noongar Claim, which encompassed 194,000 square kilometres of land and waters in the south-west of Western Australia. The first issue for determination concerned whether the Noongar people constituted a normative society at sovereignty. Wilcox J held that a society is defined as a body of persons united in and by its acknowledgment and observance of a body of law and customs. It is not necessary that the society constitute a community, in the sense that all its members know each other and live together. Wilcox J concluded that at 1829 the laws and customs governing land throughout the whole claim area were those of a single community with shared language, laws, customs and internal social interaction. Therefore, the Noongar people constituted a society for the purposes of s 223(1) of the NTA. The second issue for determination concerned whether that same society still existed and continued to acknowledge traditional laws and customs. Despite enormous forces that had assailed Noongar society since sovereignty and made it impossible for many of the traditional laws and customs to be maintained, Wilcox J found that the normative system revealed by the evidence was the normative system of traditional Noongar society, not a normative system rooted in some other, different society. Wilcox J also noted that it is unnecessary and inappropriate for the Court to determine intracommunal rights and interests. Such matters are properly subject to the internal mechanisms of law and custom within a native title holding group. (See annotation FCA appeal *Bodney v Bennell* (2008) and Chapter 10)

Butchulla People v State of Queensland (2006) 154 FCR 233 (FCA Keifel J) Considered whether authorisation for the current applicant's removal and replacement was given in accordance with s 251B of Native Title Act 1993 (Cth). It focused on whether all members of the claim group needed to be present at the meeting. Held that claim groups were obliged to use a customary process of decision making, where they still existed, rather than adopt a contemporary process.

Annotated case list

Daniel v State of Western Australia **[2006] FCA 271 (FCA Nicholson J)** Procedural determination that an appeal against a determination of native title rights does not prevent the incorporation of a PBC.

Dann on behalf of the Amangu People v State of Western Australia **[2006] FCA 1249 (FCA French J)** Procedural decision to refuse to allow the Western Australian Fishing Industry Council (Inc.) to join the native title proceedings. Neither their member's interests nor their participation in statutory committees constituted sufficient direct interest in the proceedings to be joined as a party.

Gordon Charlie v Cape York Land Council **[2006] FCA 1418 (FCA Greenwood J)** Procedural decision to reject a claim that the Cape York Land Council failed to conduct and prepare for an authorisation meeting appropriately by contacting all potential claimants. Discusses also how Land Councils should give notice and provide support for similar authorisation meetings.

Griffiths v Northern Territory **(2006) 165 FCR 300 (FCA Weinberg J)** A shift from patrilineal inheritance to cognation as the basis for taking country did not give rise to a new normative system such as would deny the Ngaliwurru and Nungali people their native title rights in the determination area of Timber Creek.

Griffiths v Northern Territory of Australia [No. 2] **[2006] FCA 1155 (FCA Weinberg J)** Final determination. (See *Griffiths v Northern Territory* (2006) 165 FCR 300 above.)

Jango v Northern Territory of Australia **(2006) 152 FCR 150 (FCA Sackville J)** Litigated determination regarding the town of Yulara in the Northern Territory. Sackville J held that the applicants had failed to establish that they lived according to traditional customs in the native title rights claimed. He held that he was unable to consider other possible arguments regarding different rights and different combinations and claimants, but must limit his judgment to the rights explicitly claimed. Further, he held that if the claimants had satisfied the threshold test for native title, their rights were unlikely to have been totally extinguished. (See appeal, *Jango v Northern Territory of Australia* (2007).)

Koara People v State of Western Australia **(2006) 226 ALR 705 (FCA Nicholson J)** Procedural determination holding that amendments to claims filed under the 'old' *Native Title Act* are still subject to transitional provisions of the 'new' Act.

Kokatha Native Title Claim v State of South Australia **[2006] FCA 838 (FCA Finn J)** Procedural decision to refuse to excise a portion of the Kokatha claim that overlaps with another native title claim. Considers the exercise of discretion under s 67 of the *Native Title Act 1993* (Cth) based on a series of factors including a lack of available funding, the significance of area to claimant group, prospects of mediation and settlement, and the efficient administration of justice.

Manas v State of Queensland **[2006] FCA 413 (FCA Dowsett J)** Consent determination recognised that native title exists in the entire determination area of Murrabar Islet, Sarbi Islet, Iem Islet, Zagarsup Islet, Kulbi Islet, Muknab Rock and Kapril Rock in the Torres Strait. The native title holders are the Mualgal people.

Mundraby v State of Queensland **[2006] FCA 436 (FCA Dowsett J)** Consent determination recognised that native title exists in parts of the determination area near Yarrabah and around Trinity Inlet and the Mulgrave River in Queensland. The native title holders are the Mandingalbay Yidinji people.

Nona and Manas v State of Queensland **[2006] FCA 412 (FCA Dowsett J)** Consent determination recognised that native title exists in the entire determination area in the Torres Strait. The native title holders are the Badualgal and Mualgal peoples.

Riley v State of Queensland **[2006] FCA 72 (FCA Allsop J)** Consent determination recognised that native title exists in the entire determination area in Cape York Peninsula in Queensland. The native title holders are the Western Yalanji people.

Risk v Northern Territory **of Australia [2006] FCA 404 (FCA Mansfield J)** Neither the Larrakia people nor the Danggalaba clan met the requirements of s 223 of the NTA because they had not maintained a system of traditional laws and customs since sovereignty. A sincere and intense desire to re-establish the laws and customs that had existed at sovereignty was not sufficient for making a determination that native title existed. Mansfield J declined to adopt the findings in a previous *Aboriginal Land Rights (Northern Territory) Act 1976 (Cth)* claim relating to the determination area, despite the Court's discretion to do so under s 86(a)(v) of the NTA. On the facts, differences in the claim area, witnesses called and legislative requirement of the two Acts made it inappropriate. (See annotation FCA appeal, *Risk v Northern Territory* (2007).)

Rubibi Community v State of Western Australia [No. 6] (2006) 226 ALR 676 (FCA Merkel J) Procedural determination that some claimants should not be considered part of the native title holding group because they were not recognised as traditional owners of the land, merely custodians. The test applied was self-identification and recognition by the native title holding group, rather than descent. Following *Neowarra*, the Court also held that practical concerns about how native title could operate within urban areas was not suitable grounds to find that native title did not exist.

Rubibi Community v State of Western Australia [No. 7] [2006] FCA 459 (FCA Merkel J) Determination recognised native title exists but is limited to the non-commercial exploitation of resources. The native title holders are the Yawuru community. The special attachment of Walman Yawuru clan members to parts of the claim area does not give rise to native title rights exclusive of other Yawuru community members. The criteria for membership of a native title holding community are:
- where a person descended from an apical ancestor had two parents who were community members: the criteria of self-identification and general community acceptance are not required;
- where only one parent of a descendant was a community member: the criterion of self-identification must be satisfied;
- people who were not descendants of an apical ancestor: the criteria of self-identification and general community acceptance must be satisfied. (e.g. via adoption or having a long-term physical association and cultural responsibilities).

Reservation of land for the purpose of a jail and police station extinguished native title rights amounting to exclusivity but did not extinguish all native title rights and interests. Construction and use of such facilities on part of the reserves extinguished native title rights and interests in the areas on which the jail and police station were constructed and on areas adjacent thereto that were reasonably necessary for or incidental to the operation or enjoyment of the jail or police station. However, the construction did not necessarily extinguish native title rights and interests in respect of the remaining areas of the reserves. Consistent with the full Court's findings in *Alyawarr*, the grant of a pastoral or mining lease does not necessarily conflict with a native title right to live on land the subject of such grant. Traditional use of an area establishes occupation, but where use is not traditional, it is a question of fact and degree whether there is sufficient occupation for the purposes of ss 47A and 47B of the NTA.

Wakaman People #2 v Native Title Registrar and Authorised Delegate (2006) 155 FCR 107 (FCA Keifel J) Procedural case that held that the Native Title Registrar's decision to refuse a claim for registration was appropriate because it is not obliged to consider whether the group seeking registration is correctly described, but merely that the description is capable of determining whether a person is part of the group or not. The Registrar should also consider whether the authorisation has been correctly made under the NTA. Also discusses the nature of the court's jurisdiction to review the requirements for registration.

Ward v Western Australia (Miriuwung Gajerrong #4 Determination) [2006] FCA 1848 (FCA North J) Concerned an area approximately seven square kilometres in the north-east Kimberley region of Western Australia that had initially formed part of the first Miriuwung Gajerrong determination (see *Ward v Western Australia* (1998)). Although Lee J's recognition of native title in that case was subsequently overturned on appeal (see *Western Australia v Ward* (2000)), his findings in relation to this particular area were undisturbed and eventually supported the recognition of native title in this consent determination. The native title holders are the Miriuwung, Gajerrong, Doolboong, Wardenybeng and Gija people.

Yankunytjatjara/Antakirinja Native Title Claim Group v The State of South Australia [2006] FCA 1142 (FCA Mansfield J) Consent determination recognised that native title exists in parts of the determination area in central northern South Australia. The native title holders are the members of the Western Desert Social and Cultural Bloc and predominantly identify as Yankunytjara people.

2007

Anderson v State of Western Australia [2007] FCA 1733 (FCA French J) Justice French considered a motion to amend a native title application to replace the existing applicants. His Honour accepted that a process of majority decision making was agreed to and adopted by a sufficiently representative section of the native title claim group for the purpose of dealing with matters arising in relation to the application.

Beattie on behalf of Western Wakka Wakka Peoples v State of Queensland [2007] FCA 596 (FCA Keifel J) Consideration of whether a native title application can be struck out. The Court found that in the present case there is nothing to suggest the continued existence of a society of Western Wakka Wakka people. If such a group did once exist, all that remains are the descendants of one person and they are said to follow family customs and practices. Also considered whether the application complied with s 62 of the Native Title Act. It was found that s 62 had not been met in a number of respects, including the failure to swear an affidavit by each of the persons who are said to be authorised to identify the claim area and its boundaries. The Court also noted that the case had been the subject of mediation since 1999 and there was an absence of any meaningful action to progress the matter. Struck out the application under Federal Court Order 35, rule 2.

Brown (on behalf of the Ngarla People) v State of Western Australia [2007] FCA 1025 (FCA Bennett J) Consent determination recognising that native title exists in parts of the determination area within the Pilbara region of Western Australia. The native title holders are the Ngarla people.

Chapman v Queensland (2007) 159 FCR 507 (FCA Kiefel J) An application to remove three of the fifteen people authorised to be the applicant in the Wakka Wakka peoples' claimant application. One was dead and the other two had allegedly refused to co-operate. Although s 66B of the NTA provides a procedure for replacement of the applicant, it had not been followed and no meeting of the claim group had been held to revoke their authority. Instead, the removal application was made under O 6 r 9(b) of the Federal Court Rules, which provides that the Court may order that a party cease to be a party where they have ceased to be a proper or necessary party. Kiefel J granted the application on the basis that the references in the NTA to the applicant do not prevent the authorisation of persons as applicant being viewed individually. Accordingly, there was no reason why O 6 r 9 should not have operation. The Register can be amended to remove the names of persons no longer authorised as applicant.

Cox on behalf of the Yungngora People v State of Western Australia [2007] FCA 588 (FCA French J) Consent determination recognised that native title exists in the entire determination area of just over 1800 square kilometres in the Kimberley region of Western Australia. The determination included area covered by the Noonkanbah pastoral lease. Rights exercised in relation to the pastoral lease prevail over native title rights to the extent of any inconsistency, but do not extinguish them. The native title holders are the Yungngora people.

Dale v Moses [2007] FCAFC 82 (FCA Moore, North and Mansfield JJ) Involved an appeal from native title determination of a single judge who dismissed the appellants' claim to native title in the determination area but found another native title claim group, the Ngarluma people and Yindjibarndi people, held non-exclusive native title. This appeal was dismissed on the basis that the Wonggoo-tt-oo people were not a group with continuing connection and were not differentiated from Ngarluma people and Yindjibarndi people.

Doolan v Native Title Registrar (2007) 158 FCR 56 (FCA Spender J) Review of the Native Title Registrar's refusal to register a native title determination application because two of the eighteen people authorised to be the applicant had subsequently withdrawn. The main issue was whether the applicant in s 61(2) of the NTA meant all of the persons authorised by the native title claim group and no fewer or all of the persons authorised by the native title claim group who, at any particular time, were willing and able to discharge their representative function. Spender J held that the proper construction of s 61(2) is the latter, and did not distinguish between a group member's capacity to act and that person's willingness to act.

Eringa No. 1 Native Title Claim v South Australia [2007] FCA 182 (FCA Mansfield J) Mansfield J refused to make an order stipulating that if gender-restricted preservation evidence was given and the judge then appointed to hear the proceeding was a woman, the applicant would be entitled not to adduce that evidence at trial. His Honour observed that such an order was unnecessary because: (i) the uncontested operation of s 46(d) of the *Federal Court of Australia Act 1976 (Cth)* was that preservation evidence is subject to judicial discretion and does not automatically become evidence in the hearing of the proceeding; and (ii) the discretion under s 46(d) is guided by s 82(2) of the NTA, which provides that the Court may take account of the cultural and customary concerns of Indigenous Australians so long as to do so does not unduly prejudice any other party to the proceedings. Mansfield J also noted that parties must appreciate that the judge hearing a matter has a role and presence that is an inevitable part of the exercise of judicial power under Chapter III of the Constitution, regardless of whether the judge is male or female.

Gamogab v Akiba (2007) 159 FCR 578 (FCA Keifel, Sundberg, Giles JJ) Involved the issue of whether a national of Papua New Guinea could be joined as a respondent. Focused on the nature and extent of the Court's discretion to do so where interests may be affected by a native title determination. The court of appeal held that Gamogab could be joined to the proceedings and remitted the matter to the primary judge to determine the terms of that joiner.

Griffiths v Northern Territory (2007) 243 ALR 72 (FCA French, Branson and Sundberg JJ) Native title consent determination recognising the rights and interests of the Ngaliwurru and Nungali persons who are members of the Makalamayi, Wunjaiyi, Yanturi, Wantawul and Maiyalaniwung estate groups in the Timber Creek area.

Gudjala People 2 v Native Title Registrar [2007] FCA 1167 (FCA Dowsett J) Involved an application for review of a decision by the Native Title Registrar not to register an application. The Court held that the Registrar was bound by statutory duty rather than a previous decision, which upheld arguments similar to those presented by the applicant in a different claim area. Also, the Court held that any errors in the decision-making process do not necessarily deny the applicant procedural fairness. Dowsett J noted that the role of the Registrar is administrative and a failure to refer to a salient fact is not within this role. His Honour also considered whether an error of law had been made in refusing to register the claim. While considering the principles of *Yorta Yorta*, he found that the overlaps in the claim area were not adequately explained and that the application fails to explain how, by reference to traditional law and customs presently acknowledged and observed, the claim group is limited to descendants of the identified apical ancestors. Dowsett J also noted that no basis is shown for inferring that there was, at and prior to 1850–60, a society that had a system of laws and customs from which relevant existing laws and customs were derived and traditionally passed on to the existing claim group. His Honour ultimately found that the claim should not be accepted for registration.

Gumana v Northern Territory of Australia (2007) 158 FCR 349 (FCA French, Finn and Sundberg JJ) A fee simple grant in the intertidal zone made under the *Aboriginal Land Rights Act 1976* (ALRA) conferred an exclusive right over the waters that flowed onto the intertidal zone, including a right to exclude those seeking to exercise a public right to fish or to navigate. In consequence, the *Fisheries Act* cannot authorise entry by the public or the issue of permits or licences to fish in that water. The contrary finding in *Yarmirr* was plainly wrong in relation to ALRA grants. However, the *Yarmirr* principle continues to apply in relation to native title. As the native title rights and interests were held communally by the native title holders, it was not necessary to enquire whether there was a connection between a clan member's spouse and the determination area.

Harrington-Smith v Native Title Registrar [2007] FCA 414 (FCA Lindgren J) An injunction was sought to prevent the removal of an entry from the Register of Native Title Claims after the claim was dismissed at first instance by the Federal Court. Under s 190(4) of the NTA, an entry must be removed from the Register as soon as practicable after the application has been dismissed. The applicants argued that a claim is not dismissed until any appeal proceedings are heard and determined. This argument was rejected by the Court. Lindgren J held that 'dismissed' bears its natural meaning, and is satisfied by the dismissal of an application at first instance following a trial.

Harrington-Smith v Western Australia [No. 9] (2007) 238 ALR 1 (FCA Lindgren J) Eight overlapping applications for a determination of native title were before the Court, all concerning semi-nomadic peoples alleged to constitute a normative society known as the Western Desert cultural bloc. Lindgren J found that none of the claims that required authorisation under the 1998 amendments were in fact authorised. In consequence, he did not have jurisdiction to make a determination. However, in light of the importance of the matter and the likelihood that it would be the subject of appeal, his Honour made a series of other findings that also led him to conclude that the appropriate outcome was to dismiss all eight applications. In consequence, Lindgren J held that internal disputes among claim groups and overlapping claims will not be overlooked by the Court merely by presenting them as one claim without further evidence of unified or common traditional laws and customs.

Hughes (on behalf of the Eastern Guruma People) v State of Western Australia [2007] FCA 365 (FCA Bennett J) First native title claim settled by consent in central Pilbara. Determination recognised that native title exists in the entire determination area.

Jango v Northern Territory of Australia (2007) 159 FCR 531 (FCA French, Finn and Mansfield JJ) Involved a native title compensation claim. Considered the nature of native title rights and interests that had been extinguished, criteria for the identification of native title holders and whether the evidence presented was sufficient to support the existence of traditional laws and customs. The Court focused on whether the trial judge ought to have determined pre-existing native title on other bases and whether he misunderstood the pleaded case. The Court concluded that there was no error by the trial judge and dismissed the appeal. In reaching the decision, the Court considered whether registration of title under the *Real Property Act 1886* (SA) had validly extinguished native title, the effect of indefeasibility provisions and the validation provisions of the NTA and *Validation Act*.

King v Northern Territory of Australia [2007] FCA 994 (FCA Moore J) A preliminary determination concerning two pastoral leases in the Northern Territory. The parties submitted a list of issues to the Court for adjudication. In response, the Court made the following findings: (1) rights of access to pastoral leases are subject to the greater rights of the pastoral leaseholder. Yet, the native title rights should still be described to their full extent, rather than include a qualifying term, such as 'limited access' or 'live temporarily'. (2) The creation of a town rubbish dump extinguishes inconsistent native title rights as it involves the state determining how land should be used. (3) Airstrips and trap yards located away from the homestead, and the area around them necessary to operate them safely and effectively, do not extinguish native title rights. (4) A gas pipeline running over the pastoral leases is not a public work and does not extinguish native title. (5) The proclamation of the town of Newcastle Waters did not extinguish native title because, as with *Alyawarr*, the proclamation did not specify how the land was to be used. The parties then used this determination as the basis of their subsequent consent determination.

King v Northern Territory of Australia [2007] FCA 1498 (FCA Moore J) Consent determination recognising that native title exists in parts of the determination area. The native title holders are the Turrutpa-Jalapirri, Pinkakujarra, Murranjayi and Liyartu-Walamarnta groups.

Kite v State of South Australia [2007] FCA 1662 (FCA Finn J) Claim struck out under s 84C. Justice Finn made this decision because there were substantial ambiguities and contradictions between the evidence and submissions made during the hearing, as well as doubt about the rights of the community of descendents advancing the claim. His Honour found that the claim 'may well owe more to concepts drawn from common law conceptions of property than from traditional laws and customs'.

Kokatha People v State of South Australia [2007] FCA 1057 (FCA Finn J) Involved the issue of whether a respondent to an application for a native title determination can seek a determination of native title in his or her favour under s 225 of the NTA. The court concluded that a respondent could not seek a determination under s 225 without following the procedures for authorisation under the NTA.

Lovett on behalf of the Gunditjmara People v State of Victoria [2007] FCA 474 (FCA North J) Australia's 100th native title determination. Consent determination recognised that native title exists in parts of the determination area in Victoria. The native title holders are the Gunditjmara people.

Moses v State of Western Australia (2007) 160 FCR 148 (FCA Moore, North and Mansfield JJ) Litigated determination recognising native title over parts of the determination area. The native title holders are the Ngarluma and Yindjibarndi peoples. This decision overturned an earlier determination to dismiss this claim.

Ngadjon-Jii people v State of Queensland [2007] FCA 1937 (FCA Spender J) Consent determination recognising that native title exists in specific lots near Malanda and Bartle Frere in far north Queensland. The native title holders are the Ngadjon-Jii people.

Patta Warumungu People v Northern Territory of Australia [2007] FCA 1243 (FCA Mansfield J) Consent determination recognising native title exists in part over 64 square kilometres around Tennant Creek. The native title holders are the Patta Warumungu people. This was the first consent determination in the Northern Territory.

Payi Payi & Ors on behalf of the Ngururrpa People and State of Western Australia [2007] FCA 2113 (FCA Black CJ) Consent determination recognising native title over 30,000 square kilometres in the Great Sandy Desert of Western Australia. The native title holders are the Ngururrpa people.

Reid v State of South Australia [2007] FCA 1479 (FCA Finn J) Involved a decision to strike out under s 84C on the basis that its authorisation did not meet the requirements of the NTA. Justice Finn found that there was no evidence to suggest that all members of the Kokatha Peoples Community were present and that the description of the claim group was only a part of the group. He also found that there was uncertainty in relation to the description of the members. Justice Finn was doubtful that there was evidence of a right of self-authorisation under traditional laws and customs and found that reliance on the elders' approval did not assist in the application because authorisation must be by 'all persons ... who ... hold common or group rights'.

Risk v Northern Territory (2007) 240 ALR 75 (FCA French, Finn and Sundberg JJ) Appeal against a decision that neither the Larrakia people nor the Danggalaba clan possessed rights and interests under traditional laws and customs. In determining whether the laws and customs were traditional, the Court endorsed the *Yorta Yorta* test. Accordingly, a court must examine the course of the claimant group's observance of traditional laws and customs to determine whether continuity can be established from sovereignty to the present, notwithstanding that some change, adaption or interruption may have occurred. In contrast, the book-end error is impermissible (to merely compare the body of laws and customs at sovereignty with those that exist today). However, on the facts, the appeal was dismissed because the primary judge did not misapply the *Yorta Yorta* test.

Annotated case list

Timothy James Malachi on behalf of the Strathgordon Mob v State of Queensland [2007] **FCA 1048 (FCA Greenwood J)** Consent determination recognising that native title exists in parts of the claimed Strathgordon area on Cape York Peninsula. The native title holders are the Strathgordon Mob.

Trevor Close on behalf of the Githabul People v Minister for Lands [2007] **FCA 1847 (FCA Branson J)** First positive determination of native title in New South Wales in a decade. Consent determination recognising that native title exists in the entire determination area, including nine national parks and thirteen state forests in northern New South Wales. The native title holders are the Githabul people.

Van Hemmen on behalf of the Kabi Kabi People #3 v State of Queensland [2007] **FCA 1185 (FCA Collier J)** Determined to dismiss the applicants' claim because they lacked proper authorisation. This decision was taken because the Kabi Kabi #2 applicants, the Gurang Land Council and Queensland South Native Title Services argued that the Kabi Kabi #3 applicants were not properly authorised and their claim should be dismissed pursuant to s 84C. The Court accepted this argument, noting that the claim overlapped with another claim and that eleven of the twelve named apical ancestors were named in both the Kabi Kabi #2 and #3 claims.

Walker on behalf of the Eastern Kuku Yalanaji People v State of Queensland [2007] **FCA 1907 (FCA Allsop J)** Consent determination recognising that native title exists over 126,900 hectares in the World Heritage-listed Daintree National Park. Within this area, the native title holders have exclusive rights of access and use over 30,300 hectares. The native title holders are the Eastern Kuku Yalanji people.

Webb v State of Western Australia [2007] **FCA 1342 (FCA French J)** A procedural determination considering the relationship between s 94C and s 66C. The report provided by the Native Title Registrar under s 66C is a 'statutory means for drawing the attention of the Court to applications which may meet the conditions of dismissal under s 94C'. The Court is not bound by the report and dismissal under s 94 is not considered unless there is failure to comply with direction under s 94C(1)(e)(i) or there has been a failure to take steps to resolve the claim. Justice French found that the area of the claim was much larger than areas covered by future act notices and the application was a part of a regional work program. Accordingly, he found that there was no occasion to consider the mandatory dismissal provisions.

2008

***Billy Patch & Others on behalf of the Birriliburu People v State of Western Australia and Others* [2008] FCA 944 (FCA French J)** Consent determination recognising that native title exists over 66,760 square kilometres in the Little Sandy Desert, Western Australia. The claim area is located roughly 900 kilometres north-east of Perth. The native title holders are the Birriliburru people.

***Bodney v Bennell* (2008) 167 FCR 84 (FCA Finn, Sundberg and Mansfield JJ)** This case concerned four appeals against the judgment of Justice Wilcox in *Bennell v Western Australia* [2006] FCA 1243. The main issue for consideration was whether Justice Wilcox correctly applied s 223 of the NTA. This involved consideration of the meaning of the term 'traditional' within the context of s 223 and the consequential requirement of continuity. The court held that Justice Wilcox had incorrectly applied s 223. Among other things, he had asked the wrong questions in determining whether the traditional laws and customs of the traditional Aboriginal society had continued to be observed and acknowledged without substantial interruption. Justice Wilcox focused on whether or not the society that existed at sovereignty had continued to exist, rather than looking at whether that society had continued to follow traditional laws and customs that were practiced at sovereignty. As a result of the erroneous application of s 223, the appeal succeeded. The full Court set aside the orders made by Justice Wilcox. The separate question relating to whether or not native title rights and interests existed in relation to the Perth metropolitan area specifically was remitted to the docket judge for consideration. (See Chapter 10.)

***Eringa, Eringa No. 2, Wangkangurru/Yarluyandi and Irrwanyere Mr Dare Native Title Claim Groups v The State of South Australia* [2008] FCA 1370 (FCA Lander J)** Consent determination that native title exists over 7770 square kilometres of the Witjira National Park, South Australia. This was the first successful native title claim over a national park in South Australia, as well as the first claim to be successfully mediated without court intervention. It resolved three distinct native title claims. The native title holders are the Lower Southern Arrente and the Wangkangurru peoples.

***Griffiths v Minister for Lands, Planning and Environment* (2008) 235 CLR 232 (HCA Gleeson CJ, Gummow, Kirby, Hayne, Heydon, Crennan and Kiefel JJ)** Decision concerning compulsory acquisition of native title by the Northern Territory Government in the Timber Creek township. The traditional owners of the area had lodged an objection to the acquisition and an application for a determination of native title over the area (*Griffiths v Northern Territory* (2007) 243 ALR 72). The Court considered two main issues: the extent of the power to acquire land 'for any purpose whatsoever' under s 43(1) of the *Lands Acquisition Act 1978* (NT) (LAA); and whether s 24MD of the NTA provides for the extinguishment of native title by compulsory acquisition where no other rights and interests, other than those of the Crown, existed in relation to the area concerned. The majority (Gummow, Hayne and Heydon JJ, with Gleeson CJ and Crennan J agreeing) found that the 'for any purpose whatsoever' in s 43(1) of the LAA must, at least, include acquisition 'for the purpose of enabling the exercise of powers conferred on the executive by another statute in the territory', in this case the *Crown Lands Act 1992* (NT), s 9, which provides that the Minister may grant estates in fee simple or lease Crown land. The majority disregarded a clear line of authority against local governments interfering with private title for the benefit of another person. Justices Kirby and Kiefel dissented. Kiefel J said that there was no proposed purpose for the acquisition within any broader plan of the Northern Territory Government. She found that the acquisition was for the benefit of a private developer. Kirby J emphasised the unique nature of native title and found that, as a result, extinguishment must be contained within 'very specific and clear legislation that unmistakably has this effect'. The native title holders argued that the NTA could not be satisfied if there were no other non-native title interests in the area acquired. Section 24MD(2) provides for the extinguishment of native title on just terms compensation if all non-native title rights and interests are also acquired. However, all the judges were of the view that s 24MD of the NTA allowed for a compulsory acquisition extinguishing native title, even where the only interests existing in the area (other than those of the Crown) are native title rights and interests, provided all of the conditions found in s 24MD(2) are met. Justices Hayne and Heydon noted that any other reading would not satisfy the RDA. However, the result achieves this very effect in removing the rights of native title holders in favour of the rights of a license holder without reaching an agreement with the native title parties. (See Chapter 8.)

***Gudjala People #2 v Native Title Registrar* (2008) 171 FCR 317 (FCAFrench, Moore and Lindgren JJ)** An appeal regarding the primary judge's review of the Registrar's refusal to register the applicant's claim. At trial the primary judge found that the Registrar had made an error of law in the test applied for registration. The full Court dismissed the appeal, stating that during the registration process:

> [I]t is only necessary for an applicant to give a general description of the factual basis of the claim and to provide evidence in the affidavit that the applicant believes the statements in that general description are true. Of course the general description must be in sufficient detail to enable a genuine assessment of the application by the Registrar under s 190A and related sections, and be something more than assertions at a high level

of generality. But what the applicant is not required to do is to provide anything more than a general description of the factual basis on which the application is based. In particular, the applicant is not required to provide evidence of the type which, if furnished in subsequent proceedings, would be required to prove all matters needed to make out the claim. The applicant is not required to provide evidence that proves directly or by inference the facts necessary to establish the claim.

Hazelbane v Doepel **(2008) 167 FCR 325 (FCA Mansfield J)** Involved a review of the Registrar's decision to register an overlapping claim over the Town of Batchelor under s 190A of the NTA. The original applicants argued that the Registrar, in deciding to accept the Town of Batchelor No. 2, did not seek submissions from them. The Court found the original applicants had standing to bring the claim as they were a 'person aggrieved' under the Administrative Decisions (Judicial Review) Act. Mansfield J found that the Registrar fell into error by identifying a wrong issue and asking himself a wrong question in addressing procedural requirements in s 190C(2) and (4). Accordingly, it was held that the decision to register the Batchelor No. 2 application be set aside.

Lapthorne v Indigenous Land Corporation **[2008] FCA 682 (Siopis J)** Concerned the dismissal of a native title application. Mr Lapthorne claimed native title over an area of land the Indigenous Land Corporation intended to sell. The Thudgari Native Title Group, of whom Mr Lapthorne claimed to be a member, was also pursuing a native title claim over the same area of land. The Court found that Mr Lapthorne had not obtained proper authorisation from the Thudgari people to make the claim, as required by s 61 of the NTA. Furthermore, he had not produced the necessary evidence to show that he was entitled under s 66B of the NTA to replace the persons named in the native title claim already commenced by the Thudgari people.

Lardil, Yangkaal, Gangalidda & Kaiadilt Peoples v State of Queensland **[2008] FCA 1855 (Spender J)** Determination of native title by consent. The issue was whether it is within the power of the Court and appropriate to make an order under s 87 of the NTA, and whether s 225 of the NTA was satisfied. The determination of native title was made.

Leslie Hayes & Ors on behalf of the Thalanyji People v The State of Western Australia and Others **(unreported, FCA, 18 September 2008, North J)** Consent determination that native title exists in parts of the determination area, in the West Pilbara of Western Australia. The native title holders are the Thalanyji people.

Mineralogy Pty Ltd v Kuruma Marthudunera Native Title Claimants [2008] WAMW3 Objection to grant of tenement. The objectors were the Kuruma Marthudurara Native Title Claimants who claim that they are:

registered native title applicants over the land on which the Applicant seeks to have the proposed tenement granted. The objectors believe that activities that might be allowed under the proposed tenement could have an adverse impact upon the exercise of native title rights, cultural heritage (including sites of significance) and lifestyles of the objectors. Work and activity allowed under the licence could also affect the environment and flora and fauna in the area, which would impact on the objectors, and the granting of the tenement would be contrary to the public interest.

Final recommendation that grant be refused.

Northern Territory of Australia v Arnhem Land Aboriginal Land Trust (2008) 236 CLR 24 (HCA Gleeson CJ, Gummow, Kirby, Hayne, Crennan and Keifel JJ) Recognised that the rights and interests held by the Yolgnu people in relation to areas of land in Blue Mud Bay under the *Aboriginal Land Rights (Northern Territory) Act 1976* (Cth) included the right to make decisions about who enters their waters irrespective of the operation of the *Fisheries Act 1988* (NT). The majority accepted the argument that even though the *Fisheries Act* controlled fishing within the boundaries of Aboriginal land and waters, a fishing licence is not sufficient to confer permission to enter or remain on Aboriginal land. The decision does not have any direct impact on native title jurisprudence. However, as noted above, it demonstrates that rights over water, even in areas subject to highly regulated licensing regimes, can sustain a right to exclude. It also indicates that the non-exclusive native title to offshore areas may be more robust than is currently presumed.

Stanley Mervyn, Adrian Young, and Livingston West and Ors, on behalf of the People of the Ngaanyatjarra Lands v The State of Western Australia and Ors (unreported, FCA, 3 June 2008, French J) Consent determination recognising that native title exists in the claimed area in the Central Desert, Western Australia. The native title holders are the People of the Ngaanyatjarra Lands.

State of Western Australia v Sebastian (2008) 173 FCR 1 (FCA Branson, North and Mansfield JJ) Involved two competing claims to native title over land and waters around Broome in Western Australia. The full Federal Court upheld the original judgment of Merkel J. In reaching its decision, the full Federal

Court made extensive comment on how the requirements of *Yorta Yorta* are met. It found that s 47B was capable of applying to areas within the proclaimed township of Broome.

Turrbal People v State of Queensland **[2008] FCA 316 (FCA Spender J)** Notice of motion brought by original applicant seeking to replace herself with another person. This motion was opposed on the basis that she did not have the authority of the claim group to make this decision. His Honour followed the previous decision of *Williams v Grant* [2004] FCAFC 178, which assumes that the original applicant was authorised. Following this decision, if she had the authority to make the original application, she had the authority to decide on an altered position of the applicant.

Western Desert Lands Aboriginal Corporation v State of Western Australia and Others **(2008) 218 FLR 362(NNTT Sumner CJ)** Tribunal decision that an expedited process for granting future acts within a determination area is available to both native title claimants and native title holders.

Wiri People v Native Title Registrar **(2008) 168 FCR 187 (FCA Collier J)** Application for a review of a decision of a delegate of the Native Title Registrar to not accept the Wiri People #2 Application for registration under s 190A of the NTA. Justice Collier held that it is also 'incumbent on the delegate to be satisfied that the claimants truly constitute such a group and the applicant should be seen to be authorised by all persons who relevantly hold the common or group rights'. His Honour also noted that the Registrar was entitled to consider information obtained as a result of searches conducted by the Registrar under s 190A(3)(b). His Honour also confirmed that s 190C (4)(b) does not confine the Registrar or delegate to the statements made in affidavit or the information provided in the application. This also includes the consideration of an overlapping claim, which had also been certified by the relevant representative body in the area.

Worimi Local Aboriginal Land Council v Minister for Lands for the State of New South Wales [No. 2] **[2008] FCA 1929 (Bennett J)** Non-claimant application under NTA seeking a determination that no native title exists over an area of land. The previous claimant applications for determination that native title exists were struck out for not meeting requirements of the NTA. The previous claimant was joined as third respondent under s 84(5) of the Act. The third respondent opposed the non-claimant application. This was the first case where a non-claimant application was actively opposed. The burden of proof is an evidentiary burden with a requirement to prove the proposition negative on the balance of probabilities. There is no presumption of native title and the third respondent is not required to establish native title but is required to adduce evidence once the applicant has adduced sufficient evidence from which the negative proposition may be inferred. The third respondent had not adduced sufficient evidence to cast doubt on applicant's case and there was no sufficient evidence that asserted rights and interests arise under normative system of traditional laws acknowledged and traditional customs observed. The Court held that the applicant was entitled to a determination that there is no native title over the land.

2009

Adnyamathanha #1 Native Title Claim Group v The State of South Australia **[2009] FCA 358 (19 March 2009) (Mansfield J)** Concerns an application for separate determinations of native title under s 61(1) NTA. The three proposed determinations relate to two native title claims. The first is a claim to a substantial area of South Australia. The second claim is over the Flinders Ranges National Park, which is within the boundaries of the first claim. It was proposed that the first claim be subject to two consent determinations, one over a large part of the claim and another over the smaller Angepena area. It was reasoned that separate determination of the native title claims would result in a mutually satisfying outcome in a timely and efficient manner. Given the complex and varied nature of the proposed land uses in Angepena, it would be better if it was the subject of a separate consent determination. Further, the work and negotiations conducted in relation to Angepena were specific to the area. Thus, the Court ordered that the hearing of the proposed consent determinations be confirmed for a later date (see case below), with a separate consent determination to be entered in relation to Angepena Station.

Adnyamathanha #1 Native Title Claim Group v The State of South Australia (No. 2) **[2009] FCA 359 (Mansfield J)** The Federal Court gave effect to three separate consent determinations of non-exclusive native title rights and interests over the Angepena Pastoral Station and other specified areas in the Flinders Ranges, central South Australia. The applications were made under ss 87 and 87A of the *Native Title Act 1993* (Cth). Section 87 sets out the Federal Court's power to make orders sought by the consent of the parties. The consent determinations recognised the Adnyamathanha people's non-exclusive native title right and interests, including the right to access and live or camp on the land, to gather, hunt and fish, and to conduct cultural and spiritual activities on the determination areas. Although a late objection was made by a pastoralist who did not consent to the determination, Justice Mansfield decided to proceed with the hearing of the application for consent determinations for two reasons. First, there are a range of prescribed notification procedures in the NTA, which the pastoralist did not seek to utilise at any time. Second, the pastoralist was aware of the Adnyamathanha claim and could have expressed any concerns at an earlier time.

Brown v State of South Australia [2009] FCA 206 (Besanko J) Considered the authorisation process that must be followed under the NTA to validly make a native title determination application. There were two issues in the case. First, was the group identified in the application a native title claim group under s 61 of the NTA? It was held that the applicant's family group was not a native title claim group but, rather, a subgroup or a group larger than specified in the application. Even if it had been established that the applicant's family constituted a native title claim group, it could not be established that the applicant obtained valid authorisation to make the application, as not all members of the claim were given a reasonable opportunity to participate in the decision-making process. The Court found that there was no evidence that any advertisement or notice was given in respect of the relevant meeting, and the connection between those who attended the meeting referred to and the native title claim group was not established in respect of attendance. Thus, the native title determination application was struck out under s 84C NTA.

Coyne v State of Western Australia [2009] FCA 533 (Siopis J) This was a procedural decision that upheld an application under s 66B of the NTA to replace the current applicant of a native title determination, known as the 'Southern Noongar claim'. Each of the applicant movers is a member of the Wagyl Kaip claim group, the current applicant. Respondents to the application contended that authority to replace the current applicants was improperly obtained. They argued that an insufficient number of people from the claim group attended the meeting at which the decision was made to replace the current applicant. Thus the meeting was not representative of the Wagyl Kaip claim group and could not properly be described as a claim group meeting for the purposes of s 66B of the Act. Furthermore, it was contended that the current applicants could not be removed, as they were elders of their respective families and their families would be unrepresented in the claim group should they be replaced. The court held that there is no provision in the NTA requiring the current applicants in a native title claim to comprise representatives from each of the family groups within the claim group. As to the issue of authority, it was determined that sufficient notification of the meeting and the business to be transacted at the meeting was provided to all members of the claim group, thus the decision was validly obtained. The number of members to actually attend the meeting was therefore not relevant. Accordingly, the application by the applicant movers to replace the current applicants was validly obtained under s 66B NTA.

FMG Pilbara Pty Ltd v Cox **[2009] FCAFC 49 (30 April 2009) (Spender, Sundberg and McKerracher JJ)** Concerned a review of a finding by the NNTT that a party did not fulfil its obligation to negotiate in good faith. It was concerned with the scope of the obligation to negotiate in good faith, in particular the relevance of the stage of negotiations and if there was a requirement to negotiate specifically about a future act. The Court held that the applicant fulfilled its obligation to negotiate in good faith and the Tribunal had the power to conduct an inquiry and make a determination under s 38 NTA. Accordingly, the Court allowed the appeal and ordered that the decision of the NNTT be set aside.

Hunter v State of Western Australia **[2009] FCA 654 (North J)** Consent determination that native title exists over most of the determined area (Determination Area Part A) located within Western Australia's Pilbara region. The orders, made under s 87 and s 87A of the NTA, gave effect to an agreement reached via court-ordered mediation. It was agreed that the Nyangumarta people are entitled to exclusive possession, occupation, use and enjoyment of the land and waters within Determination Area Part A. This was subject to some exceptions. The Nyangumarta people do not hold native title rights in relation to flowing underground waters in the determined area. Further, in relation to pastoral leases falling within Determination Area Part A, the Nyangumarta people hold non-exclusive rights, including the right to access and move through the leased areas and the right to live on the area, subject to any inconsistent rights of others. The determination area is subject to an overlap claim brought by the Karajarri people. It will be finalised at a later date. Additionally, the Court ordered under s 56 of the NTA that the Nyangumarta Warrarn Aboriginal Corporation is to be the trustee of the native title rights and interests.

Kuuku Ya'u People v State of Queensland **[2009] FCA 679 (Greenwood J)** Consent determination recognising that native title rights and interests exists over the land and waters in a determined area in far north-east Queensland. The Kuuku Ya'u people hold exclusive rights, except in relation to water, to possession, occupation, use and enjoyment of a specified area within the determination area. As to the remainder of the determination area, the Kuuku Ya'u people hold non-exclusive native title rights and interests. These non-exclusive native rights and interests included the right to hunt and gather, use the natural resources in specified areas, camp on the land, and maintain and protect significant and important sites and places under traditional laws and customs. The nature and extent of the non-exclusive native title rights and interests varied across the determination area. It was agreed that there were no native title rights and interests in relation to minerals and petroleum.

***Nambucca Heads Local Aboriginal Land Council v Minister for Lands* [2009] FCA 624 (Perram J)** The Court made a determination that no native title rights or interests exist in the land. The determination was unopposed. This determination was sought by the applicant so as to allow for the development of land in accordance with s 40AA of the *Aboriginal Land Rights Act 1983* (NSW). Section 40AA prohibits a Local Aboriginal Land Council from disposing of land vested in it if the land is subject to native title rights and interests. Because the applicant held a legal estate in the land, the Council was entitled to apply for a court determination of native title.

***Quall v Northern Territory of Australia* [2009] FCA 18 (Reeves J)** Application under O 20 r 4 of the Federal Court Rules for summary dismissal on the grounds of issue estoppel, abuse of process or because the application had no reasonable prospects of success. The determination area was split into areas A and B. An earlier determination, *Risk v Northern Territory* [2006] FCA 404, had established that no native title exists within area A because there had been a substantial interruption in acknowledgment and observance of traditional laws and customs by the traditional Aboriginal society that existed at sovereignty. Counsel for the Northern Territory submitted that these findings in *Risk* related to the ultimate facts that must necessarily found the Quall native title application. It was contended that *Risk* had conclusively determined these issues. Justice Reeves accepted that on this basis, the decision in *Risk* gave rise to an issue estoppel preventing Quall applicants from pursuing their claim.

In the event that the decision on issue estoppel was wrong, Justice Reeves considered whether or not allowing the Quall application would constitute an abuse of process. A non-exhaustive range of factors to be considered in making the decision was identified. Ultimately, the failure of the Quall applicants to raise issues now being raised in earlier proceedings, the consequential waste of public resources and the risk of conflicting decisions were key issues in Justice Reeve's conclusion that allowance of the application would constitute an abuse of process. Justice Reeves did not consider it necessary to determine whether or not the application had reasonable prospects of success. The application was dismissed. The Quall applicants have appealed against this decision.

BIBLIOGRAPHY

Articles, books and reports

Aboriginal and Torres Strait Islander Social Justice Commissioner, *Native title report: July 1996–June 1997* (Human Rights and Equal Opportunity Commission, Sydney, 1997).

Arnold, Ann, 'Turning back the tide of history', *The Sunday Age: Extra* (Melbourne), 8 January 2006, 18.

Bartlett, Richard, 'Aboriginal land claims at common law' (1982) 12 *University of Western Australia Law Review* 293.

—— *Native title in Australia* (2nd edn, Lexis Nexis Butterworths, Sydney, 2004).

—— and Simon Young, 'From rights to relics: A two part critical analysis of the role of "traditional laws and customs" in native title doctrine', Native Title Conference, Geraldton WA, 18 September 2002.

Basten, John, 'Beyond Yorta Yorta', (2003) 2(24) *Land, Rights, Laws: Issues of Native Title* 1.

—— 'The Native Title Amendment Bill and the Senate Amendments', paper presented to the Symposium on Native Title: Facts, fallacies and the future, UNSW, 20 May 1998.

—— 'Recent development in native title law and practice: Issues for the High Court', (2002) 2(13) *Land Rights Laws: Issues of Native Title* 1.

Black, Michael, 'Development in practice and procedure in native title cases' (2002) 13 *Public Law Review* 16.

Blackstone, William, 1 *Commentaries on the laws of England* 104 (Legal Classics Library 1983) (1823).

Bowe, Heather, 'Linguistics and the Yorta Yorta native title claim' in John Henderson and David Nash (eds), *Language in native title* (Aboriginal Studies Press, Canberra, 2002).

Brennan, Sean, Larissa Behrendt, Lisa Strelein and George Williams, *Treaty* (Federation Press, Sydney, 2005).

Brough, J., 'Wik draft threat to native title', *The Sydney Morning Herald* (Sydney), 28 June 1997, 3.

Brysland, Gordon, 'Rewriting history 2: The wider significance of *Mabo v Queensland*' (1992) 17 *Alternative Law Journal* 162.

Cairney, Amelia, '*De Rose v South Australia [No. 2]* (2005) FCAFC 110 (8 June 2005)' (2005) 7(5) *Native Title News* 89.

Connolly, P., 'Should the courts determine social policy', The High Court of Australia in *Mabo*, Association of Mining and Exploration Companies Inc., 1993.

Department of Justice, *Report of the Steering Committee for the development of a Victorian native title settlement framework*, December 2008. Available online at <www.justice.vic. gov.au>.

Fisher, Sally and Jennifer Saxton, 'Backyards for grabs: Kennett', *The Australian* (Sydney), 10–11 July 1993, 3.

French, Robert, 'Lifting the burden of native title: Some modest proposals for improvement' (2009) 93 *Reform* 10.

Gluyas, Richard, 'Big miners fight Mabo claims', *The Australian* (Sydney), 8 March 1993, 25.

Hagen, Rod, 'Ethnographic information and anthropological interpretation in a native title claim: The Yorta Yorta experience' (2001) 25 *Aboriginal History* 216.

Hammond, Jane, 'Diamond drilling sparks first Mabo case', *The Australian* (Sydney), 30–1 January 1993, 8.

—— 'West plots to stop *Mabo* claims', *The Australian* (Sydney), 27 May 1993.

Hiley, Graham (ed.), *The Wik case: Issues and implications* (Butterworths, Sydney, 1997).

Hulme, S. E. K., 'Aspects of the High Court's handling of *Mabo*' (1993) 87 *Victorian Bar News* 29.

Janke, Terri, *Our culture: Our future: Report on Australian Indigenous cultural and intellectual property rights* (AIATSIS/Michael Frankel, Canberra, 1998).

Land, Clare, 'Representations of gender in E. M. Curr's "Recollections of squatting in Victoria": Implications for land justice through the native title process', (2002) 5(19) *Indigenous Law Bulletin* 6.

Lane, P. H., 'The changing role of the High Court', (1996) 70 *Australian Law Journal* 246.

Lavery, Daniel, 'A greater sense of tradition: The implications of the normative system principles in Yorta Yorta for native title determination applications' (2003) 10(4) *Murdoch University Electronic Journal of Law* http://www.murdoch.edu.au/elaw/issues/v10n4/lavery104.html (accessed 26 August 2009).

Loughton, Gavin, '*Gumana v Northern Territory*' (2005) 7(6) *Native Title News* 108.

McIntyre, Greg, 'Native title rights after *Yorta Yorta*' (2003) 9 *James Cook University Law Review* 268.

McNeil, Kent, 'Aboriginal title and Aboriginal rights: What's the connection?' (1997) 36 *Alberta Law Review* 117.

—— 'The post-*Delgamuukw* nature and content of Aboriginal title' (Draft #3), *Delgamuukw* National Process Papers (May 2000) 12.

—— 'Native title and extinguishment', paper presented to the FAIRA Native Title Conference, 11 May 1995.

McRae, Heather, Garth Nettheim, Laura Beacroft and Luke McNamara, *Indigenous legal issues, commentary and materials* (3rd edn, Lawbook, Sydney, 2003).

Murray, T., 'Conjectural histories: Some archaeological and historical consequences of Indigenous dispossession in Australia' in Ian Lilley (ed.), *Native title and the transformation of archaeology in the postcolonial world*, Oceania Monograph (2000), 50.

Neate, Graeme, 'An overview of native title in Australia — Some recent milestones and the way ahead', paper delivered at 11th Annual Cultural Heritage and Native Title Conference 'Building Partnerships and Finding Better Solutions for Better Outcomes', Brisbane, Queensland, 21 July 2004.

Neave, M. A., C. J. Rossiter and M. A. Stone, *Sackville and Neave: Property law: Cases and materials* (6th edn, Butterworths, Sydney, 1999).

Nettheim, Garth, '*Mabo*: Judicial revolution or cautious correction? Mabo v Queensland' (1993) 16 *University of New South Wales Law Review* 1.

North, Tony, 'Disconnection — The gulf between law and justice', paper presented at the National Native Title Conference 2009: Spirit of Country – Land, water, life, 3–5 June 2009.

Office of Indigenous Affairs, Department of Prime Minister and Cabinet, Commonwealth of Australia, 'Towards a more workable Native Title Act', discussion paper, Canberra, May 1996.

Office of Native Title, Western Australia, 'Towards an alternative settlement framework', consultation paper, October 2005.

Owen, Richard, '*Mabo* a threat to recovery: MIM chief', *The Australian* (Sydney), 30 March 1993, 41.

Pearson, Noel, 'Concept of native title at common law', in *Land rights — Past, present and future: 20 years of land rights, our land is our life*, Conference Proceedings (Northern Land Council and Central Land Council, Canberra, 1996) 119.

—— 'Land is susceptible of ownership' in M. Langton et al. (eds), *Honour Among Nations?* (Melbourne University Press, 2004) 83.

—— 'The High Court's abandonment of "the time-honoured methodology of the common law" in its interpretation of native title in Miriuwung Gajerrong and Yorta Yorta', Sir Ninian Stephen Annual Lecture, Law School University of Newcastle, 17 March 2003. Available at <www.capeyorkpartnerships.com>.

—— 'Where we've come from and where we're at with the opportunity that is Koiki Mabo's legacy to Australia', Mabo lecture, Native Title Conference, Alice Springs, 3 June 2003, available at <www.capeyorkpartnerships.com>.

—— 'Wik: Whither the separation of powers', *The Australian* (Sydney), 2 January 1997, 11.

Perry, Melissa and Stephen Lloyd, *Australian native title law* (Sydney, Law Book, 2003).

Reynolds, Henry, '*Mabo* and pastoral leases' (1992) 12(59) *Aboriginal Law Bulletin* 8.

Ritter, David, 'The "rejection of terra nullius" in *Mabo:* A critical analysis' (1998) 18 *Sydney Law Review* 1.

Sharp, Nonie, 'Contrasting cultural perspectives in the Murray Island case' (1990) 8 *Law in Context* 28.

Slattery, Brian, 'The metamorphosis of Aboriginal title' (2006) 85 *The Canadian Bar Review* 255.

Strelein, Lisa, 'Conceptualising native title' (2001) 23 *Sydney Law Review* 95.

—— 'Indigenous people and protected landscapes in Western Australia' (1993) 10 *Environmental and Planning Law Journal* 38.

—— 'The "courts of the conqueror": The utility of the courts for the assertion of Indigenous self-determination claims' 5(3) *Australian Indigenous Law Reporter* 1.

—— 'Native title holding groups and native title societies: *Sampi v State of Western Australia* [2005]' (2005) 3(4) *Land, Rights, Laws: Issues of Native Title* 1.

—— 'A Captive of Statute' (2009) 93 *Reform* 48–51.

—— Michael Dodson and Jessica Weir, 'Understanding non-discrimination: International criticisms of Australia's compliance with human rights standards' (2001) 3 *Balayi Culture, Law and Colonialism* 113.

Sutton Peter, *Native title and the descent of rights* (National Native Title Tribunal, Perth, 1998).
Tickner, Liz, 'Cattlemen in rage as land claims loom', *West Australian* (Perth), 19 April 1993, 13.
Wahlquist, Asa, 'Judge under fire over Mabo ruling', *The Australian* (Sydney), 27 February 2006, 5.
Webb, Raelene and Sonia Brownhill, '*Northern Territory v Alyawarr, Kaytete, Warumungu, Wakaya Native Title Claim Group*' (2005) 7(4) *Native Title News* 61.
Weiner, James, 'Diaspora, materalism, tradition: Anthropological issues in the recent High Court Appeal of the Yorta Yorta' (2002) 2(18) *Land, Rights, Laws: Issues of Native Title* 1.
Wooten, Hal, 'Mabo — Issues and challenges' (1994) 1 *Judicial Review* 303.

Case law

Adeyinka Oyekan v Musendiku Adele [1957] 2 All ER 785
Adnyamathanha #1 Native Title Claim Group v The State of South Australia [2009] FCA 358
Adnyamathanha #1 Native Title Claim Group v The State of South Australia (No. 2) [2009] FCA 359
Adnyamathanha People v South Australia [1999] FCA 402
Alexkor Ltd and Another v Richtersveld Community and Others [2003] Case CCT 19/03 (14 October 2003)
Alyawarr, Kaytetye, Warumungu, Wakay Native Title Claim Group v Northern Territory (2004) 207 ALR 539
American Dairy Queen (Qld) Pty Ltd v Blue Rio Pty Ltd (1981) 147 CLR 677
Amodu Tijani v Secretary, Southern Nigeria [1921] 2 AC 399
Anderson v Western Australia [2002] FCA 1558
Anderson v Western Australia [2007] FCA 1733
Anderson v Wilson (2000) 97 FCR 453
Arnhemland Aboriginal Land Trust v Directory of Fisheries (NT) (2001) 109 FCA 488
Attorney General (Quebec) v Attorney General (Canada) [1921] 1 AC 408
Attorney-General of the Northern Territory v Ward (2003) 134 FCR 16
Australian Manganese Pty Ltd v State of Western Australia and others (2008) 218 FLR 387
Balog v Independent Commission against Corruption (1990) 169 CLR 625
Beattie on behalf of Western Wakka Wakka Peoples v State of Queensland [2007] FCA 596
Bennell v State of Western Australia (2006) 153 FCR 120
Billy Patch & Others on behalf of the Birriliburu People v State of Western Australia and Others [2008] FCA 944
Bodney v Bennell (2008) 167 FCR 84
Bodney v Westralia Airports Corporation Pty Ltd (2000) 109 FCR 178
Brandy v Human Rights and Equal Opportunity Commission (1995) 183 CLR 245
Bropho v Western Australia (1990) 171 CLR 1
Bropho v Western Australia (2000) 96 FCR 453
Brown v State of South Australia [2009] FCA 206
Brown (on behalf of the Ngarla People) v State of Western Australia [2007] FCA 1025
Brown v Western Australia [2001] FCA 1462

Buck v New South Wales [1997] FCA 1624
Bulun Bulun v R & T Textiles Pty Ltd (1998) 86 FCR 244
Butchulla People v State of Queensland (2006) 154 FCR 233
Calder v Attorney-General of British Columbia (1973) SCR, 404; (1973) 34 DLR (3d).
Calvin's case (1608) 77 Eng Rep 377
Campbell v Arnold (1982) 565 FLR 382 (NTSC)
Chapman v Queensland (2007) 159 FCR 507
Clarke on behalf of the Wotjobaluk, Jaadwa, Jadawadjali, Wergaia and Jupagulk Peoples v State of Victoria [2005] FCA 1795
Clissold v Perry (1904) 1 CLR 363
Clunies Ross v Commonwealth (1984) 155 CLR 193
Coco v the Queen (1994) 179 CLR 427
Coe v Commonwealth (1979) 24 ALR 118
Coe v Commonwealth (1993) 118 ALR 193
Commonwealth v New South Wales (1923) 33 CLR 1
Commonwealth v Tasmania (Tasmanian Dams case) (1983) 158 CLR 1
Commonwealth v Yarmirr (1999) 101 FCR 171
Commonwealth v Yarmirr (2001) 208 CLR 1
Congoo v Queensland [2001] FCA 868
Cooper v Stuart (1889) 14 App Cas 286
Corporation of Yarmouth v Simmons (1878) 10 Ch D 518
Cox on behalf of the Yungngora People v State of Western Australia [2007] FCA 588
Coyne v State of Western Australia [2009] FCA 533
Dale v Moses [2007] FCAFC 82
Daniel v State of Western Australia [2006] FCA 271
Daniel v Western Australia [1999] FCA 686
Daniel v Western Australia (2000) 178 ALR 542
Daniel v Western Australia (2002) 194 ALR 278
Daniel v Western Australia [2003] FCA 666
Daniel v Western Australia (2005) 141 FCR 426
Dann on behalf of the Amangu People v State of Western Australia [2006] FCA 1249
Dauan People v Queensland [2000] FCA 1064
David on behalf of the Iama People and Tudulaig v Queensland [2004] FCA 1576
Davis v The Commonwealth (1988) 166 CLR 79
De Rose v South Australia [2002] FCA 1342
De Rose v South Australia [No. 1] (2003) 133 FCR 325
De Rose v South Australia [No. 2] (2005) 145 FCR 290
Deeral v Charlie [1997] 1408 FCA
Delgamuukw v British Columbia (1993) 104 DLR (4th) 470
Delgamuukw v British Columbia [1997] 3 SCR 1010
Derschaw v Sutton (1997) AILR 11
Dillon v Davies (1998) 145 FLR 111
Djabugay People v Queensland [2004] FCA 1652
Djaigween v Douglas (1994) 48 FCR 535
Doolan v Native Title Registrar (2007) 158 FCR 56

Ejai v Commonwealth (1994) (Unreported, SCWA, 18 March 1994, 1774/93)
Eringa No. 1 Native Title Claim v South Australia [2007] FCA 182
Eringa, Eringa No. 2, Wangkangurru/Yarluyandi and Irrwanyere Mr Dare Native Title Claim Groups v The State of South Australia [2008] FCA 1370
Fejo v Northern Territory (1998) 195 CLR 96
Fesl v Delegate of the Native Title Registrar (2008) 173 FCR 150
FMG Pilbara Pty Ltd v Cox [2009] FCAFC 49
Fuller and Another v De Rose and Others (Unreported decision, HCA A37/2005, Hayne, Gummow and Crennan JJ, 10 February 2006)
Gale on behalf of the Darug People v Minister for Land and Water Conservation for New South Wales [2004] FCA 374
Gamogab v Akiba (2007) 159 FCR 578
Gerhardy v Brown (1985) 159 CLR 70
Gibuma on behalf of the Boigu People v Queensland [2004] FCA 1575
Goldsworthy Mining Ltd v Federal Commissioner of Taxation (1973) 128 CLR 199
Gordon Charlie v Cape York Land Council [2006] FCA 1418
Griffiths v Minister for Lands, Planning and Environment (2008) 235 CLR 232
Griffiths v Northern Territory (2006) 165 FCR 300
Griffiths v Northern Territory (2007) 243 ALR 72
Griffiths v Northern Territory of Australia [No. 2] [2006] FCA 1155
Gudjala People #2 v Native Title Registrar [2007] FCA 1167
Gudjala People #2 v Native Title Registrar (2008) 171 FCR 317
Guerin v R (1984) 13 DLR (4th) 321
Gumana v Northern Territory (2005) 141 FCR 457
Gumana v Northern Territory [No. 2] [2005] FCA 1425
Gumana v Northern Territory of Australia (2007) 158 FCR 349
Hamlet of Baker Lake v Minister of Indian Affairs and Northern Development (1979) 107 DLR (3d) 513
Harper v Minister for Sea Fisheries (1989) 168 CLR 314
Harrington-Smith v Native Title Registrar [2007] FCA 414
Harrington-Smith v Western Australia [No. 9] (2007) 238 ALR 1
Harris v Great Barrier Reef Marine Park Authority (2000) 98 FCR 60
Hayes v Northern Territory (1999) 97 FCR 32
Hayes v Northern Territory [2000] FCA 671
Hazelbane v Doepel (2008) 167 FCR 325
Hughes (on behalf of the Eastern Guruma People) v State of Western Australia [2007] FCA 365
Hunter v State of Western Australia [2009] FCA 654
Jack Billy on behalf of the Poruma People v Queensland (2005) 223 ALR 447
James on behalf of the Martu People v Western Australia [2002] FCA 1208
James on behalf of the Martu People v Western Australia [No. 2] [2003] FCA 731
Jango v Northern Territory of Australia (2006) 152 FCR 150
Jango v Northern Territory of Australia (2007) 159 FCR 531
Johnson v M'Intosh (1823), 8 Wheat 543
Jones v Queensland [1998] QSC 11
Kaurareg People v Queensland (2001) 6(2) AILR 41

Kelly on behalf of the Byron Bay Bundjalung People v New South Wales Aboriginal Land Council [2001] FCA 1479
Kennedy v Queensland (2002) 190 ALR 707
King v Northern Territory of Australia [2007] FCA 1498
King v Northern Territory of Australia [2007] FCA 994
Kite v State of South Australia [2007] FCA 1662
Koara People v State of Western Australia (2006) 226 ALR 705
Kokatha Native Title Claim v State of South Australia [2006] FCA 838
Kokatha People v State of South Australia [2007] FCA 1057
Kruger v Commonwealth (1997) 190 CLR 1
Kuuku Ya'u People v State of Queensland [2009] FCA 679
Lapthorne v Indigenous Land Corporation [2008] FCA 682
Lardil Peoples v Queensland (1999) 95 FCR 14
Lardil Peoples v Queensland (2001) 108 FCR 453
Lardil Peoples v Queensland [2004] FCA 298
Lardil, Kaidilt, Yangkaal and Gangalidda People v Queensland [2000] FCA 1548
Lardil, Kaidilt, Yangkaal and Gangalidda People v Queensland [2001] FCA 464
Lardil, Yangkaal, Gangalidda & Kaiadilt Peoples v State of Queensland [2008] FCA 1855
Lawson v Minister for Land and Water Conservation [2004] FCA 165
Leslie Hayes & Ors on behalf of the Thalanyji people v The State of Western Australia and Others (unreported, FCA, 18 September 2008, North J)
Lipan Apache Tribe v United States (1967) 180 Ct Cl 487
Lovett on behalf of The Gunditjmara People v State of Victoria [2007] FCA 474
Mabo v Queensland [No. 1] (1988) 166 CLR 186
Mabo v Queensland [No. 2] (1992) 175 CLR 1
Mabuiag People v Queensland [2000] FCA 1065
Manas v State of Queensland [2006] FCA 413
Masig and Damuth People v Queensland [2000] FCA 1067
Mason v Tritton (1994) 34 NSWLR 572
Members of the Yorta Yorta Aboriginal Community v Vic, M128/2001 (24 May 2002) transcript
Members of the Yorta Yorta Aboriginal Community v Victoria (1996) 1 AILR 402
Members of the Yorta Yorta Aboriginal Community v Victoria [1997] FCA 1181
Members of the Yorta Yorta Aboriginal Community v Victoria [1998] FCA 1606; (1999) 4(1) AILR 91
Members of the Yorta Yorta Aboriginal Community v Victoria (2001) 110 FCR 244
Members of the Yorta Yorta Aboriginal Community v Victoria (2002) 214 CLR 422
Mervyn and Others on behalf of the Peoples of the Ngaanyatjarra Lands v Western Australia [2005] FCA 831
Milirrpum v Nabalco Pty Ltd (1971) 17 FLR 141
Mineralogy Pty Ltd v Kuruma Marthudunera Native Title Claimants [2008] WAMW 3
Moses v State of Western Australia (2007) 160 FCR 148
Mualgal People v Queensland [1999] FCA 157
Mualgal v Queensland (1998) 90 FCR 303
Mundraby v State of Queensland [2006] FCA 436
Munn v Queensland (2001) 115 FCR 109

Munn v Queensland [2002] FCA 486
Mye on behalf of the Erubam Le v Queensland [2004] FCA 1573
Nambucca Heads Local Aboriginal Land Council v Minister for Lands [2009] FCA 624
Nangkiriny v Western Australia (2002) 117 FCR 6
Nangkiriny v Western Australia [2004] FCA 1156
Neowarra v Western Australia (2003) 134 FCR 208
Neowarra v Western Australia [2004] FCA 1092
New South Wales v Commonwealth (1975) (*Seas and Submerged Lands case*) 135 CLR 337
Newie on behalf of the Gebaralgal v Queensland [2004] FCA 1577
Ngadjon-Jii people v State of Queensland [2007] FCA 1937
Ngalakan People v Northern Territory (2001) 112 FCR 148
Ngalakan People v Northern Territory (Unreported, FCA, 7 February 2002, O'Loughlin J)
Ngalpil v Western Australia [2001] FCA 1140
Nona and Manas v State of Queensland [2006] FCA 412
Nona on behalf of the Badulgal v Queensland [2004] FCA 1578
Nona on behalf of the Saibai, Dauan, Mabuiag, Badu and Boigu Peoples v Queensland [2005] FCA 1118
North Ganalanja Aboriginal Corporation v Queensland (1995) 61 FCR 1
North Ganalanja Aboriginal Corporation v Queensland (1996) 185 CLR 595
Northern Land Council v Commonwealth (1987) 61 ALJR 616
Northern Territory of Australia v Arnhem Land Aboriginal Land Trust (2008) 236 CLR 24
Northern Territory v Alyawarr, Kaytetye, Warumungu, Wakaya Native Title Claim Group (2005) 220 ALR 431
O'Keefe v Malone [1903] AC 365
Pareroultja v Tickner (1993) 42 FCR 32
Passi on behalf of Meriam People v Queensland [2001] FCA 697
Patta Warumungu People v Northern Territory of Australia [2007] FCA 1243
Payi Payi & Ors on behalf of the Ngururrpa People and State of Western Australia [2007] FCA 2113
Quall v Northern Territory of Australia [2009] FCA 18
R v Keyn (1876) 2 Ex D 63
R v Sparrow (1990) 1 SCR1075; (1990) 70 DLR (4th) 385
R v Symonds [1847] NZPCC 387
R v Van der Peet [1996] 2 SCR 507
Radaich v Smith (1959) 101 CLR 209
Reid v State of South Australia [2007] FCA 1479
Richtersveld Community and Others v Alexkor Ltd and Another [2003] (6) BCLR 583 (SCA)
Riley v State of Queensland [2006] FCA 72
Risk v Northern Territory (2007) 240 ALR 75
Risk v Northern Territory of Australia [2006] FCA 404
Rubibi Community v State of Western Australia [No. 6] (2006) 226 ALR 676
Rubibi Community v State of Western Australia [No. 7] [2006] FCA 459
Rubibi Community v Western Australia (2001) 112 FCR 409

Rubibi Community v Western Australia [No. 5] [2005] FCA 1025
Rubibi v Western Australia (2002) 120 FCR 512
Rubibi v Western Australia [2003] FCA 62
Saibai People v Queensland [1999] FCA 158
Sampi v Western Australia [No. 2] [2005] FCA 1567
Sampi v Western Australia [2005] FCA 777
Sampi v Western Australia [No. 3] [2005] FCA 1716
Smith on behalf of the Gnaala Karla Booja People v Western Australia (2001) 108 FCR 442
Smith v Western Australia (2000) 104 FCR 494
Sparrow v R (1990) 3 CNLR 160
St Catherine's Milling and Lumber Company v R (1888) 14 App Cas 46
State of Western Australia v Sebastian (2008) 173 FCR 1
Stanley Mervyn, Adrian Young, and Livingston West and Ors, on behalf of the People of the Ngaanyatjarra Lands v The State of Western Australia and Ors (unreported, FCA, 3 June 2008, French J)
Stephen on behalf of the Ugar People v Queensland [2004] FCA 1574
Stewart v Williams (1914) 18 CLR 381
Te Weehi v Regional Fisheries Officer (1986) 1 NZLR 680
Thaiday on behalf of the Warraber, Poruma and Iama Peoples v Queensland [2005] FCA 1116
The Case of Tanistry (1608) Davis (80 ER); 4th ed. Dublin (1762) (English translation)
Thorpe v Kennett [1999] VSC 442
Timothy James Malachi on behalf of the Strathgordon Mob v State of Queensland [2007] FCA 1048
Toomer v Witsell (1948) 334 US 385
Trevor Close on behalf of the Githabul people v Minister for Lands [2007] FCA 1847
Turrbal People v State of Queensland [2008] FCA 316
United States v Santa Fe Pacific Railroad Co (1941) 314 US 353
Van Hemmen on behalf of the Kabi Kabi People #3 v State of Queensland [2007] FCA 1185
Waanyi People's Native Title Application (1994) 129 ALR 100 (NNTT)
Wade v New South Wales Rutile Mining Co Pty Ltd (1969) 121 CLR 177
Wakaman People #2 v Native Title Registrar and Authorised Delegate (2006) 155 FCR 107
Walker on behalf of the Eastern Kuku Yalanaji People v State of Queensland [2007] FCA 1907
Walley v Western Australia (1996) 67 FCR 366
Wandarang v Northern Territory (2000) 104 FCR 380
Wandarang, Alawa, Marra and Ngalakan Peoples v Northern Territory [2004] FCAFC 187
Ward on behalf of the Miriuwung and Gajerrong People v Western Australia (1998) 159 ALR 483
Ward v Northern Territory [2002] FCA 171
Ward v Northern Territory (2002) 196 ALR 32
Ward v Western Australia (1996) 69 FCR 208

COMPROMISED JURISPRUDENCE

Ward v Western Australia (Miriuwung Gajerrong #4 Determination) [2006] FCA 1848
Warrabur and Poruma People v Queensland [2000] FCA 1066
Warria on behalf of the Kulkalgal v Queensland [2004] FCA 1572
Warria on behalf of the Poruma and Masig Peoples v Queensland and Ors (2005) 223 ALR 62
Webb v State of Western Australia [2007] FCA 1342
Werribee Council v Kerr (1928) 42 CLR 1
Western Australia v Commonwealth (1995) 183 CLR 373
Western Australia v Ward (1997) 76 FCR 492
Western Australia v Ward (2000) 99 FCR 316
Western Australia v Ward (2002) 213 CLR 1
Western Desert Lands Aboriginal Corporation v State of Western Australia and others (2008) 218 FLR 362
Western Yalanji Peoples v Pedersen [1998] 1269 FCA
Wik Peoples (McNaught Ngallametta) v Queensland [2000] FCA 1443
Wik Peoples v Queensland (1996) 63 FCR 450
Wik Peoples v Queensland (1996) 187 CLR 1
Wik Peoples v Queensland [2004] FCA 1306
Wilkes v Johnsen (1999) 21 WAR 269
Wilkes v Western Australia [2003] FCA 156
Wilson v Anderson (2002) 213 CLR 401
Wiri People v Native Title Registrar (2008) 168 FCR 187
Worimi Local Aboriginal Land Council v Minister for Lands for the State of New South Wales [No. 2] [2008] FCA 1929
Wotjobaluk People v Victoria [1999] FCA 961
Yankunytjatjara/Antakirinja Native Title Claim Group v The State of South Australia [2006] FCA 1142
Yanner v Eaton (1999) 201 CLR 351
Yarmirr and Others v Northern Territory (Unreported FCA, 4 April 1997, Olney J)
Yarmirr v Northern Territory (1998) 82 FCR 533
Yarmirr v Northern Territory [2000] FCA 48

Legislation

Aboriginal Councils and Associations Act 1976 (Cth)
Aboriginal Land (Lake Condah and Framlingham Forest) Act 1987 (Cth)
Aboriginal Land Act 1991 (Qld)
Aboriginal Land Rights Act 1983 (NSW)
Aboriginal Lands Act 1995 (Tas)
Aboriginal Land Rights (Northern Territory) Act 1976 (Cth)
Administrative Decisions (Judicial Review) Act 1977 (Cth)
Crown Lands Act 1884 (NSW)
Crown Lands Act 1978 (NT)
Crown Lands Alienation Act 1876 (Qld)
Crown Lands Unauthorized Occupation Act 1839 (NSW)
Evidence Act 1995 (Cth)
Fauna Conservation Act 1974 (Qld)

Federal Court Act 1976 (Cth)
Fish Resources Management Act 1994 (WA)
Fisheries Act 1988 (NT)
Judiciary Act 1903 (Cth)
Land Act 1910 (Qld)
Land Act 1933 (WA)
Land Act 1962 (Qld)
Land Act 1989 (WA)
Land (Titles and Traditional Usage) Act 1993 (WA)
Lands Acquisition Act 1978 (NT)
Maralinga Land Rights Act 1984 (SA)
Mining Act 1906 (NSW)
Mining Act 1978 (WA)
Native Title Act 1993 (Cth)
Native Title Amendment Bill 1997
Native Title Amendment Bill 1997 [No. 2]
Native Title Amendment Act 1988 (Cth)
Native Title (New South Wales) Act 1994 (NSW)
Pastoral Land Management and Conservation Act 1989 (SA)
Petroleum Act 1915 (Qld)
Petroleum Act 1967 (WA)
Pitjatjantjara Land Rights Act 1981 (SA)
Public Works Act 1902 (WA)
Public Works Act 1912 (NSW)
Queensland Coast Islands Declaratory Act 1985 (Qld)
Racial Discrimination Act 1975 (Cth)
Real Property Act 1862 (NSW)
Real Property Act 1861 (Qld)
Real Property Act 1858 (SA)
Real Property Act 1862 (Tas)
Real Property Act 1862 (Vic)
Sale of Waste Lands Act 1842 (Imp)
Territory Parks and Wildlife Conservation Act (NT)
Torres Strait Islander Land Act 1991 (Qld)
Transfer of Land Act 1874 (WA)
Western Lands Act 1901 (NSW)

Treaties

United Nations, Convention on the Elimination of All Forms of Racial Discrimination, 21 December 1965, 660 UNTS 195

Other sources

1881 Petition to the Governor General of New South Wales from the Residents of the Maloga Mission

INDEX

abalone fishing, 188
abandonment, 16–17, 62–63, 79–80
  De Rose, 88–89, 93, 124
  see also Yorta Yorta v Victoria
Aboriginal Land Rights Act 1983 (NSW), 230
Aboriginal Land Rights (Northern Territory) Act 1976 (Cth), 3, 49, 132, 185, 212, 217, 225
  s 73(1)(d), 196
Aboriginal nation, 184, 185
aboriginal title (Canada), 39, 85
access, 38–39, 88, 89, 90–91, 92
  right to control, 64, 65–66, 71, 204, 209, 225
  see also occupancy
acquisition of land see compulsory acquisition
acquisition of sovereignty see sovereignty
act of state doctrine, 76–77, 128–129
adjoining Aboriginal land, 196
Adnyamathanha #1 Native Title Claim Group v The State of South Australia, 227–228
Adnyamathanha People v South Australia, 190
adoptive descent, 198
affidavits, 201
Alawa people, 194, 206
Alice Springs determination *(Hayes)*, 54, 142, 146, 191, 193
  see also *Hayes v Northern Territory* (Alice Springs determination)
alternative settlement negotiations, 149
Alyawarr, Kaytetye, Warumungu, Wakay Native Title Claim Group v Northern Territory, 204
  see also (Alwawa)
amendments to determination applications, 190

American Dairy Queen (Qld) Pty Ltd v Blue Rio Pty Ltd, 27, 31
Amodu Tijani v Secretary, Southern Nigeria, 14, 129
Anderson v State of Western Australia [2007], 214
Anderson v Western Australia (2000), 192
Anderson v Western Australia [2002], 199
Angepena Station, 227–228
animal conservation, 44–48, 188, 191
annexation, 2, 13, 15, 184 see also sovereignty
Antikirinya people, 87, 214 see also *De Rose v South Australia*
applicants, 190, 199, 201, 216, 221
  custodians, 213
  failure to participate in proceedings, 202
  removal/replacement, 210, 214, 215, 226
  representatives of, 204
applications, 191
  to combine claimant applications, 190
  parties to, 192; exclusion, 188, 204
  struck out, 214–215, 220
  unopposed, 200
Argyle project, 58
Arnhemland Aboriginal Land Trust v Director of Fisheries, 196
Arrente people, 222
artworks, 64
Atherton Tablelands, 196
attachment to area see connection with land
Attorney-General of the Northern Territory v Ward, 202–203
Aureed Island, 206
Australian Constitution, 4, 5, 19, 20–21, 46, 186, 216
authorised applicants, 190, 199–200, 201–202

Index

Badu (Badualgal) people, 206, 208, 212
Ballardong claimant application, 199
Bar-Barrum people, 196
Bardi people, 143, 209
Barron Gorge National Park, 204
Bartle Frere, 220
Batchelor township, 224
Beattie on behalf of Western Wakka Wakka Peoples v State of Queensland, 214–215
Beaumont J, 56–57, 140
beneficial construction, 84, 118, 119, 121, 122, 125, 196
beneficial interest, 14, 27, 31
Bennell v State of Western Australia (2006), 210
see also *Bodney v Bennell*
Billy Patch & Others on behalf of the Birriliburu People v State of Western Australia and Others, 222
Binhthi people, 187
biological descent, 198
Birriliburru people, 222
Black J, 124
Blackburn J, 2–3, 9, 184
Blackstone, William, 135
Blue Mud Bay, 208, 225 see also *Northern Territory of Australia v Arnhem Land Aboriginal Land Trust*
bodies corporate, prescribed see prescribed bodies corporate
Bodney v Bennell, 97–115, 124, 125, 137, 138, 140–142, 144, 222
communal title, 107–114
connection with land, 112–114, 141
continuity and change, 99–106, 140
distinction between common law native title and statutory native title, 115
Bodney v Westralia Airports Corporation Pty Ltd, 192
Boigu people, 205, 208
Brandy v Human Rights and Equal Opportunity Commission, 186
Branson J, 75–76, 78–79
Brennan J, 26–27, 121
Wik Peoples v Queensland, 28, 30, 117; bundle of rights concept, 26, 136; enforceability, 145; extinguishment, 31–32, 33–35

Brennan J, and *Mabo v Queensland [No.2]*, 79, 117, 130–131, 133–134, 137, 184–185
colonial law concepts, 2, 9–10
communal native title, 108–109; cited in *Bennell*, 108, 109
connection with land, 11, 12, 63
extinguishment, 16–18, 19–21, 30; acquisition of sovereignty and, 16, 40, 128–129; cited in *Wik*, 27, 28; freehold, 37
inalienability, 14
leases, 27; cited in *Wik*, 27
skeletal principles, 10, 18, 40, 52, 131
traditional law and customs, 10–11, 15, 16, 17, 109, 135, 138
typology of rights and interests, 109
British Columbia, 148–149
Broome, 114, 198–199, 225–226
Bropho v Western Australia, 192
Brown (on behalf of the Ngarla People) v State of Western Australia, 215
Brown v State of South Australia, 228
Brown v Western Australia, 196
Brue Reef, 209
Buck v New South Wales, 187
Bulun Bulun, 64–65
Bundjalung people, 197
bundle of rights concept, 119
Fejo, 38–39, 41, 42–43
Ward, 55–57, 58, 61–63, 121, 194, 202
Wik (Brennan J), 26, 136
Yanner, 44–45, 48
see also coexistence
Butchulla People v State of Queensland, 210
Byron Bay, 197

Callinan J, 37, 45, 48, 73, 121
Calvin's case, 135
Campbell Island, 206
Canada, 13, 14, 15, 39, 84, 85, 148–149
Cap Islet, 204
Cape York Land Council, 211
Cape York Peninsula, 212, 221 see also *Wik Peoples v Queensland*
capital cities, 97 see also Perth metropolitan area
Central Desert, Western Australia, 225

Chapman v Queensland, 215
Clarke on behalf of the Wotjobaluk, Jaadwa, Jadawadali, Wergaia and Jupagulk Peoples v Victoria (Wotjobaluk determination), 139–140, 149, 207
clear and plain intent, 17–18, 32, 53, 69, 72, 84–86, 118, 123, 132, 146 *see also* statutory construction/interpretation
Clissold v Perry, 83
Clunies Ross v The Commonwealth, 83
coastal waters *see* sea country
Coe v The Commonwealth, 3, 184, 185
coexistence, 22–35, 118
  with freehold title, 38–39, 41
  with land rights grant, 185
  with pastoral leases, 191
  with sea country, 50
  Ward, 55–59, 71–72
  see also partial extinguishment
Collier J, 226
colonial law, 2–3, 9–10, 14, 41, 42, 118, 148
  Queensland, 24–25, 28–29
  South Australia, 92, 218
  see also sovereignty
combination of applicant claims, 190
  see also groups and group claims
commercial agreements, 148
Commonwealth of Australia Constitution, 4, 5, 19, 20–21, 46, 186, 216
Commonwealth v Yarmirr (2001), 49–54, 66, 131, 132–133, 136–137, 142, 148, 196
  enforceability, 54, 144–145
  Kirby J, 53–54, 120, 148
  sovereignty, 50–52, 119–120, 127, 128, 129–130, 132–133
  traditional customs and law, 49–50, 54, 126–127
  Ward discussion of non-exclusive, differences between, 66
  Yorta Yorta, 76
Commonwealth v Yarmirr (1999), 54, 190
communal claims, 89, 94–96 *see also Bodney v Bennell*; groups and group claims
communal title, 12–13, 15, 46–47, 78, 116, 137, 138, 142–143, 213
  Bennell, 107–114

law pre-*Mabo*, 3
  South Africa, 127
  Ward, 56, 62
  Yarmirr, 142
'community', 98, 101, 107 *see also* traditional societies
compensation, 19–21, 59–61, 118, 147–148, 191, 205 *see also* Racial Discrimination Act 1975
compensation claims, 218
compulsory acquisition, 4, 19, 82–86
conflict of laws, 126–127
Congoo v Queensland, 196
connection with land, 11, 16–18, 43, 73, 75, 78–79, 139–141, 205
  Bennell, 99–100, 107, 108, 112–114, 124
  De Rose, 87–89, 90–91, 95, 140–141, 200, 207
  Gumana, 141
  Ward, 56, 61, 63–65, 93, 121, 125, 140
  Yanner, 44, 46–48
  Yorta Yorta [1997], 188
consent determinations
  New South Wales, 187, 197, 221
  Northern Territory, 202–203, 206, 219, 220
  Queensland, 187, 189, 195, 196–197, 204, 206, 207, 221, 224, 229–230;
  Torres Strait, 191, 192, 194, 197, 198, 204, 205, 209
  South Australia, 222, 227–228
  Victoria, 149, 207, 219
  Western Australia, 192, 193, 196, 198–199, 200, 206, 208, 218, 222, 224, 225, 229
conservation of wildlife/natural resources, 18, 44–48, 188, 191
Constitution of Australia, 4, 5, 19, 20–21, 46, 186, 216
continuity test, 99–106, 135, 141
  presumption of continuity, 141
Cooper v Stuart, 3, 184
Cox on behalf of the Yungngora People v State of Western Australia, 215
Coyne v State of Western Australia, 228–229
Crennan J, 223
Croker Island region, 49, 142, 189

Crown Lands Act 1992 (NT), 83
Crown Lands Alienation Act 1876 (Qld), 28
cultural knowledge, protection of, 64–65, 75, 88–89, 105 *see also* traditional societies
cultural survival, threat to, 74, 85
Curr (squatter), 75
customary practices *see* traditional law and customs

Daintree National Park, 221
Dale v Moses, 215
damages *see* compensation
Damuth people, 193
Danggalaba clan, 212, 220
Daniel v Western Australia, 190, 192, 200, 203, 207, 211
Dann on behalf of the Amangu People v State of Western Australia, 211
Darug people, 205
Dauan people, 208
Dauan People v Queensland, 192
David on behalf of the Iama People and Tudulaig v Queensland, 204
De Rose v South Australia [2002], 87–94, 96, 200
De Rose v South Australia [No. 1] (2003), 92–94, 124, 125, 138, 203
De Rose v South Australia [No. 2] (2005), 87–96, 124–125, 139, 140–142, 143, 144, 207–208
 Bennell and, 97, 110
 Sebastian and, 114–115
Deane J, 3
 Mabo v Queensland [No.2], 10–15, 27, 109, 127; extinguishment, 14–15, 17, 19, 20, 21, 38, 40, 131–132
Deeral v Charlie, 187
defeasibility *see* extinguishment
Delgamuukw v British Columbia, 148–149
derogation, 138, 145
Derschaw v Sutton, 188
determination, 135, 143, 149, 194–195
 compliance with s 225, 49–50, 62, 142, 192, 201
 National Native Title Tribunal powers, 186
 non-claimant, 200, 226–227

under s 55, 189
town areas, 193, 204, 209, 218–219
see also applications; consent determinations
Dharrpa people, 187
Dillon v Davies, 188
Dingaal people, 187
discrimination, perpetuation of, 147–148, 149
divestiture of title, 16
Djabugay People v Queensland, 204
Djaigween v Douglas, 185
doctrine of estates, 27
Doolan v Native Title Registrar, 216
Doolboong people, 214
Dowsett J, 217
Drummond J, 23, 119
Dunghutti people, 187

East Arnhem Land, 208
Eastern Guruma people, 218
Eastern Kuku Yalanji people, 221
education, 90
Ejai v Commonwealth, 184
employment, 74, 88, 89, 90, 91
enforcement, 33, 54, 67, 76, 144–145
Eringa No. 1 Native Title Claim v South Australia, 216
Eringa, Eringa No. 2, Wangkangurru/ Yarluyandi and Irrwanyere Mr Dare Native Title Claim Groups v The State of South Australia, 222
Erub Island, 205
estate groups, 108, 113, 142, 143–144, 214, 215, 216
estates, doctrine of, 27
Euahlayi-Dixon clan, 72 *see also Wilson v Anderson*
evidence, 185, 187, 188, 192, 193, 199, 204
 Bennell, 98, 99, 105–106, 114
 De Rose, 89–90, 91
 Yorta Yorta, 74–75, 79–80
 see also witnesses
Evidence Act 1995 (Cth), 192
exclusion of parties, 188, 204
exclusive possession, 23–24, 26–30, 121, 122, 125, 132, 137–138, 147

Native Title Act 1993 provisions, 58, 62, 109
pastoral leases, 22–30, 32, 192
sea country, 49–54, 208
Ward, 56, 57, 62–63, 65–70, 147
Wilson , 72
Yarmirr, 190
see also freehold land (fee simple estates)
executive power to acquire land *see* compulsory acquisition
expert witnesses, 91, 188
extinction of title, 16
extinguishment, 15, 16–21, 37, 52–53, 79, 116, 118–119, 125, 131–133, 138, 144–148
clear and plain intent, 17–18, 32, 53, 69, 72, 84–86, 118, 123, 132, 146
De Rose, 92, 207–208
Fejo, 41–43, 119
Lardil, 197
Native Title Act 1993 provisions, 5–6
Ngalakan People, 198
North Ganalaja, 23–24
Ward see Western Australia v Ward
Wik, 27, 30–35, 118
Wilson, 72, 192, 202
Yanner, 45–48, 119
see also freehold land; inconsistency; leases; partial extinguishment; *Racial Discrimination Act 1975*

Fauna Conservation Act 1974 (Qld), 44–48, 191
Federal Court of Australia, 36, 68, 115, 118, 124–125, 195
Bennell see Bodney v Bennell
Bulun Bulun, 64–65
De Rose see De Rose v South Australia
jurisdiction, 185, 189, 198
Neowarra see Neowarra v Western Australia
North Ganalanja see North Ganalanja Aboriginal Corporation v Queensland
powers, 185, 186, 190, 227
procedures, 185, 191, 193, 197, 206, 215, 230 *see also* evidence
Risk , 140

Sebastian see State of Western Australia v Sebastian
Ward, 55–57, 62, 63, 66, 69, 70, 78, 140
Wilson, 192
Yarmirr, 49–50, 52, 54, 137, 190
Yorta Yorta, 74–76, 78–79, 80–81, 123–124
Federal Court of Australia Act 1976 (Cth)
s 46, 216
s 53A, 190
fee simple estates *see* freehold land (fee simple estates)
Fejo v Northern Territory, 36–43, 73, 118, 119, 133–134, 146, 188
bundle of rights concept, 38–39, 41, 42–43
intersection of traditional law and non-Indigenous law, 39–40, 41–43
Yanner judgment, 47, 48
Yarmirr, and, 53
fiduciary duties, 3, 20, 23, 117, 192
Finn J, 100, 219, 220
Fish Resources Management Act 1994 (WA), 191
Fisheries Act 1988 (NT), 225
fishing and hunting, 44–48, 119, 120, 132
Adnyamathanha, 227–228
Bennell, 100, 104, 109
De Rose, 88, 89, 92
Derschaw, 188
Dillon, 188
Gumana, 208
Lardil, 205
Mason, 185
methods used, 78
Native Title Act provisions, 49–50
Wilkes, 191
Yanner, 191
Yarmirr, 49, 51–54, 190, 196
Flinders Ranges National Park, 227–228
FMG Pilbara Pty Ltd v Cox, 229
free passage *see* innocent passage, right of
'freehold equivalence' tests, 84, 85
freehold land (fee simple estates), 18, 30, 82, 83, 86, 188, 192
Fejo v Northern Territory, 36–43, 118, 119; cited in *Yanner*, 46
intertidal land, 189–190

Index

French J, 106, 112, 141, 143, 200, 209, 214, 221
future acts, 6, 60, 148, 191, 193, 197, 199
future generations, 16–18

Gabba Island, 206
Gadura people, 49
Gajerrong people, 37, 55–56, 61, 142, 143, 189, 202–203, 214 *see also Western Australia v Ward*
Gale on behalf of the Darug People v Minister for Land and Water Conservation for New South Wales, 205
Gamaay people, 187
Gamogab v Akiba, 216
Gangalidda people, 44, 125, 142, 193, 197
Gascoigne, 193–194
Gaudron J, 37, 50, 55
  Mabo v Queensland [No 2], 10–15, 27, 109, 127; extinguishment, 14–15, 17, 19, 20, 21, 38, 40, 131–132
  Wik Peoples v Queensland, 22–23, 31; exclusive possession, 26–27, 28, 29–30, 32
  Yorta Yorta v Victoria, 76, 78, 200
Gebara Island, 206
gender restrictions, 188, 204, 216
'generation by generation' test, 105–106, 141
  see also 'continuity' test
  see also traditional law and customs
genocide, 191
Gerhardy v Brown, 3, 60–61
Gibbs J, 185
Gibson Desert, 196
Gibuma on behalf of the Boigu People v Queensland, 205
Gija people, 214
Githabul people, 221
Gleeson CJ, 37, 50, 55, 72, 76, 78, 86, 122, 223
Gnaala Karla Booja claim group, 199
Gordon Charlie v Cape York Land Council, 211
Gove Peninsula *see Milirrpum v Nabalco Pty Ltd*
Great Sandy Desert of Western Australia, 220

Grey, Earl, 25–26
Griffiths v Minister for Lands, Planning and Environment, 82–86, 125, 146, 222–223
Griffiths v Northern Territory, 82, 211, 216
groups and group claims, 12–13, 110–111, 112, 113, 138–139, 141–144
  Adnyamathanha People, 190, 227–228
  Bennell, 97–115
  De Rose, 87, 94–96, 141–142, 144
  Gale, 205
  Harrington-Smith, 218
  Ngalakan People, 198
  Northern Territory v Alyawarr, 209
  Rubibi see Rubibi v Western Australia
  Ward, 195
Gudjala People 2 v Native Title Registrar, 217, 223–224
Guerin, 14
Gumana v Northern Territory, 106, 141, 208, 217
Gummow J, 37, 50, 55, 76, 78, 223
  Griffiths, 86
  Wik Peoples v Queensland, 24, 28, 30, 32, 118, 136
  Yanner v Eaton, 46–48, 78
Gunditjmara people, 149, 219
Gunnamalla clan *see Yanner v Eaton*
Guruma people, 218

Haldane, Viscount, 129
Hamlet of Baker Lake v Minister of Indian Affairs and Northern Development, 13
Harrington-Smith v Native Title Registrar, 217
Harrington-Smith v Western Australia [No. 9] (2007), 125, 218
Harris v Great Barrier Reef Marine Park Authority, 193
Hatches Creek, 204, 209
Hayes v Northern Territory (Alice Springs determination), 54, 142, 146, 191, 193
Hayne J, 37, 50, 55, 76, 78, 86, 223
Hazelbane v Doepel, 224
hearsay evidence, 192
heritage preservation, 12, 75, 93, 207 *see also* traditional law and customs
Heydon J, 86, 223
High Court of Australia, 3, 135

Fejo see Fejo v Northern Territory
Griffiths see Griffiths v Minister for Lands, Planning and Environment
Mabo v Queensland [No. 1] (Racial Discrimination Act 1975 decision), 4, 5, 20, 60, 184
Mabo v Queensland [No. 2] see Mabo v Queensland [No. 2]
Native Title Act case *see Western Australia v Commonwealth*
North Ganalanja see North Ganalanja Aboriginal Corporation v Queensland
Ward see Western Australia v Ward
Wik see Wik Peoples v Queensland
Wilson v Anderson, 72, 118, 122–123, 202
Yanner see Yanner v Eaton
Yarmirr see Commonwealth v Yarmirr
Yorta Yorta see Yorta Yorta v Victoria
Holroyd River Holding pastoral leases, 24, 29–30, 32 *see also Wik Peoples v Queensland*
Hopevale, 187
Hughes (on behalf of the Eastern Guruma People) v State of Western Australia, 218
Human Rights and Equal Opportunity Commission, 186
Hunter v State of Western Australia, 229
hunting *see* fishing and hunting

Iama people, 204, 209
inalienability of native tide, 13–14
inconsistency, 10, 18, 37–38, 46, 84, 118
  Anderson, 192
  De Rose, 96
  Fejo, 38, 40
  Guerin, 14
  Ward, 55–59, 62, 71, 96, 146, 194;
  inconsistency of incidents test, 68–69, 194, 202
  Western Australian v Commonwealth, 38
  Wik, 22–23, 26, 27, 33–35, 118, 146
  Wilson, 72, 122–123
  Yanner, 45–48
  Yarmirr, 50, 51–54, 132–133
inconsistent grant, compensation for, 19–21
incorporeal intellectual property, 64
Indigenous Land Corporation, 4, 224

Indigenous Land Use Agreements, 7, 149, 197
Indigenous law and customs *see* traditional law and customs
Indigenous nation, 184, 185
Indigenous title
  Canada, 39, 85
  New Zealand, 85
Indigenous witnesses *see* witnesses
Indjibarndi people, 207
  see also Yindjibarndi people
inherent vulnerability, 40–41, 48
inheritance, 17, 60, 72, 108, 138
Injibandi people, 203
injunctions, 185, 197
innocent passage, right of, 51–54, 132, 196
intellectual property, incorporeal, 64
intent *see* 'clear and plain intent'
interlocutory relief, 197
international law, 51, 52, 53–54, 127, 132, 133, 135
intertidal zone, 189–190, 195–196, 208, 217

Jaadwa people, 207
Jack Billy on behalf of the Poruma People v Queensland and Others, 208
Jacobs J, 128
Jadawadali people, 207
James v Western Australia (Martu determination), 73, 200, 203
Jango v Northern Territory of Australia, 211, 218
Jawi people, 143, 209
Jeaka Island, 204
Jones v Queensland, 189
judicial functions, 186
Jupagulk people, 207

Kabi Kabi people, 221
Kaidilt people, 125, 142, 193, 197
Karajarri people, 229
Katz J, 75–76, 78–79
Kaurareg People v Queensland, 197
Kaytetye people, 204, 209 *see also Northern Territory v Alyawarr, Kaytetye, Warumungu, Wakay Native Title Claim Group*

Keep River National Park, 70
Kelly on behalf of the Byron Bay Bundjalung
   People v New South Wales Aboriginal Land
   Council, 197
Kennedy v Queensland, 200
Keyn's case, 51
Kiefel J, 83, 84, 215, 223
Kimberley region, 209, 214, 215 see also
   Neowarra v Western Australia
King v Northern Territory of Australia,
   218–219
Kirby J
   Fejo, 38, 39, 40, 119; extinguishment,
      37, 38, 40, 42–43
   Griffiths, 84–85, 223
   Ward, 71, 85, 202
   Wik, 24, 25, 26, 27, 28, 119;
      enforceability, 127; extinguishment, 31,
      32, 33–35
   Wilson v Anderson, 122
   Yarmirr, 53–54, 120, 148
   Yorta Yorta, 76, 78, 200
Kite v State of South Australia, 219
Kiwirrkurra people, 196
Koara People v State of Western Australia, 211
Kokatha Native Title Claim v State of South
   Australia, 212
Kokatha people, 220
Kokatha People v State of South Australia,
   219
Kuku Yalanji people, 221
Kulka people, 206
Kuruma Marthudurara Native Title
   Claimants, 225
Kuuku Ya'u People v State of Queensland,
   229–230

Lake Victoria, 205
Lamer CJ (Supreme Court of Canada), 39,
   148–149
land, 2–3 see also connection with land;
   ownership
Land Act 1910 (Qld), 22–35
Land Act 1933 (WA), 70
Land Act 1962 (Qld), 15, 22–35
Land Councils, 211, 230
land rights, 3, 49, 132
Land (Titles and Traditional Usage) Act

1973 (WA) see Western Australia v
   Commonwealth
Lands Acquisition Act 1978 (NT), 82–83,
   84, 223
language and linguistic groups, 13, 74, 87,
   97, 98, 100
Lapthorne v Indigenous Land Corporation,
   224
Lardil, Kaidilt, Yangkaal and Gangalidda
   People v Queensland, 125, 142, 193, 197
Lardil Peoples v Queensland, 191, 205
Lardil, Yangkaal, Gangalidda & Kaiadilt
   Peoples v State of Queensland, 224
Larrakia people, 36–37, 41, 44, 97, 212,
   220 see also Fejo v Northern Territory
law and customs see traditional law and
   customs
law-making power, 4–5, 19, 20–21, 46,
   51, 117
   effect of Racial Discrimination Act 1975
      (RDA), 60–61
   see also normative law systems
Lawson v Minister for Land and Water
   Conservation, 205
leases, 6, 18, 26–27, 69–72, 82, 86,
   121–122
   licences and, 28–29
   in perpetuity, 122–123
   see also pastoral leases
Lee J, 55–56, 57, 65, 68, 78, 147, 189,
   194, 214
legislative extinguishment, 19–21 see also
   Racial Discrimination Act 1975 (Cth)
legislative power see law-making power
Leslie Hayes & Ors on behalf of the Thalanyji
   People v The State of Western Australia and
   Others, 224
licences, 25, 26, 28–30
   to hunt or fish, 44, 46, 53
Lindgren J, 217–218
Little Sandy Desert, Western Australia, 222
Liyartu-Walamarnta group, 219
local governments, 83, 223
Long Island, 209
Lovett on behalf of the Gunditjmara People v
   State of Victoria, 219
low watermark, 51, 100, 189
Lower Southern Arrente people, 222

Mabo v Queensland [No.1] (Racial Discrimination Act 1975 decision), 4, 5, 20, 60, 184
Mabo v Queensland [No.2], 1–2, 9–21, 91, 116–117, 122, 147–148, 149, 184–185
colonial law concepts, 2–3, 9–10
communal title, 12–13, 15, 108, 142
construction principles, 31–32
Court membership, 121
extinguishment, 15, 16–21, 37, 40, 84, 132, 147–148; *Ward,* 57, 65, 148
inconsistency, 84, 131–132, 133
legislative responses, 3–7, 62, 142 *see also Native Title Act 1993* (Cth) (NTA)
sovereignty, acquisition of, 13, 128–130, 131–132, 145; *Yarmirr,* 50, 51, 119–120
traditional law and customs, 78, 79, 126, 130–133; *De Rose,* 144; *Fejo,* 39, 43, 133–134; *Wik,* 33–34
see also Brennan J, and *Mabo v Queensland [No.2]*
Mabuiag people, 208
Mabuiag People v Queensland, 193
McHugh J, 37, 45, 77
  Mabo v Queensland [No.2], 12, 19–20, 117
  Ward, 58, 73, 121
  Yarmirr, 51, 126, 130–131
McNeil, Kent, 137, 145
Mahoney J, 13
Maiyalaniwung estate group, 216
Makalamayi estate group, 216
Malanda, 220
Manas v State of Queensland, 212
Mandilarri-Ildugij people, 49
Mandingalbay Yidinji people, 212
Mangalara people, 49
Mansfield J, 100, 105, 208, 212, 216, 224, 227–228
Marra people, 194, 206
Martu determination (*James v Western Australia*), 73, 200, 203
Masig and Damuth People v Queensland, 193
Masig people, 193, 210
Mason CJ, 12, 18–21, 60, 117, 185
Mason v Tritton, 185
Mayorram people, 49
mediation, 6, 190, 195, 199, 212, 215, 222, 229

Members of the Yorta Yorta Aboriginal Community v Victoria see Yorta Yorta v Victoria
Meriam people, 1–2, 9, 184, 198 *see also Mabo v Queensland*
Merkel J, 54, 93, 137, 139–140, 141, 199, 225–226
Mervyn and Others on behalf of the Peoples of the Ngaanyatjarra Lands v Western Australia, 208
Milirrpum v Nabalco Pty Ltd, 2–3, 9, 53, 184
Minaga people, 49
Mineralogy Pty Ltd v Kuruma Marthudunera Native Title Claimants, 225
minerals, 15, 30, 62–63, 194, 198
Mining Act 1978 (WA), 61
mining leases, 6–7, 18, 71, 121
Miriuwung people, 37, 55–56, 61, 120, 142, 143, 189, 202–203, 214 *see also Western Australia v Ward* (2002)
Mitchellton pastoral leases, 24 *see also Wik Peoples v Queensland*
Moses v State of Western Australia (2007), 138, 219
Mualgal people, 189, 191, 212
Mualgal People v Queensland, 191
Mualgal v Queensland, 189
Mukar (Mugquar) Islet, 204
Mulgrave River, 212
Munn v Queensland, 198, 201
Muran people, 49
Murranjayi group, 219
Murray Islands, 9, 198 *see also Mabo v Queensland*
Mye on behalf of the Erubam Le v Queensland, 205

Nambucca Heads Local Aboriginal Land Council v Minister for Lands, 230
Nangkiriny v Western Australia, 201, 206
National Native Title Tribunal (NNTT), 6, 186, 187, 195, 199, 229
national parks and reserves, 18, 70, 73, 121, 198–199, 204, 222, 227–228
Native Title Act 1993 (Cth) (NTA), 4–6, 22, 36–37, 98, 115, 117–119, 120–123, 126, 142, 146

Index

acquisition of land processes (NT) and, 83, 84
expedited procedures, 187
extinguishment provisions, 5–6, 57–59, 68–71, 72, 79, 146, 147; compensation, 59, 61
'freehold equivalence' tests, 84, 85
Part 2 Division 2, 57
Part 2 Division 2A, 57–58
Part 2 Division 2B, 57, 72
Part 3, 190
preamble, 135, 196
s 7, 60
s 11, 5, 57
s 12, 186
s 13, 190, 195
s 15, 57, 58–59
s 23A, 58
s 23B, 72
s 23C, 57
s 23G, 57
s 23J, 59
s 24HA, 191, 193
s 24MD, 85, 86, 223
s 24NA, 191
s 38, 229
s 45, 61
s 47, 195
s 47A, 119, 195, 198, 199, 208, 213
s 47B, 59, 73, 119, 209, 213
s 55, 189
s 56, 189, 193, 229
s 57, 189, 193
s 61, 190, 216, 224, 227, 228
s 62, 190, 215
s 66, 192
s 66B, 199, 200, 201, 215, 224, 228–229
s 66C, 221
s 67, 212
s 82, 188, 192, 204, 216
s 84(5), 195, 201, 226–227
s 84C, 219, 220, 228
s 86, 212
s 86EN, 195
s 86G, 200
s 87, 224, 227, 229
s 87A, 227, 229
s 94C, 221
s 190(4), 217
s 190A, 185, 223–224, 226
s 190C, 226
s 211, 46, 191
s 213(2), 185
s 223, 118, 124–125, 126, 135, 141, 144, 149, 190; *Bennell*, 100, 107, 108–109, 110, 112–114, 210, 222; *De Rose*, 94–95, 141, 142, 144, 200, 207; *Gumana*, 141; *Neowarra*, 143, 204; *Risk*, 212; *Rubibi*, 141; *Ward*, 61, 62, 63–64, 194, 202; *Yarmirr*, 50, 51, 76; *Yorta Yorta*, 76–77, 79, 100–101, 123, 197–198, 200–201
s 225, 49–50, 62, 142, 192, 201, 219, 224; *Bennell*, 109–110, 111
s 237, 199
s 237A, 58, 96
s 238, 59
s 248B, 70
s 251B, 210
s 253, 199
Native Title Act case *see* Western Australia v Commonwealth
Native Title Amendment Act 1998 (Cth), 7, 80, 115, 119, 120, 121, 148
Native Title Registrar, 185, 214, 216, 217, 221, 223–224, 226
nature conservation, 18, 70, 73, 204
wildlife, 44–48, 188, 191
navigation, 52–54, 132, 190, 196
necessary inconsistency *see* inconsistency
negotiation, 187 *see also* mediation
Neowarra v Western Australia, 137, 138, 141, 142, 143, 146–147, 203–204
Bennell and, 113
final determination, 206
Yorta Yorta and, 125
New South Wales *Public Works Act 1912*, 205
New South Wales v Commonwealth (1975), 51, 128
New South Wales *Western Lands Act 1901*, 122, 192, 202
New Zealand, 85
Newcastle Waters township, 219
Newie on behalf of the Gebaralgal v Queensland, 206

Ngaanyatjarra Lands, 208, 225
Ngadjon-Jii People v State of Queensland, 220
Ngalakan people, 194, 198, 201, 206
Ngalakan People v Northern Territory, 198, 201
Ngaliwurru people, 211, 216
Ngalpil v Western Australia, 198
Ngaluma/Injibandi people, 203
  see also Ngarluma people
  see also Yindjibarndi people
Ngarinyin people, 142 see also *Neowarra v Western Australia*
Ngarla people, 193–194, 215
Ngarluma people, 138, 203, 207, 215, 219
Ngayndjagar people, 49
Nguraritja see *De Rose v South Australia*
Ngurrara people, 200
Ngururrpa people, 220
Nguurruumungu people, 187
Nharnuwangga people, 193–194
Nicholson J, 192
Nigeria, 129
non-claimant determination, 200, 226–227
non-recognition, 130–133
non-statutory extinguishment of title, 19
Nona and Manas v State of Queensland, 212
Nona on behalf of the Badulgal v Queensland, 206
Nona on behalf of the Saibai, Dauan, Mabuiag, Badu and Boigu Peoples v Queensland, 208
Noongar community, 97–110, 111, 124, 210, 228 see also *Bodney v Bennell*
Noonkanbah pastoral lease, 215
normative law systems, 39–43, 53–54, 125, 126–127, 133–135, 147, 149
  Bennell, 101–106
  Yorta Yorta, 76–81, 133–134; *De Rose* distinguished from, 93
normative society, 78, 80, 98–101, 107, 123, 139–144, 203–204, 209, 210 see also groups and group claims
North America, 12, 15, 18, 39, 84, 148–149
North Ganalanja Aboriginal Corporation v Queensland, 23, 27, 186–187
North J, 56–57, 147, 148, 194, 201
Northern Land Council v Commonwealth, 3

Northern Territory *Crown Lands Act 1992*, 83
Northern Territory *Lands Acquisition Act 1978*, 82–83, 84
Northern Territory of Australia v Arnhem Land Aboriginal Land Trust, 132, 225
Northern Territory Supreme Court, 2
Northern Territory v Alyawarr, Kaytetye, Warumungu, Wakay Native Title Claim Group, 97, 101, 107–108, 113, 115, 124, 125, 144, 209
Nugal people, 187
Nungali people, 211, 216
Nyangumarta people, 229
Nyangumarta Warrarn Aboriginal Corporation, 229
Nyungar people, 37

occupancy, 10, 12–14, 17
  Bennell, 112
  De Rose, 88–89, 90–91, 93, 207
  Pearson on, 135, 138
  Ward, 62, 63, 93, 135, 194–195
  Yorta Yorta, 74–76, 78
  see also connection with land
offshore see sea country
Oilnet, 36
Olney J, 54, 139, 140, 146
  Yarmirr, 49–50, 52, 189–190
  Yorta Yorta, 74–75, 78, 80–81, 123–124, 189
O'Loughlin J, 87–94, 96, 124
Ord River project, 120
overlapping claims, 190, 218, 224, 226
overseas precedents, 39
  see also aboriginal title (Canada)
ownership, 3, 4, 23–24, 91, 137–138
  Mabo v Queensland [No. 2], 10, 13–15
  Queensland Coast Island Declaratory Act 1985 (Qld), 4
  Ward, 62, 65
  see also sovereignty
ownership of resources, 15, 62–63, 198
ownership of sea country, 51

Papua New Guinea nationals, 216
Pareroultja v Tickner, 185
parks and reserves, 18, 70, 73, 121, 198–199, 204, 222, 227–228

Index

partial extinguishment, 147
  De Rose, 92, 96
  Ward, 55–59, 71–72, 120–121, 146, 147, 194, 202
  see also bundle of rights concept; coexistence; inconsistency
Passi on behalf of Meriam People v Queensland, 198
past acts, 57–58, 59, 60
pastoral leases, 18, 38
  Alyawarr, 204
  Cox , 215
  Daniel, 203
  De Rose see De Rose v South Australia
  Hayes, 191
  King , 218–219
  North Ganalanja Aboriginal Corporation, 23, 27, 186
  Northern Territory v Alyawarr, 209
  Ten-Point Plan, 6–7
  Wandarang, 206
  Ward, 58, 69–70, 71–72, 121, 122
  Wik [2004], 207 *see also Wik Peoples v Queensland*
  Wilson , 72
  Wilson, 122–123, 202
  see also inconsistency
Patta Warumungu People v Northern Territory of Australia, 220
Payi Payi & Ors on behalf of the Ngururrpa People and State of Western Australia, 220
Pearce Cay, 206
Pearson, Noel, 68, 133, 135, 137, 138
Perth metropolitan area, 97, 107, 108, 112–114, 210, 222
petroleum *see* minerals
Pilbara, 200, 203, 207, 215, 218, 224, 229
Pinkakujarra group, 219
Pitjantjatjara people, 87 *see also De Rose v South Australia*
Poruma people, 208, 209–210
possessory title, 117, 135 *see also* occupancy
prescribed bodies corporate, 189, 193, 203, 206, 211
previous acts, 57–58, 59, 60
private benefit, 83–84
private rights to land, grants of, 17–18, 82
  see also freehold land; leases
Privy Council, 3

proof, 10–16, 114–115, 116, 117, 124, 125, 140, 141, 149
  De Rose, 95–96
  Derschaw, 188
  Ngalakan People, 198
  Pearson on, 135
  Ward, 61, 187
  Yorta Yorta, 74–81, 139–140
  see also evidence
property law, 44–45, 60, 64, 109, 136–137
proprietary interests, 14–15, 27, 56, 90, 109, 121, 137
  fauna, 44–45
  minerals, 15
  protection limits, 144–148 *see also* extinguishment
public purpose, 83–84
public rights *see* fishing and hunting
Public Works Act 1912 (NSW), 205
Pula Nguru/Spinifex People, 192

Quall v Northern Territory of Australia, 230
Queensland *Coast Island Declaratory Act 1985* (Qld), *Mabo [No.1]* decision, 4, 5, 20, 184
Queensland Court of Appeal, 44
Queensland *Crown Lands Alienation Act 1876*, 28
Queensland *Fauna Conservation Act 1974*, 44–48
Queensland *Land Act 1910*, 22–35
Queensland *Land Act 1962*, 15

Racial Discrimination Act 1975 (Cth), 137, 145, 147–148
  Griffiths , 86
  impact on state legislation, 60–61
  Mabo v Queensland [No.1] and Queensland *Coast Islands Declaratory Act 1985* (Qld), 4, 5, 20
  Mabo v Queensland [No.2], 16, 19, 20
  Native Title Act 1993 suspension provisions, 5
  Native Title Act case, 5, 186; see also *Western Australia v Commonwealth* (1995) (*Native Title Act* case)
  Native Title Amendment Act 1998 suspension provisions, 7

253

Ward, 57, 59–61, 121, 202
Yanner, 46
radical title, 13, 14, 27, 50–51, 104, 119–120, 129
Real Property Act 1886 (SA), 218
recognition, 9–21, 51–53, 54, 59, 85, 126–150
  withdrawal of recognition, 68
  'recognition level', 108, 125, 141–144, 203
Reeves J, 230
regulation of rights and interests, 45–48
Reid v State of South Australia, 220
rents, 25, 29
reports, copying or disclosure of, 198–199
reserves and parks, 18, 70, 73, 121, 198–199, 204, 222, 227–228
resources, ownership of, 15, 62–63, 194, 198
resources, use/taking of, 30, 63, 189–190, 196 see also fishing and hunting
resumption as vacant Crown land, 36–43
reversion to Crown, 23, 27–29
revival, 41–43, 119, 146
rights and interests, 'typology' of, 109–111
Riley v State of Queensland, 212
Risk v Northern Territory, 97, 99, 105, 115, 124, 125, 140, 212, 220, 230
root title see coexistence
Rubibi appeal, 97, 114–115, 143
Rubibi v Western Australia, 138, 141, 198–199, 201, 204, 213
rules of interpretation, 82–86

Sackville J, 93, 200, 211
Saibai people, 208
Saibai People v Queensland, 191
St Vidgeon's claim, 194
Sale of Waste Lands Act 1842 (Imp), 25
Sampi v Western Australia, 125, 143–144, 209
Sassi Island, 209
sea country, 49–54, 100, 132–133, 142, 189–190, 196
  Gumana, 208
  Jones, 189
  see also Commonwealth v Yarmirr
Seas and Submerged Lands case, 51, 128
Selway J, 106, 141, 208

settlement, 2–3, 10, 13–14, 24–25, 99, 101–102, 105–106, 140
  traditions and customs at time of see traditional law and customs; traditional societies
  see also sovereignty
shipping, 52–54, 132, 190
Single Noongar Claim, 97, 98, 210 see also Bodney v Bennell; Noongar community
skeletal principles, 10, 18, 40, 52, 131, 132, 133
Smith on behalf of the Gnaala Karla Booja People v Western Australia, 199
Smith v Western Australia, 193–194
'society', concept of, 100–101, 107, 143
  see also traditional societies
South Africa, 127, 135
Southern Nigeria, 129
'Southern Noongar claim', 228
sovereignty, 13, 72, 76–77, 119–120, 123, 128–130, 132, 134–138, 148–149, 184, 185
  Bennell, 98, 100, 103–104
  Mabo, 10, 15, 17, 128–130, 131–132, 145; time of acquisition, 13
  pre-Mabo law, 2–3, 9–10, 184
  Yarmirr, 50–52, 119–120, 127, 128, 129–130, 132–133
  see also normative law systems
speak for country, right to, 73
  Bennell, 100
  Neowarra, 138
  Ward, 62–63, 65, 67
special purpose leases, 70
Spender J, 216
Spinifex People, 192
spiritual connection with land, 12, 39, 141
  De Rose, 88–89, 90
  Ward, 64, 121
  Yanner, 46–48
St Vidgeon's claim, 194
Stanley Mervyn, Adrian Young, and Livingston West and Ors, on behalf of the People of the Ngaanyatjarra Lands v The State of Western Australia and Ors, 225
state legislation see law-making power
State of Western Australia v Sebastian, 97, 114–115, 124, 125, 143, 225–226

statutory construction/interpretation, 118, 119, 121, 125, 146
in *Wik*, 25–26, 31–32
see also bundle of rights concept; *Native Title Act 1993*
statutory land rights title, 115, 122, 185
statutory leases, 22–35, 70–72 see also pastoral leases
Stephen on behalf of the Ugar People v Queensland, 206
Stephens Island, 206
Strathgordon Mob, 221
sub-surface resources, 15, 62–63, 229
sui generis character, 11, 14, 30, 32, 39–40, 64, 67, 85, 109, 137, 147
Sundberg J, 100, 138, 141, 142, 143, 146–147
Supreme Court of the Northern Territory see Northern Territory Supreme Court
surrender of title, 16–17
suspension, 58, 119, 146, 188

Ten-Point Plan, 6–7
Tennant Creek, 220
terra nullius, 1, 2 see also sovereignty
territorial waters see sea country
Territory Parks and Wildlife Conservation Act (NT), 70
Tha people, 187
Thaiday on behalf of the Warraber, Poruma and Iama Peoples v Queensland, 209
Thalanyji people, 224
Thayorre people, 22–23, 27, 33 see also *Wik Peoples v Queensland*
Thiithaarr people, 187
Thorpe v Kennett, 191
Thudgari people, 224
Thuubi people, 187
tidal waters, 132, 206, 207 see also intertidal zone
Timber Creek township, Northern Territory, 82, 211, 216, 222–223
Timothy James Malachi on behalf of the Strathgordon Mob v State of Queensland, 221
Toohey J, 121
Mabo v Queensland [No 2], 11–12, 13, 15, 109, 117; cited in *Yorta Yorta*, 79;
extinguishment, 16, 19, 20
Wik Peoples v Queensland, 25, 30, 34, 120; exclusive possession, 26, 27, 31–33
Torres Strait, 191, 192, 193, 194, 197, 198, 204, 205, 206, 209, 212
town areas see Alice Springs determination *(Hayes)*; Broome; Hatches Creek; Perth metropolitan area; Tennant Creek; Yulara township
trade, 189–190, 196, 209
tradition, 74, 76, 78–79, 100, 105, 125
traditional law and customs, 8, 10–15, 116, 133–135, 140–141
Bennell, 98–106, 109–111
continuity and change, 99–106
De Rose, 87–91, 92–96, 138, 139, 140–141, 144
groups and group claims, 138–139, 143–144
inheritance, acquisition or succession of title under, 17, 138
intersection with non-Indigenous law, 76–77, 104, 108, 110–111, 118, 123, 125–127, 134, 147
Lardil, 205
law pre-*Mabo*, 2–3
Neowarra, 141
non-recognition in Australian law, 33–34, 39–40, 41–43, 126, 135
Ward, 61, 62–65, 67–68, 112
Yanner, 46–47
Yarmirr, 49–50, 54, 126–127
Yorta Yorta see *Yorta Yorta v Victoria*
see also connection with land; normative law systems; sovereignty
traditional owners see *De Rose v South Australia*
traditional societies, 11–14, 80, 139–140, 141, 205 see also *Bodney v Bennell*; *Yorta Yorta v Victoria*
traditional use see fishing and hunting
trespass, 28, 31
Trevor Close on behalf of the Githabul People v Minister for Lands, 221
Trinity Inlet, 212
Tudu Island, 204
Turrbal People v State of Queensland, 226
Turrutpa-Jalapirri group, 219

Two Brothers Island, 206
typology of rights and interests, 109–111

Ugar Island, 206
underlying title *see* coexistence
uniqueness *see sui generis* character
United States, 3, 13
unopposed applications, 200, 230
Upper Murchison and Gascoigne, 193–194
use of land, 63–67, 78
use of resources, 30, 62–63, 92, 189–190, 202 *see also* fishing and hunting
usufructuary rights/interests, 14–15, 56, 109, 129

Van Hemmen on behalf of the Kabi Kabi People #3 v State of Queensland, 221
vesting, 45, 70, 121
von Doussa J, 56–57, 140
'vulnerable title', 40–41, 48, 71, 117, 119, 147, 149

Waanyi case *see North Ganalanja Aboriginal Corporation v Queensland*
Wagyl Kaip claim group, 228–229
Wajarri people, 193–194
Wakaman People #2 v Native Title Registrar and Authorised Delegate, 214
Wakay people, 204, 209
Walker on behalf of the Eastern Kuku Yalanji People v State of Queensland, 221
Walley v Western Australia, 187
Walman Yawuru clan, 213
Wandarang, Alawa, Marra and Nagalakan Peoples v Northern Territory, 206
Wandarang v Northern Territory, 194
Wangkangurru people, 222
Wanjina-Wunggurr community, 142, 143
see also Neowarra v Western Australia
Wantawul estate group, 216
Warburton Range stock route, 208
Ward on behalf of the Miriuwung and Gajerrong People v Western Australia, 55–56, 65, 189
Ward v Northern Territory, 201–202
Ward v Western Australia (1996), 187
Ward v Western Australia (Miriuwung Gajerrong #4 Determination) [2006], 214

Wardenybeng people, 214
Warraber people, 209
Warrabur and Poruma People v Queensland, 194
Warria on behalf of the Kilkalgal v Queensland, 206
Warria on behalf of the Poruma and Masig Peoples v Queensland, 210
Warumungu people, 204
water resources, 201, 202, 204, 205, 207–208, 229 *see also* sea country
Webb v State of Western Australia, 221
Wellesley Island, 142
Wergaia people, 207
West Kimberley, 209
Western Australia v Commonwealth (*Native Title Act* case), 4–5, 24, 117, 118, 186
 extinguishment, 38, 50, 128–129
 sovereignty, 128–129, 132
 validity of Commonwealth law, 4–5
 validity of other acts, 60–61
Western Australia v Ward (1997), 143, 188
Western Australia v Ward (2000), 56–57, 140, 147, 148, 194–195
Western Australia v Ward (2002), 55–73, 109, 117–125, 135, 146, 147, 202, 203
 abandonment, 62–63, 79, 89
 Bennell and, 110–111
 bundle of rights concept, 55–57, 58, 61–63, 121, 194, 202
 connection with land, 56, 61, 63–65, 93, 112
 De Rose judgment and, 89, 92, 93, 96
 extinguishment, 121
 Griffiths judgment and, 85
 Kirby J, 71, 85
 leases, 69–70, 92, 121–122
 Miriuwung and Gajerrong relationship, 142, 143
 policy setting of common law development, 148
 possessory title, 117, 147
 use of resources, 62–63, 96
 Wilson judgment and, 72, 122
 Yorta Yorta judgment and, 78–79
Western Australian *Fish Resources Management Act 1994*, 191

Western Australian Fishing Industry Council, 211
Western Australian *Land Act 1933*, 70
Western Australian *Land (Titles and Traditional Usage) Act 1973 see Western Australia v Commonwealth*
Western Australian *Mining Act 1978*, 61
Western Desert cultural bloc, 218
Western Desert Lands Aboriginal Corporation v State of Western Australia and Others, 226
Western Desert peoples, 87, 90, 93–95, 144, 214 *see also Bodney v Bennell*; *De Rose v South Australia*
Western Lands Act 1901 (NSW), 72, 122, 192, 202
Western Wakka Wakka people, 214–215
Western Yalanji people, 212
Western Yalanji Peoples v Pedersen, 189
Wik Peoples (McNaught Ngallametta) v Queensland, 195
Wik Peoples v Queensland, 22–35, 73, 117–121, 146, 187
 bundle of rights construction, 26, 136
 content of title, 136
 Court membership, 121
 enforceability, 127, 145
 Fejo judgment, 38
 legislative response, 6–7
 Ward judgment and, 57, 63, 69
 Wilson judgment, 72, 122
 Yanner judgment, 45
 Yarmirr judgment, 53
Wik Peoples v Queensland [2004], 207
Wilcox J, 93, 97–108, 112–114, 124, 140, 210, 222
wildlife conservation, 44–48, 188, 191 *see also* national parks and reserves
Wilkes v Johnsen, 191
Wilkes v Western Australia, 204
Williams v Grant, 226
Wilson v Anderson, 72, 118, 122–123, 192, 202
Wimmera River, 207

Wiri People v Native Title Registrar, 226
Witjira National Park, South Australia, 222
witnesses, 75, 88–89, 91, 99, 106, 143
 gender, 188, 204
Wonggoo-tt-oo people, 215
Worimi Local Aboriginal Land Council v Minister for Lands for the State of New South Wales, 226
Wororra people, 37, 142, 186 *see also Neowarra v Western Australia*
Wotjobahlk People v Victoria, 191
Wotjobaluk determination, 139–140, 149, 207
wrongful extinguishment, 19–21, 59–60
Wunambal people, 142 *see also Neowarra v Western Australia*
Wunjaiyi estate group, 216

Yalanji peoples, 189, 212
Yam Island, 204
Yangkaal people, 125, 142, 193, 197
Yankunytjatjara/Antakirinja Native Title Claim Group v The State of South Australia, 214
Yanner v Eaton, 44–48, 51, 118, 119, 120, 137, 191
 fishing method, 78
 Ward judgement and, 63
Yanturi estate group, 216
Yarmirr v Northern Territory, 188, 189–190, 195–196 *see also Commonwealth v Yarmirr*
Yarrabah, 212
Yarriambiak Creek, 207
Yawuru community, 141, 198–199, 213 *see also Rubibi v Western Australia*
Yindjibarndi people, 138, 215, 219
Yirrkala people, 2–3
Yolngu people, 225
Yorta Yorta people, 37
Yorta Yorta v Victoria (1996)], 186
Yorta Yorta v Victoria [1997], 188
Yorta Yorta v Victoria [1998], 74–75, 78, 189
Yorta Yorta v Victoria (2001), 75–76, 78–79, 80–81, 197–198
Yorta Yorta v Victoria (2002), 74–81, 117, 120, 123–125, 133–134, 139–140, 200–201, 203

Bennell and, 97, 98, 99, 100–104, 105
concept of 'society', 100–101
De Rose circumstances distinguished
from, 93
Ward judgment and, 143
Yulara township, 211
Yungngora people, 215
Yunkunytjatjara people, 87, 89, 90 *see also*
De Rose v South Australia

Zagai Island, 204

Inconst - case by case basis, a factual inquiry